As American as Mom, Baseball, and Apple Pie

As American as Mom, Baseball, and Apple Pie:

Constructing Community
in Contemporary American Horror Fiction

Linda J. Holland-Toll

Bowling Green State University Popular Press
Bowling Green, OH 43403

Copyright 2001 © Bowling Green State University Popular Press

Library of Congress Cataloging-in-Publication Data

Holland-Toll, Linda J.
    As American as mom, baseball, and apple pie : constructing commu-
nity in contemporary American horror fiction / Linda J. Holland-Toll.
        p. cm.
    Includes bibliographical references and index.
    ISBN 0-87972-851-5 -- ISBN 0-87972-852-3 (pbk.)
    1. Horror tales, American--History and criticism. 2. American fiction
--20th century--History and criticism. 3. Community life in literature.
4. Community in literature. I. Title.

PS374.H67 H65 2001
813'.0873809--dc21
                                                                2001037998

Cover design by Amy Smolar

CONTENTS

ACKNOWLEDGMENTS

This book, such as it is, would not have come into being without the assistance of many people. I especially wish to thank my dissertation advisor, Dr. Robert W. Merrill, who unrelentingly demanded the best possible work of which I was capable, even when I knew, positively and absolutely, that I could not summon the strength of will to rewrite one more chapter, one more time. And even when we somewhat acrimoniously (on my part, at least) disagreed on rhetoric, punctuation, and the value of the texts I chose, he never failed in attention or patience. The question, "Why these particular texts?" will haunt me to my grave. Dr. Edward Ingebretsen is owed thanks for serving on my committee from the far reaches of Norway and Georgetown, and for his constant encouragement, especially welcome when I knew I could not possibly write a dissertation, and his cogent criticism, which helped keep me on track. I also wish to thank Dr. Susan Palwick, who criticized little and encouraged much. Her belief in the value of this particular study often kept me going. I also wish to thank Dr. Richard G. Hunt, who agreed to index this manuscript, and also provided invaluable assistance to me during the entire writing process, and Dr. Charles Horn for his assistance on scientific topics.

Perhaps most of all, I owe a great and incalculable debt, and quite possibly my sanity, to my friends Gail Lee McDermott, Diana M. Binder, and Rita E. Rippetoe, who, depending on what I most needed to hear, sympathized, bullied, or cajoled me into one more day working on "The Damned Thing." Without their constant encouragement, long-distance sympathy, critical opinions on both my writing and my interpretations, cups of hot tea, and polite, inexorable nagging, I would have quit a million times.

The mistakes, and of course there are some, are my own; the editing, commentary, alternate readings, and all other useful suggestions, are theirs.

"Souls that have toiled, and wrought, and thought with me"—I thank you.

1

TWO PARTS GORE AND ONE PINCH WALKING DEAD:
WHAT EXACTLY IS HORROR FICTION?

from ghosties and ghoulies
and long-leggety beasties,
and things that go bump in the night
Lord God, deliver us.[1]

Once, shortly after reading Stephen King's vampire novel, *'Salem's Lot*, I was sitting in a chair at my optometrist's in total darkness when I suddenly noticed two small red dots of light. These dots immediately reminded me of the descriptions of sullen red eyes glowing in the dark in *'Salem's Lot*, and I re-experienced the dis/ease which that particular text had produced in me.[2] For weeks, I had glimpsed those same sullen red eyes out of the corners of my eyes during my evening walks, even though vampires do not exist, and I know that vampires do not exist. Nevertheless, the lines, "Even from the rise we could see the sullen red glare of those eyes. They were less human than wolf's eyes" reverberated dis/easefully in my mind.[3] To questions like, "Why do you read that stuff, anyway?" I could return no satisfactory answer. But I felt that whatever role horror fiction plays in American life was important, and more than an easy couple of hours' worth of thrills-n-chills. The result of my cogitations follows.

My purpose in writing about horror fiction is to explore, in Jane Tompkins' terms, what kind of cultural work horror texts perform. Tompkins attempts to redefine literature and literary study "not as works of art embodying enduring themes in complex forms but as attempts to redefine the social order [. . .] they offer powerful examples of the way a culture thinks about itself."[4] Redefining and reordering the socialscape is something about which horror fiction is obsessively concerned. Tompkins' view that "a novel's impact on the culture at large depends not on an escape from the formulaic and derivative but on its tapping into a storehouse of commonly held assumptions" also works quite well within the paradigms of horror fiction, as much horror fiction deploys formulaic elements and repetitive plot structures when it rifles this storehouse, which it then subverts on many different levels. As Tompkins so cogently contends, "When literary texts are conceived as agents of cultural formulation rather than as objects of interpretation and appraisal, what counts as a 'good' character or a logical sequence of events changes accordingly."[5] I will explore exactly how horror fiction works to subvert commonly accepted cultural models by illuminating these commonly held cultural assumptions and exposing their dark side, a process which generates cultural dis/ease within the society at large. Such a reading will cut across the grain and read communities from a perspective which emphasizes the exclusionary rather than the inclusive, refuting the critical theories which postulate horror fiction as working within inclusive, conservative paradigms.

In *The Monster Show: A Cultural History of Horror*, David Skal notes,

One place the dream [the American dream] is permitted to perish, with noisy, convulsive death rattles, is in horror entertainment. The American nightmare, as refracted in film and fiction, is about disenfranchisement, exclusion, downward mobility, a struggle-to-the-death world of winners and losers.[6]

Such a point of view, which I share, is in direct opposition to Stephen King's main view on horror fiction, which sees disestablishment as resolving into affirmation and reconfirmation of cultural values. I contend that the most effective horror fiction, disaffirmative horror fiction, is that which subverts and lays bare the cultural assumptions which we use to avoid facing certain unpleasant realities.

Within American society, a widespread fear exists that we are more threatened, less safe, more under siege than at any previous time. We check the back seats of our cars; leave hitch-hikers, even men and women with small children, stranded on the road; lock ourselves within our increasingly fortress-like homes; live in "gated communities," those fortresses against the barbarous "other"; glance over our shoulders, even while walking in broad daylight; cross the street to avoid threatening (e.g., Black/Hispanic/punk-like/skinhead) Others. We fear the loss of our possessions and our lives, and in so doing we lose, through erosion, our accepted values, especially those concerning community. A desensitization towards man's obligation to the rest of mankind is the unhappy result of this fear of our fellow man. Thus we are constantly alienating ourselves from our own accepted values, a condition which disaffirmative horror fiction replicates and confronts.

Horror fiction reveals the body beneath the sheet, so to speak, and actively denies and resists the more affirmative cultural models which we use to tell reassuring stories about ourselves and our communities.

The sense of a *doppelganger* effect, of horror lurking not only in a text ostensibly restricted to fantastic elements but also in its real-life themes, adds to the dis/easeful effect.

As Clive Barker, a noted horror writer and critic, claims, "The kind of horror I write is primarily interested in tearing away the veil."[7] Judith Halberstam notes that horror fiction constructs the monster in order to discuss the human condition; she further argues that the monster is the "site of humanity" and is always read in terms of monstrous multiplicity. Such readings produce, I would argue, not only a monster/human inter-coupling, but also the dis/ease such interpretations fuel. Halberstam points out that the nineteenth century Gothic is a historically specific monster-producing text for monster-consuming readers; such a text uses the monster not only to construct the human, but also to talk about the dis/ease-provoking topics of race, class and gender, topics the monster embodies.[8] Siting the monster within the human body rejects the argument of evil as other-positioned. Furthermore, if the monstrous is not then limited to gender, but must also include class and race, as Halberstam argues, the sites for the production of cultural dis/ease increase radically. I contend that a text which cannot be contained in one type of reading, stressing gender, class, or race, must inevitably produce lingering dis/ease because of the unresolvable anxieties it creates for its consumers.[9] A text which transgresses convenient barriers and resists convenient pigeon-holing creates cultural dis/ease simply because it cannot be easily contained. As the sites for the monstrous multiply, so multiply the cultural dis/eases. And who could not identify a site for the monstrous? Gay men, women of color, ethnic Albanians, college professors, adjunct faculty, working-class college students, threatened white males, welfare mothers—the list is endless.

But how exactly does this study, which is not primarily a generic or definitional effort, discuss horror fictions without providing a map for the reader? It cannot, of course, so the following definition, by no means final or all-inclusive, is no more than a way to offer certain paradigms to discuss certain kinds of horror texts which I find most effective in generating the cultural dis/ease so intrinsic to horror fiction.

What makes a horror text a horror text cannot be reduced to certain "must haves" any more than poetry, for example, can be objectively quantified, although, as in other genres, there are certain conventions or elements which do generally appear to define horror fiction. Attempts to define horror fiction solely in terms of genre and to reduce its manifold complexities to a neatly wrapped package of formulaic elements are almost always unsuccessful. Horror may be subsumed entirely within the fantastic, as critics such as Tvetsan Todorov and Rosemary Jackson argue, or it may be a separate genre but closely related to fantasy and science-fiction, as other critics have pointed out.[10] Gene Wolf's view of horror as "the only genre named for its effect on the reader" is probably the most useful example.[11] Unlike detective fiction which usually lends itself to more neatly packaged definitions, horror fiction tends to elicit the same type of definition as that of the man who says, "I don't know much about art, but I know what I like." Like our man gazing at canvases and reacting on the basis of simple preference, the reader of horror fiction can readily recognize a horror text but may well resort to the lame and rather exasperating argument based on, "I know what it is when I read it." What may horrify, terrify, or revolt one reader may not be recognizable or definable as horror to another reader. Most readers of Stephen King's *Pet Sematary*, for example, acknowledge its horrific qualities, but in my view, *Pet Sematary* is one of the horror fictions which, in King's words, "seem personal and . . . hit you around the heart." As such, it is an exemplar of disaffirmative horror fiction.[12]

Generally speaking, the reader of horror fictions expects at least some of the following elements to surface: an aspect of the supernatural—an actual physical monster embodied in the vampire, werewolf, ghost, or aliens; fantastic or inexplicable events which may or may not have a non-fantastic cause, or which, as Todorov argues, may or may not be explicable;[13] characters with super/paranormal powers; extreme emotions, melodramatic situations and sensational plots; emotional engagements of terror, horror, or revulsion; and, of course, the paradoxical feeling of enjoyable terror.

The term "monster" as I use it is a kind of cultural shorthand, which encompasses a wide range of beings from such certifiable monsters as vampires through people identified as human monsters to people "just like us." In *Monster Theory*, Jeffrey Jerome Cohen discusses monster culture as

a cultural fascination with monsters—a fixation that is born of the twin desire to name that which is difficult to apprehend and to domesticate (and therefore disempower) that which threatens. . . . [T]he monster is . . . a code or a pattern or a presence or an absence that unsettles what has been constructed to be received as natural, as human. . . . The monster is that certain cultural body in which is condensed an intriguing simultaneity or doubleness.[14]

While I agree with Cohen, my definition, by encompassing people who are "just like us," includes and defines as monsters not only Dracula but also the friendly residents of Shirley Jackson's unnamed village, the ones who are, indeed, "just like us."

As Terry Heller points out in *Delights of Terror: An Aesthetics of the Tale of Terror*, a reader who cannot attain some distance, who cannot finish a novel by Stephen King or watch the shower scene in *Psycho,* has been unable to achieve the "aesthetic distance" necessary to read horror fiction in the first place.[15] In *Supernatural Horror in Literature*, H. P. Lovecraft defines atmosphere as the essential component of anything which claims to be horror fiction.[16] Jettison the things that go bump in the night if you will, but something must be present to induce the horrific elements. As David Hartwell states in the introduction to *The Medusa Shield*, "The emotional transaction is paramount and definitive and we recognize its presence even when it doesn't work."[17]

I tend to agree with Hartwell's assessment with the *caveat* that if it doesn't work, recognition is not enough to qualify it as effective horror fiction. If one can read indifferently of encounters with monsters, some necessary engagement is lacking in the relationship between the reader and the text. Perhaps, as King notes when he encounters people who cannot read horror, "the muscles of the imagination have grown too weak."[18] The emotional transaction to which Hartwell and King refer is closely linked with the dis/easeful feeling which I contend horror fiction generates when resolution and closure are actively resisted. As I read Hartwell, he is referring, within the usual boundaries of horror fictions, to the emotions of terror, horror, and revulsion; if these emotions are not present and the necessary engagement is lacking, the reader will neither experience nor react to the social and cultural anxieties and dis/ease which I contend are the *sine qua non* of the most effective horror fiction.[19]

The reasons for this uncertainty of definition are many: a great many fictions which are not readily recognizable or strictly definable as horror yet have such strong elements of horror embedded within them that the emotional engagement many readers experience locates them in horror territory. Many so-called horror texts, on the other hand, have completely implausible and perfectly happy endings which sabotage the necessary effect of the text. In *Nightmare on Main Street: Angels, Sadomasochism and the Culture of Gothic*, Mark Edmundson terms this type of discourse as "the culture of facile transcendence," which he defines as "anti-Gothic" and sees as marked by "the belief that transformation is as simple as a fairy tale wish."[20] An ending that completely negates the text's horrific issues denies the horror and says, in effect, that there are no monsters under the bed, no waking-nightmares-turned-real, no societal problems which hit home in a personal way, and in the absence of a pervasive and lingering sense of dis/ease, nullifies the main effect of horror fiction.

Thus, as is often the case in generic considerations, the questions become confused: Is there some recipe for writing horror? Take two parts gore and one part walking dead, throw in a pinch of ghost and forbidden knowledge, and there you have it? Does the effect on the reader define horror or is it a matter of authorial intentionality, and in any case can intentionality be completely separated from effect? Are there certain elements which are absolutely necessary, without which a reader will categorically refuse to accept the novel as a horror book? And if so, what are they, these elusive paradigms? Must a horror text have some supernatural construct? Are monsters *de rigueur*? If the text does not have the supernatural, if it does not use the monster, if the haunted house looks, and is, perfectly normal, or the nice next-door neighbor does not, literally, embody the monster, is one reading a horror text? These are questions which have long interested me, and while I will not propose definitive answers, I will contend that many of these arguments revolve around the affirmation-resistant structure of the most effective horror fiction, which must in some way reflect the sense of dis/ease so pervasive in the culture.

For the purpose of this analysis, therefore, horror fiction will be handily defined as any text which has extreme or supernatural elements, induces (as its primary intention and/or effect) strong feelings of terror, horror, or revulsion in the reader, and generates a significant degree of unresolved dis/ease within society. The key definition employed is that of a significant degree of unresolved dis/ease or conflict significant enough that the reader who inhabits the society cannot simply gloss it over and return to business as usual. Spreading glossy white frosting over the burned and lumpy cake is not enough; people know that the frosting only hides the ghouls, whatever those ghouls may be, without destroying them. It is the knowledge that horror fiction, rather than reflecting unreal horror, is metaphorically or allegorically discussing everyday horror that causes dis/ease. A fiction which cannot be marginalized or defined as fantastic and thus easily resolved and categorized is much more threatening than a fiction which actually occupies the margins, which is clearly demarcated by the fantastic. A text in which the boundaries are intentionally blurred and the "Other" hard to isolate is more anxiety producing than a text in which the "Other" is easily isolated and has no connection with the characters and, by extension, the reader.

I should, however, re-emphasize the essential slipperiness of almost any generic definition. One cannot expand the definition of horror fiction and equate it with any manifestation of cultural dis/ease without rendering generic distinctions meaningless. Hundreds of texts, after all, grapple with social problems without automatically falling into horror fiction. Although texts such as *The Scarlet Letter* and *Huckleberry Finn* generate dis/ease and strong reactions in their readers, neither is horror fiction. Both have elements of conventional horror fiction, and both deal with man's inhumanity to wo/man, but neither leaves the reader in No Man's Land; both achieve resolution and affirmation in ways which the most effective horror does not. *Hamlet* and *Macbeth*, for example, have the *soi-disant* "litmus test" of horror fiction, the supernatural presence; *King Lear* has many emotionally wrenching and dis/ease-provoking scenes. And yet, most readers do not place these texts in the same category as *Dracula* or *Pet Sematary*.[21]

These uncertainties in classification occur because horror fiction is a fiction of the margins, a fiction of the outer limits of humanity, a fiction of "Otherness," and thus is often embodied in scenarios which reflect "Otherness." This sense of the unreal colliding with the mundane is one element integral to horror fiction. What Eric Rabkin defines as "structural ambiguity" in *The Fantastic in Literature* is intrinsic to the genre.[22] The reader no sooner accepts the mundane paradigm of events and sees a cohesive interpretation then the events deconstruct into something defined as unreal or fantastic, something on the outer limits, or even beyond, the bounds of credibility and rational explanation. Horror fiction cannot be read like a realistic or naturalistic novel, even though it shares many realistic and naturalistic techniques; the constantly shifting paradigms of horror force a more ambiguous or indeterminate reading on the reader. As Steffen Hantke states, "Fantasy operates within the same hermeneutics of reading as realistic modes of discourse, yet unlike its counterparts, it emphasizes the gaps, disruptions, and gray areas of transitions that exist between the successive elements of the interpretive sequence. It aims at derailing the safe or predictable interpretive sequence."[23] Thus, a reader who wishes to engage a text in which the realistic sequence of events does not suddenly, inexplicably, and continuously reverse itself would be well advised to avoid horror fiction since it works by the process Hantke labels "derailment."

In *Powers of Horror*, Julia Kristeva notes the horrific effect of the abject, which she expresses in terms of loathing and its alienating effect on the self: "The corpse, seen without God, and outside of science, is the utmost of abjection. It is death infecting life. . . . It is thus not cleanliness or health that causes abjection but what disturbs identity, system, order. . . . [A]bjection is elaborated through failure to recognize its kin; nothing is familiar, not even the shadow of a memory." Kristeva goes on to argue that abjection is fueled by revulsion, by fear, by emptiness. These elements are all components of horror fiction, a type of discourse which "will seem tenable only if it ceaselessly confront [*sic*] that otherness, a burden both repellent and repelled, a deep well of memory that is unapproachable and intimate: the abject."[24] The role of the abject is similar then to the role of horror fiction: a constant confrontation with the antinomous feelings intrinsic to the alien, the other. As Noel Carroll correctly points out in *The Philosophy of Horror*, revulsion is a key factor in the interaction between human and Other, and something which causes anxiety within the character and within the participating audience.[25] The initial feeling of revulsion, according to Stephen King the least fine emotion engendered by horror, quite often metastasizes to feelings of horror and terror as the Other draws closer.[26]

I agree, to some extent, with the arguments of various critics, among them Edith Birkhead, Steffen Hantke, Terry Heller, Walter Kendrick, and Stephen King, that horror fictions often provide displacement in vicariously experienced fear, thrills and chills, thus exorcizing these fears, and denying such realities as death; I would therefore also agree that many horror fictions do work conservatively to reaffirm the values of the society with which they are concerned. But these views are too limiting to be definitive, implying as they do a move towards resolution and closure which is distinctly uncharacteristic of the most effective horrific fiction.

If we were to establish a spectrum of horror, one which moves from the affirmative text in which the monsters are completely but temporarily defeated, life resumes much of its normal placidity, and the dis/ease is subtle, such a text would be at the affirmative pole of the spectrum, whereas texts which not only call societal constructs into question but leave them deliberately unresolved and which affirm nothing but the Void would occupy the disaffirmative pole of the spectrum. The middle ground of the spectrum is marked by those texts, the vast majority, which couple together a degree of affirmation and a degree of dis/ease, texts in which the resolution is permanently compromised. While these are by far the most common of horror fictions, and the disaffirmative texts I will examine the distinct minority, it is the latter, I will argue, which are the most effective. I will deploy this structure to examine the construct of community, which will include the role of the individual as human monster; the social community and how it is constructed; and the political community, which for the purposes of this study will be defined as dystopia.

The texts I will discuss in the course of this study are many and varied, and my reasons for selecting these texts among the eight hundred plus candidates for inclusion are as varied as the texts themselves. I have limited the texts I discuss in detail to contemporary horror fictions, generally American. Although numerous examples of dis/ease-provoking texts exist as far back in literature as *Beowulf* and the Norse sagas, and much Gothic and Victorian is dis/ease-provoking, contemporary horror fiction is the arena in which I see my contentions most dramatically displayed.

In *Sensational Designs*, Tompkins writes,

Because I was trying to understand what gave these novels traction in their original setting (i.e., what made them popular, not what made them "art") I have looked for continuities rather than ruptures, for the strands that connected a novel to other similar novels. . . . I have seen them in Foucault's phrase, as "nodes within a network. . . . I do not argue for the value of these texts on the grounds of their *difference* from other texts. . . . My aim rather has been to show what a text had in common with other texts."[27]

In a manner similar to Tompkins, I have been less concerned about the intrinsic or aesthetic value of the texts I have selected and more interested in how the texts work to illustrate the ways I see horror fiction functioning. To someone studying horror fiction, Tompkins' assertions about the value of the stereotyped, the sensational, and the trite are very useful indeed. Tompkins cogently argues that seeing "literary texts as agents of cultural formation rather than as objects of interpretation and appraisal" changes the way we value those texts. Setting aside "modernist demands," and considering the text as a "blueprint for survival under a specific set of political, economic, social, or religious conditions" . . . produces a "text which succeeds or fails on the basis of its 'fit' with the features of its immediate context [and] on the degree to which it provokes the desired response."[28]

Thus, my choice of texts ranges very widely: such classics as Shirley Jackson's "The Lottery" share shelf space with texts as relatively unknown as Edward Bryant's "A Sad Last Love at the Diner of the Damned." Some of the authors are well known, as are Stephen King, Thomas Harris, and Peter Straub; some like Carol Orlock or Manly Banister are less well known. Some of the texts, particularly Anne Rivers Siddons' *The House Next Door* might seem no more a horror fiction than Jerzy Kozinski's *The Painted Bird*, and yet I will contend that these are, in the reading I deploy, horror fictions. Some of the texts, such as Robert McCammon's *The Wolf's Hour*, seem nothing more than lightweight adventure-types stories and certainly not worth a serious reading. Some texts might well be more accurately generically defined as science fiction, fantasy, or even detective fiction, but the elements which I see as integral to horror fiction are foregrounded in these texts. Some texts, such as F. Paul Wilson's "Midnight Mass" and Rod Serling"s "The Monsters Are Due on Maple Street" were selected because they are exemplary instances of texts which reflect extratextual dis/ease. Some were selected simply because I liked them, and some were selected because I did not like them. In this particular storehouse, gifted authors like Thomas Harris are packed higgeldy-piggeldy alongside formulaic authors like Dean R. Koontz. Thus, while in some cases, I will have a very specific reason for discussing a particular text as opposed to the many other texts I could discuss, in some cases, the reason I chose the texts I chose was, in Tompkins' terms, "what allowed them to operate as instruments of culture self-definition."[29]

My interest lies in reading texts within this paradigm, concentrating on the texts I see as most effectively horrific, those texts which actively resist resolution and closure or reaffirmation or resolution/restoration motifs, which work not only to deny affirmative motifs, but which actively produce feelings of extreme dis/ease and cultural dread. Thus the texts in which I am most interested do not necessarily discuss blueprints for survival or solutions to problems, as do Tompkins' texts; my choices lay bare the problems and reveal the constructs, but often leave the solution out of the discussion. For the purposes of a clear-cut definition, I have labeled this type of fiction as disaffirmative horror fiction. The reader cannot close such books with a satisfied thump but is haunted by the text. Perhaps Terry Heller's concept of being "haunted" by certain texts, but on a level more visceral and less cerebral, is *apropos*. Heller contends that certain texts, by their very ambiguity, "haunt the reader" and force him or her to construct a resolution to nullify the "anti-closure" in the text. In this argument, such texts as Poe's "Ligeia," "The Fall of the House of Usher," and Henry James' novella *The Turn of the Screw* are dis/easeful precisely because of the element of ambiguity and "anti-closure."[30]

Taking a related line of attack, I contend that disaffirmative horror is that fiction which does not supply a happy ending, however qualified, and allow people to retain intact their basic assumptions about such value systems as those embedded in communities; on the contrary, it works to deconstruct those value systems and lay them bare as the agenda-ridden social constructs they undoubtedly are. Horror fiction tends to continually point out that those "accepted values," the cultural models and unarticulated rules which many people endorse, do not come straight down from Mt. Sinai but are human constructions. As such, these constructs have an agenda. And an agenda is always to someone's benefit as well as to someone else's liability. Horror fiction tends to point up the gaps, discontinuities, and deliberate exclusions which must take place to allow people to accept the values in the first place; it then relentlessly presses "the phobic pressure points" of contemporary life.[31] Disaffirmative horror fiction, far from working to reassure us that the monsters are not us, forces a dis/easeful confrontation with the monstrous, with ourselves, from which we cannot, *pour cause*, walk away. Such an effect is unlikely to uphold or confirm affirmative values because the construction of "monsters-r-us" lays bare the monstrous and exposes the tacit agreement to gloss over the monstrous. Thus, critics who read horror fiction conservatively are missing one of the main elements of horror fiction, that which propels the human/monster nexus and forces us to examine the more dis/easeful elements of society. Hantke argues that "horror fiction almost always pretends to take sides with its most conservative readers, [but] the conciliatory ending of many mainstream horror fictions does not preclude the reader's profound sense of unease at being reminded that social realities remain fundamentally ambiguous, even though the social Other might be controlled at the present moment."[32] I would argue that the pretense that Hantke sees is actually a rather thin veneer of accepted reality; the difference between a pretense and a veneer is small, perhaps, but significant: a veneer is an established part of the furniture integral to the finished piece. By constantly deconstructing the reader's nascent idea of the reality within the text and the commonly held assumptions of which Tompkins speaks, much horror fiction challenges directly the authority of the conservative as well as the acceptance of the *status quo* by being distinctly nonconciliatory.

Stephen King usefully defines "the danse macabre" in his critical work of the same name devoted to the nature and art of horror fiction:

The work of horror really is a dance—a moving, rhythmic search. And what it's looking for is the place where you, the viewer or the reader, live at your most primitive level. . . . Such a work dances through these rooms which we have fitted out one piece at a time, each piece expressing—we hope!—our socially acceptable and pleasantly enlightened character. It is in search of another place, . . . the simple and brutally plain hole of a Stone Age Cave-dweller.[33]

The fact that this room exists in all of us creates dis/ease; the fact that someone may see this room and expose the occupant for what he or she actually is provides one good working metaphor for the horror text, one which can be centered entirely in the mundane everyday life familiar to us all. Once that room, that secret real self, is exposed, or once an individual or a society has seen the reality behind the conventions, the profound dis/ease which defines horror cannot be so readily banished or ignored. David Skal's phrase *catharsis interruptus*, which denies the cathartic effect and echoes the interdiction on completion or satisfaction, is apt cultural shorthand for the effect of horror fiction.[34] Horror fiction deconstructs our expectations by constantly subverting those beliefs and situations wherein we think we know what we believe because we live in a society that makes fervent claims for commonly accepted values. Horror fiction, in effect, holds up a carnival house mirror which reveals the often warped and ironically true image of our society, our community, and ourselves.

For the purposes of this study, then, I will argue that horror fiction functions best in terms of emotional effect and intentionality inextricably coupled with the degree of disaffirmation within the text. The lack of closure, the sense of dis/ease unarticulated and lurking within the text, and the sense that all is not all well are prime causes of the societal dis/ease generated by the lack of affirmative resolution. The effect on the reader cannot be separated from the degree of affirmation postulated as one drives the other. It is this pairing which defines a text as horrific and not necessarily the usual panoply of conventions associated with horror fiction.

Such seemingly positive cultural models as the importance of the individual in the community, the social construct of community, the political manifestations of community and, of course, the belief in the essential humanity of people are relentlessly and minutely scrutinized by horror fiction, which often finds these societal norms to be little more than empty husks. Horror fiction quite frequently points out, with all the subtlety of a sledge hammer, often with grossly graphic and offensive scenes, that things are not what they seem, not as we would have them, or even as we pretend they are. This is the value and function of horror texts, from the ill-written mass-market formulaic novels to the classics in the field. Like Socrates the gadfly, they examine beliefs we cling to and sometimes even validate them; in a substantial number of cases, however, affirmation and validation are rejected. The "magic mirror" device, which reveals the nature beneath the smiling surface, the monster under the man, and the skull beneath the skin, is a device common in horror fiction; like the carnival mirror which delivers the warped/true image, it can be turned on the culture with uncomfortable yet truly fascinating results. By concentrating on the skull beneath the skin, on the reality of the skeleton society instead of on its smoothed-out skin, horror fiction lays bare one truth: all of the qualities on which we pride ourselves as Americans are as subject to alienation and subversion as they are to validation and reaffirmation. One of the main sites for this contention is the concept of community, a concept which I will examine in the following chapters by employing the spectrum discussed above as it applies to the individual, social and political levels.

Chapter 1 introduces my arguments and provides both a working definition of horror fiction and a map. Chapter 2 will examine the critical structures which I see as fueling the dis/ease-provoking elements in horror fiction. Chapters 3, 4, and 5 will examine the range of the human monster from the paradox of the affirmative human monster through the mid-spectrum human monster to the disaffirmative human monster. Chapters 6, 7, and 8 will examine the social construction of communities, arguing that community is constructed not from the cultural model which postulates a coming together but by its antithesis, the strategies of exclusion. Chapters 9, 10, and 11, will discuss political communities in terms of dystopia, again moving from the paradoxical affirmative dystopia through the extremely disaffirmative dystopias

My interest is community and the intersections between community and horror fiction. The move from the individual through the social to the political emphasizes the importance of communities in our life; to look at communities through the eyes of horror, while dis/ease provoking, also illuminates a very much taken-for-granted concept and sheds light, perhaps the light of the Cymric *cannall gorff*,[35] but light all the same.

2

HOW DOES IT WORK?
THE STRATEGIES OF EXCLUSION AS STRUCTURE

"Every one of us stood alone, and the sooner a man realized that all
... were expendable, the better for him."[1]

In this chapter I will discuss structures which contribute to my contention that the most effective horror fiction is antinomous, Dionysian,
exclusionary, and often in direct and dis/ease-provoking conflict with
the cultural models which order society. Cultural (cognitive) models function much like Jane Tompkins' views on common cultural assumptions.
Naomi Quinn and Dorothy Holland define the phrase as follows: "*Cultural
models* are presupposed, taken for granted models of the world which are
widely shared (although not necessarily to the exclusion of other alternative models) by the members of a society and that play an enormous role
in their understanding of the world and their behavior in it."[2]

Cultural models explain how meaning systems are organized within
a culture. When James B. Twitchell discusses the "unarticulated rules of
a culture," or Jane Tompkins discusses "commonly held cultural
assumptions" as societal underpinnings, or Stephen King defines horror
fiction in terms of "phobic pressure points,"[3] they are speaking of cultural models. More importantly for my purposes, Quinn and Holland,
et al., postulate the importance of cultural/cognitive models as imposed
order: "Undeniably a great deal of order exists in the natural world we
experience. However, much of the order we perceive in the world is
there only because we put it there."[4]

Much horror fiction, especially disaffirmative horror fiction, works
by exposing the contradictions embedded in social reality, contradictions which cultural models often "paper over" in order to achieve and
maintain accepted social order. Thus, horror fiction not only frequently
postulates an alternative model which lurks beneath the shared under-
standings, but also consistently undercuts and subverts the more usual
model. If, for example, cultural models view the human condition as distinctly separated from the bestial, and community as a coming together
(a denial of the essential alienation of the human condition) and if community is viewed as the cynosure of human social order, and political

14

systems as positive organizing tools, horror fiction—most notably the disaffirmative type—creates rampant dis/ease by calling the accepted cultural models into question and deconstructing and exposing them as social constructions. If such fictions do indeed cause a person to reassess reality, to shift paradigms of belief and reality, the effect is extremely dis/ease-provoking.

The absolute dismissal of the supernatural, the slow coming to belief, and the reluctant discarding of previously accepted paradigms of reality occur quite often in horror fiction. The move from "Nonsense, you know there is no such thing as a werewolf," to forging a silver bullet is typical of the genre. What paradigms have shifted, what new and irreversible Dionysian intrusions have occurred to accomplish an acknowledgment of a werewolf? Invoking the horrific as the rational explanation for an otherwise inexplicable event directly challenges the social constructs through which we construct "reality." Everyone knows that monsters, at least inhuman monsters, do not exist; if a text or author forces the reader to consider the monster as real and as monstrous as a condition of engagement, then preconceived notions of reality are under attack for the duration and sometimes beyond. If one agrees with deconstruction or postmodern theory, reality has no absolutes but is built upon subjectivity and perception, foundations which may shift beneath the feet of the unwary builder. What we call reality has no separate external existence; it is a construct and as such has an agenda. Agendas are devices which exclude: they demarcate boundaries, limit participation, and often demonize other points of view.

Central to my discussion of horror fiction is the concept of antinomy—of apparently valid laws in contradiction, of contradictory elements inseparably fused into one oxymoronic element, e.g., the twenty-four hour "night and day" cycle we label day, or the opposite facets of heads and tails which define one coin. As we can define night as the absence of daylight, so that one term means nothing without the other, so horror fiction, with its frequent evocations of the unreal and the exaggerated, cannot function in the absence of everyday reality.

Horror fiction is driven mainly by antinomy, however unrecognized and unarticulated. Antinomy, irony, and paradox, which often result in ambiguity, gaps, and slippage, are strong presences in horror fiction; the sense of a text in irresolvable conflict with itself is usually present and is one of the means by which pervasive cultural dread is both produced and intensified. Donna Haraway's comment that "Irony is about contradictions that do not resolve into larger wholes, even dialectically, about the tension of holding incompatible things together because both or all are necessary and true," speaks to the importance of horror fiction as "a world changing fiction." Haraway's insistence on "Social reality as lived social relations, our most important political construction" figures very strongly in my reading of horror fiction.[5] To successfully engage in horror fiction, the reader must be able to juggle Haraway's unresolved wholes and have a sense of irony keen enough to recognize the slippage inherent in irony without permitting that recognition to ruin the engagement. During the day there are no monsters, but with nightfall the possibility of the monstrous emerges and takes on life with the deepening darkness. As there is no light in the absence of darkness, as a concept is usefully defined in terms of what it is not, antinomous elements are crucial among the structures which work to produce horror. Quite frequently the antinomy is expressed in terms of cultural dis/ease and such common conventions as supernatural elements, an extremely unrealistic as well as fantastical situation, closely juxtaposed to and inseparable from a very detailed, very realistic evocation of daily life are vehicles to treat, allegorically and metaphorically, deep-seated societal dis/ease. As both Todorov and King suggest, to discuss the fantastic is therefore to discuss reality allegorically, on at least one level.[6]

While horror fiction has much in common with novels which invoke realistic representation, it differs in three important ways. As mentioned previously, one is the line of demarcation marked by the Dionysian intrusion of the supernatural, the closest thing extant to a litmus test for horror fiction; the second is the emotional response of terror, horror, or even revulsion effected by a horror text. The third, and I would argue the most essential, is the sense of extreme, exaggerated and unresolvable antinomy, which effectively resists closure and resolution more radically than most other fictions. The sense that closure cannot be achieved, that one can close the text, so to speak, but not walk away, or that one can walk away but not close the text, demarcates horror territory.

Another dis/ease-provoking element is the realization that a monster is not always easily recognizable. The be-fanged and be-clawed monster concretizes some deeply seated element agonistic to the accepted cultural model. Metaphorizing the monster from the abstract to the concrete brings the dis/ease to the light of day. While this concretization may be a step in the process towards de-monsterization, I contend that the concretization does not always work to either provide a relief valve or to affirm the cultural model. As Cohen states baldly in *Monster Theory*, "The monster always escapes because it defies easy categorization."[7]

A vampire, for example, functions on many different levels in many different times. Bram Stoker creates Dracula as a disorderly Dionysian eruption into an ordered society; closely wedded to the destruction of Dracula, however, is the destruction of Lucy Westenra and the containment of Mina, the penalties Stoker assesses for their transgressions. Moreover, Halberstam persuasively argues that *Dracula* reflects anti-Semitism, an extension of her argument that monsters should be read as a triad of race, class, and gender. "Dracula, then, resembles the Jew of anti-Semitic discourse in several ways: his appearance, his relation to money/gold, his parasitism, his degeneracy, his lack of allegiance to a fatherland, and his femininity."[8] Concerns with the Jew as a parasitic or vampiric "Other" battening on good Englishmen are, of course, well established in British history; in the late nineteenth century concern with Jewish business practices and capitalization was on the rise in Great Britain, and Stoker's monster can be easily related to dis/ease with the Jewish presence. If one reads Stoker's monster as draining the bourgeoisie, parasitical aristocrat that he undoubtedly is, yet another level of dis/ease concerned with class antagonism surfaces. But as the times change, so change the vampires. In *Carrion Comfort* (1989), Dan Simmons, a contemporary American, uses the metaphor of vampires as Nazis, monsters who subvert the mind and will of their victims. The dis/ease engendered by the Third Reich still resonates frequently in today's society because, among other reasons, an explanation for the horrors of the Holocaust is still lacking. Perhaps Simmons uses the mind vampires, one of whom was a Nazi, as a metaphor for Germany's apparent inability to resist such an atrocity. Stephen King sees vampires as destroying faith in community, and Poppy Z. Brite's vampires are alien beings, whose prey humans are, while Anne Rice seems to be trying to make Louis a sympathetic member of the human community. Laurell K. Hamilton, a relative newcomer to the field, places the vampires as citizens, as neighbors, and as "us."

In all cases, however, the presence of the embodied unDead produces a dis/easeful situation. How does one deal with an immortal, blood-drinking, monstrous body except to be aware that, however much the vampire may resemble a human being, *mon semblable, mon frère,* this creature is essentially in/unhuman? But if it once was us, as is the foundation myth, and looks like us, and often acts like us, and feels the same emotions we feel, but must be demarcated as un/human, demonized as the unDead must be, and sacrificed for the good of the living community, such demarcations must inevitably produce dis/ease. After all, a stroll at the wrong time of night and we could be a vampire, or a victim. Or both. Louis, Anne Rice's victimized hero in *Interview with the Vampire* (1976), at one time attempts to restrict himself to cats and dogs as a source of blood, although this makes him a laughing stock among other vampires; but we are aware that at any time the deeply rooted Dionysian elements in Louis' very nature might well take over and then humans will be his prey. King's, Simmons', and Brite's vampires prey on humans routinely, for humans have no other function; like the Morlochs' view of the Eloi in Wells' *The Time Machine* (1895), humans are the herd, the prey, and nothing more. Hamilton's vampires use the fascination with monsters to elicit willing victims. For the human capable of a muscular enough imagination to imagine vampires and humans co-existing, such images produce great dis/ease.

One of the frequent structures connected with the dialectical conflict between the rational and the intuitive is the Apollonian/Dionysian interface originally postulated by Frederich Nietzsche in *The Birth of Tragedy*. This conflict has been extended in horror fiction criticism, specifically by Stephen King, to encompass the dialectical move from the existing order to the loss of order to its subsequent restoration.[9] The Apollonian reflects order and harmony, the importance of the intellect and the rational in society and man's ever upwardly mobile journey to perfection. It is from the rational, the explicable, and the comprehensible that order is derived. Apollonian fiction, including some horror fiction, is interested in questions of restoration and reaffirmation. It is fiction in which, despite the sudden eruption of the Dionysian, Apollonian order is restored, however qualified this reversion may be. In affirmative horror fiction, such constructs have at their heart an attempt to dispel evil and dis/ease.

The Dionysian, on the other hand, represents disorder and dissonance, and the supremacy of the emotional and the irrational. It is a paradigm of disorder, of human beings run amok. The Dionysian is connected with the dismal knowledge that far from being on the upward path, making steady progress, we are, in our very nature, bestial, disorderly and uncontrolled. The Dionysian ascendant inevitably means the antinomous descent of the Apollonian into disorder, chaos, or dystopia. In Dionysian fiction, order cannot be restored, and the Apollonian interface does not work.

Texts which privilege the Dionysian, such as Hawthorne's "Young Goodman Brown" (1835) or "The Minister's Black Veil" (1837), short stories in which order is not restored, provoke discussions which often attempt, unsuccessfully, to mitigate or resolve the dis/ease. But whether Young Goodman Brown was dreaming or actually witnessing a witches' *sabbat*, the effect is irremediably Dionysian, at least for Goodman Brown. In this text, Apollonian order is defeated by Dionysian ceremonies which take place in the secret recesses of the dark wood, but which also taint village life. In "The Minister's Black Veil," Mr. Hooper swathes himself in a black veil. Because the fragile construct of community must be protected, the strategies of exclusion come into play almost immediately. Rather than moving to internalize their dis/ease concerning this rather trivial scrap of crêpe, the congregation basically demarcates and demonizes Hooper from any Christian communion. Instead of acknowledging a rather common religious doctrine, to whit, that man is by nature sinful, his community scapegoats him. Consequently, the Reverend Mr. Hooper lives a lonely and alienated life and dies a solitary death because he wishes to call attention to the sinfulness of mortal man, not excluding the Elect, and thus wears a black crêpe veil. "How strange," said a lady, "that a simple black veil, such as any woman might wear on her bonnet, should become a terrible thing on Mr. Hooper's face" . . . "I would not be alone with him for the world. I wonder he is not afraid to be alone with himself."[10] This is, of course, an ironic commentary on the human condition, as thinking human beings must, of necessity, be at times afraid to be alone with themselves. The macabre comment that "good Mr. Hooper's face is dust; but awful still is the thought that it moldered beneath the Black veil" again works to deny resolution and to foreground the dis/easeful realization that the knowledge of sin and evil do not stop at the grave. Here lurks the horrific element, the core of the dis/ease. Says Mr. Hooper, "I look around me, and lo! on every visage a Black Veil!"[11]

As mentioned above, Stephen King postulates the intrusion of the Dionysian into an Apollonian society as a means of producing the deep-seated dis/ease so intrinsic to horror fiction. However, King reads this intrusion as temporary and postulates that since horror fiction is a conservative genre, one which upholds accepted conservative values, Apollonian order must be restored. King further argues that horror fiction is essentially reaffirmative in nature, is concerned with the restoration of order in society, and is a force for the harmonic and Apollonian as opposed to the dark excesses of the unbridled Dionysian.[12] Specifically, King says that "[Horror fiction] has an effect of reconfirming values, or reconfirming self-image and our good feelings about ourselves."[13] This view is not always incorrect: in fact, quite often horror fiction does reaffirm existing *mores* via the restoration of order and the vindication of social values. I do, however, contend that King's reading is too simplistic and too monolithic, as it does not account for those texts in which King's move toward affirmation does not take place.

Reading against the grain, or in a dis/orderly fashion, so to speak, I contend that horror fiction is most effective when the Dionysian cannot be contained, when the Apollonian is not completely restored or not restored at all, or when the Apollonian/Dionysian cannot be separated.

Far from being conservative fiction, "as conservative as an Illinois Republican in a three-piece pin-striped suit,"[14] the type of fiction with which I am concerned is better characterized by David Hartwell's contention that this fiction embodies "radical doubt."[15] If the Apollonian privileges the rational, comprehensible, and ordered, one must acknowledge that, cheek by jowl, the threads of irrationality, incomprehensibility, and rampant disorder have also permeated Western discourse. In terms of a storehouse of cultural assumptions, the rational is jumbled higgledy-piggledy on the same shelves as the mad, the insane, and the completely irrational. Rationality, for example, fails in the face of Hiroshima, though a rational and scientific progress resulted in Hiroshima. Rationality fails to explain an Adolf Hitler or a Pol Pot, or even the homegrown horrors of a Jeffrey Dahmer. Such evidence of pure evil or rampant disorder exists, Janus-faced, alongside the Enlightenment idea of the continued and rational perfectibility of humankind.

Depending on the text, the Apollonian/Dionysian interface is almost entirely resolved, affirming the values posited within the text; or is partially resolved, in which case some of the values are affirmed, but some are not; or is left in an irreconcilable stasis, which I argue creates the greatest degree of cultural dis/ease.

In affirmative horror fiction, order and harmony are achieved only when a community is cohesive, when an accepted set of values not only predominates, but is perceived as life-affirming. Typically in this type of horror text, a stable society is threatened by either an internal or external force. This society may be an entire country, a village, a neighborhood, or a unit as small as a family. It may be threatened by government forces such as biological warfare, a decline in employment, corrupt government agencies, radiation-induced gigantic grasshoppers, an alienated and indifferent citizenry, psychopaths, the end of life as we know it, or monsters from elsewhere, ad *infinitum*. And it is this threat to individuals within their ordered environment with which much horror fiction is essentially concerned. In this type of affirmative horror fiction, order is restored at the end of the text, which implies a satisfaction with communal *mores*. The brave townspeople save their community from the voracious and carnivorous grasshoppers, the remnants of humanity re-form communities and start, in the best pioneering tradition, from scratch in a brave new land, the oppressive, fascist agency is defeated and exposed, the community either destroys or contains the psychopath, or the townspeople kick alien butt. The monster, in other words, is defeated. It is not the biological warfare, not the grasshoppers, not even the lone psychopath which is, in and of itself, the concern, but the preservation of the community and its accepted values.

Mid-spectrum texts attain partial resolution, and the Apollonian, although compromised or co-opted, regains a compromised ascendance, although knowledge of the submerged and temporarily defeated Dionysian elements remains prominent and is definitive for this type of horror fiction. Whatever Dionysian contagion has erupted within the stable and ordered society has been defeated but is neither forgotten nor entirely resolved. The realization that the victory is temporary, that another Dionysian event could call the stability and coherence of the community into question is something of which both the characters and the reader are all too aware. While such mid-spectrum texts all acknowledge the fragility of such societal constructs as the role of the individual, social community, or political community and work to reveal not only the fragility but also the actual construction of these institutions as edifices made by society for reasons of exclusion and control, their preservation, however compromised, still works antinomously. By fusing the Apollonian/Dionysian together and by revealing the necessary dependence on artificial and internal constructs, these texts work to generate dis/ease, however mitigated it may be. Surprisingly, considering King's critical stance, which argues validation and affirmation, much of his work fits in this mid-spectrum.

What happens when nothing is positively reaffirmed? What is the effect, the reader's response, when the values under consideration are negative values? What is the use, the function, of leaving us in the wasteland, staring, so to speak, at desolation, with all the comforting, but false, illusions which typically shield us from reality lying about in shreds, tatters, and bloody gobbets? One might well question whether such horror fiction has any purpose whatsoever and believe that skimming the morning newspaper can ruin the day as effectively. One might also argue that calling attention to a negative condition is, in effect, an affirmation because the negative condition is recognized, and implicitly addressed, thus leading to affirmation.

While it is true, algebraically speaking, that two negatives create a positive, in reality the active acceptance of negative values, values which espouse inhumanity, denigrate the value of the individual life or the value of a community, and set up a scenario in which good is powerless and justice non-existent, cannot affirm anything. One definition for horror fiction as well as society is that man's inhumanity to man, *Homo homini lupus*, is a good working definition of evil, and that one who is inhuman to his fellow creatures is evil. As the concept of evil is not usually defined as affirmative, texts which deal ambiguously with evil, or which deliberately resist closure of evil situations cannot be read as affirmative in their effect. While they may be affirmative in a back-handed fashion, affirming there is indeed something to worry about, these disaffirmative texts do not function to assure the reader that all is well. Affirming the negative may draw one deeper into the Pit, may make one a denizen of the Void, but it cannot create a positive set of values. Like fighting fire with fire, the result is either a conflagration or a desolation. More purely Dionysian fictions insist that order cannot be restored, that the Apollonian interface does not work, and that no remedy for a dis/eased society can come into play. Not only do many texts exist which do not reaffirm the existing *mores*, many reaffirm the negative side of the community with assumptions which range from the concept of *privatio boni*, in which evil is no more than the absence of good, to active reaffirmation of the Void.[16] As Lance Morrow points out in an interesting meditative essay on evil, "The end of the 20th century is sorting out different styles of malignity. Evil has been changing its priorities, its targets, its cast of characters."[17] Since one of the main concerns of horror fiction is to address whether order and justice exist, those texts which seem to answer in the negative are of particular interest for the dis/ease with society which they project. Such novels occupy the Dionysian extreme of the spectrum because Apollonian order can never be restored. The Apollonian surface may survive, but, as in my earlier metaphor, it can only conceal the burned cake; the cake remains inedible despite its glossy white frosting.

As I noted above, more horrific situations arise when the invested values are negative values, and community takes on darker and more evil meanings. Sometimes the seemingly positive society is not positive, or the society is so corrupt that the only course possible is further corruption, or the negative force is so overwhelming that restoration and subsequent re-affirmation are not possible. Worse yet, sometimes the negative values are reaffirmed and stand unchallenged. In fact, if, as I contend, disaffirmative structures are a key element of the more effective horror fictions, then the most Dionysian horror fiction would be those works which not only induce as the predominating effect feelings of terror, horror, and revulsion, but those fictions which leave the reader with these feelings completely unresolved and paramount.

Within the paradigms defined above, for example, Jerzy Kosinski's *The Painted Bird* is an example of a novel which is not generally read in terms of horror fiction but which fits the paradigm under discussion. Kosinski posits a community so hopelessly corrupted by mindless and casual cruelty that no possible salvation exists. *The Painted Bird* reflects the Dionysian aspect of life in which order is not recoverable, and the *status quo* is irremediably and irrevocably altered for the worse. This novel, depicting numerous horrific scenes and showcasing the ultimate horror theme, which, in the twentieth century at least, is man's seemingly unending capacity to deal out inhumanity to his fellow creatures, is an excellent example of the Dionysian ascendant. Societal dis/ease appears on nearly every page of this sparely written work, set in Eastern Europe in the middle of World War II, a dystopic period in twentieth-century history, and one which certainly reflects a society in conflict with certain accepted values.

Kosinski's bird, painted and doomed to "other" status by the sadistic peasantry, is the ruling metaphor for a death-dealing, life-denying society which, by embracing the evil which surrounds it, becomes actively evil itself. As Kosinski says, in his problematic foreword, ironically entitled "Afterward," "it [*The Painted Bird*] offered a topography for those who perceived the world as a battle between the bird catchers and the birds."[18] Kosinski's protagonist is subject to much the same treatment as the painted raven: he is demarcated, demonized, and scapegoated. While his physical body is not sacrificed, his ability to live as part of any community is sacrificed.

Many of the scenes in Kosinski's book inspire the reader with loathing and revulsion: the fate of the painted bird within the flock, the fate of a human being who has the misfortune to be different, is horrific. When one of the peasants traps, paints, and releases a raven, a desperate battle ensues:

The ravens flew amuck in the skies and suddenly the painted raven plummeted . . . It was still alive, opening its beak and vainly trying to move its wings. Its eyes had been pecked out and fresh blood streamed over its painted feathers.[19]

Add in the gratuitous cruelties dealt out to man and beast alike, which occur and reoccur with gut-wrenching effect, the narratives wherein the Eastern European peasantry takes great delight in the unnecessary torture of brute animals and in the inhuman treatment meted out to a war orphan, and *The Painted Bird* fits more neatly in horror fiction than in other genres.

Take, for example, the scene in which the child narrator has attempted to rescue a crippled horse and has brought it to a peasant's farm. The point is not that the horse cannot recover; even today, horses with shattered legs are routinely dispatched. But consider how the peasant dispatched the horse:

[H]e threw a noose over the crippled horse's neck and tied the other end of the rope to the plow. The strong horses twitched their ears and looked with indifference at the victim. He [the crippled horse] breathed hard and twisted his neck, which was being squeezed hard by the rope. I stood by wondering how I could save his life, how I could convince him that I had no idea that I would be bringing him back for this . . . the cripple suddenly turned his head and licked the farmer's face. . . . The man did not look at him but gave him a powerful openhanded slap in the muzzle. . . . Suddenly the farmer spat on his hands, grabbed a knotted whip and lashed the rumps of the two strong horses. They bolted forward violently, the rope grew taut and the noose tightened on the neck of the condemned. . . . When the panting horses stopped, the farmer walked up to the victim and kicked him a few times.

There are no supernatural motifs here, and no monsters lurking in the closet, merely the unmitigated and indifferent cruelty detailed time and nauseating time again throughout the text. The complete repudiation of any degree of compassion, whether for boy or beast, and the delight in the cruelty inflicted defines this text as one in which man's inhumanity to man defines the entire culture. It is not the fact that the horse is only useful to the peasant-farmer dead; it is war-time and too much to expect the farmer to send for a vet for a horse for which nothing can be done. But is it too much to expect a small shred of mercy? For the boy, if not for the horse? The boy must not only know he has betrayed a helpless animal, but, worse, in order to survive, he must also be complicit in betrayal: "I spent the rest of the day helping the farmer skin off the hide and cut up the carcass."[20] *Homo homini lupus* indeed.

Perhaps an even more horrific moment in *The Painted Bird*, however, is the scene in which the boy realizes that his long-lost parents have found him and he is as unable to escape them as any other long-caged animal would be. He remembers a wild hare caged a long time; when it was finally released, it crept back into its cage: "Every one of us stood alone and the sooner a man realized that all . . . were expendable, the better for him."[21] Or as King emphasizes in *'Salem's Lot*, *"Alone. Yes, that's the key word, the most awful word in the English tongue. Murder doesn't hold a candle to it and hell is only a poor synonym."*[22]

Nor can the weak ending of *The Painted Bird* entirely mitigate the preceding horrors. The child narrator in *The Painted Bird*, mute from an overdose of horror, regains his voice at the end, thus restoring, perhaps, at least a small chance for some sort of affirmation, but what anodyne could possibly exist to redefine his community as something other than cruelty personified and himself as other than a doomed and painted bird? We do not know what, if any, degree of community Kosinski's character attains or whether he will ever be able to identify with any creature other than the doomed and painted bird. And if he cannot identify with his community, if he remains frozen in the raven/painted bird state, what kind of life will he live? An even worse scenario obtrudes: perhaps he will decide that it is better to be one of the flock of unpainted birds or the bird catchers than to accept his status as "other."

Out of these antinomous structures comes a pattern which appears in texts that concern the human monster, social community, or utopia/dystopia. The strategies of exclusion: demarcation, demonization, scapegoating, and sacrifice work to define the very purpose of horror fiction as exclusionary, divisive, and, ironically and antinomously, the methods by which cohesion and community can be both attained and maintained. These strategies, unpleasant as they are, are part and parcel of the "cultural work" which Tompkins sees texts as performing. Like the texts Tompkins discusses in *Sensational Designs*, which "provid[e] society with a means to think about itself, defining certain aspects of a social reality which the author and readers share," horror fictions "express and shape the social contexts that produced them."[23] By unrelentingly deploying this particular pattern, which points up how we really form communities, how we really relate to other people, what kind of world we really live in, disaffirmative fiction resists the easy answer, the happy ending, the *faux* resolution. This pattern places horror fiction beyond King's reaffirmation, Twitchell's relief valve, Heller's vicariousness and even beyond Hartwell's "radical doubt" or Gibson's view of horror as diagnostic. The most effective horror fiction is relentlessly confrontational in its refusal to accept compromise or resolution; the exaggeration and the graphic nature of much horror fiction, the relentless rending of social constructs, even the constantly recurring strategies of exclusion function to deny even "carrion comfort."

Communities, Monsters, and "Us"

INTRODUCTION

"Yes, he's a monster."
Katey Painko, mother of a child at a North Valley Jewish Community
Center in Los Angeles, where a gunman shot three small boys and
two adults, when her young daughter asked her if the police outside
the building were trying to catch a "monster."[1]

Chapters 3, 4, and 5 will examine one of the more common subjects
in horror fiction, the loosely defined motif of the human monster, the
entity that appears human but is actually monstrous. As will be the case
in future chapters, a spectrum which ranges from an affirmative use of
the motif through the disaffirmative use is clearly present.

An early and potent exemplar of the beast within is, of course, Mr.
Hyde, Dr. Jekyll's alter ego. In his novel *Dr. Jekyll and Mr. Hyde* (1886),
Robert Louis Stevenson emphasizes the dichotomy people feel in Hyde's
presence: "There is something wrong with his appearance; something
displeasing; something downright detestable. I never saw a man I so disliked, and yet I scarce know why. He must be deformed somewhere; he
gives a strong feeling of deformity, although I couldn't specify the point.
. . ."[2] In other words, while those who encounter him react viscerally to
him as a monster, the truly frightening thing about Hyde is that he looks
like one of us.

In Hyde's case, people react to the concealed/cloaked inner bestiality; in more recent fiction, the sense of otherness is often even less
apparent than is Hyde's and thus more dangerous because of the contagion implicit in contact with the monstrous. Such beings generate
extreme dis/ease precisely because although they are not monsters, but
human, they are not human, but monsters. Thus the many types of
"human monsters," i.e., people who are actually human/beasts, such as
werewolves or shapeshifters; people with unusual psychic powers, like
psychometry or pyrokinesis; psychopaths, serial killers, and other
deranged individuals. All these characters are considered inescapably
monstrous. Whether we label them human monsters, as Jeffrey Dahmer
is so conveniently labeled, or refer to the concept of the "beast within,"
or like my recent horror fiction class, decide that "one sick puppy" provides a working definition, we are still talking about the inhuman
"Other," the one that cannot be, but inescapably is, part of us.

The demarcation process, the process of setting boundaries between us and the monster, is no easy task. As horror critics have nearly universally commented, the alien from outer space, a convention beloved of 1950's horror fiction, is easily demarcated. But the monster that looks like us, acts like us, and feels like us is infinitely more difficult to demarcate. If we identify and demarcate the human monster, we also, inescapably, acknowledge and demarcate ourselves. Thus we label the human monster as monstrous as if denying his human condition is enough to provide the necessary separation. But this monstrous discourse is one to which we repeatedly return because we are uneasily aware that simple denial will not serve. The relation between ourselves and the human monster, in other words, is one of commonality, not difference, which is why we are simultaneously dis/eased by and fascinated with human monsters. And it is the denial of the existence of "the beast within," the fear that mankind is inherently monstrous, which creates the cultural dis/ease.

As Richard Tithecott argues in *Of Men and Monsters*, we are fascinated by both the construction and the spectacle of serial killers.[3] In his foreword to Tithecott's book, James Kincaid sardonically notes that "one person (0.0002%) [in 5,000] can locate Lake Huron on a map. Yet a solid 100%, every single adult and child, identifies him [Jeffrey Dahmer] as a serial killer, homosexual, cannibal, ghoul—now dead, killed by a righteous man, albeit a prison inmate, who had enough."[4] What American would claim anything in common with Jeffrey Dahmer or Ted Bundy or John Gacy? Conventional thinking would claim that they are self-constructed, self-demarcated monsters. Not us, but Other. And yet there is always a voice in the narrative that claims the alleged killer was an All-American boy. That old chestnut of normality—that he was nice to old ladies or adopted stray dogs—often surfaces as well. In fact, such "true crime" accounts of such "monsters" as John Gacy and Ted Bundy emphasize their seeming normality, their uncanny ability to be "just like us."[5] We read these statements with emphasis on the "seemed." Obviously, we were deceived; he only appeared to be a regular guy or a nice person; he was actually a monster wearing a human mask, a beast in human clothing. He was nice to old ladies and stray dogs as a cover for his horrific activities, but he could not possibly have really been kind or caring, because he is Other, a monster, and cannot, *ipso facto*, have anything in common with real human beings. Except, of course, he can care for stray dogs, help old ladies cross the street, and still be a serial killer. But if the conventional wisdom concerning human monsters is accepted, it does provide a panacea for the fear that the human monster lurks in all of us. Tithecott, for example, emphasizes the discourse that works to cast the serial killer as monster, to distance him from the community, and to neatly categorize him. In what I would define as a scapegoating ritual, society is purified by recognizing the monster, categorizing him, and then imprisoning or executing him. These rituals, carried out by the FBI or the police force at the expense of understanding the motivations of the serial killer, safeguard society and allow the lines of demarcation between us and the monster to stand unchallenged.

One of the more common subversions employed by horror writers counters the strategies of exclusion by forcing reader identification with the Other, the character who stands far outside accepted values. By creating a character of the Void, one who lacks the basic connections by which we define the human, and then subverting this character's evil or "otherness" just sufficiently to manipulate the reader into seeing the world through the eyes of a monster, the horror writer subverts the once clear boundaries between society and Other and between human and beast, consequently blurring the margins between black and white, good and evil. As James Kincaid comments, "We build them up as Others so we can fear and despise them, while we long for them and admire them."[6] But of course, no one really wants to contemplate the idea that this "beast within" personality could be an integral part of the human animal, that a Dahmer, a Bundy, or a Gacy is actually one of us, a member of the community.

The following triad of chapters will explore how the human monster functions in horror fiction. These texts also generate questions about how a monster is produced as well as recognized. Are human monsters the product of some genetic flaw? A contagious virus? Is the environment responsible? The mother? The father? Are human monsters the product of random accident? Atavistic throwbacks or the accursed of God? If any of these concepts prove true, the rest of society has successfully invoked the strategies of exclusion to protect themselves from identification with this "Other." Substantially less comforting is the idea that the family or the community or accepted societal mores have had a role in shaping the monster; such a point of view, after all, would make society complicit in monster-making.

The question of identification is one that becomes increasingly more confusing and conflicted. How does anyone know whether the neighbor harbors the "beast within"? In contemporary America, one might know very little about one's neighbors. The days in which everyone knew not only their neighbors but also their neighbors' entire genealogy and family history are long gone. The familiar knowledge based on folklore and legends is either unknown or discredited.

In more traditional horror fiction, the monster is readily identifiable as bestial or monstrous despite its ostensibly human shape, as with, for example, the archetypal werewolves and vampires. One can employ the folklore and myths to locate and destroy the inhuman monster. When in doubt, watch your spooky guest. No image in the mirror? Never seen by day? A sort of moldery dust on his clothes? Unusual hairy appendages? These monsters are easy to spot. The werewolf shot in the paw paralleled by the new bandage on the preacher, for example, in King's *The Cycle of the Werewolf*, is a dead giveaway, a convention previously employed in texts such as Howard Wandrei's "The Hand of the O'Mecca," or Frederick Marryat's "The White Wolf of the Hartz Mountains," or Hugh Walpole's "Tarnhelm." The point, of course, is that a member of the community who knows and accepts these myths, legends, and folk-tales as authoritative discourse can locate the monster and know the means by which it can be destroyed. This leads to less dis/ease. There may be a monster out there, even though no one believes in such things, but if there were such a monster, which of course is a nonsensical fear, the monster could be identified and destroyed. The identification and destruction of the monster functions to restore the accepted orderly paradigms to society. In the more affirmative texts in this spectrum, social order is basically restored, even if the "human monster" pays an unfair price. The "watch for the mutant" has been successfully completed, and the community can return to its normal ordered and stable state.[7] Unfortunately for this belief, it is not the readily identifiable mutants which make society so uneasy but the antinomous mutants, the ones who carry the monster successfully cloaked within them. The more conflicted the texts, the less social order can be successfully restored. In the disaffirmative texts in the spectrum, social order, if ever it existed, cannot be restored because the human monster cannot be successfully contained.

Some more contemporary texts simply spotlight the monster and provide no particular explanation for what caused the monstrous. Monsters just are. They inhabit the same space we inhabit, work at the same jobs, live in the same homes. Until they mark themselves as human beasts, of course. Once they do identify themselves, King's watch for the mutant can begin. Then they are clearly and comfortingly "Other," a mutation outside the normal. But this comforting fiction is precisely that: a fiction. The demarcation of boundaries between us and the monster is not so readily explained. Thus, the most memorable and effective horror fictions, the type which leave the unwary reader lying awake at 3:00 a.m. analyzing creaking planks, for example, discards the unreal situations and supernatural monsters and demonstrates that the true horror, the true heart of darkness, is found within typical men and women. In many ways an easily identifiable monster, one that can turn into a wolf or a bat, or has tentacles and comes from outer space is less fearsome than the unsuspected human monster, who may after all flourish in our midst and not be easily identified as the mutant or the Other. Lovecraft's monsters are easily identifiable as monsters; if they "get" you at least you know what got you, small comfort though that may be. But if you are targeted by Hannibal Lecter, Thomas Harris' cannibalistic cultural icon of the monstrous, how will you recognize him as a human monster?

HUNTING THE LAUGHING TIGER:
COMMUNAL CONTAINMENT STRATEGIES

"Inside the beast-skin, a man, yes. But inside the man-skin, a beast."[1]

The human monster is an antinomy—at one and the same time, monster and human as well as human and other. The Apollonian/Dionysian conflict, embodied in the human monster, reflects the fears that social order will disintegrate to the point where the Dionysian will take over. The more affirmative texts manage to restore order within their societies at a reasonable cost even as they acknowledge the dis/ease provoked by the price paid. Thus, a slight dis/ease is unavoidable; these texts are not sanitized versions of fairy tales like *Little Red Riding Hood* or *Cinderella*, but serious attempts to work out the intrusion of the Dionysian.

An important concern, therefore, arises from how aware communities deal with a tiger in a man suit. How does a community react to discovering that the tiger in the man suit inhabits the same space the community inhabits, and having learned about the beast, how can they deal with the beast who masquerades as a man? First, how a community defines a human monster is often called sharply into question. Second, how a community deals with a situation in which an individual who was once one of them has now been set apart, frequently by circumstances beyond any individual's control, is of concern. In a typical formulaic werewolf novel, for example, the person who becomes a werewolf does not choose this fate. These people were at one time part of "us" and most of the time are still "us." Except, of course, when they turn into ravening beasts and pitilessly rend the members of their communities limb from limb. Obviously, the disease these people have contracted is no more their fault than is multiple sclerosis or rabies; just as obviously, they cannot be permitted to live in the community. However defined, the monster is invariably an entity who has in some way either abrogated its humanity or had it abrogated by outside forces. But the abrogation, whether a matter of choice, or random chance is not easily processed. Essentially, this chapter will examine how the community deals with the individual who cannot be part of the community, but who, however paradoxically, functions in an affirmative manner, as well as how a community restores social order when confronted with a human being who is undeniably monstrous. It will trace a movement from the simple self-demarcation which occurs in *The Wolf's Hour*, through the more complicated exclusions which occur in *The Dead Zone* to the self-containment postulated in *Rose Madder* as a means of keeping the beast within safely under control.

In tales of shapeshifting gods like Dionysos, Cerwyn, and Cernunnos, or such semi-divine progeny as minotaurs and centaurs, or such monstrous beings as werewolves and manitous, the image of human as beast or "Other" has long had the Dionysian power to both exalt and horrify. Either emotion upsets the Apollonian applecart and deconstructs an ordered society. Over time, however, the image has transmuted; the beast is no longer as readily recognizable as a minotaur or a centaur would be. In some horror fictions, the beast as shapeshifter can pass as human, and judging its status in society becomes extremely problematic. Werewolves, for example, are almost always viewed adversely, but some horror fictions use werewolves to point out the sad fact that wolves have their admirable side and humans their decidedly abominable side. The effect on the reader when the werewolf motif is subverted is worth examining in terms of how a text with an affirmative human monster can work as horror fiction.

While most werewolf tales evoke horror or revulsion and validate generally accepted cultural norms, Robert McCammon's *The Wolf's Hour* (1989) almost entirely subverts the "beast within" motif, while recognizing the essential inability of a human monster to be one of us. While McCammon's text is in some ways incredible, even for horror fiction, it reflects an extratextual dis/ease and is one of the few decently written examples extant of the affirmative beast within/human monster model. In this case the werewolf protagonist is the hero, and men more often than not the real beasts. Wolves adhere to a code of honor, and men reflect the bestial qualities usually assigned to wolves. Thus, the novel immediately plays against both accepted horror conventions and ingrained cultural prejudices. The negative archetype of the wolf comes into play here, as does the fear of bestiality and the discomfort associated with species slippage.

Western literature is full of the wolf as an evil creature. *Little Red Riding Hood, The Three Little Pigs, Peter and the Wolf,* and *Henri and the Loup-Garrou* all come to mind, amid countless others. Stephen King, for example, playing to the archetype, always classifies the wolf as a servant of Evil, whereas the dog is almost always a positive force.[2] Until recently, this archetype was accepted knowledge in Western culture. In everyday life it often still holds true, as the timber wolves exterminated in New Mexico and facing annihilation in Yellowstone Park stand mute witness. Despite numerous field studies, notably Farley Mowat's *Never Cry Wolf*, which indicate that wolves' diets are much lower on the food chain than is commonly believed, ranchers ascribe nearly genocidal killing powers to them.[3] The wolf, constructed as a glutton, a killing machine, and a remorseless predator who kills for the sheer love of slaying, is a creature of excess, a Dionysian figure. In addition, bestiality is prohibited in contemporary cultures; unless the bestiality occurs in accepted myth or fairy tale, it is defined as hard-core pornography. A werewolf, a human-beast, can couple with females of either species, thus blurring ordained and accepted boundaries. These werewolves, after all, can produce hybrid offspring, creatures which are not only limited to one species, but can shift at will also.

But McCammon's human monster, the wer-beast Michael Gallatin, is a werewolf fighting on the side of the Allies against Nazi Germany, fighting Hitler's evil Third Reich behind enemy lines at considerable risk to his own skin, or hide, as the case may be. As a child, he was bitten by a werewolf and captured to be part of their dwindling community. Werewolfdom is caused by a virus, somewhat like rabies, which liberates an atavistic part of the brain that human beings have lost. Thus, he has no agency: his demonization does not occur through his own choice. He survives the change, however, and learns to accept and use his dual nature. His werewolf teacher Wiktor, who used to be a university professor until he lost his position to the politics of the time and his family to starvation, teaches him the ways of humans and wolves. Wiktor not only teaches him the Great Books of the Western World and several languages, as well as science and mathematics, he also teaches him to live like a wolf. According to Wictor, humans are the beasts; as he tells Michael, "I would know the wolf's way from birth, and be ignorant of that beast called a human being."[4]

The fact that one of these lessons takes place in the den and culminates in a successful rat hunt is a bit dis/ease-provoking. Mikhail "put the rat's head between his teeth and bit down on the tough little neck" He offers the head to Wiktor, as "it was good manners to offer the best portion of any meal to Wiktor." The essential antinomy here is perhaps best captured by the narrator's commentary: "The man and boy ate their rat in the dark chamber, with the echoes of civilized minds in the shelves all around them." The scene deliberately juxtaposes the human and the bestial: "That rat was as slow as a muffin-stuffed grandmother. . . . [T]he brain reminded him [Mikhail] of a sweet potato pie."[5] Thus McCammon blurs the boundaries between man and wolf, for what need has a man to learn to hunt rats, and of what use to a wolf are Great Books?

Wiktor may see the werewolf positively, but the overall cultural archetype of the wolf is still negative. Thus, Mikhail Gallatinov really has no place in the world. Wiktor impresses the absolute necessity to "live free" on his pupil and frequently describes England as a place where "they don't execute their teachers. . . . They don't burn your books in England and they don't kill for the love of it."[6] England, in other words, is less beastlike than post-Tsarist Russia. Eventually, the human beasts destroy the werewolf community, and Michael, remembering his teacher's comments, goes to England. Since he is extraordinarily useful to British intelligence, his arcane powers are kept absolutely secret. While one of his covers is the eponymous Baron von Fange, he is able to operate successfully because almost no one knows he is a werewolf. Or would believe their eyes were they to witness the change. Thus, he can accomplish almost impossible intelligence operations, use wolf packs when he has need of them, call on the agility, strength, speed, sensory capabilities, and woodscraft of wolves, but always keep his human brain. When the Nazis are planning to use a fatal poison gas to wipe out London and effectively neutralize the D-Day invasion, Michael is the prime force in stopping the attempt.

Wiktor has asked Michael, "What is the lycanthrope in the eyes of God?"[7] Established legend, folklore, and myth answer the question one way. The werewolf is the accursed of God, a minion of Satan, and evil incarnate. Michael sees things slightly differently. He says, after witnessing the concentration camps, with the piles of dead bodies, the hair shorn for sale to wigmakers, the callous and bestial cruelty displayed, and after bringing the Commandant to his death, "The lycanthrope was God's avenger."[8] If there is a genocidal killing machine at work, it is not the werewolf, but the human. But how can Michael be a monster and a hero at one and the same time? He can only be a hero by concealing his true nature and refusing communion with his community, because allowing his wolfish nature to be known will result not only in a swift descent to villainy but an attempt by narrow-minded Apollonians to destroy the Dionysian intruder. However heroic Gallatin has been, however useful in preserving society, the same society which praises Gallatin the freedom fighter would turn on him in the blink of an eye were he to acknowledge his true nature.

This very affirmative tale is tinged with dis/ease as Michael Gallatin can never admit his true identity, not to his neighbors in the remote Welsh fastnesses where he lives, and not to his lovers, either. On the other hand, he is a werewolf because of random chance, and he does control his nature. Thus, he is not subject to the fear and loathing to which he would be subject were his true identity known. But he is a werewolf and the only way he can maintain his acceptance in the human world is to live on the margins of that world as a solitaire. He must self-demarcate because otherwise the remaining strategies of exclusion will spring into play, and he may well end up killed by the very people whose lives he has safeguarded. Thus, the werewolf is conflicted biologically, archetypally, and politically, and even an affirmative text which challenges these conflicts must still have a slight tinge of dis/ease to it.

Another affirmative use of the motif occurs when the societal values and political institutions work as they are supposed to, and the human monster, whether a shapeshifter or an "unnaturally empowered" human being, is contained. This "monster," however affirmative in behavior, must be contained because someone with paranormal abilities can see behind the social facades of the community and reveal too many unpleasant truths. Stephen King's *The Dead Zone* (1979) is an excellent example of such a text, as the unnaturally empowered John Smith uses his ability to see the past and the present in order to preserve social order. This novel is more conflicted than *The Wolf's Hour*, as the protagonist has been a member of his community all his life, until he is changed by circumstance. Such a plot structure generates more dis/ease than one with a marginalized character because the community has more at stake. King's very vivid evocation of the processes by which community members are subject to the strategies of exclusion, regardless of their previous status or motivation, and the way he resolves the conflict while still resisting complete affirmation make *The Dead Zone* an effective example of affirmative horror fiction.

In *The Age of Sex Crime*, critic Jane Caputi refers to *The Dead Zone* as a novel concerned with "a sex killer as the pure creation of his monstrous mother" with "a fully developed subplot about a Ripper-type killer of young girls."[9] While there is certainly a subplot concerning a serial killer, the most important point King makes is that the "unnaturally" empowered John Smith is perceived as no less monstrous and just as threatening as the serial killer Frank Dodd, who, incidentally, does not limit his victims to young girls. While King does employ the monstrous mother trope rather too frequently, *The Dead Zone* is less about serial killers than it is about the perception and definition of human monsters. John Smith does not choose human monsterdom; his Dionysian powers are the unhappy result of an accident. Like Gallatin, he was in the wrong place at the wrong time.

John Smith is a young, excellent teacher whose life is normal in nearly every way. He has flashes of precognition dating from a childhood head injury, and when he and his girlfriend Sarah go to the County

Fair, he wins a large amount of money from a rigged Wheel of Fortune. He has no idea how he does this, nor has he any way to control it, but this talent sets Johnny slightly off from other people. One of the metaphors King employs for the "beast within" is the Jekyll and Hyde mask which Johnny wears when he and Sarah go to the fair: "The left side of the face, the half with the open eye, appeared to be normal. But the right half was the face of a monster, drawn and inhuman."[10] In some ways, this metaphor describes friendly, popular, outgoing Johnny Smith perfectly. As he spins the *Wheel of Fortune*, Sarah thinks "how strange his face was in this bold yet furtive lighting. She thought of the mask again—Jekyll and Hyde."

Coming home from the fair, Johnny is involved in a head-on collision. Johnny goes into a coma in late October 1970 and awakens in May 1975 to find his personal life has been unalterably shattered. After three years of waiting and hoping for Johnny's recovery, Sarah has married Walter Hazlett. He also awakens to a world where he has the psychic abilities of precognition and psychometry. He accurately predicts the future and displays uncanny knowledge about the past. He tells his doctor, Sam Weizak, for example, that his mother did not die in Warsaw in the battle for Poland during World War II but survived in a state of temporary amnesia, married an engineer, had several children, and is now living in Carmel, California. He also tells Sam that his mother still dreams of him, dreams that "the boy is safe."[11] Weizak decides, after phoning his mother and recognizing her voice, to let the whole matter drop. As he says, "The boy is safe, the woman is safe in Carmel. The country is between them, and we let that be."[12] While Weizak can accept Johnny's abilities, many other people cannot, even when they benefit, and so the strategies of exclusion come into play. When Johnny tells his physical therapist, Eileen Magown, that her house is on fire, he saves not only her house but her beloved cats. But he pays a price. Not only do the nurses who witness his call and the confirmation of the fire stare at him accusingly, so that Johnny thinks dismally of *Jury's eyes*, but even as Eileen says, "God bless you, Johnny" and kisses him on the cheek, "the expression on her face was very much like superstitious dread."[13] When Johnny meets the local press, an extremely skeptical reporter, Roger Dussault, demands he prove his abilities and hands Johnny a medal from his dead sister. Unfortunately for the reporter's skepticism, Johnny reveals that the man's older sister died of a drug overdose but tells the reporter that she always loved him. The reporter collapses, and Johnny is suddenly not a seven-day wonder, but a freak, a person to be demarcated and demonized. When Johnny tries to explain that he meant no harm, the pattern becomes starkly clear:

"I didn't mean to hurt him," he said. "Honest to God, I never meant to hurt him. I didn't know."

The TV reporter backed up a step. "No," he said. "Of course you didn't. He was asking for it, anybody could see that. Just . . . don't touch me, huh?"[14]

Johnny feels responsible for his knowledge, and such power, of course, is problematic. But the press, particularly the tabloid press, does not take such a humanistic outlook on life. Johnny is an immediate celebrity, and the sight of the news film results in a fatal stroke to his mother. On her deathbed, she makes Johnny promise to carry out what she sees as God's will:

"Don't run from him, Johnny. Don't hide away in a cave like Elijah, or make him send a big fish to swallow you up. . . . You'll know the voice when it comes. It'll tell you what to do. It told Jeremiah and Daniel and Amos and Abraham. . . . And when it does, Johnny . . . *do your duty.*"[15]

While Johnny agrees with her so that she will die in peace, he does not accept his mother's dying injunction. The notion of prophecy, after all, is not a particularly comfortable one. Prophets or seers are those people who must occupy the margins, tell people what they do not want to hear, and be roundly cursed for their pains. So it is with Johnny. Like the prophets, Johnny is more or less called by God; unlike the Old Testament prophets, whose dis/easeful status is directly protected by Yahweh, Johnny cannot distance himself from the general population. Like Teiresias in Sophocles' Oedipus cycle, he is both feared and blamed for events over which he has no control but can only predict.

While Johnny has been comatose, two real human monsters have been busy in the area. As is the case with the dis/ease-provoking human monster, neither of these monsters are easily differentiated from the average person. A series of sexually oriented serial killings has terrorized Castle Rock, and the sheriff has been unable to crack the case. Sheriff George Bannerman, both outraged at the constant killings and fearful for his job in the next election, asks Johnny for help solving the murder. Johnny at first refuses, but when the next victim is a nine-year-old girl, he finally decides he has a moral duty to assist if he can. The scene in which he clutches an empty pack of Marlboro cigarettes and melds with the killer, chanting, "Slick, I'm slick, I'm so slick," both frightens and convinces Bannerman:

His [Johnny's] voice rose to a crazy triumphant shriek that competed with the wind, and Bannerman fell back another step, his flesh crawling helplessly, his balls tight and cringing against his guts. "Let it stop," he thought. Let it stop now. Please."[16]

Bannerman is convinced, but he is also frightened and repelled. But the real problem arises when Johnny tells the sheriff who the killer is. When he describes the killer, Bannerman accuses Johnny of being a fake and a publicity hound, and threatens to "break his back" if he makes his accusations public. Johnny cuts to the crux of the matter:

"You don't *want* it to be Dodd, do you? . . . Because . . . Frank looks up to good old Sheriff George Bannerman, oh, Frank's bloody Christ down from the cross, except when he's raping and strangling old ladies and little girls, and it could have been your *daughter*, Bannerman."[17]

Reluctantly, because he is a good lawman and also because he must prove Johnny wrong, Bannerman investigates. But Johnny also realizes that however thankful Bannerman may be once the killer is captured, he will be too uncomfortable to associate with him. Johnny is thus increasingly marginalized in the community of which he was once a part. People are either uncomfortable around him, want something from him, or want to expose him. And even when his prescience results in good, people demarcate him.

Johnny is right, of course: Frank Dodd, a police officer and Bannerman's protégé, the man he thinks of as a son, is indeed the killer. Bannerman says to Johnny, just before they confront Dodd, "If you really can see such things, I pity you. You're a freak of God, no different than a two-headed cow. . . . I'm sorry. That's a shit thing to say, I know."[18] Consequent to the capture of the Castle Rock killer, the Board of Education at Cleaves Mills revokes Johnny's newly offered teaching contract because he is "*too controversial to be a good teacher.*" Although Johnny is acting from the highest of motives and does indeed restore societal order by capturing the serial killer, he is nevertheless demarcated and demonized: "*All they can see is that your picture was in* Newsweek *and the* New York Times *and that the Castle Rock story was on the national news broadcasts.*"[19]

Thus, Johnny rapidly becomes the scapegoat. He manages to get employment as a short-order cook and then as a tutor. He is, as the reader expects, extremely successful as a tutor, but again he is victimized by his inability to let tragedy happen if he can avoid it. He warns the people at Chuck's graduation party that the restaurant where the senior class is holding its graduation party will burn to the ground with extensive fatalities. Although he frightens some of the people who hear him into staying away, many of the senior class disregard his warning, and the place burns. Once again, hounded by the survivors, the press and the needy people who contact him, he moves on, trying, unsuccessfully as it turns out, to escape the crushing obligation his powers place upon him.

While tutoring Chuck, Johnny notices a promising new political candidate, Greg Stillson, but even the sight of him strikes a chord of dis/ease in Johnny. Greg Stillson is a Dionysian figure pretending to be Apollonian. In the reader's first encounter with Stillson, he kicks to death a dog guarding the farm at which he has stopped: And while he wonders if he is going crazy, he feels no remorse, only chagrin that he will be unable to sell a Bible and that he might lose his job. Although Stillson presents himself as a Populist, someone who stands for the common man, his thoughts on that man are very revealing. After he has kicked the dog to death, he thinks, "Wouldn't do him any good if Clem Kadiddlehopper and his wife and their six kids came back from town now in their Studebaker and saw Fido dying out here with the bad old salesman standing over him."[20]

Stillson is a completely ruthless and amoral psychopath as well as a man of great personal charm. Thus, he is another human monster, like Dodd, shrouded by his apparent status as one on the side of social order. It is Stillson who has drug offenders carrying out much needed community projects like landscaping and designing children's playgrounds; it is also Stillson who drastically cuts library and social service funding. Stillson, running independently for a seat in the House of Representatives after a stint as mayor of Ridgway, is also the man whom Ngo, the Vietnamese gardener, recognizes as a human monster, one who has "taken the game of the Laughing Tiger a step further. Inside the beast-skin, a man, yes. But inside the man-skin, a beast."[21] Johnny meets Greg Stillson, shakes his hand, and has an extraordinary experience:

Everything came at him at once . . . like some terrible black freight train . . . like a speeding engine . . . and the headlamp was knowing everything, and its light impaled Johnny Smith like a bug on a pin. . . . Perfect knowledge ran him down, plastered him as flat as a piece of paper . . .[22]

What Johnny sees is Greg Stillson bringing apocalyptic destruction on the world. Later, Ngo, who has experience with human monsters, says Stillson should be killed, either politically or physically, but Johnny rejects that solution, thinking to himself, *Killing only sows more dragon's teeth . . . I believe it with all my heart.*[23] Johnny researches Stillson, keeps notebooks, and falls just short of the model of an obsessed assassin. But his dreams, dreams in which a laughing tiger pads through miles of scorched earth still torment him, and he realizes that he cannot ignore his knowledge. He therefore asks a question which is at the core of the section entitled "The Laughing Tiger": *If you could jump in a time machine and go back to 1932, would you kill Hitler?*[24] Eventually, he decides to kill Greg Stillson. He knows his behavior will be adjudged like that of the Oswalds, the Sirhans, and the Bremmers, and that to assassinate Stillson is to set himself on the same level as the human monsters of the world, but he nevertheless decides to proceed. His plans go awry, but Stillson, who grabs a small child to shield himself when he hears the first rifle shot, is politically dead. Johnny, who has recently been diagnosed with a brain tumor, dies of a hemorrhage, but not before his grasp on Stillson's leg confirms that the man's destructive power is gone.

While the plot structure of this novel clearly falls within the affirmative portion of the spectrum, it is still dis/ease-provoking. Clearly, while there are three "human monsters" in this text, only two of them are actually evil. People love Greg Stillson, the political psychopath, but they demonize Johnny, despite the fact that John Smith is a moral and decent man who refuses to profit by his powers. Johnny, by accepting the burden of power, accepts not only the demarcation which comes with his psychic powers, but also the subsequent scapegoating and sacrifice.

It is this antinomy that causes dis/ease in *The Dead Zone*. John Smith should not be demonized at all; he is the main force by which two truly harmful individuals are contained or neutralized, yet the community puts him in the same category of human monster as Frank Dodd and Greg Stillson. This text is also dis/ease-provoking because the hero does and does not win in the end. His sacrifice is affirmative in nature and recognized as such, yet he is still labeled as a freak. As a witness at the Senate Hearings says, "If he did have such a curse—yes, I would call it a curse—I hope God will show pity to that man's tortured soul."[25]

While the first two texts in this chapter explore questions of definition and identity, Caleb Carr's *The Angel of Darkness* (1997) is concerned not only with the containment of the human monster but also with problems of identification. In McCammon's *The Wolf's Hour*, the very lack of identity makes the affirmative werewolf possible; in *The Dead Zone*, John Smith is easily defined as a human monster. In Carr's text, however, the human monster must first be identified so that she/he may be contained. The monster in this text is closer to the mid-spectrum human monsters explored in the following chapter because no marker sets them off from the rest of society.

The Angel of Darkness is an important novel in a discussion of human monsters, as it is a thoughtful discussion of the much maligned monstrous mother, who permeates serial killer and horror fiction. It is much to Carr's credit that he manages to deploy the monstrous mother in such a manner as to contextualize the mother archetype, relate it to both the late nineteenth century and the present day, and look at the elements behind the construction of the "mother as monster," avoiding all the stock images and facile judgments."[26] The dis/ease in this text arises from several points: first, the human monster is a female serial killer, which reverses the male serial killer convention; second, the serial killer is that most dis/ease provoking of characters, a monstrous mother. Libby Hatch, the antagonist, kills children—her own and other people's—in a vain attempt to fulfill the societal expectations which she can neither perform nor avoid. Third, Carr's novel acknowledges that the gender role which assigns nurturing nonviolent status to women is often erroneous. Carr's contention, articulated in the "Acknowledgments," is worth quoting at length:

Women are just as prone to violent crime as are men. But their victims are most often children—frequently their own children. . . . [W]omen generally abuse or murder people with whom they have strong personal connections unlike men, who often select strangers as the victims of their violent tendencies, since they are easier to objectify."[27]

Carr further acknowledges that any similarities to present day female violent crime are intentional, and this extratextual element is the fourth *locus* of interest in his novel. Since Libby Hatch, his serial killer, not only kills two of her three children, but blames a mythical black man, the contemporary parallels are not too hard to recognize. The recurring question in the horrifying Susan Smith case was "how could a mother do such a thing," as if being a mother exempted her from the usual motives for homicide. In Smith's case it is generally acknowledged that she thought her affair with her employer's son would culminate in marriage. In breaking off the affair, her lover claimed he was not ready to be a father, and the children, far from being the center of Smith's universe, became commodities to be disposed of in a manner that would allow her to emerge as the grieving mother. Thus the nine-day charade in which Smith, quite convincingly performing the grief-stricken mother, begged for her sons' return, and her nearly universal demonization when the truth came out. What generally goes unexamined is the automatic assumption that giving birth equates with a nurturing female role, commonly labeled "mother," even though thousands of mothers mistreat, abuse, and even murder their offspring yearly, clearly indicating that motherhood does not come into being simply through impregnation. And yet mothers and motherhood hold such a valorized position in the culture that each case is greeted with the same disbelief.

Libby Hatch, the dark angel of Carr's title, is a serial killer living in *fin-de-siècle* New York. No one, except protagonist Dr. Laszlo Kreizler, can easily accept that she could possibly be a serial killer because she is a woman and women are, by reason of biological differences, nurturers. Narrator Stevie Taggert recalls the story some twenty-odd years after it happened. Muckraking journalist John Schuyler Moore is embittered that his book that details the Beecham case remains unpublished because of its offensive contents.[28] As Stevie notes, sardonically but honestly, "Maybe it *is* a story that needs telling, like Mr. Moore claims; but there's plenty of stories that need telling what never get told because people can't bear the hearing. . . . The Beecham case was strong stuff, maybe too strong . . . Could be you should've . . . started with something that didn't involve talk about slaughtered boy-whores, cannibalism, and eye-balls in a jar."

Resonances of the Jeffrey Dahmer case are hard to miss, and it is as true today as 100 years ago that such accounts make uncomfortable reading, although the discomfort level is evidently not high enough to discourage people from reading them. Stevie suggests the Libby Hatch case, and the effect is interesting: "My friend goes a little pale." Such a comment is interesting, as it is hard to see how a woman's name, twenty-odd years after the fact, could produce a worse effect than the previous catalogue of horrors. Moore says, "You just couldn't . . . How could anyone. . . . I thought you were talking about a case that wouldn't be as gruesome as Beecham's. In the Hatch case, you've not only got kidnappings, but murdered infants, grave robbing."[29] Stevie, who has wagered that he can tell Libby Hatch's tale, concedes that

> "The tale of Libby Hatch was more frightening and disturbing than any-thing we ran across in our hunt for the butcher John Beecham . . . [It] may hor-rify you, reader, and it may strike you as too unnatural a story to have ever happened. . . . But you can take this from me: if the story of Libby Hatch teaches us anything at all, it's that Nature's domain includes every form of what society calls "unnatural" behavior. "[30]

The idea of the natural as in natural women, natural law, and natural behavior linked to gender roles is at the root of the dis/ease generated in the novel. Miss Sara Howard, a female private eye whose practice is lim-ited to women, is retained on a case of kidnapping, which quickly takes several new twists, and most of the novel is concerned with the detection and capture of Libby Hatch, childsnatcher/slayer and human monster.

What gives this novel the tinge of dis/ease which defines the type of affirmative horror fiction I am discussing is the conflict within the monster and Carr's scrutiny of the construction of gendered roles in a society in which society creates and then condemns the human monster. Libby Hatch has neither the talent nor the instinct for marriage or motherhood, and yet that role is the only really acceptable role for her in late nineteenth century society. Even Sara Howard, who has money of her own and can afford to indulge her eccentricities, is aware that she is a "spinster detective," and that she will not really be a woman until she has a family: "A man can be a bachelor, and still be a man. . . . But a woman without children? She's a *spinster*, Stevie . . . always less than a woman."[31]

Dr. Laszlo Kreizler is an alienist who is pioneering the theory of "context," i.e., that actions cannot be accurately interpreted outside of the cultural matrix which produced them. More prosaically, he feels that in order to understand the aberrant, he must attempt to see the world the way the aberrant sees it. While Kreizler is less interested in executing Libby Hatch than in treating her, he has a problem. Despite the proofs he has amassed, which link Hatch not only to the kidnapped Ana Linares, a Spanish diplomat's child, but to the murder of several other children, no one believes him. In most people's opinions, she is a brave and grief-stricken woman.

Kreizler quotes the eminent social thinkers of the day to the effect that as soon as a wife becomes a mother, the center of her world shifts, and she subordinates herself completely to her child's needs. He also quotes a certain Professor James to the effect that "Parental love is an instinct stronger in woman than in man—the passionate devotion of a mother to a sick or dying child is perhaps the most beautiful moral spectacle the world affords."[32] While Kreizler scoffs at these comments as mawkish sentimentality, Sara points out the unresolvable conflict in a woman who either cannot have or nurture children but is only identifiable in society in terms of her ability to do so, a situation which creates an irresolvable double bind: "It's a cruel standard—especially to women who can't achieve it. Libby couldn't, and the failure broke her."[33] Further detection reveals new information, and eventually Kreizler, Stevie, Moore, and Howard come to the conclusion that she kidnaps children and then kills them because they

> "Reject her attention and her care, no matter how much effort she puts into it. She tells herself it's their fault. She has to. Because the alternative—"
>
> Mr. Moore finally picked it up. "The alternative—is to admit that she has *no* nurturing skills." He let out a low whistle.

"My God . . . do you mean to tell me this woman has structured her whole life around something she can't *do*?"[34]

The point Moore is still missing is that Libby Hatch has not structured her life around being a mother; her life has been structured for her by the demands of the society she has the misfortune to inhabit. Libby Hatch has almost no chance to escape her environment. Behind Libby Hatch lies a trail of dead children from her first child, her wet-nurse days, her marriage, her nursing days, and also her kidnappings. And yet her story about the black man who killed her children is believed by the authorities. When Kreizler eventually gets enough evidence to bring her to trial, Clarence Darrow is very nearly successful in bringing in an acquittal because people cannot believe that Libby Hatch could do such a thing. The inviolable status of the home and the sanctity of motherhood as cultural models are too strong to be easily dismissed. A last-minute investigation reveals her first murder, that of the illegitimate child she killed and buried with her dog. The connecting clue is inscribed on the gravestone in her family home, *Love Always, from Mama*, the same sentiment engraved on her murdered children's grave. Faced with this revelation, Libby Hatch accepts a plea bargain, kills the guard she has managed to seduce, and escapes, but is finally brought to justice by Kreizler and company.

In an interesting echo, when the final hunt for Libby Hatch and her kidnap victim is underway, El Niño, a Filipino aborigine who has joined the party to help find his employer's child, likens her to a man-eating tiger. He is in favor of executing Hatch as that is what one does to maneaters: "Will you hunt the tiger with me [he asks] or will you try to 'understand' it?"[35]

In the final confrontation between Kreizler and Hatch, Kreizler once again offers to help and Libby replies, *"But I've done nothing! . . . Can't you see that? . . . No, no of course you can't. You're a man.* What *man* could understand what my life has been like—why I've had to make the choices I have?"[36] In a final speech, which reveals the unresolvable conflict within her, Libby says,

"I did *everything* for those children. . . . For *what*, Doctor? . . . They never stopped needing. . . . I did everything I could, *everything*, but it never stopped! It was *all I could do*—it should have been enough! But it never was . . . it never was. And so—can't you see? They were better off after I—. . . . They didn't need *anything* then."[37]

Naturally, this is not an acceptable reason for killing several innocent children; equally obviously, she believes they are better off dead, although Stevie believes that they were simply in the way of a new life, like Susan Smith's unfortunate children. El Niño shoots Libby with a poisoned dart and she dies, murmuring, *"always needing."*[38]

Thus, this somewhat dis/easeful novel falls in the affirmative section of the spectrum as the human monster is contained and order is restored. But the dis/easeful effect lingers as one realizes how very contemporary this ostensibly historical-detective novel is. Stevie, supplying a coda to the narrative, points out that

> "True to the doctor's beliefs, the real monsters continued, then as now, to wander the streets unnoticed, going about their strange and desperate work with a fever that looks to the average citizen like nothing more than the ordinary effort required to get though an ordinary day."[39]

My strongest example of an affirmative yet dis/ease-provoking text is King's *Rose Madder*, one of the first of his novels to feature a woman as a strong proactive protagonist. *Rose Madder*, like Carr's *The Angel of Darkness*, concerns the Dionysian aspect of the female, the female as potentially monstrous. King resists the standard "and she lived happily ever after" formula and devises an ending which resists the many fairy-tale aspects of *Rose Madder* in favor of a more realistic scenario. As is the case in many of his other works, King writes an apparently affirmative novel in which the values he sees as conservative and reassuring are validated. While this is true, it is only part of the truth. The rest of the truth, that human monsterdom is inherent in the human condition and contagious, is considerably less reassuring. Although Rose Madder moves from a Dionysian society masquerading as Apollonian to an Apollonian society, awareness of the contained Dionysian and its possible recurrence lurks just below the surface. The beast within is of major interest as King not only ties it to the myth of the Minotaur but also emphasizes the impossibility of full containment.

The novel's primary male character, Norman Daniels, is a detective, a man theoretically dedicated to preserving society from the human monsters which prey upon it. Daniels is part of a police organization where extreme and totalitarian control, one manifestation of which is wife-beating, is acceptable—not only to the policemen but to their wives as well. Early in the novel, in fact, Norman is linked, in a word play on cop, with a bull, and thus with the human beast. Thus, King depicts an Apollonian society in which all the accepted societal values are perverted and corrupted. This concept of community may be accepted by both the cops and their wives, but neither Norman Daniels' claim nor Rosie Daniels' acceptance can make this community affirmative in nature.

To summarize briefly, Rose McClendon Daniels is a woman who has endured long-term abuse, emotional, sexual, mental, and physical. Norman, who is sexually stimulated by violence, routinely beats, bites, burns, and sodomizes Rose. When she is four months pregnant, he beats the child out of her belly, and after that Rose goes into a type of mindless existence, totally contained within his wishes and terrified into near catalepsy. Rose does not dare press charges; she believes Norman when he tells her that cops are a family, a band of brothers. If she ever runs away, he says, he will have all the help he needs in tracking her down. Norman's talismanic police academy ring is engraved with *Service, Loyalty and Community*. Since the motto on Norman's ring is often impressed on Rosie's breasts, she believes him absolutely.

It occurs to Rose Daniels one day that her problem is not that her husband will kill her; the problem is that he will only incapacitate her. The litany of abuse runs through her mind:

"Fourteen years. Fourteen years of having him talk to me up close. The miscarriage. The tennis racket. Three teeth, one of which I swallowed. The broken rib. The punches. The pinches. And the bites, of course. Plenty of those Plenty of—."[40]

Since she cannot call the domestic abuse hotline and have her husband arrested, she does the next best thing. Despite being scared witless of being caught by Norman and utterly terrified of being out on her own, Rose Daniels runs away.

Rosie makes her move from an extremely stable but inherently perverted community to a new life, one in which she hopes to be free of Norman. She finds an affirmative Apollonian community to replace the corrupted Apollonian community which she has rejected. She starts a new life with the aid of Daughters and Sisters, an activist feminist self-help group which runs a halfway home for battered women. Daughters and Sisters provides her with a sanctuary, a job, and a new start, and she slowly forges a new life. Rose discovers she has a perfect voice for recording audio books, rents her own apartment, trades her wedding ring for a picture for which has a strong and inexplicable attraction, meets a new man, dramatically changes her hair color, and seems to be well on her way to starring in a feminist success story. Ironically, Rosie succeeds so well as a reader because she has fantastic breath control; Rhoda, her director, says,

"You have great voice management, but the absolutely incredible thing is your breath control. If you don't sing, how in God's name did you get such great control?"

"I don't know," she had told Rhoda. . . . "I guess it's just a gift."

The truth is somewhat darker:

A nightmarish image had occurred to Rosie then: sitting in the corner with her
kidneys swelling and throbbing like bloated bags filled with hot water . . . Sitting there breathing with long flat inhales and slow soft exhales, because that's
what worked best.[41]

While Rosie does not wish to share her private torments, she cannot
deny them either, and part of the affirmative nexus which works so successfully in this novel is that she uses what she can from her previous
life and tries to discard the rest.

But Norman, incensed by her flight, infuriated over her "theft" of
the ATM card, and incandescently inflamed by the fact that "little creepmouse Rose" has dared to escape, uses a technique he calls "trolling" to
trace his errant wife. Rose is aware that Norman will try to track her
down and will certainly kill her if he does so. She still does not dare ask
for police protection, so Rose must guard herself as best as she can.

But this is horror territory, and Rose has magic on her side. She has
no effective defense against Norman—except the picture, for which she
traded her engagement and wedding ring.

The picture shows the remains of a vine-cloaked Greek temple and
foregrounds a woman, dressed in a *zit*, with a blonde chignon, and a gold
armlet, her back to the viewer. The picture, which exercises a strong and
irresistible fascination for Rose, turns out to be animated. Every time
Rose looks at it, she sees a little more of the landscape; what is more,
she dreams of being in the picture, and in the morning finds crickets and
grass from the picture in her apartment. This picture reveals a world in
which women have power, a sisterhood which Rosie, whose name
echoes Rosie the Riveter, would like to join. In a motif which echoes
Oscar Wilde's *The Picture of Dorian Gray* (1890), the picture hides a
corrupted world.[42] Rose Madder, the woman in the picture, is a mirror
image of Rosie, but a decayed and diseased Rosie who defines men as
beasts and is as unstable emotionally as Norman; the woman's baby
recalls the child Rosie lost, the child she had named Caroline; and the
bull in the maze is, of course, Norman. What Rose is most conscious of
in Rose Madder is a sense of barely controlled rage which might spill
over at any time under any pretext.

Norman successfully trolls for Rosie, killing several of her friends
from Daughters and Sisters in the process. When Norman eventually
traps Rosie and Bill in Rose's apartment, they escape him by going into
the painting. It is in this corrupted world that Rosie permanently escapes
her husband, learns some unsavory truths about herself, and also forfeits

an important part of her painstakingly acquired new identity. She successfully lures her husband to his death, taunting him in a way she would not have dared in the "real world." Instead of fearing his rage and planning ways to mitigate his rage, a very unsuccessful strategy, she uses the rage to manipulate him into going to his death at the hands of Rose Madder. Rosie also learns that Rose Madder, her *alter ego*, is being eaten by the barely restrained rage she feels: Underneath the beauty was madness. . . . *It's a kind of rabies—she's being eaten up with it . . . she's apt to fall on me and do whatever she did to Norman.*[43]

As she is leaving the diseased world of the picture, a place she will no longer need to inhabit, she asks Rose Madder, "Am I you? Tell me the truth—am I you?"[44] This question is at the crux of the beast within trope. Are Rose McLendon Daniels/"creepmouse Rose,"/*Rosie Real, a great big deal*, and Rose Madder the same woman? It is this question with which Rose must somehow come to terms.

As readers, we may (or may not) be able to accept the motif of an animated picture; if this fiction is to engage us, however, what we must accept is the idea that power corrupts both individuals and societies, and that one always pays a price for power. Victimization and the denial of victimization do not always result in a strong and affirmative personality; an emergent sense of identity and agency may lead to the corrupt use of power by women as well as by men. Rose cannot deny her past without risking replaying it in the role of the abuser. For Rosie, there can be no forgetfulness; she is given a small vial of the waters of Lethe for Bill, but she herself is prohibited from using it and warned to "remember the tree." Rose, who has thought the admonition refers to the tree in the maze in the picture, finally discovers that it is the tree in her own world, where she and Bill had gone on a picnic for their first date. Under the tree is a vixen's den, and the vixen symbolizes both Rosie and Rose Madder. The vixen might be a carrier of rabies or she might not, and this is what Rosie needs to remember. She saves the few drops of water for Bill and keeps the memories for herself. She does not have the luxury of forgetting; in fact, her diseased other self has enjoined her most strictly to remember. As she thinks to herself, in a slight misquoting of Santayana, "Those who do not remember the past are doomed to repeat the bastard."[45]

The unsavory truth Rose learns about herself is that she and the diseased woman of the portrait are indeed sisters. If she does not wish to become more like the diseased woman and less like *"Rosie Real, a great big deal"* she must forever watch for that uncontrollable rage. The situation Rose faces when she discovers the down side of power is dis/ease-provoking because she has not entirely escaped the corruption. Like the woman in the picture, she has been permanently infected and must be forever on guard against the abusive side of her own personality. She does not walk, unscathed, back to a happy ending. Although this novel is basically affirmative, I have informally interviewed several abused wives concerning King's apparently overdrawn portrait of abuse: not one woman to whom I spoke thought the portrait exaggerated. All of them thought it reasonable that Rosie could also discover a dark, even murderous side of her own personality.[46]

Several years after she has married Bill and has a daughter, Rose finds herself experiencing a rage similar to Norman's. Ostensibly, she is reacting to a disagreement over which house they should purchase, but her rage is entirely out of proportion. Bill thinks she is still angry, but she is actually in

a black rage, almost a killing rage and she must make a frantic effort to (*remember the tree*) keep from seizing the pot of boiling water . . . and throwing it in his face. . . . [T]hat night, as she lies sleepless in bed, two words play over and over in her mind: *I repay.*

Rose Madder's function was to repay and now it seems as if she has infected Rosie, after all. Rosie finds herself nearly flying into rages at work as well, as when she fantasizes

hooking her nails in Rhoda's throat and *shoving her face into the hot spew of blood, wanting to baptize this new life she has been so stupidly struggling against. . . . She is repaying, that's what,* repaying, *and God help anyone on the wrong side of her account books.*[47]

Finally she knows what she must do. She buries the artifacts from her old life, completely breaking with the past when she buries the one seed from the tree in the maze and Norman's ring, given to her by Rose Madder as a keepsake, under the vixen's tree. After this pilgrimage, she goes to the tree yearly, and the rages abate.

Thus, in *Rose Madder* Rosie does escape from a perverted community, but in order to escape, she must confront and control, but perhaps not ultimately defeat, the corruption within herself. This leaves her, at best, in a compromised Apollonian world, a world in which she must always be aware that rage is a function of power, not an easily articulated and categorized masculine pattern of behavior, from which being gendered female she is exempt, but one which can overtake her at any time. Rosie escapes, to be sure, but lives the rest of her life attempting to disempower the corruption through which she has successfully escaped.

She must struggle, married to Norman's antithesis, not to become Norman. Does she succeed? The narrator claims Rose has reached safe harbor, but Rose, less sanguine, feels that coming to the tree once a year Ais the renewal of an unstated covenant, [which] if it keeps her from hurting anyone is time well spent."[48]

The dis/ease in this text, although fairly well resolved, is nevertheless real. Rose cannot simply forget her experience in the diseased world of the picture because the latter is not a separate world; as the woman in the picture has reality in the outside world, so the corruptive possibilities in the picture have a base in reality. Were Rosie entirely a victim and completely immune to anger and power, this would be an entirely affirmative text, but she is not, and it is not. The reader sees Rosie struggle to control her rage and realizes that conserving the Apollonian in an increasingly Dionysian world is neither easy nor likely to end. In this text, the dis/ease is generated from the human condition. King recognizes that abuse is not necessarily a gender-restricted problem and thus denies us the facile and easy ending in which Rosie escapes, lives a deservedly happy existence nurturing Bill and her much-longed-for child, and never comes into contact with her dark side. In King's novelistic world, it seems, communities are more fragile and more constructed than many readers would wish to think.

Thus the better affirmative horror fictions, while they do value Apollonian community, also confront the problems of forming and maintaining community in the face of the infections of the Dionysian. As I noted earlier, the paradigms of monsterdom have changed; the monsters no longer have easily identifiable human characteristics, and the early warning system cannot work as easily. By not simply denying the Dionysian intrusions, the texts I have discussed work effectively to confront and assimilate them. By resisting a complete defeat of the Dionysian, however, these texts leave a lingering feeling of dis/ease. Social order is important in these particular texts, and that makes containment of the human monster necessary. It is extremely unlikely that a creature like Michael Gallatin could ever be accepted within a "normal" community, despite his heroic actions. Johnny Smith, despite his many good qualities, is the societal equivalent of a mutant; his deformity may be internal and invisible, but it is present enough to make the people who benefit by his sacrifice too uncomfortable to accept him. Libby Hatch is both a monster and a victim of her society, which both shapes and condemns her. Rose is uneasily aware, from first-hand knowledge, that the diseased Rose Madder and Rosie McClendon are one and the same. None of these characters walk unscathed and unaccountable back to a society in which all ends well, although their societies do survive very nicely.

4

HE AND WE AS MONSTERS:
BREAKING DOWN THE MONSTER DEMARCATIONS

"He's a monster. Beyond that no one can say for sure."[1]

Several factors differentiate mid-spectrum horror fiction from either affirmative or disaffirmative. Mid-spectrum texts, like disaffirmative but unlike affirmative texts, often create cultural dis/ease simply by spotlighting the monster and providing no reasonable explanation for monsterdom. If one does not know what causes a human monster, both identification and containment are difficult to achieve. Unlike disaffirmative horror, mid-spectrum horror fiction depicts a human monster who is generally contained, but the containment carries a higher price tag than is the case in affirmative horror fiction, and the containment is often very fragile and occasionally even ineffective. In addition, the human monster may be so horrific and so inexplicable, so monstrous, that even the containment does not leave the reader feeling as though social order has been entirely vindicated or restored. But if the monster is safely behind bars, social order is reaffirmed, and the community can breathe more easily, how can the resolution and affirmation be defined as compromised? Perhaps the economies of loss are partially responsible, perhaps the callous disregard for the intrinsic meaning of human life plays into the dis/ease, and perhaps the terror, horror, and revulsion generated by one who appears to be one of us, but is not one of us, are responsible.

One of the two important patterns I will discuss in this chapter involves a clearly delineated human monster, a being with whom we do not identify. This pattern generates horror and dis/ease, but does not result in identification with the monster. We remain us, and the monster remains the monster. The second and more dis/ease provoking pattern occurs when the demarcations between human and monster are not as clear, and we cannot identify the human monster without identifying ourselves. While the lack of specific guidelines on the production of human monsters is dis/ease provoking, as is our fascination with them, the most troubling source of dis/ease in mid-spectrum horror fictions occurs when the boundaries between the antagonist and the protagonist, the monster and the monster-catcher are blurred, and the author humanizes the evil human monster sufficiently to compel reader identification. Mid-spectrum fictions of this type often have characters whose humanity is both affirmed and denied. By contrast, in *The Wolf's Hour*, Michael Gallatin, however quasi-monstrous, is obviously the hero, and if the reader can accept the paradigm shift from werewolf-as-enemy to werewolf-as-hero, no further subversion is necessary. In King's *The Dead Zone*, Smith himself finally embraces the role as willing sacrifice for the community. The price Johnny pays, in other words, buys something worth the sacrifice, and the economies of loss are not so monstrously unbalanced.

Not even containment balances the economies of loss in Charles King's *Mama's Boy*, although the human monster is both identified and contained, and little danger of reader sympathy exists. Stephen King's *The Dark Half*, and Thomas Harris' *Red Dragon* and *The Silence of the Lambs* with their masterful blurring of the boundaries between the human and the monster, and their insistence on the universality of infection intentionally provoke the dis/easeful reaction which I contend is the *sine qua non* of horror fiction. These are fictions in which the scorecard becomes a little blurred in the monsters vs. us game. If the human monster comes out of an environment that shapes him as monster but is not itself a monstrous environment, the dis/ease arises from the blurring and the inexplicability of affect. The dis/ease arises not only from the psychotic reaction but also from what is absent. And what is absent, some essential connection with the ethical/moral nexus or with simple humanity, provokes dis/ease whether the monster is caught or not. We fear not only that which threatens us but also that which is beyond our comprehension. "Nothing human is alien to me" may be one of the aphorisms of philosophic discourse, but in this type of fiction, the dis/ease arises precisely because there is something alien, something inhuman, jostling for space with the human. Even though much of this fiction has a protagonist who is clearly non-monstrous, clearly a monster-catcher, sometimes the blurred borders on which I commented earlier surface.

Jonathan Kellerman, Ph.D., a practicing social psychologist as well as author of the Alex Delaware psychological thrillers, provides an extremely useful definition of the human monster:

He's the beast who walks upright. Meet him on the street and he'll seem normal, even charming. But he roams those streets, parasitic and cold-eyed, stalking his prey behind a veneer of civility. . . .

He's the psychopath and psychiatry understands '.'m even less than it does the schizophrenic. The symptoms of madness can often be altered with medication, but there is no therapy for evil.[2]

This definition, stressing as it does the incomprehensibility of the monster, foregrounds the concerns of mid-spectrum horror fiction, with its emphasis on the beast within and our inability to understand him. The clear claim that nothing can effectively be done to neutralize him captures the essence of the characters I will discuss in this chapter and the next.

Although Charles King's *Mama's Boy* is not particularly well-known, it exemplifies perfectly a pattern which I define as intrinsic to mid-spectrum horror, that of the clearly delineated human monster with whom we do not identify. Clearly, the main character is a monster; just as clearly, the boundaries between us and him remain unchallenged. *Mama's Boy* also shares in the storehouse of stereotypical cultural assumptions about serial killers which postulate "nurturing," often by a monstrous mother, as the main reason for the construction of human monsters, foreground a sense of inexplicability about their actions, and emphasize in graphic detail the sadistic brutality of the killings.

Charles King's *Mama's Boy* (1992), as the title indicates, locates gender role conflict at the root of human monsterhood. Evan Highland, a/k/a professor Julian Lamb, is born into a dysfunctional family. Until he is ten years old, he thinks his mother is a Vietnam War widow. His mother, who is mentally disturbed, has sexual relations with him, telling him, "You're mine. I've given you everything. . . . I have a right." Evan is extremely unwilling to participate and also extremely unwilling to hurt his mother, who chants "marital, *sexual* . . . marital, *sexual* . . . ,"[3] linking incest and sexual relations and ostensibly destroying young Evan's chance for a normal life. That same summer, he discovers that his father is not dead at all. He rides over to his father's house, thinking, "He would have a dad! Like he always did in his dreams!" His father completely rejects him, saying, "If I ever see you around here again, I'll cut off your mother's checks for good. You got that? Then she'll be in an institution where she belongs. And so will you." When Evan starts to cry, his father says, "She's turned you into a regular little fairy, I see. How the hell could you be any son of mine?"[4] Evan's mentally disturbed mother and his father's brutal rejection indisputably explain a certain amount of disturbance, but they are still not sufficient to account for his subsequent behavior. Evan becomes obsessed with spying on his "father's" family, as he feels that the new family has the life he should have had. He lives in a run-down house without the material possessions and sense of community of his father's replacement family. The spying is his way of forming a community, but a community that is fatally flawed as it has no basis in reality. He becomes obsessed with the family's secret language and his father's second wife, Marilyn. His forcible exclusion from the intimacy on which he spies but in which he cannot take part evidently also makes him a human monster. He spies on their lovemaking and masturbates to climax, "with his father's wife. In his father's tree. Speaking his father's secret language."[5] His father has certainly employed the strategies of exclusion against him, and the young Evan Highland is effectively demarcated and scapegoated, forcibly relegated to outside status. Given his mother's unnatural fixation on him, his unnatural fixation on his mother, and his inability to have a normal sexual relationship as a result, one can see reasons for a very disturbed young man, but we must recall that not all victims of a disturbed parent, an absent parent, and brutal rejection become human monsters.

Not surprisingly, Highland majors in languages, at which he is brilliant, and ends up in the CIA because he has a definite predilection for spying as well. After spending some years on internal surveillance of politically sensitive families, e.g., environmental and political activists, he amasses a collection of videos. Dis/ease rears its ugly head here as well, because, as we all know, the CIA is expressly prohibited from spying on American citizens, particularly American citizens exercising their constitutional rights as citizens. He becomes a hired assassin on the usual secret and totally deniable government assassination team, until, of course, the government no longer needs him and attempts to achieve complete deniability by killing the entire team. He then escapes, changes into Professor Julian Lamb, gets a tenured position, and continues killing, which he enjoys. He chooses families from his video collection, families who have attractive wives and secret languages, uses them for sexual release, and slaughters them mercilessly. Again, the exaggerated and seemingly disproportionate reaction so typical of horror fiction creates dis/ease. After all, if he abandoned his mother and stalked his father's family, his actions would make sense. Instead, he supports Claire, his mother, until she dies, and leaves his father alone. Nor does he attempt to kill the man who tried to kill him or the CIA Director who ordered the hit. While the typical reader would not condone killing his father's second family, such actions would reflect comprehensible causes and effects. If Highland decided to kill the men who tried to kill him, the logic would also be understandable. But if he made comprehensible choices, he would not be a human monster in the first place.

The lack of humanity in *Mama's Boy* generates cultural dread; being a caring, loving, ethical family who just happens to possess a secret language and supports worthwhile causes precipitates butchery by a psychopath. The FBI postulates that it is the close-knittedness of the brutalized families which attracts the killer, which in a way is true, as the private language the families employ is a sign of both a closely knit family and the trigger which sets off the psychopathic killer. When Lamb goes after the Grant family, who speak *Dolphone* and are passionately and actively involved with endangered species, he slaughters the children, dragging eight-year-old Geraldine out from under the couch, thinking, "Pretty little thing—her fear excited him. He would have enjoyed screwing her as he slowly choked the life out of her, but he had not time."[6] But worse is yet to come. His main interest is Juleth Grant, who reminds him of Marilyn Highland, his father's second wife. After she unsuccessfully attacks him with an iron, he overpowers her, gags and ties her to the bed, and tortures her with a steam iron, telling her,

> "That's snake language for *hot love. HISSS. HISSS.*"
> He held the iron just above her left nipple, scorching it with steam. She made loud muffled noises behind her gag and twisted her body frantically to escape. . .
> "The steam iron was your idea, don't forget. You started it. . . ."
> He loosened her gag. "Any last words before the Grants join the passenger pigeon?"
> In a muffled voice she asked, "Why are you doing this?"
> In a high-pitched singsong, he squawked, "Why are you doing this? TURCLEW TURCLEW. Why are you doing this? ARKA ARKA ARKA . . . ." He hopped on the bed and knelt between her legs, holding the red-hot iron high, and whispered,
> "Just think of me as your reward for being happy."[7]

What is dis/easeful, aside from the pornographic details, is the raw and utterly senseless hatred with which Lamb butchers the families. The sadistic delight he takes in turning Juleth's secret language against her, violating her private life before he violates her body, and the incomprehensible glee he displays as he tortures her generate not only horror and repulsion, but terror. Lamb has now slaughtered twenty-three people, including thirteen children, and his murders are getting increasingly more gruesome. None of the victims even know him; needless to say, they have done nothing to deserve their awful fate, except "being happy" and possessing those attributes he does not. Lamb not only tortures his victims, he hates them personally and uses their most intimate moments against them. *"Dolphone*, the Endangered Speechies" may be cloyingly cute, but it is this family's way of communicating among themselves, their way of establishing the close bonds so hated and coveted by Lamb. When Lamb taunts Juleth Grant as he sadistically tortures her to death, telling her, "Papa's gone to the elumPHant graveyard.

So have Rosi and Gerri and Linkie. Poachers shot them for ivory. You Grants love endangered species—now you're an endangered species yourself," the scene produces horror and terror.[8] It is not only that the Grants are caring, committed people, that the family is defenseless, that Juleth Grant is described as a person of courage, conviction, and kindness, that the violation of their lives is complete and ruthless; it is the complete abnegation of humanity which makes this text impossible to resolve affirmatively.

Lamb will end up dead, shot down by the police detective brother of one of the families he slaughtered. Jake Harrow catches Lamb, not by any empathy with the monster, but by painstaking and dogged police work. Even the certain knowledge of the monster's death, however, and the knowledge that "the Family Murderer" is incontrovertibly dead, does not entirely mitigate the horror of this novel. Societal order is reaffirmed; Jake, the representative of the forces of social order not only successfully tracks the killer down, but also eradicates him. Julian Lamb will never again butcher innocent families, and the remainder of society is now safe because Lamb is dead. But several factors resist an affirmative reading and make this a mid-spectrum text.

Harrow, though successful, does not act within the New York Metropolitan Police to solve the crime because Captain Douglas Cowen almost ruins the investigation, alienates the FBI, and tries to frame Jake on drug charges when he will not cooperate with the Captain's megalomaniacal need for publicity. Furthermore, Cal Ordway, the CIA operative who ran agent Highland, fears adverse reaction (budget cuts) if anyone discovers that "the Family Killer" is a renegade CIA assassin and decides the easiest way out of the situation is to neutralize Jake. This subplot also works to increase dis/ease, as the knowledge that the forces of law and order on which we depend to maintain social stability are corrupt, is not precisely comforting. As the Director of the CIA says to Ordway:

"What if the walk-in [Jake] is right? That means one of our own people is out there, murdering moms and kids. . . . This isn't dirty tricks in some Third-World country Rand never mentioned to McNally; it's multiple murders right here in the U.S. of A. We trained this guy at taxpayers' expense to kill taxpayers. We become the guard dog that ate the baby. Think how that will play at appropriations time."[9]

The dis/ease rises when the forces of law and order are difficult to differentiate from the monsters. The CIA deliberately used Highland, knowing he was dangerously unbalanced; in fact, Ordway pushes Highland out of surveillance and into assassination by threatening Highland's mother. Later, when he realizes Highland was not killed as planned but is killing men, women, and children who are also, let us not forget, American taxpayers, his only concern is to cover up the whole scenario by killing Highland, if he can find him, and Jake if he cannot. Not only are we not safe from human monsters, the CIA is training them and turning them loose. Considering how truly monstrous Highland is, this is a profoundly dis/easeful premise. Thus, *Mama's Boy* discusses the clearly delineated human monster, the one we fear because we cannot understand him, the comfortably "othered." No transgressions in empathy have as yet appeared to muddy the lines and create even more dis/ease. We may not "understand" this particular man in a tiger skin, but we also do not feel the need to empathize with him. Hunting him will do.

By contrast, Stephen King's *The Dark Half* (1990) works effectively to create cultural dis/ease primarily because the protagonist is not a monster, but to all appearances, one of us. As Richard Tithecott so cogently points out, "We are happier if our monsters remain gargoyles."[10] By reworking the classic *doppelganger* convention of Stevenson's *Dr. Jekyll and Mr. Hyde*, in which Apollonian and Dionysian personalities coexist, and having two seemingly separate individuals, King makes it easy for the reader, at least initially, to keep the lines of demarcation intact, identify with the human being, and reject his evil second self. The reader realizes rather early on, however, that separate though the two personalities may appear, they are actually one person. Thus, *The Dark Half* provides a bridge between texts of the first pattern, which are relatively uncomplicated, and Harris' extremely disturbing fictions, which center on the human monster's infection of the detective, and by extension, the reader.

King's Thad Beaumont is a fragmented personality: one half of him is stereotypically Apollonian—the mild-mannered English professor who writes literary books which do not, alas, sell well. Thad is a gentle family man, a popular teacher, and a respected member of the community. Dionysian George Stark, Thad's pseudonym and dark half is "a high-toned son-of-a-bitch" who writes remunerative hard-boiled thrillers which make Mickey Spillane look like Casper Milquetoast. Stark's protagonist, Alexis Machine, is a completely amoral psychopathic killer who is also the creation of gentle, self-effacing Thad. The conflict between the two selves is thus almost immediately established. After Frederick Clawson, a two-bit blackmailer, threatens to expose Thad Beaumont as George Stark, Thad and his wife Liz decide to "kill" George off. Liz is very relieved, because profitable though Stark is, she does not like his effect on Thad. Since George is a construct, a fictional

representation, he cannot really have an effect on Thad: he has no independent existence. But this is horror fiction territory and strange things
happen: Stark is a part of George both physically and metaphysically.
Thad is dark haired, slight in stature and clumsy; he drives a family car,
is a faithful husband and a loving father, but is rather a passive and
mediocre character. No one would notice Thad in a crowd. George Stark
is none of these things. George Stark is fair-haired, tall, broad-shoul-
dered, graceful, drives a high powered car, and is extremely active. Perhaps George is more than a handy pseudonym, a vehicle for making
money. Perhaps George is what Thad would like to be.

After George Stark is exposed, killed off, and buried, complete with
publicity shots in *People* magazine, strange things start to happen. The
"grave" in which Liz and Thad have "buried" him is found clawed open
and a series of murders occur. All the victims are those people in any
way connected with the story on George Stark. Sheriff Alan Pangborn is
absolutely convinced that Thad Beaumont is the murderer, and for good
reason: Thad's fingerprints are all over the crime scene. But, of course,
the killer is not Thad; it is George Stark, who has somehow assumed cor-
poreal reality. And since the *persona* of George Stark is carefully constructed by Thad from all he represses and denies, constructed out of the
Dionysian side of his personality, George murders everyone without any
compunction whatsoever to send a message to Thad. Eventually, he kidnaps Liz Beaumont and their twins Wendy and William, in order to force
Thad to help him write another George Stark novel. Thad, who is perfectly aware of his creation's proclivities, agrees, but he manages to call
up millions of psychopomps, in this case sparrows, and Stark is dragged
away, back to the land of the dead, thus apparently restoring order.[11]

The interplay between George Stark and Thad Beaumont is the
most dis/ease provoking element in the novel. When George Stark
finally forces Thad to cooperate with him and write a new Alexis
Machine novel, a novel that will prevent his physical disintegration and
restore his somewhat problematic existence, the two tend to reflect each
other. Liz realizes that bumbling Thad is also George Stark. In turn, the
twins, Wendy and William, respond to George exactly as if he is their
father. They do not see the psychotic killer, the remorseless murderer
who revels in killing. They see someone they accept as "daddy." Liz is
absolutely horrified at their reactions, for when Liz sees them together,
the revelation is, again, much like the reaction of people to Mr. Hyde:
"They looked nothing whatsoever alike. . . . Yet they were mirror
images, just the same. The similarity was eerie precisely because there
was no one thing the protesting, horrified eye could pin it on. It was *sub
rosa*, deeply buried between the lines but so real it shrieked."[12]

Alan Pangborn, forced to accept the fact that Thad Beaumont cannot be in his summer home in Maine and simultaneously killing people in New York, does the research which disinters the secret twin.[13] George Stark is and is not a separate entity: in many ways he is a ghost, excised years before, but in other ways, he is not excised at all, but *sub rosa* still. As Thad says, laughing George's crazy laugh, "the laughter of a man, [Alan thinks] who was dancing on the edge of oblivion. *He* is [crazy] and he came from me, didn't he? Like some cheap demon from the brow of a third-rate Zeus."[14] Earlier, Thad has stated uncategorically that "Words on paper made him, and words on paper are the only things that will get rid of him."[15] And yet, when Thad and George prepare to carry out the ritual which will resurrect George Stark, writing the manuscript in Black Beauty Berol pencils, Thad's desire to get rid of George, stated so strongly a few moments earlier, is called into question:

"You're kind of up for it, ain't you, hoss [says George]. No matter what you say, part of you is just *raaarin* to go."

"Yes," said Thad simply, and Alan didn't think he was lying.

"Alexis Machine," Stark said. His yellow eyes were gleaming.

"That's right," Thad said, and now his eyes were gleaming. "Cut him while I stand here and watch."

"You got it!" Stark cried, and began to laugh. "I want to see the blood flow. Don't make me tell you twice."

Now they both began to laugh.

Liz looked from Thad to Stark and then back at her husband again and the blood fell from her cheeks because she could not tell the difference.[16]

The writing is more than ritual, more than an exchange, more than the explicit trade of Thad's family for the novel. What will happen, inevitably, because Thad and George are not separate identities, is that Thad will fade as George reintegrates. Part of Thad knows this, but he also knows that the sparrow psychopomps will come for George, who does not know about them. As part of Thad wants to write *Steel Machine*, so part of him wants to be George Stark. What Thad discovers, though, is that he wants to write the words that will call the psychopomps more than he wants to write the Stark novel.

After the birds have carried Stark away, the price becomes starkly clear. Alan Pangborn meditates on the whole unbelievable experience:

You don't understand what you are, and I doubt you ever will. . . . Standing next to you is like standing next to a cave some nightmarish creature came out of. The monster is gone now, but you still don't like to be too close to where it came from. Because there might be another.[17]

Alan Pangborn is aware that Thad did not ask to be twinned or maliciously devour his twin *in utero*. If he is a cannibal, a murderer, and a monster, it is not by his active agency. Nevertheless, Alan cannot forget the similarity. For him, as well as for Liz, Thad is tarred with the monster brush.

Thus King writes a conflicted story which acknowledges that Jekyll and Hyde cannot be separated. One cannot get down and boogie as Hyde and still keep Jekyll uncontaminated. One cannot be Thad Beaumont, mild-mannered English professor by day and predatory George Stark at night and reasonably expect to keep the selves separate. Thus, *The Dark Half* serves as a bridge between those fictions which have a clearly demarcated, distinctly unempathetic human monster, one moreover, which ends the tale either dead or imprisoned, and Thomas Harris's extremely conflicted, slouching towards disaffirmation texts, in which we are forced into empathy and understanding of men who are no less monstrous than Evan Highland. King's careful examination of Thad Beaumont's very conflicted halves sets the stage for the second pattern in mid spectrum horror fiction: that of the monster with whom we do identify.

In this type of human monster fiction, another method of generating cultural dis/ease comes into play: the monster, while still monstrous, yet has some humanity to differentiate him from an Evan Highland, or even a Beaumont/Stark. We can, in other words, see similarities, not just comforting differences. In addition, the monster-catcher is infected by the human monster and often generates almost as much dis/ease as the monster. The dis/easeful question which arises then is not only how we can catch the monster, or how we can identify the monster, but also how we can avoid being infected by that monster. Identification with the monster, whether on the part of the monster-hunter who must understand and empathize with him in order to capture him, or people with whom the monster bonds, plays out as infection. These people are, so to speak, tarred with the monster brush, and to a considerably greater degree than Thad Beaumont. And so is the reader, who in the the earlier texts can easily maintain the demarcations between human and monster. Harris resists such easy solutions, in the development of both his protagonists and his antagonists, and the resulting reading experiences are both riveting and far removed from a comfort zone. Steffen Hantke shrewdly argues that horror fiction "aims at derailing the safe or predictable interpretive sequence." Hantke further claims that this type of fiction is not as concerned with "coherence, stability and the reconciliation of conflicts," as with "gaps, disruptions, and the gray areas of transition."[18] This useful paradigm, with its constant sense of disruption, of things falling apart and centers failing to hold, is central to much horror fiction, and works especially well with texts such as *Red Dragon* and *The Silence of the Lambs*, texts in which Harris shows unparalleled skill in first establishing the monstrous and then contextualizing the monster in terms of human experience. An encounter with the monster, the beast within, I would argue, must necessarily foreground the sense of discontinuity and fragmentation. When detective fiction is merged with horror, the result is the derailment about which Hantke writes. A "safe interpretive sequence" does not make strong connections between the hero and the villain, as do Harris' novels, *Red Dragon* and *The Silence of the Lambs*. Certainly there is nothing supernatural about Harris's characters; certainly the text seems firmly grounded in the detective/police procedural tradition. I would argue, however, that since human monsters are of paramount concern in Harris' texts, and since the reader's attention is often riveted, however unwillingly or uncomfortably, on the characters of Francis Dolarhyde, Jame Gumb, and Hannibal Lecter as well as on those of Jack Crawford, Will Graham, and Clarice Starling, that interest inevitably centers on the horror of the psychopath, undoubtedly one of contemporary society's nightmares. This doubled genre therefore makes for antinomous reading. What exactly is the reader's principal expectation? Is this a horror story about a serial killer or a detective novel which will resolve the fears the monsters have created? As this reading suggests, my answer is that Harris's novels embody generic hybridization in which the elements of detective fiction and horror are uneasily but masterfully conjoined.

Unlike *Mama's Boy*, but like most detective fictions, Harris's novels place a high value on a morally stable and ordered society. Unlike much government involvement in other horror fiction, the FBI plays a redeeming role here. For the most part, no renegade agents or private agendas within the FBI exist to call the role of the FBI into question.[19] The FBI is a strong community heavily invested in working with the state police forces toward the laudable goal of capturing monsters. The action within these novels moves toward a restoration of stability which is achieved by removal of the monster from society. The horror and fascination evoked by the monster/monster-hunter connection, however, complicates the movement toward stability. This leaves the reader in an essentially compromised position in a world in which at least one of the heroic monster hunters survives his collision with the monster, but is damaged, perhaps fatally, in the process.

The main plot of *Red Dragon* (1981) concerns Will Graham's attempts to capture Francis Dolarhyde, a family-killing serial killer. Dr. Hannibal "the Cannibal" Lecter, the infamous protagonist of *The Silence of the Lambs*, functions as the third corner of a triangle. His interest lies in amusing himself, but he also functions like the Greek Choragos figure, laying bare the dis/eases within Will Graham and analyzing Dolarhyde as well. Lecter adds to the dis/ease generated by this novel because while we understand the process which went into making Dolarhyde a monster, Lecter is an enigma. Confronting Lecter as a human monster does not arouse the reader's empathy; Lecter is evil because he enjoys being evil. Judged criminally insane, he knows that he will never be de-institutionalized; he has, therefore, nothing to do but create his own amusement wherever and however he can. In *Red Dragon*, he finds this amusement in calling attention to the link between himself and Will Graham and also in sending the *Red Dragon* (Francis Dolarhyde) after Will Graham and his family.

Prior to Graham's unwilling involvement in capturing Dolarhyde, he has captured Gareth Hobbs, "the Minnesota Shrike," and Hannibal "the Cannibal" Lecter. After Lecter nearly costs him his life, Graham quits the FBI. Graham has discovered a capacity for identifying with the Other, which is completely unacceptable to his self-identity. So horrific is this revelatory knowledge that rather than continue to work in the field in which he is both useful and indisputably proficient, he pastes his diploma over a crack in the ceiling and fixes boat motors for a living in the Florida Keys, a geographical entity, it should be noted, as far on the border or margins of the United States as he can manage. As his boss Jack Crawford notes, "There's nobody better with evidence, but he has the other thing, too. Imagination, projection, whatever. He doesn't like that part of it."[20] As the omniscient narrator notes, "There were no effective partitions in his mind. . . . His learned values of decency and perception tagged along, shocked at his associations, appalled at his dreams; sorry that in the bone arena of his skull there were no forts for what he loved."[21] While he is highly lauded for his ability to read the minds of the monsters, the serial killers whom he pursues, this uncanny ability distances him from the rest of his society. His co-workers, for example, feel just a little uneasy around Will. And why not? Can one really identify with the monster and still avoid being one?

In a telling vignette, even Jack Crawford, who both likes and values Will immensely, shows distaste at his ability to read the killer:

"Mrs. Leeds was a good looking woman," Graham said. "You've seen the family pictures, right? I'd want to touch her skin in an intimate situation, wouldn't you?'"

"*Intimate?*" Distaste sounded in Crawford's voice before he could stop it. Suddenly he was busy rummaging in his pockets for change.

"Intimate—they had privacy. Everybody else was dead. He could have their eyes open or shut, however he liked."[22]

Thus, even Graham' co-workers tend to discuss him, eye him with morbid curiosity, and fall into uneasy silences around him, in a manner similar to that of his prey's co-workers; not because he actually has the monster within, and they are actually threatened by this knowledge, but because they realize that he is, in effect, infected by his contact with the mutant. Chief Springfield, a police chief in whose jurisdiction Graham is investigating, for example, is both impressed and uneasy with Graham. He is impressed because Graham intuits the killer's actions, and his intuition results in a few partial fingerprints. He is uneasy because when he comments, "That's by God remarkable," Graham does not respond: "Graham's face was blank: closed like a lifer's face."[23] Springfield classifies Graham as remarkable, but also as a lifer, a man who cannot be permitted to live in a normal community.

Like Johnny Smith's, Graham's "gift" has the effect of cursing him and of making him a pariah, though an eminently useful one. His gift also forces him to confront the certain knowledge that one cannot entirely distance oneself from the beast: like calls to like. As Dr. Alan Bloom, a behavioral psychologist, says in conversation with Jack Crawford:

"Will wants to think of this as purely an intellectual exercise, and in the narrow definition of forensics, that's just what it is. . . . What he has in addition is pure empathy and projection. He can assume your point of view or mine—and maybe some points of view that scare and sicken him."[24]

Of all the characters in the novel, it is, ironically, Hannibal Lecter, the indisputable human monster, who best expresses the dis/ease Graham generates. When Will Graham goes to see him, Lecter says,

"You just came here to look at me. Just to get the old scent again, didn't you? Why don't you just smell yourself?"
"Do you know how you caught me. Will?"
"The reason you caught me is that we're just alike" was the last thing Graham heard as the steel door closed behind him.[25]

Will, walking away to freedom, conscious that there are only five doors between Lecter and freedom, "had the absurd feeling that Lecter walked out with him," but perhaps it is not absurd: Will Graham goes to see Lecter because he needs to refresh a certain mind set that he has lost living at the Keys.[26]

The fragile and compromised nature of the affirmation in this novel becomes very apparent, even though the serial killer is captured and contained, because the demarcations between protagonist and antagonist are hopelessly blurred. Monster-catcher Will Graham, is, at the very least, infected with the human monster virus in the eyes of both his antagonists, the serial killers Francis Dolarhyde and Hannibal Lecter, and in his co-workers. At one point, as Graham is closing in on him, Dolarhyde thinks, "Graham knew because he knew. The son of a bitch was a monster."[27] Coming from the mouth of a socio/psychopathic necrophiliac, this is an interesting comment. Dolarhyde is killed and order more or less restored, but the price Graham pays is tragically out of proportion to the victory. By the end of *Red Dragon*, Will Graham has successfully captured three serial killers; in the process, he has also lost his wife and step-son, been brutally assaulted, and permanently disfigured. Later, Clarice Starling, the protagonist of *The Silence of the Lambs*, thinks, "Will Graham, the keenest hound ever to run in Crawford's pack, was a legend at the Academy. He was also a drunk in Florida now, with a face that was hard to look at, they said."[28] Such a fate is neither fair nor comforting, because Will Graham is a genuinely good man, a man who works to protect the rest of society from the monsters. To define him in the same terms as a monster, someone with a face hard to look at, not only deconstructs the affirmation implicit in the containment of the serial killer but also redefines Graham as a monster.

Red Dragon, then, works with a doubled perception of the monster. We not only have incontestable monsters like Francis Dolarhyde and Hannibal Lecter, but we also react negatively to the people who understand them. Will Graham's undoubted success in tracking the monster does not, as one would expect in an affirmative paradigm, net him the wholehearted respect of the community; instead, he is almost as much a pariah as is Lecter or Dolarhyde. At one point, Will, intensely drunk, attempts to literally make Dolarhyde appear and talks to the image he brings into being:

> "You've got to try to stop, just hold off until we find you. . . . Help me a little. . . . It's you and me now, sport." He leaned across the table, his hand extended to touch, and the presence was gone.[29]

Such a communion is impossible. As the narrator points out, "to begin to understand the Dragon, to hear the cold drips in his darkness, to watch the world through the red haze, Graham would have had to see things he could never see, and he would have had to fly through time."[30] However unfortunate his community's response may be, and one can see why his community would respond with dis/ease, he is, unlike the conventional good guy in the conventional Western film, outside of the accepted social structure.

And yet, at the end of the novel, the deformed and broken Will Graham, a victim of his environment as much as is the serial killer antagonist, wonders if "the vicious urges we control in ourselves and the dark instinctive knowledge of those urges function like the crippled virus the body arms against. He wonder[s] if the old, awful urges are the virus that makes vaccine."[31]

In *The Silence of the Lambs*, the infection generated by the monster functions similarly. Hannibal Lecter finds pleasure in dissecting the innermost being of Clarice Starling, Will Graham's counterpart. Harris's very sympathetic characterization of Clarice, who is, in some ways, a lamb to the slaughter, evokes as much dis/ease in the reader as does Will Graham's predicament. She is also tracking a serial killer, again with the "help" of Lecter. As Jack Crawford sternly reminds Clarice,

> "Do your job. Just don't ever forget what he is."
> "And what's that? Do you know?"
> "I know he's a monster. Beyond that, nobody can say for sure."[32]

Clarice is much more vulnerable than Will Graham, who can walk away from Lecter. And while Graham carries baggage of his own from encounters with the monster, he is not a beginner desperate to succeed. Unlike Will, Clarice has little choice except to cooperate with Lecter. Crawford suspects that Lecter has information about Buffalo Bill, the latest serial killer, and sends Clarice to talk with Lecter, who will only deal with her on a *quid pro quo* basis. Any information he gives her must be paid for by either a petty humiliation or a violation. Lecter immediately labels Clarice, unkindly and inaccurately:

> "You're a well-scrubbed, hustling rube with a little taste. Your eyes are like cheap birthstones—all surface shine when you stalk some little answer. And you're bright behind them, aren't you? Desperate not to be like your mother. Good nutrition has given you some length of bone, but you're not more than one generation out of the mines, *Officer* Starling."[33]

Such a cruel yet perspicacious comment on the background she has so painfully left behind rendered by a human monster must at the very least crumble her sense of accomplishment, her sense of painfully acquired integrity and self-worth. To acknowledge the ambivalence she feels about her background and to trade her innermost nightmares for the insights that Lecter can provide immediately creates great discomfort for both Clarice and the reader. Lecter's insights will aid her in containing the monster, thus advancing her career and leaving the raw cracker girl of West Virginia a little farther behind; on the other hand, a trade this tawdry, a bargain with a human being so monstrous, has a very high price tag: a tag infinitely higher than the price tag on her one good bag or carefully acquired "add-a-bead" necklace—that necklace gained by sweaty grapplings in back seats, the sweaty grapplings a matter more of the body than anything else, a matter easily bathed away. And Lecter's acute eye, assessing the good bag and the bad shoes, knowing that Clarice has the beads to which he so cuttingly refers, seeing so clearly the secret room, and dismissing all her efforts so casually, immediately sets up a conflict Clarice cannot win.

Nevertheless, Clarice has no choice. The FBI is stymied in its efforts to catch "Buffalo Bill," Crawford has lost Will Graham, and the killer is stepping up the timetable of his killings. Buffalo Bill (a.k.a. Jame Gumb) kidnaps a senator's daughter, and the stakes become even higher. Eventually, tantalized, obfuscated, and aided by Lecter, Clarice puts the parts of the puzzle together and rescues Catharine Martin. But in order to get the information she needs to capture Jame Gumb, she must render to Lecter her most closely kept memory, the essential reason she is who she is. After her father died, Clarice was sent to a ranch in Montana, where they fed horses bound for the slaughterhouse. She fears for Hannah, a horse she has befriended, and one dark night is awakened by screaming:

> "I woke up in the dark and the lambs were screaming."
> "They were slaughtering the spring lambs?"
> "Yes."
> "What did you do?"
> "I couldn't do anything for them. I was just a—"

Lecter, far from unprescient, says, "Do you think if you caught Buffalo Bill yourself, and if you made Catharine all right, you could make the lambs stop screaming, do you think they'd be all right too, and you wouldn't wake up in the dark and hear the lambs screaming? Clarice?"[34]

She does rescue the horse, but when she and the horse are running away, she must leave the lambs to their bloody fate, and this is the memory that haunts her, the memory that Lecter savors. It is also the only currency he will accept, so to avoid the demarcation she has experienced in her childhood, she must sell bits of herself to Lecter in return, not for answers, but for tantalizing bits of information. Unfortunately, the more she knows, the more infected she becomes.

Senator Martin finds Clarice investigating her daughter's belongings and accuses her of theft. Possibly because Clarice is hyper-sensitive about her underprivileged childhood, such class labelings really anger her; they also function to demarcate her from that which she wishes to be, and she is "afraid that there was something tacky that Senator Martin saw in her, something cheap, something thieflike." On a day in which she endures various humiliations ranging from insults to taunts, "one thing stung the worst: being called a thief."[35] Resentful though she is, she knows she can pull herself together and be "approved, included, chosen and not sent away." Obviously, this need to wipe out her childhood experiences is what drives Clarice so relentlessly.

What makes *The Silence of the Lambs* mid-spectrum is not only the successful containment of one human monster, but the fact that Clarice comes to terms with her mother and her heritage. When she is preparing to examine and photograph one of the victims of Buffalo Bill, she realizes two very important things. One is that she and the victim are sisters, and that she owes the victims her best work, not for advancement, but because it is her obligation. She owes the women who are just like her the same degree of dedication she owes the senator's daughter. It is only when she is back in West Virginia, the place Lecter accurately sees her as wanting to escape, that she realizes the validity of her heritage. As she faces the corpse she realizes she needs

. . . a prototype of courage more apt and powerful than any Marine parachute jump. The image came to her and it helped her but it pierced her, too: *Her mother, standing at the sink, washing blood out of her father's hat, running cold water over the hat. Saying, "We'll be all right, Clarice."*[36]

Clarice does eventually rescue Catharine Martin, kill Jame Gumb, beat the charges of unfitness brought against her, and successfully complete her academy training. But again, the price is a high one. Hannibal Lecter manages to escape and kill several people who get in his way. Although she has been in close contact with the monsters, successfully captured one, attained self-knowledge and become reconciled with her background, she still has to face the knowledge that Hannibal Lecter is loose on the same planet with her, and that someday she may have to face him again. Only this time he will be unconfined. What is more, in the note he writes her, he tells her that the lambs will never stay silent for her: "Because it's the plight that drives you, seeing the plight, and the plight will not end, ever."[37]

All this hard-bought knowledge, however, tends to de-emphasize the affirmative qualities of life. Neither corruption nor evil can be prevented from seeping into the protagonists' personal lives. Graham loses his wife and step-son, and very nearly his life, as a direct result of the impingement of the monsters. Clarice Starling, who tracks down and kills Jame Gumb, discovers that not all monsters can be safely caged. And even when the monsters are safely caged, the knowledge the monster may have of you is not caged. Clarice must live with the fear that Lecter so mercilessly exposes. Perhaps there is something trashy about her, perhaps all her education and her skills mean nothing in a world that judges her for what her family is. Even the protagonists are dis/ease-provoking in these novels, if only because Will Graham pays a completely unfair price, and Clarice must come into intimate contact with a monster.

The other side of the antinomous coin, the most dis/ease-provoking aspect to Harris's novels is their human monsters, who are much more conflicted and developed than Charles King's characters. Dolarhyde, Gumb, and Lecter are extremely intelligent and almost entirely amoral. Communities are no more than their playgrounds; they are as fearsome to contemporary society as were Jack the Ripper or the fictional Dracula to Victorian London. As Dracula embodied substantially more than a fear of the unDead for the Victorians, so Lecter, Dolarhyde and Gumb embody more than fear of a serial killer. This triad of human monsters embodies the fear of a society about the members which comprise it. Indeed, what is frightening about the human monsters, who do not shape-shift, who are not harmless by day, is that they are not readily recognizable as monsters. Dolarhyde manages a film processing lab, Gumb has a business, and Lecter is an extremely proficient and brilliant doctor of psychiatry. What is frightening about these characters is that we could live next door to them for years, and if our luck held, we might never know that we lived next door to monsters. What is even more frightening is that in the case of Dolarhyde or Gumb the same societal forces which misshaped them could misshape us as well. Even more frightening than being a helpless victim of the society in which one lives but cannot function is that sometimes there is no convenient scapegoat to blame. And then what price our certainties?

Unlike the previous texts I have discussed, *Red Dragon* reveals in intimate and excruciating detail why Francis Dolarhyde is a monster. Dolarhyde, moreover, is more than a flat character, the serial killer as bogeyman. In some way, on some intuitive level, Francis Dolarhyde triggers the same atavistic fear as Mr. Hyde. One could argue that on a subliminal level, people are aware of the beast and wish to placate it, but there is nothing to directly identify Dolarhyde as a serial killer.

While Francis Dolarhyde is not easily recognizable as a monster, he is so internally warped and twisted that no other epithet will define him accurately. Dolarhyde was born with a severe and untreated harelip and looked more like a "leaf-nosed bat than a baby."[38] Whether this harelip is the cause of his warped *persona* is open to question; certainly it marked him as other, but so did the upbringing he endured. He still has a very slight speech impediment; far more important, he is still frozen in time as a deformed pariah and reacts to people as though he were still monstrously deformed. Dolarhyde was raised by his demented, hate-ridden grandmother as an instrument of revenge aimed at the daughter and the world which rejected her. He learns hate and rejection earlier than he learns to be a person. And out of this rage and pathetic need for communion and acceptance, he selects his victims and kills them. In a chilling reminder of the lack of safety in our society, Dolarhyde, who manages a film processing department and has thousands of feet of film from which to select, knows that "families are mailing their applications to him every day."[39]

What is most horrifying about *Red Dragon*, though Dolarhyde's actions are horrible enough, is his doomed attempt to break out of the socio-psychopathic mode and into humanity. Like Lamb, he kills entire families out of some thwarted attempt at communion; also like Lamb, he is more interested in the women than the men or children; and again like Lamb, he employs videotapes in his perverted bonding with his victims. But unlike Lamb, Francis Dolarhyde attempts to escape his own monstrosity. He meets, bonds with, and has a normal sexual relationship with Reba McClane, a blind woman. Reba cannot see the monster that Dolarhyde feels he is; she accepts him simply as another human being. "With Reba, his only living woman, held with her in this one bubbleskin of time, he felt for the first time that it was all right. . . . Dolarhyde, damned murderer of eleven, listened time and again to her heart."[40] Since Dolarhyde has absolutely no experience with normal human beings, and since he has been treated as a monster since childhood, it is not surprising that he does not understand what he feels for Reba.[41] Since he is a shattered personality, who has subsumed Francis Dolarhyde into the *Red Dragon*, a process he calls Becoming, it is not surprising that he in unable to accept himself. Francis Dolarhyde hates himself and uses his *alter ego* the Red Dragon to find a way to avoid being the despised Francis Dolarhyde, the demarcated, demonized scapegoat. Thinking about Reba, he reveals himself:

Maybe she liked Francis Dolarhyde.
That was a perverted despicable thing for a woman to do.

He understood that he should despise her for it, but oh God it was good.

Reba McClane was guilty of liking Francis Dolarhyde. Demonstrably guilty.[42]

Dolarhyde tries to save Reba from the Dragon. In an epiphany, he realizes that he can kill himself to save Reba, except that he fears that the Dragon will still be able to kill her. Not only does he fear that the Dragon will kill her, but he also fears that the Dragon will tell her that he, Dolarhyde, is nothing. And this he cannot bear. So he flies to the Brooklyn Museum and eats Blake's print. Mistakenly, he believes that he can choose, that he can in some way reverse the strategies of exclusion. That essentially his nature and his acts preclude success is a large part of the horror of *Red Dragon.*

For it is not the knowledge of Dolarhyde's crimes alone which horrifies us: he is even more horrifying because somewhere within his warped persona is an ability to bond with another human being; his struggles and eventual scarifying failure to accept a loving relationship are as horrifying as any of Lecter's excesses. Furthermore, as his background is filled in, we see that he was born to be warped, that the society we live in and feel fairly comfortable with has shaped the monster we know on a gut-wrenching level as Francis Dolarhyde, serial killer and human beast.

Jame Gumb, the human monster in *The Silence of the Lambs,* is fixated on the mother who abandoned him and wishes to reinvent himself as a woman; he does not, however, pass the required tests necessary to diagnose him as a true transsexual. Thus, while what he does, in this case stalking and killing women for their skins, marks his gender identity in his own mind, society identifies him as male and rejects his attempts to change his sexual equipment. His rejection fuels his rage and drives him to tailor "a suit with tits." There are, of course, slight problems in obtaining the necessary material for this article, but nothing that Gumb, master tailor and soulless psychopath, cannot overcome. Gumb thinks of his victims as "its," troublesome detours in obtaining the material he needs to be beautiful, to effect his transformation from man to woman.

Both Gumb and Dolarhyde have the indicators associated with psycho/sociopaths, but their records are hidden. Gumb's psychological assessments define him as disturbed, but he was convicted as a juvenile; in Dolarhyde's case, his mother, who married a rising politician, kept both his existence and his "crimes" hidden.[43] Both Gumb and Dolarhyde learn their useful trades, their covers and enabling devices, in institutions. Dolarhyde learns film processing in the U.S. Army, and Gumb learns to tailor in a California penal institution. In an ironic echo of

Stevenson's seminal novel, Gumb is employed by "Mr. Hide." In a further masterful use of antinomy and subversion, both of these institutions exist not to aid human monsters but to protect society.

To some degree, the warped souls of Dolarhyde and Gumb, like Mr. Hyde's, are reflected in their physical appearance, which, echoing the stark medieval world view, warns the beholder of the evil within. Yet Dolarhyde and Gumb seem to live at least marginally normal lives within their society. "Mr. D" may not be the world's most popular boss, but no one articulates a suspicion of him as a monster, either. None of Gumb's neighbors have any idea what his little hobbies may be. In any case, it is not the recognizable psychopath who creates true and lasting horror in us, but the secret psychopath, the one who has hidden the beast successfully, who is horrifying.

Lecter, for example, is far from identifiable as a human monster. As Will Graham notes, "He's a monster. I think of him as one of those pitiful things that are born in hospitals from time to time. . . . Lecter is the same way in his head, but he looks normal and nobody could tell."[44]

Cultured, sophisticated, extremely reputable, and professionally successful, Lecter would seem to be the last person to be an active psychopath. He is surely the ultimate Other—the civilized cannibal. When Lecter cannibalizes one of his unfortunate victims, the victim does not end up in a savage's stewpot, but as the featured entreé in a gourmet dinner. And no one, encountering the charming Dr. Lecter, would feel the need to be on guard. Who, invited to a dinner hosted by a renowned gourmet, would suspect that the sweetbreads were not the body parts of a calf but the body parts of a fellow human being? And who, having consumed this forbidden fare, would not end up treated for an eating disorder? What makes Lecter the cynosure of horror is his absolutely normal façade. How can a society deploy the strategies of exclusion or containment, if it has no measurable quantifiers with which to work? While Lecter is certainly a Dionysian intrusion into an ordered society, he wears the Apollonian mask with absolute success.

It is extremely tempting to classify Lecter as a psychopath, an Other, pure and simple, who has, who can have, no relation to those of us us who are human. More than Stevenson's dualistic Hyde, more than the fearsome Teenage Werewolf, Hannibal the Cannibal is the perfect monster. And yet the antinomy between humanity and inhumanity does exist. Clarice Starling is safe from him. Alone of all his acquaintance, evidently, she touches some chord of humanity within him. "The world," he says, "is more interesting with you in it."[45] As he tells her this, he is planning to continue his hobby; whatever action Clarice Starling may take or not take has a price tag attached.

This beastliness hidden within a man is always infinitely more horrific than that same beastliness openly on display. The outward manifestations of monstrosity are there to see in those figures; guards exist against these monsters. The well-known garlic at the windows, the cross, the stake, or the silver bullet will repulse or destroy these creatures, but no device exists to identify and destroy a Hannibal Lecter. And what solution can exist, except defining him as completely separate from the human race and confining him somewhere as much out of sight as possible? But out of sight is not out of mind, a sad fact to which the Will Grahams and Clarice Starlings of the world can attest. This effect not only leaves the discerning reader uneasy over the state of society, but leaves that reader uneasy over the state of him or herself. These particular texts strongly reflect the growing fear within the community of other members of the community. Yes, say Harris, King, and various other authors, you are frightened and there is a good reason for it. These characters could be your quiet well behaved neighbors. And in *Silence* Lecter has escaped. . . .

Thus, while critics who affirm the affirmative element in horrific fiction are frequently on solid ground, as even a cursory scanning of the basic horror text confirms, the constant process of subverting these values must eventually erode their affirmative qualities and call the very values we have founded our society on into sharp question. What happens to a long cherished value when the character discovers that it is no longer true? What happens to the childlike belief in the efficacy of ritual monster banishing when the ritual no longer works? Worse than a failed ritual is the knowledge that beings exist who are completely unaffected by any of the rituals or conventions of society. Worst of all is the knowledge so unacceptable to Graham or Starling: in Pogo's memorable words, "we have met the enemy, and he is us."

THE HIDDEN MONSTER:
PROBLEMS IN CONSTRUCTION AND IDENTITY

"Everyone is interchangeable anyway. It doesn't really matter."

In the more disturbing human monster texts, the pattern of disaffirmation unfolds in several ways. Implicit in a disaffirmative pattern is the idea of the human monster as uncontained. However monstrous such figures are, in less horrific texts they are neutralized by either prison or death, and thus constitute a contained threat.

More radical dis/ease is provoked when the community has, to some degree, made the monster itself, which occurs in Stephen King's *Carrie* and in Joyce Carol Oates "Extenuating Circumstances." The community actively forces monsterhood on King's protagonist; Oates' self-referential narrator feels ostracized and demonized by the society in which she cannot function. On one level these works provoke the most emotionally horrific responses because the community and the individuals which produced a human monster do not seem to understand their responsibility. The monsters thus generated are both monstrous and horrific as well as human and pitiable.

A greater level of dis/ease involves problems of identity, since in order to contain the monster, we must first recognize him/her as monstrous. In Patrick Süskind's *Perfume: The Story of a Murderer*, the monster is a source of repulsion for all "normal" people who encounter him; he is defined as unnatural because he lacks a human odor. In *The Other*, the monster seems to be safely contained at story's end, but the identity of the monster is uncertain. The text deliberately refuses answers, and the ensuing narratorial ambiguity contributes greatly to the sense of dis/ease. Perhaps the most dis/easeful type of human monster, however, is the monster who is not only uncontained but unrecognized as a monster within his society and thus unconstrained by any societal forces. Such a monster creates the deepest dis/ease merely by its existence. Brett Easton Ellis' *American Psycho* is distasteful, disgusting, and dehumanizing. Repellent as the novel is, however, it does provoke great dis/ease; the central character at novel's end is not only free but completely unrecognized as a monster.[1] The lack of humanity, the lack of containment, and the kind of damage done, which is often irremediable, mark these texts as disaffirmative. *American Psycho* is simply an extreme instance of this kind of horror fiction.

In Stephen King's first novel, *Carrie* (1974), one of the most effective depictions of the consequences involved in casual demonization, the human monster is both pitiable and fearsome, which sets up a dis/easeful dichotomy in the reader.[2] Her peers define Carrie as a pariah, and thus her status is externally dictated; if she can be defined as a monster, or at least a monstrous body, by outside forces, she bears no responsibility for that designation. However, when finally pushed too far, Carrie not only accepts her status as a pariah and a monster but also actively chooses to become truly monstrous. Carrie's eventual deployment of her telekinetic power results in the destruction of many innocent people, including Carrie herself, and no real resolution.

Carrietta White has been subject to the strategies of exclusion for as long as she can remember. Raised by a hyper-fanatical "Christian" mother, abused and tormented by her mother for the sin of being born a woman, made a scapegoat by the children with whom she attends school in the small town of Chamberlain, Carrie White lives a life of unremitting misery. Her mother, her religious beliefs, and her repellent appearance all work to demarcate her off from the accepted groups. Such qualities mark her as the scapegoat, especially for the more popular girls. Anyone can torment Carrie because no one could possibly be less popular. In effect, Carrie is the *sine qua non* of community; the school cliques are formed relative to Carrie. And Carrie, who is an intelligent girl, realizes her predicament but cannot change the environment in which she is trapped.

The novel opens with the infamous shower scene and makes Carrie's position perfectly plain. As she stands in the shower, "a frog among swans . . . she looked the part of the sacrificial goat, the constant butt."[3] At sixteen she has her first menstrual period during the group shower and is entirely ignorant of its significance. The girls, who hate her and are repelled by her, start chanting "Plug it *up*, plug it *up*" and pelting her with tampons.[4] But Carrie, who has endured years of cruel taunts and pranks, suddenly starts gibbering and howling, and the girls dimly realize fission has occurred. Research done *post facto* will inaccurately link the blossoming of Carrie's paranormal powers with the late onset of menstruation, but Carrie has always had telekinetic and psychometric powers; it is after the shower scene that she starts to work actively to develop her power. Previously, she has blocked all memories of her telekinetic power from her consciousness, equating her budding powers with the evil associated with female sexuality.

On the way home from school, she imagines one of the worst offenders, Chris Hargensen, *"bloody and screaming for mercy. With rats crawling all over her face."* She remembers a thousand incidents of abuse and a hundred ways in which she has "tried to erase the redplague circle that had been drawn around her."[5] Five-year-old Tommy Erbter, riding his bike, sees Carrie, says, "Hey, ol' fart face! Ol' praying Carrie!" and falls off with the bike on top of him. Carrie, who has been wishing she could take revenge on the world at large, and Tommy in particular, stops dead in her tracks as she realizes that what she has wished for has come to pass. At this point Carrie realizes that she may be a scapegoat and a pariah, but she has power, power which she starts to actively develop. She deliberately flexes her mind muscle, exercising and strengthening it in the same manner as biceps are strengthened, by increasing weight and repetitions. From this point on, any destruction Carrie wreaks will not be the result of directionless emotion as has happened in the past, but a decision to use her power for vengeance.

Part of the dis/ease engendered by *Carrie* derives from the fact that it is not just a bunch of cruel adolescent girls and boys who make Carrie's life a living hell, but, from all indications, much of the town of Chamberlain. The gym teacher, Rita Desjardins, is disgusted by Carrie, although "she would certainly repress her feeling that Carrie is "a fat, whiny bag of lard."[6] The assistant principal, Mr. Morton, defines Carrie, whom he calls Cassie and Miss Wright, solely in terms of her mother, who was once suspended for hitting a girl she had seen smoking a cigarette. "I've placed her, I think, Margaret White's daughter."[7] He has not recognized Carrie; he has merely slotted her into the weird people category and defined her in terms of her mother. Although the entire neighborhood knows that Margaret White is quite literally a religious nut, no one interferes. At age three Carrie is already a victim of her mother, who has told her that sex is evil, that only women who sin by having sex grow breasts, which she calls *dirtypillows*, and who, when she sees Carrie talking to the "Whore of Babylon" (a/k/a Stella Horan, a fifteen-year-old next-door neighbor who sunbathes wearing a bikini), literally scourges herself with her nails. Stella Horan, recounting the anecdote, says,

"I could hear her [Margaret] . . . praying and sobbing and screeching. . . . and Margaret telling the girl to get in the closet and pray. The little girl crying and screaming that she was sorry, she forgot."[8]

Shortly after this episode, a rain of stones falls on Margaret White's house and the neighbors hear a scream; again no one interferes. And since this community is one that any of us might inhabit, the disquieting question arises: on which side would we stand? Further dis/ease is generated by the fact that the person most responsible for Carrie's physical and emotional well being is the most destructive. Margaret White, creator/destroyer, nurturer/retarder, lifegiver/deathdealer, and mother/monster is one of the most significant sources of dis/ease in this text, for Carrie, convinced that her mother has beaten the "Black Man" and driven forth all sin from her body, both loves and hates her mother. More important, she has no chance of developing into a person as long as her mother lives. And her mother, in her final subversion of any maternal feelings, has decided to kill Carrie rather than see her develop into a normal, i.e., sexual, human being.

Yet another source of dis/ease is Susan Snell, one of the popular but nice girls. Susan was a participant in the stoning by tampons and feels genuine remorse. Such an action does not fit in with her view of herself, and she is too uncomfortable to either justify or dismiss it. Her mind's eye replays the scene until she decides she must make a significant expiatory gesture. In making this gesture, Susan Snell brings on the mass destruction of Chamberlain. In disaffirmative horror fiction attempts to set the situation right do not succeed. Susan asks her much-loved boyfriend Tommy Ross, a popular student, teen-age heartthrob, and jock-of-all-sports to take Carrie to the Spring Ball, the culmination of four years of high school and an event which she herself desperately wants to attend. But Susan understands that a small and meaningless act of atonement will not do. This is not like giving up chocolate-covered watermelon seeds for Lent when one doesn't like them; this gesture must hurt Susan as much as she has hurt Carrie. Although Sue knows that she has done "a suck-off thing," as she admits to herself, one of the reasons she attends Miss Desjardins' punitive detention "had nothing to do with nobility. She wasn't going to miss her last Spring Ball for anything. For *anything*."[9] But Susan literally cannot stand to accept this image of herself, so she asks Tommy to ask Carrie to the Spring Ball. Chris Hargensen, the ringleader of the disaffected, resents the trouble to which the attack on Carrie White leads. She refuses to attend detention, forfeits tickets to the Prom, and with Billy Nolan, her loutish boyfriend, decides to wreak vengeance on Carrie. At the prom, when Carrie and Tommy are crowned King and Queen, at the moment when Carrie feels acceptance is within her grasp, she is "crowned" with a bucket of pig's-blood: "Pig's blood for a pig."[10] Tommy Ross is killed by the falling bucket, but he soon comes to seem one of the few lucky ones. Carrie has spent a great deal of time flexing the mind muscles that allow her to move things, and her power has increased to astronomical proportions. Standing on the stage, drenched with blood, her initial hopeful feeling of being "dusted over with the enchantment of the evening"[11] annihilated, she believes that the entire senior class was complicit in her humiliation. And the entire senior class does start laughing; some with the laughter that erupts at funerals, but some because as Norma Watson says, "Carrie had been the butt of every joke. . . . It was either laugh or cry, and who could bring themselves to cry over Carrie?"[12] Unfortunately for her tormentors, this is not little Carrie White, the powerless goat, but a human monster who decides to use her power. So Carrie deploys her telekinetic power, the power her classmates do not realize she has, for retribution. As she thinks to herself, "there was still enchantment and wonder, but she had crossed a line and now the fairy tale was green with corruption and evil."[13] Indeed, Carrie reacts as a monster. She decides to get every last one of them, innocent or guilty. She has already turned on the sprinkling system, but now she also shorts out the electricity. Seeing one of her fellow students being electrocuted, she thinks, "He looked funny. She began to laugh. (By christ then let them all look funny)."[14] Having incinerated the gymnasium, Carrie roams the streets of Chamberlain, killing many of the townspeople, quite a few of whom have done nothing at all to her. Mrs. Simard, one of the survivors, says that she watched people being electrocuted and knew that Carrie was "*Glad!* I could *feel* her being glad."[15] When Carrie tracks down and kills her mother as well as Chris Hargensen and Billy Nolan, the actual perpetrators, and then dies of a coronary thrombosis, the reader feels justice may have been served, but too much of Chamberlain has been destroyed. Too many innocent people, people who did nothing to Carrie, have died to allow the affirmation of containment to take place. It is also difficult to dismiss the agony Carrie experiences in the final hours of her life, much of which she does not deserve.

Another source of dis/ease lies in Susan Snell's experiences. Like Clarice Starling in *The Silence of the Lambs,* Susan Snell gains two-edged knowledge about herself, but unlike Clarice's knowledge, which connects her past to her present, Susan's knowledge leaves her more fragmented and less complete. Susan was telepathically linked to Carrie when she died, and like Addie Bundren in Faulkner's *As I Lay Dying*, Susan must decide how to live a life that is defined as lasting until "the time when my light is carried down that long tunnel into blackness."[16] In order to deny the reality of Carrie and her power, the townspeople and the White Commission, the official government inquiry, subject Susan to the same strategies of exclusion to which Carrie was subjected. Since she has done nothing particularly horrendous, and indeed has made an honest attempt at atonement, it is difficult to see why she should feel responsible.

The investigators do not believe that Susan could be selfless enough to act out of altruistic motives. As one of the academics argues, echoing Jerzy Kosinski,

"It would be uplifting if we could believe that adolescent human nature is capable of salvaging the pride and self-image of the low bird in the pecking order . . . but we know better. The low bird is not picked tenderly out of the dust by its fellows; rather it is dispatched quickly and without mercy."[17]

The official narrative provokes further disaffirmation by defining adolescents as monsters incapable of any degree of mercy or compassion. *Carrie* is therefore dis/ease-provoking on several points: any one of us could be either Carrie or her tormentors; her mother, rather than nurturing her, tries to kill her; the institutions of power fail her; and, finally, all attempts to make the situation right are doomed to utter failure. *Carrie* is disaffirmative because society makes the human monster, cannot control the monster, and still denies the possibility of actual monsterdom while simultaneously defining humans as monsters, thus rejecting any possibility of effective resolution at the same time as it rejects human sympathy and empathy.

Joyce Carol Oates' "Extenuating Circumstances" (1992) develops much the same thematic as *Carrie*, a thematic in which the human being designated as other or pariah takes vengeance. The retributive action is limited to the woman's husband/lover as opposed to an entire group, but the vengeance is almost unbearably horrific as well as unbearably pathetic. Because the most effective horror fiction is necessarily linked to the dis/ease partially generated by a reader's visceral reaction, I have chosen to include Oates' disturbing story. Written almost entirely in dependent clauses beginning with "because," which neatly reflect the narrator's fragmented view of reality, this short story details a woman's decision to boil her toddler son. The evocation of madness, of a woman marginalized and rejected, is horrible enough, but what places this short story solidly in the disaffirmative matrix is the last line of the story, addressed to the absent husband/lover: "Because I wanted to tell you these things. Just like this."[18] As with reader reaction to *Carrie*, one does not know what to feel. Pity for someone so wretched and obsessed, so unable to deal with abandonment, is certainly an emotion evoked, but so is sheer revolted horror at images like "Because the washcloth soaked in his saliva will dry on the line and show no sign," or "Because I wore rubber gloves to spare myself being scalded," or "Because my neighbors' TV was on so loud, I knew they could not hear even if he screamed through the washcloth."[19]

Part of the dis/ease is produced by the first-person narrative, which works much like Poe's narratives. We are in the grip of an insane narrator, who may yet be reliable. No information exists beyond the narrator's twisted account. The woman is obviously now a single mother, with a partner who wants nothing to do with her, but whether this was a one-night stand, a short affair, a long-term relationship, or a marriage is never addressed. She, left with her memories, their child, and a slowly disintegrating grasp on reality, has been forcibly othered. Because she cannot accept the finality of her lover's rejection, the eventual focus of the narrative closes in on the child, who acts as a locus for her hatred of both her lover and herself. She is victimized by the strategies of exclusion, living in a society in which she cannot function, in which everyone excludes her—the judge who heard the court case, her lover's sister who will not tell her his whereabouts, shopkeepers who sell her sleeping pills made of flour and chalk, cashiers who cannot remember her name, other mothers who criticize her, employers who "will not believe me when I list my skills" and who, she believes, tear up her misspelled job applications as soon as she leaves.[20]

In turn, she deploys these same strategies to demarcate her son. She describes him as wetting his pants, having a runny nose and a weak eye, and flinching, whimpering, and crying. She claims she boils him to death to spare him the cruelties to which she thinks she has been subjected and to which, in turn, she subjects him. The conflicting but inseparable reasons for her actions deny closure and render this a deeply disaffirmative text: "Because then I could speak to you in this way, maybe in a letter [. . .] over the telephone or even face to face. Because then you could not escape. . . . Because in this there is mercy. . . . Because I loved him. Because love hurts so bad."[21] Not only does her narrative, with its paranoid elements, create deep dis/ease with its randomly juxtaposed justifications for her actions and numerous narratorial gaps, the vivid images of her life and its despair and hopelessness also deny any affirmative readings. Which narrative are we to believe? She boiled her child alive to spare him pain? Or she boiled her child alive to force her ex-partner to acknowledge her existence? Or was it simply to get back at him and displace her responsibility onto his shoulders? None of these questions are ultimately answerable, and all of them contribute to the slippage which also provokes dis/ease. Like Heller's earlier examples, this text forces dis/ease as the reader tries to construct a story which fills in the gaps and explains away the inconsistencies. The question of reliability, of provenance, while not as central as in Thomas Tryon's *The Other*, is still important in producing dis/ease. Has she been demarcated and demonized as she thinks, for no good reason, or is she indeed delusional and paranoid? If horror does indeed validate the cultural norms and make us feel better about our culture, how does this narrative work to good effect? She boiled her son alive, she says in the last line, "Because I wanted to tell you these things. Just like this."[22]

Identifying the monster is crucial to all human monster fiction. After all, to safely contain a monster we must be able to say with assurance who is and is not a monster. My first two examples in the disaffirmative chapter comprise a monster consensus; however sorry we may feel for the characters, we can easily identify them as monsters. Carrie, unlike John Smith, does not turn her power to positive uses; Oates' nameless narrator, like Libby Hatch, kills her child for reasons we can neither accept nor understand.

But what if the monster is not so easily identified?

Patrick Süskind's *Perfume: The Story of a Murderer* (1985) is a unique horror fiction in terms of the manner in which the human and the monstrous is discussed. This text explores the premise that one cannot be human without possessing a characteristically human odor but, being invisible, can nevertheless become a successful monster. If containment is necessary to preserve social order, how can this laudable goal be accomplished if one cannot ever locate the monster?

Jean-Baptiste Grenouille, "one of the most gifted and abominable personages in an era that knew no lack of gifted and abominable personages," has been forgotten, not because he fell short in wickedness, but because he restricted his efforts to "a domain that leaves no trace in history: to the fleeting realm of scent."[23] Since the narrator ranks him with such figures as de Sade, Saint-Just, and Fouché in terms of sheer evil, but claims he has been forgotten, the question of identity arises immediately. If he is as immoral as de Sade, why is his name not part of the pantheon of infamous blackguards?

The narrator opens with a discourse both wonderful and revolting on the appalling stenches of eighteenth-century France, "a stench barely conceivable to us modern men and women" and points out that his protagonist was born in the most putrid spot in Paris, a fish stall located near the *Cimiterie des Innocents*.[24] His mother dumps him under the gutting table with the other offal, is caught when he squalls, and hanged for attempted infanticide; the infant is then handed over to a monastery and a series of wet nurses. And here the first indication that all is not quite right surfaces. One of its wet nurses returns him to Father Terrier, claiming he not only sucks her to the bones but is possessed by the devil. She says, "This baby makes my flesh creep because he doesn't smell as human children ought to smell."[25] The priest reasons that a child, being sinless, that is, free of the odor of fleshly sins, should perforce be odorless, but he is also soon instinctively, even irrationally, repelled by the child. Terrier compares it to a spider, a devil, and a monster, simply because it awakens, sniffs at him, and starts squalling. Interestingly, once Father Terrier returns to the cloister, having disposed of the child, which is referred to as "a bellowing basket," to further emphasize its lack of humanity, he engages in what amounts to rituals of exorcism. He "cast his clothes from him as though they were foully soiled, washed himself from head to foot, . . . crossing himself repeatedly."[26] Obviously this child evokes strong reactions from everyone it encounters, but as yet, nothing except a lack of human odor accounts for such strong repulsion.[27]

The only person who can tolerate his presence is Mme. Gaillard, who runs a foundling house in the Fauborg St. Germaine; in another indication of the importance of the sense of smell, she can neither smell nor consequently feel any emotion. But the other children are so repulsed and revolted by Grenouille that they attempt to suffocate him: "He disgusted them the way a fat spider that you can't bring yourself to crush in your hand disgusts you."[28] The narrator's ruling metaphor for Grenouille during this time is that of a tick, a bloodsucking parasite which can preserve a tiny spark of life for years until it latches onto a new victim. Defining Grenouille thus adds to the repulsion factor, as this particular phylum is one which evokes dis/ease precisely because it is so inhuman and so voracious.

According to the narrator, "He was an abomination from the start."[29] He is thus defined as a monster, something other than human, something with an essential lack. In his early years, however, he discovers his one talent. He may be illiterate, incapable of emotion toward people, despised and reviled by humanity, but he has a nose for scent and an eidetic memory.

When Mme. Gaillard sells him to a tanner, like the tick the narrator has labeled him, "stubborn, sullen and loathsome,"[30] he conserves his energy and waits. One day he is delivering a load of hides to master perfumer Giuseppe Baldini and snatches the opportunity to work for him. He does so by analyzing *Cupid and Psyche*, a competitor's perfume, mixing a batch, and then improving it on the spot. Naturally, the perfume maker, a competent craftsman but no innovator, recognizes an *idiot savant* when he sees one and takes Grenouille as an apprentice. The tick has landed. He learns all he can from Baldini and finally departs in search of more knowledge. In a clear indication of his essentially monstrous nature, he has already killed a young woman with whose scent he is enraptured, but he is unsuspected because his lack of scent conceals him from notice. What makes Grenouille such a monster is that he has no conception of the value of human life except in terms of scent, which is, of course, something he does not possess on his own and for which he has an insatiable appetite.

After leaving Baldini, Grenouille ends up living in a cave for seven years. He is driven from his cave by a horrible discovery; he discovers that he, Jean-Baptiste Grenouille, greatest nose in the world, has no human scent. Since Grenouille identifies things and their importance solely in terms of scent, his nonscent signals his nonexistence. He is, in other words, not a part of the only significant hierarchy he recognizes.

When he emerges into the world of men from the cave, Jean Baptist discovers that he can masquerade as a human being with a "few clothes, the haircut, and the little masquerade with cosmetics."[31] Convinced he needs a personal odor so that he can blend in among the citizenry, Grenouille compounds a personal odor out of such fragrant ingredients as cat-shit, vinegar, decomposing cheese, rancid fish, rotten egg, and castoreum. "The bilge," notes the narrator, "smelled revolting."[32] He tops off the base with fragrant and aromatic scents, and when he has finished, he has a perfume which induces people to think that he is one of them. And although as he walks out into the street he fears that he stinks, he finds that he is treated, for the first time, like a normal person. But what makes this man a human monster is not his desire for community, but his counterfeiting of it and the use to which he puts his ability to blend in.

Having achieved acceptance, Grenouille's next ambition is to create a scent which will force people to love him. "He would be the omnipotent god of scent . . . in the real world and over real people. . . . And he wanted to do it because it was evil, thoroughly evil."[33] Thus, the production of a monster is complete; Grenouille, like Carrie, has decided to be a monster instead of a scapegoat. Carrie does it because she is driven past the point of no return; Grenouille does it because he hates the people who have rejected him. He is the more dis/ease-provoking character, because his choice is deliberate, consciously evil, and unjustified. Grenouille could well have been the eminent perfumer in all France, but he deliberately chooses evil. Once Grenouille has discovered the few paltry tricks necessary for acceptance, he uses them, not to be accepted, as Carrie would have done, but to completely subvert the strategies of exclusion and move from demarcated to demarcator, demonized to demon.

Grenouille moves on to Grasse, the perfume capital of France, in order to learn the techniques he needs to rob materials of their odors and capture those essences. And what does this advance? All this learning occurs because he has located the scent that inspires love and is plotting to possess it. The fact that the scent belongs to a living child means less than nothing. The child is not a pre-adolescent girl, not Laure Richis, but a container of scent he is determined he must possess. The narrator, who obviously loathes him, makes Grenouille's perverted point of view perfectly plain:

Grenouille, the solitary tick, the abomination, Grenouille the Monster, who had never felt love and would never be able to inspire it, stood there beside the city wall of Grasse on that day in March and loved and was profoundly happy in his love.

    True, he did not love another human being. . . . He loved her scent—that alone and nothing else, and only inasmuch as it would one day be his alone.[34]

The parallels to Buffalo Bill in Thomas Harris' *The Silence of the Lambs* are inescapable. Both texts have human monsters who pretend to be normal, covet another person's possessions, and have absolutely no feeling for the person *per se*. Buffalo Bill hunts his prey, refers to the women as "it," and covets their skins; Grenouille hunts women, thinks of them as objects, and covets their scent. As Buffalo Bill imitates, like a talking magpie, the screams and pleas of his victims, so Grenouille imitates the behavior of human beings. Both pursue goals which are supposed to result in transformation, but the goals pursued are monstrous because they do not consider other people as important. Buffalo Bill is considerably less adept at gaining acceptance, and in the end is neutralized. Grenouille cannot be neutralized because he is the monster who blends in perfectly. What can be worse than a monster one cannot recognize?

    And so Grenouille experiments and bides his time. Meanwhile, young virginal maidens start showing up dead. The panicked townspeople, employing some exclusionary strategies themselves, suspect the gypsies, the Italian field workers, the Jews, the monks, lunatics, charcoal burners, beggars, the nobility, and finally the Italian field workers again, which doesn't work because it is their young women showing up dead— all are suspected, but nothing can be proved. Eventually, Laure is murdered as twenty-four other girls have been murdered, so Grenouille can appropriate her scent for his own use. The citizenry of Grasse are utterly terrified and carry out a great many activities designed to buy protection, activities ranging from intercessions with the saints to black masses: "The people of Grasse awaited the murderer's next blow. . . . And secretly, everyone yearned to hear the horrible news, if only in the hope that it would not be about him, but about someone else."[35] This generates another source of dis/ease because it reveals community as an empty construct in which everyone is solitary, as Grenouille is solitary.

Eventually, Grenouille is caught red-handed with the clothing and hair of Laure Richis and cursory digging finds the remains of the other twenty-four victims. He is swiftly tried, convicted, and sentenced to twelve blows with an iron rod and crucifixion; the usual strangling after the blows is expressly forbidden. As was typical at this time, people prepared for the execution as for a holiday. But when Grenouille appears, the mood of the mass abruptly changes. Instead of an execution, the crowd, "overcome by a powerful sense of goodwill, of tenderness, of crazy, childish infatuation . . . of love for this homicidal little man," engages in a frenzied orgy.[36]

Grenouille, filled to the brim with hatred and contempt, feels his triumph at having made a perfume that inspires adoration turn to disgust. In times past, he has dreamed of drowning in his own odorlessness, his own lack of identity, but this time it is no dream but a waking nightmare, in which

no scream would help to wake and free him, no flight would rescue him and bring him into the good warm world. For here and now, this was the world, and this, here and now, was his dream come true. And he had wanted it thus."[37]

In complete despair, wishing only for death, Grenouille returns to Paris and anoints himself with his precious perfume, which counterfeits human scent as Grenouille counterfeits humanity, "pulling the corners of his mouth apart, the way he had noticed people do when they smile,"[38] wearing clothes, makeup, perfume, and mingling with the citizenry. The perfume can do everything for him but enable him to smell himself; it can enslave the whole world, but for Grenouille the perfume is meaningless. The one thing it cannot do is reverse his self-demarcation. Finally, Grenouille returns to the cemetery, to the putrid place of his birth, and awaits nightfall and the coming of the riff-raff. He saturates himself with the perfume and is promptly attacked by a mob who, believing him divine, rend him to pieces and devour him. The riff-raff do not feel conscience-stricken but quite light-hearted. "They were uncommonly proud," runs the last line of the novel. "For the first time they had done something out of love."[39]

In participating in this demonized rite of communion, the mob has not acted out of love any more than the mass assembled to see justice done acted out of desire. What does this perverted communion accomplish? The people who encounter Grenouille are victims of his monomaniacal desire to enslave them by inspiring love. This goal does not in any way affect his nature, which remains un/in/human and unapproachable;

he seeks literal obliteration because he has no place in the real world. There is no closure in the novel in terms of the containment of the human monster. A satisfactory resolution would indicate that the monster was knowingly contained and social order restored, as would have been the case had Grenouille suffered for his crimes in Grasse. And while one might contend that the serial killer is quite literally contained, I would argue that the cannibalistic communion by which all traces of Grenouille are obliterated only reveals the essentially animalistic nature of humanity, a point the narrator has made previously when he catalogues the odoriferous substances which make up human scent. Grenouille the murderer/human monster is not contained, rather the mob seizes and consumes a being they see as an angel.

One could argue that consuming serial killers does contain them; however, these people are not acting to restore social order. Any restoration is purely a by-blow of the Dionysian frenzy Grenouille generates. The mechanics of social order have failed utterly, as not only did the magistrates release a guilty man, they executed an innocent man. Grenouille never escapes from the strategies of exclusion because he carries them within his very nature, and society cannot escape from the "Grenouille" within for the same reason, so where in this text lies anything but a disaffirmative view of life?

While both *Perfume* and Thomas Tryon's *The Other* (1971) are concerned with the problems involved in identification and containment of the human monster, *The Other* deals, in an extremely effective, dis/ease-provoking way, with ambiguity in both the plot structure and the identity of the monster. In *Perfume*, as well as the other texts in this triad, the identity of the monster is beyond dispute. Dramatic irony is also clearly present; the readers know, from the beginning of the novel, both the identification and motivation of the monster. In *The Other* the all-pervasive situational irony adds a layer of dis-ease to the already dis/ease-provoking text. As in Edgar Allan Poe's "Ligeia," or Henry James' *The Turn of the Screw*, the reader is unable to ascertain exactly what is going on in the text, which denies any possibility of resolution or closure. While the reader is certain that either Niles or Holland Perry is a monster and best contained at the Babylon Insane Asylum, the identity of the monster remains in doubt. Is Niles a deeply disturbed adolescent unable to accept the death of his twin brother Holland or a teenage boy possessed by the malevolent spirit of his dead twin? Is he Holland, or is Holland a construct, a mask behind which Niles hides his nefarious self? Tryon, however, by deliberately obfuscating the identity of the human monster and, narratively speaking, actively leading the reader down the primrose path, goes a step further than Poe or James.

The novel is narrated by an unidentified speaker, who addresses his readers in an authoritative tone which assumes a familiarity with the situation which the reader does not possess. Thus a disjunction exists in the relationship between the narrator and the implied reader. Such statements as, "I know what you must be thinking: Madness," and "I think in some strange, awful way, I miss—*him*," assume that the narrator and audience are close enough for intimate discourse, and that the reader does indeed know to whom "him" refers.[40] Such a narratorial strategy sets up a dis/ease in the actual reading experience. As the novel progresses, the narratorial voice intrudes directly, commenting on the situation and always working to deconstruct what the reader thinks is known. The story itself echoes the narrative ambiguity as it is intentionally unclear exactly what is going on, and the reader's inability to either accept the narrator's version or construct a cohesive account of events contributes to the dis/ease.

The Other is set in Pequot's Landing, Connecticut, in 1935, and concerns the tribulations of the Perrys, an eminent family who has experienced a rather unfortunate run of events. Vining Perry has died of an accident while hauling apples down to the cellar; Russell, Niles and Holland's cousin, has a fatal accident with a pitchfork; Alexandra Perry, the twins' mother, is crippled by a fall down stairs; Aunt Fannuschka is nearly killed and permanently hospitalized by a wasp sting; Eugenia, Torrie Perry Gannon's infant daughter, is kidnapped and killed; the matriarch of the family, Ada Vedrayna, is burned to death; and one of the neighbors, Mrs. Rowe, is deliberately frightened to death. That the events take place in the past is clear, as the narrator informs us that he has been told that the Perry place, two-hundred-years old, is gone.

The actual tale opens with Holland Perry hanging his grandmother's cat and, according to the narrator, "darn near hanging himself." The narrator's initial account is fairly clear, or so we are led to believe; the cat is killed, and Holland, one of the thirteen-year-old twins, is injured. Niles, the other twin and the central figure in the novel, is quite clear on this, but the narrator's comment is not: "—and there was one who thought, for a quick moment, that Holland was—but no, he told himself, no, he's only hurt."[41] Much later in the novel, the hapless reader will discover that the narrator is one of the twins, although which twin is open to question; that Holland, who was supposedly only hurt, has been dead since the story opened; and that Niles, ostensibly the hero, may or may not be a positive figure.

Throughout most of the story, the reader is led to believe that Niles is the good twin and Holland the evil twin. The hanging of the cat is a case in point, as is a comment that Miss Josceline-Marie, the proprietor of the general store, makes to a customer who accuses Niles of riding his bike recklessly and knocking her down. "Tut, dear, you don't mean *that* one. That's Niles. . . . Why if I didn't know better, I'd think you were talking about Holland. . . . Only it couldn't have been him."[42] Ada, coming into the store in time to hear Niles' furious denials, drags him forcibly to the graveyard and confronts him with his brother's grave. The narrator points out, with a dispassionate tone clearly at odds with his identity, that

"the boy is in thrall to a cadaver, obsessed by a ghoulish inamorato, not a ghost, not a vision, but a living breathing thing of flesh and blood; Holland, *he himself.* . . . With this—creature—he acts out his little pageant of blissful agony, the happy subtle tyrannies, loving his twin yet supplanting him, idolizing him yet tearing him from his place; it is not enough to be Holland's twin, he must become Holland himself."[43]

Niles has the peculiar ability, encouraged with disastrous results by Ada, to "become" an object if he concentrates long and intensely. She is attempting to give Niles something to do to take his mind off his grief. What Ada knows, but what the reader does not, is that Niles has lost his twin and is not coping well. But, as is typical of the pattern in disaffirmative horror fiction, she worsens the situation rather than ameliorating it. For Niles, unable to exist without his twin Holland, "becomes" Holland. It is Niles who commits all the murders, all the while vehemently and doggedly claiming that Holland is the perpetrator. And since many of the deeds are either relatively insignificant, like poisoning a pet rat, or pass as accidents, as does Russell's death, the family is slow to see that Niles has, in some fundamental and irrevocable way, broken with material reality and forged his own. By the time either Ada or Alexandra realizes what has happened, it is too late for any epiphanies to change the situation. In fact, it is Alexandra's realization which causes her nearly fatal accident. While Niles has steadfastly denied his twin's demise, he also has a treasure which he takes great pains to keep hidden—and for good reason. The family ring, a gold ring with a peregrine falcon engraved on it, was awarded to Holland upon his father's unfortunate death; Niles covets the ring, which as far as anyone knows, is still on the dead boy's finger. Niles, however, has gone to the coffin and clipped Holland's finger off. He keeps the ring and the finger in a Prince Albert tobacco can, along with, we are finally apprised, several other souvenirs of the murders. Alexandra's discovery of the ring and the finger precipitates her crippling fall. She does not believe Niles when he says that Holland gave him the ring: "Curiosity killed the cat, as Holland would say. . . . What else could Holland have done—what else could *anybody* have done—except to reach out and push her down the stairs?"[44]

Such a statement is strongly at odds with what we have seen of Niles, who is always sweet and helpful, clearly beloved of all the household. So it is extremely difficult for the reader to reconcile the disparate images of Niles tearfully burying the rat Holland has ostensibly poisoned and buying his mother a puppet with the monstrous acts which have occurred.

Then there is "the Other." According to both Niles and often the narrator, Holland is a vicious psycho/sociopath: he tortures and poisons small animals, kills people who annoy him, inflicts pain for pleasure, enjoys watching the death agonies of his victims, and is in general a monster. All or part of this may even be true. Holland almost certainly did hang the cat, thus resulting in his timely demise. But if Niles is a sweet, gentle, and loving character, at least as presented by the seemingly objective omniscient narrator, then who has actually poisoned the rat, killed Russell, crippled Alexandra, frightened Mrs. Rowe to death, kidnapped, drowned, and concealed the corpse of Torrie's baby in the keg of wine customarily drunk at the annual dinner celebrating the Perry family's civic pride, and burned Ada to death? Clearly, it cannot be Holland. Holland is dead and buried, whether Niles wishes to believe it or not. And so it must be Niles, but this cannot be either because Niles is clearly not a monster. Niles' game, taught to him by Ada, of looking deeply and becoming what he looks at, is rather central to any possible resolution of this conundrum. Has Holland come back from the grave and possessed Niles' body and personality? In this scenario, the evil and dead *doppelganger* has taken over Niles' body, subverting both his body and his will. In this guise, Holland has used his more subordinate twin to accomplish his evil. Or is Niles a Dr. Jekyll/Mr. Hyde character? Beneath the sweet helpfulness he may have a Hyde-like desire to do evil he cannot recognize or admit as his own, which accounts for his hysterical insistence that Holland has done everything.

Naturally, Niles must also deny the fact of Holland's death. Niles sees himself as completely separate from Holland, and, in fact, as trying to keep Holland's secrets and stop him from committing his horrible acts. When Eugenia, Torrie's infant daughter, is kidnapped, no one seems more upset than Niles, or more anxious to help. He even goes so far as to try to force Holland to tell him where the baby is. But by this time, Ada, his beloved grandmother, has realized that her equally beloved grandson is a human monster. She also realizes that he has confused his own world with reality and will never be able to separate reality from fantasy. Once again Ada tries to force him to acknowledge that Holland is dead; she is finally able to make him say the words, but she is unsuccessful in making him understand that the game of becoming Holland is dangerous and must stop. Again, the dis/ease surfaces. Ada has only tried to help Niles overcome his grief and the result is this monstrous situation: "It broke my heart to see you so unhappy. . . . I thought in time you would outgrow it."[45]

Murderer though Niles is, Ada cannot stand the thought of him being confined to an insane asylum: "Where would they take him? To that barren place, that place of brick and iron bars . . . like some dangerous animal?"

On the other hand, distasteful though this prospect may be, where else can Niles be contained? Clearly Niles, whether he is possessed by Holland's restless spirit or "becomes" Holland in the course of a game, or is Holland as well as Niles, evil as well as good, cannot be allowed to continue his present course. This becomes apparent to Ada even as she thinks to herself that she "would never consider such a thing, never such an end for her beloved." She convinces herself that since Niles has said the words, has admitted that Holland is dead, she will be able to make him confront that fact that he has committed all the crimes, done all the awful things: "Perhaps she could get him to face it somehow; and seeing, recognizing it, perhaps there was help at hand. . . . It was a beginning in any case, a first step." But when the idea comes into her mind that it would be like teaching a baby to walk, it abruptly reminds her of the latest tragedy. When she asks him who knows about Eugenia's whereabouts. "His answer came, not so much as an answer but as a scream. "*Holland knows! Ask Holland!*"[46] Ada realizes that "He would never give it up, this incredible, this most monstrous delusion, these *remains* he was obsessed with. . . . And this outburst she had just witnessed, so unlike *him* . . . but so like . . .the Other . . . It was almost as though. . . ."[47] And as she walks away, she still does not realize that her hunch is correct.

Ada is, in other words, unaware that the monster is permanently ascendant, that Niles will never be able to separate himself from the evil twin he has in fact become. Unable to commit her beloved Niles to the insane asylum, unable to allow him to live and endanger everyone around him, she eventually attempts to immolate both Niles and herself, but Niles, ostensibly with Holland's aid, escapes and claims that she was mad. He is believed at first, but Mr. Angelini, the hired man, also suspects Niles and catches him with the grisly relics of his deeds. Thus Niles ends up at Babylon, the end of the line, the terrible place the narrator describes in the beginning of the novel.

The novel's dis/ease lies in the fact that Niles is both a sweet and helpful child and a serial killer/human monster. For if Holland is dead and buried before the story opens, and the narrative is fairly clear on this point, but Niles claims that Holland is not dead and is carrying out all these horrible deeds, who is to be believed? The narrator, who seems to have the inside story on all the events, who seems omniscient but is actually rather limited, and who is, in fact, completely unreliable from word one? On the final page of the novel, the narrator is self-identified as Holland, "They call me Niles; Niles, for god's sake, isn't that crazy? When I have told them, for years I have told them, my name is Holland. Holland William Perry."[48]

This "objective" narrator, with his slightly sardonic tone and detached point of view, turns out to be the most unreliable character in the novel. And if Holland has actually possessed his dead twin, as seems possible, then the story is told to exculpate Holland and is also unreliable. The character now labeled as Holland can no longer access his twin, "the Other": "I began to miss him, felt the lack of him, began to seek him out, to look for him. . . . But he was gone . . . he truly was dead then, he who *I* had been, the Other. . . . I could not conjure him up, as he had me."[49] The phrase "he who *I* had been" is somewhat problematic as it makes less sense applied to Holland than it does if the narrator is actually Niles. He (Niles) who *I* (Holland) had been runs directly counter to all the established pieces of knowledge we have accumulated. If the phrase were read as he (Holland) who I (Niles) had been, it would be in accordance with what we think we know. If, however, Holland has taken over Niles' physical body, then Holland has, at times, actually been Niles. However, that attempt to apply logic to the novel dissolves as the narrator thinks he is Holland. And unless the entire novel is constructed on disinformation, the line "I could not conjure him up, as he had me" must refer to Niles' ability to "be" Holland and Holland's inability to conjure up Niles. This essential slipperiness creates dis/ease on the narratorial level as the story line creates dis/ease on the plot level. Thus the gaps between what we know and what we think we know, and between who is speaking and who we think is speaking, all contribute to a dis/easeful reading.

As in other disaffirmative novels, the problem of the human monster is central. In many ways, Niles, if/when he actually is Niles, is an extremely good child, certainly not evil enough to be locked up in an insane asylum. But if he has actually succeeded in becoming Holland, at least part of the time, then he must indeed be contained, for Holland is a ruthless, amoral, cold-hearted murderer. The problem is to separate them, and this cannot be done. The situation here arises out of Ada's well-meaning but catastrophic attempt to help Niles. Intrinsic to this type of horror fiction is the inability to restore order or balance. Even Ada's death, which Niles/Holland explains as caused by a broken neck when she flings herself down to the cellar to immolate both herself and Niles, cannot redress the balance. The instability in the narrative linked with a human monster on the loose, a human monster unintentionally created by the one who loves him most, is very unsettling. Being unable to isolate the monster and say, this, this, and this caused the monster, and we can catch it, contain it, and breathe more easily at night, leads to a story which even Heller's idea of constructing an ending does not satisfactorily resolve. Why is Holland the monster? Why is Niles not? Or vice versa? What has caused one twin to be good and the other to be the infamous "evil twin"? And if we cannot figure out what produces human monsters, how will we ever be able to contain and avoid them? *The Other* provides no answers, only a series of conundrums and traps.

While both Süskind's *Perfume* and Tryon's *The Other* work with the problems generated when the monster is not recognized as monstrous, one is considerably more dis/ease provoking than the other. In *Perfume*, the monster is both contained and consumed by a mob, but since the monster is never recognized as monstrous and the cannibalistic containment is more akin to an exalted communion than containment, the text concludes in a very disturbing fashion. *The Other*, with its deliberately excessive structural ambiguity, its futile attempts to redress order, and its depiction of love as a destructive emotion, is even more disturbing, but neither of these texts can hold a candle to Brett Easton Ellis' infamous *American Psycho*.

My final text, Ellis' *American Psycho* (1991), is an extreme example of the unidentified and uncontained human monster.[50] The novel is gratuitously offensive and elicits the visceral horrific response so necessary to my argument. Since Patrick Bateman, the central character, is never identified and demarcated as a human monster, it follows that he is never caught. The strategies of exclusion cannot come into play because no one knows that a monster exists; the community cannot safeguard itself. Not only is Bateman not identified as a human monster, he is often not even correctly identified as Patrick Bateman, as he lives in a yuppie culture composed of interchangeable people. While the class known as yuppies is the major concern in this novel, and the strategies of exclusion invoked by them exclude everyone else, the reader gets no sense of these characters as real people, and consequently has a hard time caring about any one of them. Essentially, they are cardboard cut-outs, caricatures of the 1980's yuppie, caricatures with whom it is impossible to feel any degree of engagement.

David Skal, critiquing this novel in *The Monster Show: A Cultural History of Horror*, notes that both King and Ellis "depict from radically polar perspectives, the monstrous spectacle of the consumer consumed." Skal sees the essential difference as rooted in class distinctions, noting quite accurately that

The hideous progeny of Stephen King could be tolerated, or ignored, as long as they kept their place in the peasants' quarters in Brooklyn or New Jersey, but let them start tracking blood up the staircase of the Manhattan castle and there'd be hell to pay.[51]

Conversely, from another class perspective, the fact that Bateman preys upon, and is himself, as a New York cabdriver says, "yuppie scum," is not enough to mitigate the dis/ease produced by a completely inhuman monster masquerading successfully as a fellow human being. What happens when he turns his attention (as he often does) to the people who do not fall into the convenient category of "yuppie scum"? Skal's reading of the class distinctions between Stephen King, "readily available at the supermarket display rack," and Ellis, published by Vintage, points up yet another source of cultural dis/ease.[52] After all, in Ellis's consumer-ridden and driven vision, class protects Bateman, who is free to prey upon whomever he wishes, from fellow yuppies to homeless bums.

Bateman, who throughout the entire novel revolts the reader with extremely graphic accounts of perverse sex, rape, sadism, torture, murder, cannibalism, and necrophilia, is considered by Harold Carnes, the man to whom he confesses to killing fellow yuppie Paul Owen and numerous other people, "such a bloody ass-kisser, such a brown-nosing goody-goody"[53] that not only does Carnes not take him seriously, he addresses our "hero" as Davis and Donaldson in one five minute conversation. What is more, his girlfriend Evelyn Richards consistently refers to him as "the boy next store," while he whispers to himself, "I'm a fucking evil psychopath."[54] From the textual evidence, he does not look like a human monster (whatever that entity looks like) but like the iconic boy next door. He is also repeatedly described as looking like his fellow yuppies. The gap between appearance, that of a normal human being, and reality, that of a ravening amoral beast, produces dis/ease as does the easy interchangeability of humans, which confirms fears of a faceless mechanistic society. The fact that the society in which Bateman is an important cog can so misread him has dis/easeful ramifications, because human monsters must be contained if individuals and societies are to be safe; the fact that he can, repeatedly, tell his associates that he is an evil psychopath and be completely disregarded is also dis/ease-provoking. Does no one listen to this man and consider his statements at all?

Bateman frequently tells the people with whom he socializes that he fears he will hurt someone, yet no one takes any action. When Craig McDermott asks him what he wants to do, Bateman replies, "I want to . . . pulverize a woman's face with a large heavy brick." *"Besides* that," Hamlin moans impatiently.[55] In another scene, he tells Daisy, a model he has picked up intending to torture her to death,

> "I beat up a girl today who was asking people on the street for money. . . . She was young and seemed frightened and had a sign that explained she was lost in New York."
>
> Daisy stares at me blankly for a minute before asking, "And then?"
>
> "And then? I beat the living shit out of her. . . . She had misspelled disabled. I mean, that's not the reason I did what I did, but. . . . You know. She was too ugly to rape."

Uncharacteristically he sends Daisy home, telling her, "I think I might . . . hurt you. I don't think I can control myself." Daisy shrugs and says, "Okay. . . . I don't want to get too involved anyway."[56] But her reaction can be summed up by the present day adolescent shrug off, "Whatever." Bateman's actions and warning are of equal indifference to her. It does not seem to occur to her that beating up a homeless person (or any other person) is wrong, and even if in her particular milieu it is no more than harmless amusement, like offering money and snatching it back, or blinding a homeless beggar and crippling his dog, as Bateman does, one would think she might have some sense of responsibility or second thoughts about the somewhat dangerous knowledge she possesses, but she is also a surface creature and such thoughts slough off her glossy well-kept hide.

Throughout most of the novel, Ellis depicts, in mind-numbing detail, a materialistic world composed entirely of concerns with "who's who," money, brand-names, money, material objects, money, reservations, and money, which are evidently supposed to secure status in this world for the narcissistic people who inhabit it. The main concerns are looks, booking reservations, looks, defining clothes by brand, designer, and price, looks and engaging in constant one-up-man-ship. If one interchangeable yuppie has an expensive tanning salon membership, the next must own his own tanning bed; if one can make a reservation at the restaurant of the week, the others are consumed by envy. Bateman is thrown into deep depression and has to choke back tears, for example, when he loses in a "who has the best business card" contest. Ironically, each of them is completely self-absorbed in how they look, although all the male characters, the only characters who count, are always described as having slicked-back hair, suspenders, and horn-rimmed glasses. The narrative is larded with self-referential commentaries, a neat trick since none of these people have selves; reviews of CDs, rendered in minute detail; descriptions of food ordered but rarely eaten and never enjoyed; prices, along with provenances of each item; descriptions of offices, but never actual work; descriptions of shopping, travel, and money, behind which lurks an awful void. No one seems to get any satisfaction from buying an object except for the temporary satiation of the greed complex; no one values an object for the object itself, but only for its status markers, defined as designer/brand names.

Even during the gruesome descriptions of murder, Ellis inserts brand-name details, and I cannot help wondering what, if anything, is served by this juxtaposition. Does the fact that "a bag from Zabar's loaded with onion sourdough bagels sits on the kitchen table while I grind [human] bone and fat and flesh into patties" really have any importance?[57] Since Bateman is very clear on his feelings for the rest of humanity, to whit, they are prey, why would bagels from Zabar's matter? Perhaps they are the best possible type of bread on which to put the patties of human flesh? No positive values exist in this somewhat grubby, extremely commodified sub-society. Any attempt to consider a human being in terms of an inner life or as possessing real emotions is utterly taboo. The sections of the novel which are not saturated with the ravings and blatherings of a saturated consumer society are concerned with increasingly demented and graphically gruesome accounts of sexual perversion, torture, murder, cannibalism, and other aspects of Bateman's meaningless life.

Patrick Bateman is the only character about whose internal workings we know anything. And what we know is not precisely comforting. He is, by his own admission, "a fucking evil psychopath." In general, such a statement acknowledges monstrosity, but is not generally made by the psychopath himself as psychopaths are notorious for their inability to recognize their pathology. But Bateman is certainly correct. At various points in the book he is sad (often over something totally inappropriate), envious, anxious, annoyed, spiteful, and malicious; in general Bateman's feelings, like the society of which he is a part, are those of extreme alienation. Late in the novel, as he becomes increasingly more psychotic, Bateman, contemplating the impossibility of a relationship with Jean, his secretary, thinks,

"And though the coldness I have always felt leaves me, the numbness doesn't and probably never will. . . . The question *Why not end up with her?* floats into my line of vision. An answer: she has a better body than most other girls I know. Another one: everyone is interchangeable anyway. One more: it doesn't really matter."[58]

Bateman repeatedly makes the point that people are nothing more than interchangeable parts; even his fellow yuppies cannot keep their identities straight. Bateman, for example, is admiringly described as "*total GQ*" and routinely mistaken for a model.[59] He is also, ironically, mistaken for a number of other people, notably Marcus Halberstam, which "is a logical *faux pas* since Marcus works at P & P also, in fact does the same exact thing I do, and he also has a penchant for Valentino suits and clear prescription glasses and we share the same barber at the same place, the Pierre Hotel, so it seems understandable, it doesn't irk me."[60] Later, he will kill Paul Owen, perhaps for having the Fisher account, perhaps for mistaking Bateman for Halberstam, perhaps for any emotion Bateman can generate by killing.

Almost everything Bateman and his coterie does is emotionless and meaningless; even when Bateman is involved in killing someone, the absence of connection is very evident. Previous monsters have at least made something that can be labeled an attempt at some type of communion, however perverted, but Francis Dolarhyde, George Denkin, or even Hannibal Lecter are paradigms of positive communion compared to Bateman. To employ the metaphor used by both Stephen King and Caleb Carr, it is less important to "understand the tiger" once it is safely caged; it is only when the tiger is hunting that an understanding of its nature is important. Even Hannibal Lecter, the creature closest to Bateman in conception (and to whom Ellis owes a great if unacknowleged debt), shows an ability, however marginal, to bond with another human being. Bateman is more terrifying because he lacks the ability to achieve communion, however negative, is aware of this lack, and chooses to be as he is. A monster like Carrie, or Highland, or Dolarhyde, a monster who can be safely categorized and explained, is less frightening than a monster like Lecter or Bateman. Explanations of child abuse or rejection or even social pariahdom attribute the monstrous to external and easily recognizable factors. If the physical appearance of the human monster plays into the definition of monster, this is another easily identified monster sign. But Bateman has no physical deformity, no history of abuse, no status as pariah to account for the monster. Monsters simply are: Bateman simply is. And the idea that the monster could be someone who would never be suspected, would never give himself away or be taken seriously if he claimed monsterdom is as dis/ease-provoking as anything in horror fiction.

Unlike Holland Perry, Bateman does not seem to get very much satisfaction out of his monstrous acts; while Holland takes great pleasure in his actions, Bateman seems to act either from boredom or pique. Holland anticipates the effect of the many cruel acts he commits with great eagerness; whether poisoning a rat, or simply running pedestrians down, Holland's enjoyment is boundless. But Bateman simply performs his atrocious acts. He evidently does not eagerly anticipate the action in advance, as do the other serial killers we have examined, nor does he think about his victims afterwards. Once done and disposed of, they seem to disappear from his consciousness. Although he does keep videotapes in order to terrify future victims, he does not obsess over his victims. The voice describing these acts is detached and matter-of-fact, the voice perhaps of a medical examiner dictating an autopsy report, or a jaded homicide detective describing a murder scene. In the following scene, Bateman is killing a former girlfriend stupid enough to have accompanied him to his apartment.[61] Once there the negative emotion of jealousy surfaces. Over lunch he has discovered that she is seeing the chef at Dorsia, a restaurant at which Bateman has not been able to make a reservation. While this motive may seem ludicrous to the normal human being, Bateman is a creature filled with negative emotions, and her relationship with Robert Hall incites him to jealousy. The emotion involved here is one of a lack, as Bethany has something that he does not, and this type of emotion is the only type Bateman seems capable of feeling. Bateman offers this account of what he does after he clubs her unconscious:

I drag her back into the living room, laying her across the floor over a white Voilacutro cotton sheet, and then I stretch her arms out . . . nail three fingers on each hand, at random, to the wood, by their tips. This causes her to regain consciousness and she starts screaming. After I've sprayed Mace into her eyes, mouth, into her nostrils, I place a camel hair coat from Ralph Lauren over her face, which drowns out the screams, sort of. . . . During this period, I keep shouting "You bitch" at her and then my voice drops to a raspy whisper and into her ear I drool the line, "You fucking cunt. . . . Scream, honey," I urge, "keep screaming. . . . No one cares. No one will help you."[62]

Bateman is correct; no one will notice, no one will care. People disappear all the time. Bateman manages to kill an astounding number of people, even the occasional yuppie, without anyone except a cab-driver noticing the absence of a fellow cab-driver. Bateman kills hookers, bartenders, women he has picked up, fellow yuppies, ex-girlfriends, and children and is never called to account. His crimes become ever more gruesome and obvious but go unnoticed. And this is also at the root of the extreme discomfort caused by this text: none of these people matter;

they are meat for the machine, and their absence is no more noted than their presence.

As the novel progresses, Bateman's actions become increasingly horrific and excessively grotesque as he attempts to fill the void within him, and since he lives in a subculture dedicated to excess, only the most extreme experiences can stimulate his jaded senses. In one particularly revolting scene, he is torturing a nameless girl.

The hands are shot full of nails and her legs are spread as wide as possible. A pillow props her ass up and cheese, Brie, has been smeared across her open cunt and some of it even pushed up into the vaginal cavity. She's barely regained consciousness and when she sees me, standing over her, naked, I can imagine that my virtual absence of humanity fills her with mind-bending horror.[63]

Later, Bateman will introduce a half-starved rat into the woman's vagina, and when he does, he thinks, "I can already tell it is going to be another characteristically useless, senseless death, but then I'm used to the horror. It seems distilled, even now it fails to upset or bother me."[64] The effect it has on the reader is quite different. Nausea, outrage, and bewilderment jockey for position here, unless, of course, one reads the text as parodic, in which case I suppose an argument could conceivably be made for black comedy.

In my reading, horror and repulsion, those litmus markers for horror fiction, are certainly present throughout this text and make the point that disaffirmative horror fiction does not validate social norms. But, what else, if anything, does this text do? One problem in answering this question lies in the answers and explanations we are not given. What remains unanswered is why Bateman is completely unable to feel anything resembling positive human emotion; why he is a void, a complete absence; why the only emotions he ever shows are those that involve either covetousness or vindictive satisfaction; and why torturing and murdering fellow human being are the only vehicles to this satisfaction. His life, he says, "is an isolation ward that serves only to expose my own severely impaired capacity to feel. . . . If I were an automaton, what difference would there really be?"[65] To him, nothing. But to those unfortunate enough to encounter him, quite a bit.

As noted above, several critics have reviewed this novel as "a serious novel that comments on a society that has become inured to suffering" or "a disturbing book . . . written from the deepest purest motives," and Norah Rawlinson comments that "the horror does not lie in the novel itself but in the society it represents."[66] This may be an accurate assessment of the novel's intended effect, but the author does not seem to have any sort of moral stance concerning the protagonist's actions. While one cannot speak with any certainty of an author's intentions, let alone whether that author successfully engaged a myriad of readers in the manner he planned, the distanced and indifferent authorial stance works to further dis/ease the reader, at least this particular reader. Paradoxically, I would argue further that this is exactly what makes this novel the apotheosis of disaffirmation. Not only does the human monster remain unidentified and uncontained, his actions are essentially of no moment in a society reduced to commodities. Of what value is a text which denies the importance or even the necessity of being human? This text is many things: disaffirmative, repelling, revolting, degrading, and as a friend of mine fears, possibly even conducive to catching a social disease, but to label it a serious novel which examines a society inured to suffering implies a certain degree of scrutiny, of assessment, which I find lacking. A novel which says, in effect, that suffering is unimportant and that people are commodities, a novel which refuses any sense of affirmation and seethes with a complacency both smug and hopeless cannot claim the moral ground implicit in writing a didactic novel. What do we learn, if anything from this novel? To avoid yuppies? To bring into play the strategies of exclusion on a group of young urban professionals simply because one of them might be a monster? In its purest form, this type of disaffirmative horror fiction does not function affirmatively or didactically; its only function seems to be to reveal some of the unpleasant aspects of a consumer society without offering any amelioration. And, perversely, this lack of value is precisely where its valuation lies.

The fictions under consideration here, those I have defined as disaffirmative range from texts which, like King's *Carrie*, provide the reader with a specific cause and effect of monster-making to Ellis' *American Psycho*, which is of "the monsters just are" school of thinking. But one thing these texts have in common: from the comparatively predictable *Carrie* to the Grand Guignol of *American Psycho*: they display a world and people whom we would much rather did not reflect in American society. If, as Nora Rawlinson claims, the horror does not lie in the novel, but in the society it reflects, and we are all infected with the monster, then perhaps the frequently expressed feeling that we live in an unsafe society, surrounded by monsters is not fictional. Who would want Patrick Bateman, Niles/Holland Perry, the tot boiler, Carrie, or Grenouille as a neighbor?

The Construction of Social Communities

INTRODUCTION

"It was a Saturday afternoon on Maple Street . . ."[1]

Community, the concept of a group or society which shares a common ideology and values, is both a privileged subject of fiction and an integral part of our everyday lives. Thus community itself is an antinomy, composed as it is of an idealization and a concretization in direct and inseparable conflict. It is, in other words, simultaneously abstract and concrete. While we live in a concrete everyday community, a community composed of mundane interrelationships with a particular group of people, the abstraction is frequently at loggerheads with reality.

Mass media define community within the culture in many different ways, but the more popularly accepted mainstream films and television programs tend to stress the idealized and sanitized versions that are often more comforting than the reality. The positive types of constructs and resolutions reinforce the mythopoeic construct of community in which we believe, however much evidence to the contrary accumulates and however often we are confronted with that contradictory evidence. These television shows and films play out community-based sound-bites for Americans who want to believe the community myth and who desire to confuse the ideal with the real, for who can avoid community? As individuals we live within concentric spirals of community; our nuclear and extended families, our friends and acquaintances, our employment, our neighborhoods, our town or rural areas, cities, counties, states and countries—all are communities: no one can escape a community of some sort or another. We form communities to enable ourselves to live in the world; we also use the very word iconically: We speak of the academic community, the world community, the need for community, the loss of community, the failure of community, the resurgence of community, etc. Newspapers and magazines discuss community and its essential importance whether they are discussing the breakdowns likely when adolescent "superpredators" or sex offenders are released within communities, or communities gather to clean up a neighborhood or feed the hungry.

The July 7, 1997, issue of *Time*, "America: The Inside Story," featured an article entitled "The Backbone of America," which illustrates the cultural model of "small town America." One accepted but mythic cultural model reads as follows:

The deep American nostalgia for rural life may owe more to fantasy than memory, but it is a theme that has grown more powerful as the pace of change picks up. At a time when the search for a Real Life is becoming a marketing tool . . . a lot of towns are . . . deciding it is easier to restore an evocative Main Street than build one from scratch.[2]

Small town America, then, contrary to the hard realities of twentieth century life, is popularly believed to be crime-free, community-minded, not a part of the rat-race, a place where individuals are known and valued within a specific social matrix. No wonder so many sub/urbanites flee the horrors of the brutal, impersonal individual and community destroying cityscape. No wonder so many horror fictions are set in small towns.

"But you know what's going to happen? The small towns are going to become the big cities all over again."[3] The *Time* article explored the recent flight to small towns, for example, in almost exactly the economies of loss which drives the construction of community in horror fiction: the move to the small town destroys the small town ambiance which people seek: reality destroys the ideal.

Certainly the concern over community indicates both its ideological centrality in American life as well as its problematized actuality. When Colin Powell talks about volunteerism he is talking about investing in the community; when a gang leader defends the "boyz in the 'hood," he is also talking about investing in the community. If any term is reverenced, it is community. But community is a positive American value that does not really play out all that positively in American society. Community covers a wide variety of types in American society and not all of them are warm and fuzzy. Militias and skinhead organizations like the Aryan Brotherhood, after all, form communities; Charles Manson, David Koresh, Marshall Herff Applewhite—each had his own little community. Communes and other communal living arrangements are often looked at unfavorably today, reflecting as they do a more radically liberal definition than is presently politically correct. In recent years, the concept of community articulated by conservative ideologues, most infamously Dan Quayle, evoke a 1950's situation comedy mindset set in "Never-never land"; in this evocation, family values are conservatively monolithic, and no gap exists between the abstract and the concrete; gendered roles are easily differentiated; everyone knows his/her place and the general view of life is extremely agreeable and placid. Mothers stay home, fathers are loving disciplinarians, and children have small and occasional problems, with which the fathers promptly deal. Everyone in the neighborhood or small town looks out for the interests of everyone else, all injustice is absent and all problems easily resolvable—all in a single episode. Such evocations of community are extremely comforting models, and the rampant popularity and continuing syndication of such situation comedies indicates a need to believe in the idealistic version of community. And yet the ways we live our lives, and the problems we see and deal with on a daily basis undercut any idea of a monolithic working sense of community, however much such a value is nostalgically idealized.

Much horror fiction, but particularly disaffirmative horror fiction, works with community in terms of dis/ease provoking models. At the very least, even the most affirmative horror fiction questions the agenda-ridden social constructs and unthinking valorization of community; mid-spectrum horror confronts and illuminates the interstices in which the gaps, lacks, and ambiguities of community lurk. In disaffirmative horror fiction, the strategies of exclusion, encompassed by the mechanisms of demarcation, demonization, scapegoating/sin-eating, and sacrifice form communities. The dis/ease which I think so important arises because these mechanisms, however unacknowledged, are also used to form actual real world communities. The texts which I will examine in the next three chapters will be concerned mainly with communities in which the physical place as well as the idealizations are foregrounded, which use these mechanisms and the following patterns of unknowing/unaware outsider as unwilling sacrifice, and aware but demonized insider as unwilling sacrifice to construct a dis/ease-provoking articulation of community. Some of the texts examine corrupted people in corrupted communities, good people corrupted by the mechanisms which construct community, evil "people" forming a strong community, and, most dis/easeful of all, good or innocent people victimized by the mechanisms of an evil community. Whatever horror fiction uses as the vehicle—a lottery, a plague, haunted houses, supernatural monsters, aliens from outer space—horror fiction is concerned with in some way examining the strategies of exclusion.

American history reflects this dichotomous thinking about community: one of the first goals articulated by the Puritans, who formed a marginalized and persecuted community in England, was to found "a city on a hill," the "New Jerusalem." As Edward Ingebretsen notes in *Maps of Heaven, Maps of Hell*,

In the extreme of their narcissism they likened their New England settlement to a city on the hill, a light lit for all the world, rising phoenix-like from the ashes of old theological hopes. It was to be a Promised Land where they could take their rest, as they left the lost (or perhaps abandoned garden?) behind them.[4]

As is typical of the workings of community, however, they were no sooner free of the constraints and persecutions which they endured in England than they immediately implemented the same attitude in their newly articulated community. Within a decade and a half, religious boundaries were demarcated through persecution, specifically the demonization and expulsion of Anne Hutchinson and Roger Williams as well as the persecution of the Quakers, events which reflect community as antinomously composed.

The Salem Witchcraft trials, for example, show the workings of community in early America as well, if not better, than any other single event. Again, as Ingebretsen points out, "As an act of communal finger-pointing, it defined the abstract, ideological boundaries of a community."[5] Mass hysteria, religious mania, and the necessity for communal control resulted in nineteen women hanged and one man pressed to death. In this case, the demarcation and demonization rested on the testimony of three young girls and numerous tests and signs which most people today would view as ludicrous. And so it is, until one remembers that within living memory one Joseph McCarthy flourished a list which purported to be names of "commies" in the State Department; the ensuing witchhunt was based on little more than the testimony of frightened individuals and certain "signs" such as homosexuality, which served the mechanisms of demonization as well as moles and sixth fingers had served the Puritans.

How and why such ambivalencies exist are among the major concerns of horror fiction; as might be expected, community plays out very differently in horror fiction than in other genres. Texts in which a member of the community, evidently a part of and in good standing within the community, is suddenly and incomprehensively re-defined as an outsider or a scapegoat, are more dis/ease provoking yet. If anyone in the community can be suddenly excluded and scapegoated, the level of cultural dis/ease which these texts produce invariably skyrockets. The inexplicable is more provocative of dis/ease than a reason-specific exclusion. A rational assumption can be argued as there is at least a common ground from which to proceed; but an inexplicable and random exclusion, one that taps into an intuitive and irrational matrix, is productive of dis/ease simply because it exists and must therefore be accounted for, but is simultaneously beyond the margins of the explicable. Thus, fictions in which a community does not reflect the valorized ideality of American life, but represents the actualized functioning of community, are extremely likely to produce anxieties and dis/eases both lingering and unresolvable. The more antinomous the text, the greater the resistance to closure and the less likely that the reader will be able to "close a book" in which he/she has had a satisfactorily gruesome but palliated and resolved experience. The question of possible resonances is also a troubling one; when a horror fiction text posits a random, arbitrary, and inexplicable sense of exclusion, the text may be inexplicable on the surface but have subtextual levels in which the inexplicability is less problematized than the complicity. Quite often in addition to the literal exclusion, horror fiction, being by nature allegorical, is tapping some quite clearly defined and very specific exclusion. While the exclusion may be quite specific and historically located as well, thus on one level providing a specific way to read the text, the reason for the exclusion may indeed still be beyond a good and comfortable explanation.

Community in horror fiction is by no means monolithic; sometimes the demarcations and demonizations are entirely or satisfactorily resolved; sometimes the antinomy between insider and outsider, sacrificer and sacrificed, is partially resolved, and in both structures, the reader's experiences are considerably less horrific because the mechanisms of affirmation and denial come into play, permitting both closure and resolution. In what I contend is the least effective type of horror fiction, such as, for example, many of Dean R. Koontz's novels, the resolution occurs through a simple refusal to acknowledge the importance of the community-denying mechanisms; in the more effective fictions, the disruptive mechanisms are actually resolved.

AFFIRMATIVE COMMUNITY:
THE GOLDEN RETRIEVER LIVES!

"Do the dead sing? And do they love the living?"[1]

I noted earlier that the idea of community in horror fiction is by no means monolithic. Sometimes the demarcations and demonizations are entirely resolved, regardless of the apparent demands of the plot, and sometimes the antinomy between insider and outsider, sacrificer and sacrificed, is resolved as affirmatively as possible. In both structures, the reader's responses are less than fully horrific because the mechanisms of affirmation and denial come into play, permitting both closure and resolution. In novels like Dean R. Koontz's *Midnight*, for example, the mechanisms which tear communities apart and reveal the social constructs and agendas at work are neatly, all too neatly, resolved. By contrast, short stories like Charles de Lint's "Waifs and Strays," Carol Orlock's "Nobody Lives There Anymore. Nothing Happens," and Stephen King's "The Reach," achieve affirmation because the mechanisms which could function to dismantle community are both acknowledged and resolved.

One pitfall to the former type of horror fiction is that quite often, however unfortunately, the happy ending is produced *deus ex machina* and does not follow from the logic of the plot sequence. Thus, the resolution is achieved by means of the more pejorative type of melodrama, which achieves a "happy ending" by ignoring the unresolved or problematic incidents in the text. When this ersatz validation is achieved, the more critical reader is frequently left with a bad taste and the image of Little Nell snatched out of the path of the train by the Hero. Writers who routinely spare the heroes and manufacture a happy ending which violates reader expectations attempt to gloss over dis/eases in society. In the sense that such novels cheat the reader of either the necessary *catharsis* or the realistic plot culmination, they function as well as a band-aid over gangrene.

Dean R. Koontz's novels offer excellent examples of the community-at-any-cost plot structure in which reasonable causality and the reader's expectations are derailed by an ending which is absolutely positively one of the community triumphant. Troublesome teenagers, children mute from trauma, women hurt by love, and people lost in an alienated world—all are neatly cured in the final sequence, and all the horror disappears in a highly affirmative ending, typical of much adventure-suspense fiction but generally not found in even the most reassuring horror fiction.

David Punter's disturbance/comfort dialectic, which he discusses in *The Literature of Terror*, and sees as essential to the Gothic, and which I would certainly argue extends to contemporary horror fiction, is softened by Koontz to the point where the ongoing disturbance is easily transmogrified to a comfort zone at novel's end.[2] Much of the action of Koontz's works falls clearly in Punter's disturbance zone, but it invariably deconstructs to a comfort zone in which the reader who has been wriggling uncomfortably on the horror hook is released and restored to a comfortable society. Koontz's novels are notable for introducing strong elements of extreme societal disturbance, which almost invariably deploy conservative *mores* to achieve an affirmative resolution and satisfactory closure. This structure, in turn, encourages the reader to experience various extreme emotions and horrific situations, but also provides the reader with enough clues to fit a reassuring subtext together. The hesitation which both Todorov and Heller see as a structure intrinsic to fantasy fiction is invariably resolved and almost invariably dismissed at novel's end. In adopting this rhetorical strategy, however, Koontz runs the risk of disappointing the more critically oriented reader of horror fiction who may feel that the horror elements fall out of the plot a little too conveniently, or are resolved with too much reliance on the somewhat unsatisfactory and melodramatic plot devices. Koontz manipulates the œsthetic distance postulated by Bullough and Heller in such a way as to initially dis/ease the reader but also, through the recognizable adventure-suspense motifs and plot structures, to gloss over any real dis/ease the reader feels.[3]

In Koontz's *Midnight* (1989), in a convention beloved of horror fiction, a megalomaniacal scientist type has developed a serum which will create a New World Order in which rationality will be valorized and emotion banished. It sounds as though the Enlightenment idea of man's perfectibility is about to be realized. It sounds positively Apollonian. Biogenetic engineering, promulgated and carried out on the community of Moonlight Cove by Thomas Shaddack, whose favorite boyhood reading was *The Island of Dr. Moreau*, is supposed to remove all negative urges from the people of the town.

Midnight Cove is a very tightly knit community, one in which people know each other, care for each other, and watch out for each other—at least, they do so until the new and improved residents of Midnight Cove are released to prey upon them. Unfortunately, the "New People," formed by forced evolution, carry a regressive quality and quite often shapechange to sentient wolf-like beasts who hunt and kill members of their community for the fun of it. Thus, the Apollonian promise is subverted by the worst type of Dionysian excess.

The sheriff, Loman Watkins, who has undergone treatment, but who is increasingly uneasy about the effects, feels his humanity steadily eroding. He is increasingly distanced from the unchanged members of his community and keeps repeating the mantra Shaddack has instilled in him. The dialogue between Watkins and Shaddack is extremely instructive:

"You've got the power in you now to transcend human emotional limitations, and when you *do* transcend them, you'll know true peace and happiness for the first time in your life."

After awhile, Loman Watkins raised his head. . . . "Will this really lead to peace?"

"Yes."

"When there's no one left unconverted, will there be brotherhood at last?"

"Yes."

"Tranquillity?"

"Eternal."[4]

In the name of a brotherhood of peace and tranquillity, surely Apollonian and community-oriented values if ever such values existed, Watkins and his team cover up the murders committed by their fellow "brothers," and forcibly regress the remaining members, rejecting the tenets of community in which people shape a community together. In a rather interesting attack on 1960's liberalism, Watkins, knowing quite well what killed his best friend's young son, blames a liberal society run amok for his disappearance: "The country's rotten with drug freaks these days. . . . No morals, no goals but cheap thrills. They're our inheritance from the recent Age of Do Your Own Thing."[5] But the Age of Do Your Own Thing was considerably less harmful to the individual than Shaddack's forced evolution.

The disappearances mount, and eventually word leaks out beyond the confines of Moonlight Cove. Two outsiders come to Moonlight Cove—Sam Booker, an undercover FBI agent, and Tessa Lockland, a woman who has lost her sister and does not buy the official coverup. They forge an alliance with two insiders, Chrissie Foster, a precocious eleven-year-old girl, the plucky heroine type, who has witnessed her parents regressing and has fled, and Harry Talbot, a disabled Vietnam vet, complete with his Golden Retriever, Moose. These four people (and Moose) combat the increasing menace. Miraculously, or perhaps more accurately, incredibly, they emerge unscathed, although the whole town is after them, and restore order to the disordered society at no cost; in this particular ending even the Golden Retriever, thought to be dead, survives.[6] In *Midnight* the good guys win, without any losses at all, and the ravaged town, a town in which the regressives run rampant, a town in which scores of innocent people have been savagely killed or unwillingly turned, is subjected to a "necessary" coverup. Tessa and Sam unite in marriage. Sam Booker, who has an alienated heavy-metal-listening, drug-taking, Satan-worshiping son, knows, although we don't quite know how, that a hug or two will turn his son around. Even Moose, whom Koontz apparently sacrificed to those dark gods who exact a price for happiness, is spared.

All is sweetness and light and comedy in its traditional form by novel's end. The main characters, we know, will form an extended family, a community, in which no problems of alienation will exist. But this ending leaves out most of the major issues raised by the book: what about all the victims of the change? Is the survival of the fearless foursome (and Moose) really enough to balance the death of nearly a whole community? None of the questions raised are satisfactorily answered. The price of a shattered community is not addressed, nor is the fact that the regressives, innocent or guilty, willing or unwilling, are rapidly disposed of. The strategies of exclusion involved, those melodies of fragmentation and disestablishment, are not dealt with in this novel; they are merely papered over in favor of a somewhat too facile and slick re-evocation of community.

In this type of fiction, which I sardonically but affectionately label "the Golden Retriever survives type," all ends in harmony and bliss; but this is, at best, an ersatz resolution, which denies the power and problems created by science run amok by imposing a comedic ending over the very real evocation of horror. It does indeed gloss over the social unease generated by mad scientists, genetic engineering, and the fear of the monster, all of which are foregrounded and then denied in the ending, but the denial does not work to effectively resolve the dis/eases; it merely ignores them. In a world in which scientists are constantly pushing the envelope of the possible, a world in which a sheep has been cloned (and according to the *National Enquirer* turned cannibal), and genetic engineering is raising as many problems as solutions, *Midnight* should be a very disquieting text.

The affirmative ending exists at the cost of denial, which may be fair enough in a fantastic escapist novel, which, according to Eric

Rabkin, is the function of horror novels.[7] But horror functions in ways other than escapist, and the escape and entertainment occur here at the expense of organic unity and reader credulity. The other problem is David Hartwell's point: the emotional transaction is incomplete, the horrific emotions denied.[8] This novel functions in much the same way as watching a Greek tragedy like *Antigone* and discovering at the end that Haemon arrives in the nick of time, the EMT's have revived Eurydice, and Creon has signed up for an anger management class.

In this chapter, I will also discuss three short stories, Charles de Lint's "Waifs and Strays," Carol Orlock's "Nobody Lives There. Nothing Happens," and Stephen King's, "The Reach," all of which occupy a more affirmative side of the spectrum. Affirmative community is the theme, and these texts seem to me to resolve the problems with community while still leaving a lingering acknowledgment of dis/ease behind. Despite their fantastic qualities, these stories all acknowledge the antinomous qualities of community and all successfully explore the problems of creating and maintaining community in a world which pays lipservice to it but does not wish to take the actions necessary to maintain it.

"Waifs and Strays" (1993) is a ghost story in which Maisie, a teenage homeless person, is visited by her dead friend Shirley. Maisie used to collect junk for a living and squat in a burned out building with Tommy, a retarded waif, and the canine strays she takes in, but she is now attempting to be a "productive citizen." At first, the reader thinks that the waifs and strays of the title refer to these characters, but as the story unfolds, it becomes apparent that this might not be the case. When the first visitation occurs, Maisie is walking at night; as she passes her squat, she says, "I belonged here once. Not anymore, though. I'm not even supposed to be here. . . . I should be Getting Things Done like the good little taxpaying citizen I'm trying to be.[9] She meets up with the ghost of Shirley Jones, her street mentor, who is four years dead. Shirley (a/k/a Granny Buttons), was "the person who first taught me that family didn't have to be an ugly word." She remembers being a twelve-year-old runaway and going on "treasure hunts." "We'd head out with our shopping carts, sensei bag lady and her apprentice on a kind of Grail quest. But what we found was never as important as the zen of our being out there in the first place."[10] Shirley disappears, and it is not the ghost which creates the sense of dis/ease but the fact that it is evident from this conversation that Maisie does not feel as though she has taken a step up.

Maisie has met Angel, a community activist, gotten a job with Quicksilver Messenger Service, and started school to get her G.E.D., but she finds something lacking. This so-called productive life is very dissatisfying. What she lacks is the time she used to spend with her family: between the job, her education, and commuting, she has no time for her waifs and strays. Each day, as she goes out to spend the day as a productive, non-homeless, non-parasitical, community-approved type person, she realizes that her family is unhappy and growing unhappier: "I was so proud of myself for doing the right thing. . . . I rejoined society—not that society seemed to care that much, but I wasn't doing it for them anyway. I was doing it for Tommy and the dogs. . . . But I just didn't see it as better than what we'd had before." She is exhausted from the never-ending round of work and classes: "Always tired, impatient, unhappy."[11]

The ghost of Shirley appears again, not for murder or vengeance or even to point out hidden material treasure as most ghosts in horror fiction do: Shirley asks her, "What is more important? To be happy or to bring happiness to others?" Maisie replies, "I kind of like to think they go hand in hand. . . . That you can't have one without the other." Just before Shirley disappears for the second time, she asks, "Then what have you forgotten?"[12]

At their third and final meeting, Shirley tells her that being dead is being stuck somewhere unable to finish a journey, like the bus she never took back home, like the story of her life. The next day, Aunt Hilary, Maisie's landlady, tells her that her friend stopped by, hugged Tommy, "and patted each of the dogs with utter concentration as though she wanted to remember them, and then she left."[13] Maisie finally consults Bones, a Kikaha shaman, who tells her that "Ghosts have their own agendas. Maybe you both have something to give to each other."[14] When she gets home, she again realizes that everyone is unhappy, but still cannot think what to do about it. Instead of going to school, she goes to the bus station and buys a ticket for Rockcastle for Shirley, so that she can get home to the people she loved and lost.

The story concludes with a double affirmation—Maisie not only leaves a bus ticket, paid for out of her conventional day job so that the ghost can complete the journey, but she also confronts Angel, her social worker, and explains her problem:

"I've got the straight job, the straight residence . . . The things that are important—Tommy and the dogs—it's like they're not even a part of my life any more . . . I'm providing for my family . . . that should be enough, right? But it doesn't feel that way. It feels like the most important things are missing. I remember something Shirley's ghost asked me, and add, 'Maybe it's selfish but I figure charity should start at home, you know? I can't do much for other people if I'm feeling miserable myself.'"[15]

The bus ticket is gone when next she checks, and she chooses to think that Shirley came and got it and completed her journey even though she acknowledges that some homeless person may have copped it and cashed it in. The ability to acknowledge the possibility that Shirley did not appear and finish her journey is where this text differs from the glossier affirmative type.

This is a story in which the forces of affirmation do triumph, but the triumph, for more conventional society, is a somewhat Pyrrhic victory. In a situation which rings dismally true in the contemporary society, Maisie finds that pursuing her job and her education leave her with no time: no time to spend time with Tommy, the retarded man who depends on her; no time to lavish on the canine strays who have been abandoned once already; no time for anything, in fact, but "bettering" herself. As she says, "Margaret. She's the one who goes to school and works at QMS and deserts her family five days and four nights a week. She's the traitor."[16] In a very satisfying ending, Maisie decides to cut back on her working hours, continue to collect junk, which is a family expedition, and cut back on her education. She buys time, in other words.

Where, one might ask, does cultural dread or dis/ease exist in a tale which so firmly espouses such cultural values as putting one's family first? What produces the dis/ease, even the almost completely resolved dis/ease, which I contend is so important? The cultural dis/ease is generated by the realization that, in some ways, the success for which we strive is not essentially satisfying. Here is a homeless poster child: she has been rescued, uplifted, and made a productive member of society. She is in fact both a conservative and liberal icon of the paths out of homelessness. Homelessness no longer demarcates, demonizes and marginalizes her. The system works! But as Angel points out, "Things just seem to get complicated when you're around."[17] They do indeed: complicated for Maisie, for Angel, and for the reader. The dis/ease lies in the fact that resonates with so many of us: we buy our success at the price of our own personal "waifs and strays," those who in the final analysis, really matter. We buy our success, in education and in employment, by absence. We are absent from our loved ones, and the antinomy, the inseparable contradiction, arises because we are doing this to make life better for those for whom we lack time. The dis/ease arises because we will not, like Maisie, decide that time is more important; in a society as materialist and consumerist as American society has become, we will not, cannot, accept subsistence in order to have time.

"Waifs and Strays" is one of the few horror fictions I have encountered which manages the very difficult task of being genuinely affirmative; the problems are not glossed over, the losses are not ignored. The ghost, rather than being threatening, is one who warns Maisie and reminds her that family is the important value, not the nine-to-five "white bread" society of which she is striving so hard to become a part. And Maisie heeds the message. The demands of the family and societal expectations are neatly balanced in this text; her compromise provides the way out of her trap and permits the reader to feel that societal expectations and family values are not necessarily in irremediable conflict. Maisie's community supports her, but she can also accept what many of us cannot accept; thus there is still that slight and lingering dis/ease present. How many Americans would accept a subsistence existence, devoid of glittery "things," in order to spend time with their families? And yet how many people would be comfortable admitting that the materialist consumerist culture in which we live takes precedence over human beings?

In my second example, Carol Orlock's short story "Nobody Lives There. Nothing Happens" (1988), community is also affirmed despite various losses, in a way which is positive and which recognizes the integral importance of community without ignoring or glossing over the problems. The problems revolve around the propensity of insiders to shift community problems to outsiders in order to preserve the accepted community model. Were the "blame the outsiders" trope to stand unchallenged, this would be, at best, a mid-spectrum text, a text in which community is compromised, but this assumption does not stand unchallenged. One thoughtful voice acknowledges that it was not the outsiders who were to blame but the insiders themselves, and this does much to mitigate the dis/ease.

The setting is a quaint little town on the Washington state coast; in some ways it is a town which depends on tourists, but in other ways it is a town which has turned its back on twentieth-century values and opted for Victoriana. What started out as a tourist attraction has become more or less of a way of life. But it is clearly a closely-knit town, with people whose values resonate clearly and comfortably. People in this community are honest, caring, hard working, and supportive of each other. Perhaps the quality that comes through most clearly is a tolerant kindness.

A new couple, the Marquettes, who may or may not be ghosts, move into the old mansion which has stood unoccupied for a century. A robber baron built it for his Eastern bride, who took one look at the fuschia-colored High Victorian monstrosity (complete with five widow walks), went for a walk, and never returned. The text hints that the ghostly couple is the Robber Baron and Bride. The furniture the neighbors observe, for this is a small town, with a small town's avid curiosity, is a strange mix of Victorian antiques and modern furniture. No one ever sees the couple, invitations are politely declined, the occasional light flickers, but small gifts appear at odd intervals—never anything much, just a jar of honey lying in the grass, a rose-colored scarf lying on the lawn, an apron caught on a bush, and a child's scooter lying in the front yard of the Jeffersons, a poor but proud family. This "ghostly" couple brings the community even closer in kindness. The narrator, Virginia, who is telling a story that is a patchwork of surmise and observation, believes what she is saying, but admits it is speculation. She is certain about the aura of kindness which hung around the town, however, for she witnessed it.

As time passes and no one sees the couple, pranks and tricks, "clever and unpredict able and as cold as the frost," occur. All the residents who benefitted from the kindnesses are victims of the crueler pranks, pranks which strike at what each resident either loathes or loves as well as striking at a sense of community. For Virginia it is finding "three dead snakes tangled in a knot on my screen door," for Emma Gilchrist it is discovering that someone "strangled all twelve kittens recently born to one of the variegated cats."[18] Like the kindnesses, responsibility for the nasty pranks is assigned to the "ghostly" neighbors:

"Certain people," said the Courier's editorial page, "might like acting invisible and pulling mean pranks on their neighbors. They had better understand that this town knows the effect of kerosene and matches on blackberry bushes and dry old Victorian houses."[19]

Thus the language of exclusion comes into play, as "certain people" and "they" obviously refer to the Marquettes, the outsiders.

A week later the couple moves, and the town returns to its pre-ghostly visitation status. Writing years after the event, the narrator admits that she knows it was not the outsiders who were driven away by threats of arson, but residents of the town who perpetrated the mean tricks which were so disturbing. Very ironically, the children of the Jeffersons, the "poor but proud family," whose parents refuse any help, are the perpetrators of the nasty pranks. But the town, which Virginia believes knows the truth about the pranks, closes ranks and brings the strategies of exclusion into play. The outsiders are demonized and scapegoated—"It was the Marquettes' own fault if people disliked them." What finally makes the story affirmative, however, is the acknowledgement by one of the townspeople that it was not the Marquettes, but one of their own. "I knew in my heart all along, but my heart's thoughts seemed far away by then. . . . I knew with certainty and my heart leapt to my throat instantly, an hour after the moving van drove away.[20] The affirmation in this story comes not from demonization and demarcation, the unjustified driving out of the ghostly outsiders, but from the bittersweet acceptance of the knowledge that the insiders and not the outsiders were responsible. "One minority of one," the narrator musing on the knowledge she has gained, assigning responsibility to the insiders and speculating that everyone else also knows who is responsible for the pranks, does a great deal to create a strong sense of affirmation while acknowledging the dis/easeful fact that she was a part of the town and complicit in driving out the Marquettes. The lingering dis/ease is greatly dissipated by her acknowledgment that the heart knows the truth; thus the mechanism of denial is disabled and the resolution, though perhaps as bittersweet as the narrator's meditations, is fully achieved. But the bittersweet dregs remain. Having been driven out, the Marquettes do not return. The Jefferson boys, having been exempted, remain and behave increasingly badly.

My final example, Stephen King's "The Reach" (1985), can, perhaps, only be classified as a horror text by its slight supernatural motif and as such is an odd choice, except for its perfect evocation of effective affirmation. Like "Waifs and Strays," ghosts are an integral part of the narrative, and they are not malevolent ghosts. By virtue of its plot, in which an old woman, Stella Flanders, faces a cruel death by cancer and often sees her dead husband and her long lost friends, it has at least the supernatural element, which is one of the litmus tests which help define horror fiction. At story's end, Stella, who has lived on Goat Island her whole life without setting foot on the mainland, sets out to walk to the Maine-land in what turns out to be the worst blizzard of the year and is found frozen to death.

The short story deals with a very isolated and self-demarcated community, one which takes care of its own, and one which prefers to keep itself to itself. Stella Flanders' reminiscences of her life make this perfectly clear; the inhabitants of Goat Island have their own community in which charity, justice, and a helping hand are impartially administered by the inhabitants of Goat Island to the inhabitants of Goat Island for the inhabitants of Goat Island. This is a self-contained society, one which does not look to others to solve problems, and one which does not need the Maine-land. Perhaps when Stella starts seeing her old friends and her dead husband, horror ought to intrude, but it does not do so; the haunting question, *do you love*, "had begun to plague her, and she did not even know what it meant."[21] Eventually the body of water named "The Reach," freezes, and Stella sees her husband, dead for twelve years, "seeming to tell her by gesture that the time was late if she ever intended to step a foot on the mainland in this life," and she replies, "If it's what you want, Bill, God knows I don't."[22] She does go out and meet her husband and all the other dead and finds out that dying isn't too bad, not when one goes from a community in which one is loved to a community in which one is loved. Death is not the great separator, anymore than the Reach is an impassable physical barrier:

> They stood in a circle in the storm and sang, the dead of Goat Island and the wind screamed around them, driving its packet of snow and some kind of song burst from her. . . . They sang and Stella felt herself going to them and with them, finally across the Reach.

When her frozen corpse is found, on the mainland, her son says nothing about what he found:

> *Was Alden* [her son] *to tell David and Lois* [his sister and brother-in-law] *that the cap on her head had not been his?. . . He had not lived long enough to forget his dead father's cap. . . . They are questions of the Reach maybe: do the dead sing? And do they love the living?*[23]

Since the answer is obvious, to Alden and even more so to the reader, and since this text denies any difference between the living and the dead, both affirmation and resolution are encouraged in the reader's mind. The fear of death, a theme central to the effect of horror fiction, is almost entirely mitigated by the knowledge that the Reach can be spanned, that there is no painful non-transitory gap between the living and the dead. Like Stella, the reader does not fear the dead of Goat Island; they are not restless, hungry, malevolent ghosts, but the people one has known and loved.

Nevertheless, there is one passage which does prevent "The Reach" from being sentimental and too slickly affirmative: *Do the dead sing? Do they love? On those long nights alone, his mother Stella Flanders at long last in her grave, it often seemed to Alden that they did both.*[23] Thus, while the affirmation of community triumphant in the face of death is important, dissolving as it does the demarcation between the living and the dead as well as denying the demonization of the often feared dead, there is still that niggling phrase, "*at long last in her grave*" to contend with, the reminder that even in the best of communities, a slight degree of demonization and demarcation exists. Is Stella at long last in her grave, free from all suffering and united with her husband, or is Alden, her rather slow and stolid son who often gets the sharp side of her tongue, now free? Is he happy that his mother, who has suffered silently from cancer, is now dead and at peace? Probably. Is he also secretly and silently glad to be free of her strictures, free to live his life as he pleases? Probably. The text does not say and the reader can only surmise. The "at long last" is a slight but powerful reminder that the strategies of exclusion are almost always present. This slight gap, this slight ambiguity of effect, saves the text from a too easily affirmed sense of community.

Even in these basically affirmative fictions, a lingering sense of dis/ease exists. Readers may purposely ignore the resonance of dis/ease, may, as in my earlier metaphor, concentrate on the frosting and ignore the ghoul cake, or in Heller's terms construct an ending that is satisfactorily happy, but these strategies ignore the basic function and structure of horror fiction.

In this chapter, I have discussed those texts which deny any problems and paper over, with melodramatic conventions, the real issues involved in community, and contended that those texts quite simply do not function as horror. According to Koontz, all is well with the citizens of Midnight Cove at tale's end. The Golden Retriever lives! But to accept this ending is to ignore the truly horrific and unresolved plot actions. To accept this ending discounts all the human suffering and unresolved issues which Koontz has deliberately emphasized throughout the novel. The reader's comfort zone is secured at the expense of many important issues, which Koontz also emphasizes throughout the novel and then discards.

The texts which call affirmation into question but resolve it while acknowledging the difficulty of maintaining community fall into the left hand spectrum of community, that which leaves a slight lingering dis/ease in the reader's mind. This lingering dis/ease is not enough to deny community or to be too unaware of the fragile nature of community, but it is enough to avoid "the golden retriever lives" syndrome. While most of the horror is mitigated and resolved, the awareness of dis/ease lingers, even if it is only a slightly uncomfortable feeling that we ought to make Maisie's choice (but won't), or feel that the unnamed narrator has hit the mark on who the villains of the piece are, or even acknowledge, uneasily, that Alden might be secretly happy that his overbearing mother is dead. And this dis/ease, which will be more and more foregrounded as we venture deeper and deeper in to horror territory, is the *sine qua non* of horror fiction. Why else would we read a fiction which promises to say not that everything is all right, but that everything is not all right?

COMPROMISED AFFIRMATIONS:
INHABITING THE CORRUPTED COMMUNITY

"All the World Is a Vampire."[1]

Texts which occupy the mid-spectrum of our theoretical continuum are those in which the awareness of the fragility of the construct of community actively resists easily attained resolution or affirmation. Unlike previously discussed texts, in which affirmation is nearly complete, or those to be discussed later, in which affirmation, resolution, and closure are impossible, these are texts in which the reader is uneasily aware that such concepts as community are social constructs which have no independent existence and are vulnerable to various transmogrifications. The communities I will discuss are quite diverse: apparently "good" communities which fall victim to a force which reveals how very problematic the very idea of community is; and evil communities, such as werewolf and vampire communities, which maintain strong and in many ways admirable models of community. In the texts I will treat here, the ruling structure is the inability of communities to maintain cohesive bonds without some sort of exclusionary ritual. And if good communities fail and evil communities flourish, what then happens to the much vaunted model of community?

Such novels as Peter Straub's *Ghost Story*, Stephen King's *It*, and *Needful Things*, and Bentley Little's *University* suggest the problems inherent in maintaining even affirmative communities. Such communities fall prey, with almost ludicrous ease, to outside forces which effortlessly subvert the inhabitants. Gary Brandner's *The Howling* and Poppy Z. Brite's *Lost Souls* are novels which completely invert the affirmative idea of community, but nevertheless illustrate strong communities. Whatever these differences, all these texts amply reflect the previously discussed strategies of exclusion. In these works, unlike the more affirmative texts discussed in Chapter 6, the affirmation and resolution are significantly darker and more qualified, and the reader is more aware of the fragility of the construct we call community.

Peter Straub's *Ghost Story* (1979), a major novel in the late 1970's horror renaissance, concerns a town which falls victim to manitous and barely manages to survive the experience. One of the elements which concerns Straub is how a community can meet, or fail to meet, challenges to its sense of itself as a positive entity. *Ghost Story* has two very important communities: the town of Milburn with all the people who would not live anywhere else, and the community-within-the-community, the Chowder Society, a very exclusive group of five elderly gentlemen who meet monthly to tell a story. These men are envied in the community for their material solidity, their communal solidarity, and their rather elitist standards. The Chowder Society is what Milburn would like to see itself as—elegant, cultivated, and exclusive rather than the somewhat provincial small town it actually is.

Stephen King sees the novel as developing a conflict between the Apollonian and Dionysian and also argues that the novel's

moral stance, like that of most horror fiction is firmly reactionary. Its politics are the politics of the four old men who make up the Chowder Society—Sears James and John Jaffrey are staunch Republicans, Lewis Benedikt owns what amounts to a medieval fiefdom in the woods, and while we are told that Ricky Hawthorne was at one time a socialist, he may be the only socialist in history who is so entranced by new ties that he feels an urge, we are told, to wear them in bed. . . . All of these men are perceived by Straub as beings of courage and love and generosity, and as Straub himself has pointed out . . . none of these qualities run counter to the idea of reactionism; in fact, they may well define it.[2]

These definitions, however, set up artificial lines and qualities. Is Lewis Benedikt not, in his sexual politics at least, rather liberal instead of reactionary? Certainly he has no respect whatsoever for conventional and conservative views on marriage. Benedikt's preferred choice in relationships is "pseudo-marriages" in which he and various town wives have intense affairs which, while they are more than purely sexual liaisons, are clearly outside reactionary *mores*. Sears James, when he was younger, conservative Republican or not, attempted to better the lives of people in a lower socio-economic class than the one to which he was born; like the young liberals who joined Vista, for example, he tried to teach school and improve the lives of the more victimized students. The fact that he was unsuccessful and settled into a stodgy law practice in a conservative law firm does not entirely obviate his earlier liberalism. John Jaffrey, respected physician and demon drug addict, scarcely fits a conservative model. Ricky Hawthorne, as King correctly points out, is a Socialist, a position not usually associated with conservative values. Ricky accepts the fact that his wife Stella is flagrantly unfaithful to him, yet another indicator of a less than reactionary set of values. The knee-jerk linkage of conservative-reactionary politics with courage, generosity, and love simply does not work, implying as such a statement does that only conservative-reactionary politics attracts these qualities. As George Lakoff points out in *Moral Politics: What Conservatives Know That Liberals Don't*, liberals have allowed conservatives to co-opt such ideologies and values as "family values," and the end result has been to define family values solely in conservative terms, putting liberals both behind the eight-ball and in the constant position of seeming to possess neither morals nor common decency. As Lakoff notes, "Because conservatives understand the moral dimensions of our politics better than liberals do, they have been able not only to gain political victories but to use politics in the service of a much larger moral and cultural agenda for America."[3] Newt Gingrich's infamous "Contract on America," for example, pandered shamelessly to a rigid, moralistic and inhuman set of ideas concerning social welfare; nevertheless, it was extremely popular among conservatives, an example of the co-option of which Lakoff speaks.

Since conservative ideology is readily linked with both community and accepted cultural values, King and many other horror critics tend to see horror fiction as largely conservative. I contend that horror fiction actually attacks the conservative mind set, particularly in the arena of "family values" and Lakoff's "Strict Father" conceptual metaphor.[4] Even were the idea that courage, generosity and love are conservative values allowed to stand unchallenged, the dis/ease-provoking element would still be present. In *Ghost Story*, being a conservative parent gains one nothing. Following conservative rules does not guarantee survival, either. In fact, following conservative values like obedience to a parent can result in a child's untimely death. Rather than upholding conservative values, a close reading of Straub's *Ghost Story* reveals the essential hollowness of the ideology which King sees as conservative-reactionary and positive. The manitous can be controlled neither by a conservative or a liberal ideology, anymore than a human being concerns him or herself with the politics of the slaughterhouse. The character most emblematic of conservatism, Sears James, dies. He does not, it is true, "die passively at their hands," but the reluctance to go passively to death, like a steer in the slaughterhouse, is a human trait, not a political one. It is ineffective, as well, since go to his death he does.[5] Stella Hawthorne, Ricky's rather liberal, feminist, and unfaithful wife, survives quite nicely. Since she does not allow the conservative patriarchy to dictate her actions, she does not hesitate to use a hatpin to stab one of the manitous to death. The manitou is masquerading not only as a religious man, but also as "a prim little man who would tell hitchhikers it was against his principles to pick them up."[6] The manitou thinks of her as a woman, stupid and easily controlled—at least until she stabs him to death. Since conservative values tend to reflect such time-honored qualities as sexual conservatism, "family values," and patriarchal power, a novel in which these values are ineffective and qualities which run counter to the conservative are effective necessarily generates a dis/easeful sense of slippage.

The Chowder Society is bound together by more than mutual politics, wealth, and standards. Ricky Hawthorne, Sears James, Edward Wanderley, Lewis Benedict, and John Jeffrey share a secret history which both demarcates and, to a degree, demonizes them. As the tale unfolds, it also becomes evident that all of them have experience with the supernatural, although only Lewis and Sears are aware of it. In 1929, the members of the as-yet-unnamed Chowder Society met and were dazzled by a woman named Eva Galli; they accidentally killed her and, fearful of the consequences, secretly and illegally disposed of her corpse. All five have since kept the entirely undiscussed secret. Thus they are bound by, if not a homicide, certainly an unreported death. Their social standing is thus based on a secret action which runs counter to their status and expressed philosophies.

However, Eva Galli was a manitou or shapechanger and hence was not killed at all. She returns, under various guises, and wreaks vengeance on the Chowder Society. After the first victim, Edward Wanderley, is killed, the four surviving members decide to invite Don Wanderley, Edward's nephew and author of *The Nightstalker*, a horror fiction piece that in the life/art nexus echoes their experience, to try to discover what is going on. Don has fictionalized his experience and used the novel to write himself sane, but his actual experience very closely reflects the Chowder Society's experiences in which a woman with no traceable history appears, wreaks havoc, murders, and disappears. For the first time they discuss Eva Galli and formulate a plan. Simultaneously, Milburn is inundated by an unremitting series of winter storms, inexplicable animal mutilations and deaths occur, and people see strange beings which often drive them mad. Casualties mount as the shapechangers kill the citizens of Milburn or drive them to kill their loved ones or themselves. Anna Mostyn, the latest guise of the shapechanger who has appeared previously as Eva Galli, Ann-Veronica Moore, and Alma Mobley, is stalking not only the enclave of privilege represented by the Chowder Society, but all of Milburn. She is accompanied by two other shapechangers, Gregory and Fenny Bates, both of whom Sears James has already encountered during his stint as a rural school teacher. They turn Milburn from a pleasant town to a killing ground because they consider human beings of no more worth or interest than cattle or cheap entertainment. Says the voice of "Alma Mobley," caught on tape,

"I have lived since the times when your continent was lighted only by small fires in the forest . . . and even then our kinds abhorred each other. Your kind is so bland and smug and confident on the surface: and so neurotic and fearful and campfire-hugging within. We could have poisoned your civilizations long ago, but voluntarily lived on its edges, causing eruptions and feuds and local panics."

The knowledge that the monsters inhabit the fringe, in effect self-demarcating themselves but also revealing the dis/easeful truth about our childish and imagination driven fears, is not affirmative, but may nevertheless be true. The knowledge that, according to the manitou, "We chose to live in your dream and imaginations because only there are you interesting" denigrates the human experience, and also poisons the well of wonder.[7]

By the time the Chowder Society manages to dispose of the latest manifestations, only Ricky Hawthorne and Don Wanderley are still alive; in a very frequent horror motif, they leave Milburn, which is barely surviving as a community. Thus the Chowder Society's long ago "sin" has reached into the present to destroy the community. So many people have died during the winter of the manitous that Milburn, rather than being a pleasant place to live, is fast becoming a ghost town. Ricky and Stella decide to travel extensively in Europe, and Don Wanderley kidnaps a small girl, with the dis/ease provoking name of Angie Maule, who does not seem to have a history or a family. Like Don Wanderley, the reader does not actually know whether he has kidnapped and intends to dispose of a manitou or a human child; this ambiguity is dis/ease provoking because while the other children do not like Angie and refuse to play with her, and while Don feels her essential inhumanity, to all intents and purposes she behaves like a typical seven-year-old girl. If Don disposes of her and is wrong, he will have committed murder, however justifiably he thinks he is acting. In fact, the narrative opens with Don and Angie fleeing Milburn after everything is over. As it turns out, the issue is settled when Angie metamorphoses to other characters. Don kills the shapechanger and everything is restored to normalcy, except of course for the fear that shape-changers do live among us, defining us as the herd and preying upon us for both emotional and physical satisfaction. Community is no protection in this case as the manitous can easily stalk individuals within the community and kill them with impunity because the community is slow to realize that its nightmares have become real.

The Chowder Society, that elegant evocation of a previous time, is disbanded. Milburn slowly comes back at least partially to normal small-town life, but putting flowers on the graves of the manitous' victims is a time-consuming affair, and all who were part of the Great Manitou Hunt are indelibly marked. The destruction of the Chowder Society and the death of most of the original members are necessary precursors to the survival of Milburn, so the victory is compromised at best and the resolution fragile. Who is to say, after all, that another shapechanger will not materialize some where?

Perhaps the most dis/ease provoking element in this particular novel is the fear that outside forces are indeed controlling us. This fear of external control is the root fear of aliens-are-coming texts, but in this case, since the shapechanger looks like us, acts like us, and is gladly accepted as one of us, it is a bit difficult to mark and guard against the essential inhumanity of a shapechanger. Not only is this problematic, but the shapechangers, having infected one's neighbors and family, can use those animated corpses to make even more of Milburn's human residents their victims. Peter Barnes and his mother encounter the shapechangers and Peter gets away. When his mother Christina runs up to him later, he is at first vastly relieved that she also managed to escape; but she has not escaped, and this realization is shattering to her son. His joyful reaction, "You got away," turns to grief as he realizes that his mother is no longer human and is in league with the manitous. "Oh, Mom," he said. "You didn't get away from them."[8] His mother denies it but wants him to get into a car Peter knows is full of manitous. Not only must Peter deal with death, but simultaneously with one of the worst betrayals possible. One never knows who is really who in Milburn. The inhabitants may be friends, family, and parents, or they may be soulless shapechangers. Thus, while *Ghost Story* is dealing with a model in which most positive values are indeed affirmed, the losses necessary to sustain the community of Milburn and defeat the shapechangers make this a less affirmative novel than the examples discussed in the previous chapter. While Milburn is still a somewhat viable community, it is unlikely that Don Wanderley will return to Milburn or that Ricky or Peter Barnes, Christina's son and Ricky's protégé, will continue to live in Milburn. Certainly the sense of Milburn as an exclusive and perfect community has been hopelessly shattered.

In Stephen King's *It* (1986), a novel which deploys a group of children against a monster ("It") and a complicit, corrupted community of uncaring adults, the price of victory is substantially higher and the resolution considerably more compromised than in previous texts. The children who confront the monster are outcasts, outsiders to Derry, Maine. Stan is a Jew, Richie a loudmouthed, smart-alecky "four eyes," Bill a stutterer, Bev from the wrong side of the tracks, Ben obese to the point of revulsion, Eddie a "sickly" mama's boy, and Mike the only black child in Derry. They are not really of Derry, and they form the Losers Club out of simple self-defense. Since the usual gang of bullies preys on them, and there is also a horrible child-killer loose in Derry, such banding together makes sense but does not change their status as outcasts. *It* shifts back and forth between the original conflict between the monster "It" and the children and a recurrence twenty-seven years later in Derry in which the adults, who have completely forgotten their childhood experiences and sense of community, must once again forge a magic circle and at least try to defeat the monster.

But what is possible as children is less possible as adults. Belief in the magic of friendship and the invincible strength of community has been eroded by maturation. Belief in fantasy has also nearly disappeared as their imaginations have shriveled and reality has impinged on their lives. In King's dark city, it is the children's imaginations which make them both most monster-resistant and the easiest of casualties. While the adults in King's novel know that the monster exists, they are unsure of their ability to invoke the imagination necessary to believe in the fairy tales which alone can defeat the monster. Not only imagination but the will to believe is lacking. Adults no longer have the childish naiveté necessary to believe in such things as Santa Claus, the Tooth Fairy, and Captain Midnight, and that type of belief is necessary to defeat a monster:

"It," ruminating on the danger the seven children unexpectedly posed to it, thinks, *If there are ten thousand medieval peasants who create vampires by believing them real, there may be one—probably a child—who will imagine the stake necessary to kill it. But a stake is only stupid wood; the mind is the mallet which drives it home.*[9]

Whether the adults, already lacking one member of the magic circle of seven, can summon back their innocence as well as their unquestioning belief in the strength of community is at issue. To do so, they must lose their cynical adult knowledge and believe as children believe. In a recurring image, all six are childless—barren, sterile, and perhaps farther from their previous imaginative ability because of their childlessness.

Nevertheless, when the twenty-seven-year cycle erupts again, the adults, now late thirtyish Yuppies, no longer losers but highly successful in their various fields, do return to do battle with the monster. The members who have left Derry are recalled by Mike Hanlon, the keeper of the torch. Almost immediately the mechanisms of exclusion gear up as Stan is unable to face a return to Derry and commits suicide, abandoning his loving/loved wife and a successful accounting business in Atlanta. The novel soon makes clear that this is only the first such disaster.

The monstrous entity "It" and the town of Derry exist in a complicit, symbiotic relationship. "It" preys on the children of Derry, and the townspeople rather placidly ignore the extremely high casualty rate in Derry. "Runaways" is the sheriff's usual explanation, even though such an explanation is plainly ludicrous in the face of the disappearance of a three-year-old child. But to confront the unlikelihood of a three-year-old runaway would be to take action, action which might make the sheriff himself monster-bait. As the tale unfolds, the history of Derry is revealed as one in which children disappear on a regular basis, and twenty-seven year cycles of incredible violence erupt. The old timers remember these cycles, and the town historian has charted the occurrences back to the original Puritan settlement. The townspeople of Derry, however, will-fully ignore these occurrences; in many ways, it is as if they are blind to them, as if some monstrous external force has deprived them of the ability to react. But this is not the case. Secret knowledge is the key to Derry, for some of the older residents know perfectly well what is going on but prefer to deny any responsibility. Above all, they prefer to do nothing. The townspeople of Derry do not oppose the sacrifices because they do not wish to get involved. Such incidents as gay-bashing and murder, overt racism, missing children, a father attempting to murder his daughter, constant and recurring spousal and child abuse—all go completely unremarked by the residents of Derry. Beverly Marsh, running from her father, who has literal murder in his eyes, looks around the neighborhood and sees the blinds slowly drop over the eyes of the adults in Derry.

"It," which often appears as a clown named Pennywise, is the emblem of the diseased town. Beneath the history of the monster/town and the inexplicable cycles of violence, lurks the same demarcations and scapegoating as appear in Shirley Jackson's "The Lottery." Thus, in *It,* the strategies of exclusion, of demarcation, demonization, scapegoating, and ritual sacrifice surface yet again. What is truly horrifying and discomforting is that the adults buy their lives and prosperity with their children's lives. The sheriff, the councilmen, and the "movers and shakers" all willfully ignore the unexplained/able killings and disappearances. This hostile evocation of such institutions, one which sees them as corrupt and agenda-ridden, is often present in dis/affirmative horror fictions. Such constructions rend the veil from a conservative world wherein the police and governmental agencies are upholders of the moral and the good. In the compromised world of *It*, the forces of law-and-order are either actively complicit or indifferent.

The good guys, now older, cynical, and disillusioned, do defeat the monster, at least as much as such monsters are ever defeated, but in *It* the price of victory over the monster is loss of community. On both occasions, when they are pre-adolescents and successful late-thirtyish Yuppies, they forget the bonds forged between them. At novel's end, with the monster defeated, they cannot remember the experience at all; worse yet, they cannot remember the other members of The Losers Club.

The price becomes apparent after Mike talks to Richie:

I believe [Mike Hanlon thought] we were both thinking the same thing: it was over, yes, and in six weeks or six months, we will have forgotten all about each other. It's over and all it's cost us is our friendship and Stan and Eddie's lives. I've almost forgotten them, you know it? Horrible as it may sound I have almost forgotten Stan and Eddie.[10]

The Monster is finally dead, but so is the community; in a mortal symbiosis, the death of the monster leads to the death of community. As Mike Hanlon puts it, "I think that, after a long and ghoulishly vital existence, Derry may be dying . . . like a nightshade whose time to bloom has come and gone."[11] At this point, the protagonists' barrenness and sterility is re-invoked; not only are they childless Dinks (double income, no kids), lacking that most essential community of a family, they have also lost the community most integral to their lives. And while the movement of the text makes it seem inevitable and even expected, the dis/easeful truth is that the loss of community should not seem inevitable.

With the destruction of "It," the town of Derry starts to deconstruct as well. The loss of community by the survivors seems to imply that without a monstrous other there can be no community. Again, an antinomous structure surfaces: destroy the monster, and you destroy both the magic circle and the town. What does this say about horror fiction as a vehicle for dis/ease? To have the community, says King, we must accept the corruption inherent within it even though that very corruption will kill the community. Such a construction is dis/ease-provoking indeed; friendship, family, and love depend on a murdering monster, which inhabits the chthonic sewers of Derry. Rid the community of the monster and deprive the community of its ability to survive.

Such losses cannot be reconciled with an entirely affirmative closure. It is as though Tolkien's fearless band, having saved the West from Sauron and destroyed the magic ring, were to shoulder their swords, shrug, and go their separate ways, oblivious of their fellowship. Wealthy and successful as they are, the "Losers" are indeed losers, even though they separate claiming they will always love each other, and even though some of them have in fact died for one another and for the children of Derry. Their gallant battle won, it seems unfair that no Rivendell or Uttermost West awaits them; what they receive instead is unwilled oblivion, imposed by whatever force has manipulated them. This forgetfulness denies the importance of the community and makes a strong comment on the fragility of the constructs that make up community in the first place. Is community only a means to an end, something that can be dissolved when its purpose is fulfilled? As chunks of downtown Derry fall into the Androscoggin River, so chunks of the community fall into oblivion. Reading the fate of Derry back against the fate of the Losers, the plot structure demands the dissolution of the fellowship. The antinomous and symbiotic tie between the Losers and Derry is not broken so easily. As Derry dies, so dies the Losers Club. But whether the community of Derry survives at all, and this prospect is extremely uncertain, the Losers Club does not. Community has served as a catalyst for its own destruction. The evil community limps on, but the community defined in terms of love, courage, and generosity, is almost completely nullified.

In a second King novel, *Needful Things* (1991), this darker vision of community becomes even more apparent. While the monster is defeated and killed in *It*, the monster simply relocates in *Needful Things*. The citizens' complicity in the destruction of community is foregrounded in both texts. In *It*, the citizens deploy the "ABM Syndrome," (Anyone But Me) and in *Needful Things* the inhabitants privilege objects over people. Both texts point up the difficulty of maintaining community in a world which does not value community. Castle Rock, unlike Derry, seems, at least initially, a community well worth preserving, but only until the individuals in the community tear it to pieces in their selfish pursuit of material objects.

Needful Things is a conventionally Faustian tale of the dangers involved in deals with the devil. Early in the novel, Leland Gaunt moves into Castle Rock, opens a shop named Needful Things, and does a landslide business. In stereotypical New England fashion, he loves to bargain and *caveat emptor* is his motto. The residents, who understand this to mean that they are buying a pig in a poke, do not consider the further ramifications of their purchases. Since Gaunt is a demon, and bargains with the devil never work out as the unwary buyer thinks they will, the consumers are buying a glamour as well as a worthless object. What they see is indeed in one sense what they get, but in another sense is often a worthless piece of drek which has glamour only in the glamour ized one's eyes.[12] Such a device works extremely well as pointed commentary on a consumerist society, a society in which people buy to fill a void or a perceived need. In many ways, Gaunt is nothing more (nor less) fearsome than a Madison Avenue shill who spends his days dreaming up manipulative language to create both the product and the need. Gaunt promises people their heart's desire, which he always just happens to have on hand, not in return for mere cash, but for some action destructive of community, which starts a reaction like that of nuclear fission. Not only does Gaunt demand a prank as part of the price, but the pranks are also carefully calculated to be as divisive as possible. The fact that the required actions are random is further cause for dis/ease; quite frequently the perpetrator of the "harmless pranks" has nothing whatsoever against his or her victim, but does not see, or does not wish to see, the harm the prank causes.

In order to get his hands on a much coveted Sandy Koufax baseball card, for example, twelve-year-old Brian Rusk agrees to throw mud on Wilma Jerzcyk's sheets. Wilma is sure that Nettie Cobb did it, and the game of deconstructing the civilized community is underway. Although Brian may be unaware, Leland Gaunt knows, and the reader knows, that there is bad blood between Wilma and Nettie. The result is murder. Hugh Priest, in order to secure a foxtail which reminds him of his unblasted and promising youth, kills Nettie's beloved dog Raider and leaves a note saying, "Nobody slings mud on my clean sheets. I told you I'd get you!" Nettie, who knows that Wilma has threatened to have Raider destroyed, immediately jumps to the not entirely unwarranted conclusion that Wilma has killed Raider. The two women meet and literally hack each other to pieces. But in fact it is Leland Gaunt, puppet-master supreme, who has set this event in motion using Brian and Hugh, neither of whom can bear to give up his prized possession. Hugh Priest, for example, likes dogs and is appalled, after the fact, that he could kill a harmless dog whose belly he has just been scratching:

> [Hugh] suddenly felt very bad about what he had done—almost ill. . . .
>
> Yes, he had done it and he knew it, but he could hardly believe it. It was as if he had been in a trance or something.
>
> The inner voice, the one that sometimes talked to him about the AA meetings, spoke up suddenly. *"But you weren't in any fucking trance: you knew just what you were doing."*[13]

A reader who likes dogs is even more appalled than Hugh at the vicious image of someone stabbing a trusting and harmless dog to death over a worthless piece of fur. But Hugh fears loss of his foxtail more than he fears the loss of basic human decency; the fact that he fears the loss of an already lost identity (Hugh will never again be the conscientious adolescent who refused to drink while driving) is not enough reason to excuse him. At some point in the demonization process, Hugh knows perfectly well, as does Brian, who hides his card from the light of day as though he had indeed stolen it rather than purchased it honestly, that he is an active participant and complicitous in his own demonization as well as in the destruction of his community.

Unfortunately for any sense of community in Castle Rock, by the time some of the perpetrators do see the chain of events and understand their responsibility, it is far, far too late for amends. Brian Rusk, for example, feeling he has at least two murders on his hands, first makes his younger brother Sean promise never to go into Gaunt's shop; he then blows his brains out with his father's shotgun: "Never go there," he said. "Needful Things is a poison place and Mr. Gaunt is a poison man. Only he's really not a man, Sean. He's not a man at all."[14]

At this moment, Brian's mother Cora is locked in her bedroom indulging in some rather graphically sexual fantasizing over Elvis. She has bought what she believes to be "The King's" favorite sunglasses which take her to Graceland; when the police come to question her about Brian's motives for suicide, all she can think about is getting rid of them: "She had even managed to squeeze out a tear or two, thinking not about Brian but about how sad Elvis must feel, wandering about Graceland without her."[15]

The breakdown of the family mirrors the breakdown of the community. Cora is so deep into a fantasy concerning Elvis that literally nothing else matters, not the gun-shot from the garage, her hysterical younger son's shriek of horror, the questions from the police, or the fact that her younger son is in a state of shock in the emergency room. Sean had come to her, minutes before the suicide, worried about his brother, but Cora, intent on her fantasy, pushed him out of her room and locked the door. Eventually, breaking yet another bond, she will kill her best friend Myra over who is "screwing" Elvis Presley. By the time that Gaunt is ready to close up shop, murders will be too mundane even to comment upon, and Castle Rock will be a perfect, miniature, all-too-human hell.

Leland Gaunt sees himself as "an electrician of the human soul" and uses a mechanical metaphor which fits a post-industrialized society rather well:

In a small town like Castle Rock, all the fuse boxes were lined up neatly side by side. What you had to do was open up the fuse boxes . . . and then start cross-wiring. . . . [A]nd then you turned on the juice. All the juice.
All at once."[16]

Gaunt takes his amusement where he can find it, and his amusements come from community busting, from a masterful deployment of the strategies of exclusion. For Gaunt, as well as for the shapechangers in *Ghost Story*, human beings provide his entertainment, and all he needs for success is a supply of worthless objects and an understanding of basic human nature. He can then break a community down piece by piece, person by person, blowing the emotional circuits one by one and destroying a community quite thoroughly in the process. Both the strengths and fatal weakness of Castle Rock are suggested by the fuse box: lined up side-by-side and easy to cross-wire.

By the time Gaunt's little amusement is finished, Castle Rock is virtually destroyed, as are King's fictional communities of Chamberlain in *Carrie* and Derry, Maine, in *It*. The citizens delude themselves that one small action, such as throwing mud on a neighbor's sheets, making a crank phone call, or sending anonymous letters, is a cheap price to pay for the one material object they must have. *Caveat emptor*, indeed. Many of them carry out their "pranks" with great pleasure, and some act reluctantly, but all do so from fear of losing their coveted possession. Almost no one who visits the store and purchases something refuses to carry out the prank or decides that the price tag, even for their heart's desire, is too high.

In horror texts with strong didactic overtones, chaos and catastrophe result from the transgressions involved, whether these transgressions involve greed, lust, disobedience, pride, or covetousness. But once the lesson is learned, the situation achieves resolution. In the more commonly read version of "Little Red Riding Hood," Red Riding Hood will, in future, stay on the path and avoid talking to strange wolves. In the original version, Red may learn to obey her mother; it is, unfortunately, the last thing she does learn. Her consumption by the wolf results in her digestion and not her resurrection.[17] The more common version has a softened ending. In much the same manner, King softens the ending of *Needful Things* slightly because there are a few stalwart citizens who do avoid the demonization process, or who are rescued and become stronger. They are stalwart and worthy of emulation, certainly, but they are by no means the general rule, nor do they escape unscathed. In fact, when the two main characters, Sheriff Alan Pangborn and Polly Chalmers, decide, so to speak, to get out of Dodge, their survival, like that of the surviving Chowder Society members, seems to hinge on leaving their community permanently.

Aside from the ending, and the general mayhem implicit in a model where consumption is paramount, this evocation is too apt and resonates too easily with twentieth-century American consumer culture not to cause a dis/easeful and unwilling identification with people for whom things have replaced every other consideration. Community members, friends, lovers, family, spouses, and children: all pale in importance beside the chance to get the thing the soul craves. Considerations of morality and ethics dwindle to nothing; these people, our recognizable friends and neighbors, fall into a feeding frenzy where material goods are concerned, and too many Americans can recognize the incessant marketing and culturally driven desire to desire to feel perfectly comfortable reading *Needful Things*. On the other hand, despite the dis/ease generated by the text, several of the main characters do survive, and the invidious comedic ending of marriage occurs. Thus while *Needful Things* does produce a dark view of community destroyed and corrupted, illustrating the dangers of rampant capitalism and unchecked consumer greed, and while individual desires and the community are in constant conflict, the survivors, the ones who put Satan behind them, so to speak, have learned the value of community. They have also learned how very fragile and societally constructed communities are. Unfortunately, their knowledge will do nothing to aid the community in which they live. All it takes is an influx of greed, a mindset which posits my satisfaction and damn the cost, to destroy community. It is significant that even when denying the demonic power Polly employs consumerist imagery:

> "What really happened in this goddamn town?"
> It was Polly who answered.
> "There was a sale. The biggest going-out-of-business sale you ever saw . . . but in the end, some of us decided not to buy."

And minutes later, as Alan and Polly leave Castle Rock:

> My town, he thought, It was my town. But not anymore. Not ever again.[18]

Here the elements cannot actually be resolved or affirmed in more than a fragile and compromised manner. Like some Vietnam-era dogfaces, they can only save the vill by destroying it; in this case, they can only preserve a semblance of community by leaving the town and its residents, who are Alan Pangborn's sworn responsibility and Polly's friends, to their fates, whatever those fates may be. Thus, while the centrality and importance of the concept of community is valorized, the reality is abandoned. Like Derry, Castle Rock is disintegrating because the fragile constructs of community have gone hopelessly awry. More than the novel's main plot, however, the coda generates extreme dis/ease. Leland Gaunt has not been destroyed; rampant consumerism is alive and well in America. At novel's end, in a coda entitled "You've been here before," in Junction City, the nicest little town in Iowa, a new store is opening.[19]

Bentley Little's *University* (1995), the final and most exemplary text in the good community category, is a horror fiction about a university, a living malignant entity, which foregrounds and actively encourages the most exclusionary and hateful of human traits. Like Stephen King, I believe that one way to define horror is in terms of personal engagement—that which does not engage us, does not affect us. "It is," says King, "a combat waged in the secret history of the heart."[20] Since I am a member of académe, the idea of the university as a site for horror is perhaps more effective for me than for someone who considers universities unimportant.

In Little's text, the students begin displaying hostile apathy, which is bad enough (but still familiar territory, to academics at least), but this behavior rapidly metastasizes to full blown xenophobia, racism, homophobia, gynophobia, and misogyny. Violence against "Others," against Asians, African-Americans, gays, and women, skyrockets. Professors lecture on racist topics like the positive economic benefits of slavery, taunt black students with their demonized status, flunk Asian students out of the engineering programs, and torture helpless animals to loudly expressed approbation, as almost all the students eagerly join in. Violently reactionary "nativist" movements run by proto-Hitlers spring, like death angel mushrooms, from previously tolerant soil. The university community, widely considered tolerant and diverse, a bastion of liberal policies like affirmative action and diversity, appears instead as something out of the Third Reich. If the universities are apt breeding grounds for such arrant prejudices, if such hatemongering can surface seemingly overnight at the UC Brea campus, in a state well known for its liberal proclivities, then what forces are at work outside the rarefied atmosphere of académe?

Again, the divisive strategies of demarcation, demonization, and scapegoating are nearly unchecked. The fact that a heroic professor of English, Dr. Ian Emerson, and several students, primarily Jim Parker and Faith Pullen, manage to confront the cancerous entity and stop the horrific trends marks only a partial affirmation. The good guys do win, but they have been incurably infected by the monster; nor are they certain that the entity which infected UC Brea has actually been destroyed. While Ian Emerson escapes unscathed, unlike many of his colleagues, and even attains another position in the UC system, the two heroic students, Jim and Faith, have been infected, perhaps mortally. One of the results of the victorious students' exposure to the malignant university is a taste for sado-masochistic sex. The novel closes with the acknowledgment of contained infection and its strange attraction: "He dragged her down, slapped her breasts. She grabbed his penis, squeezed, nails drawing blood. And it was good."[21]

This is uncomfortable enough in its graphic explicitness, its linking of pain with pleasure, but what really produces a feeling of acute dis/ease is that the earlier violence is not only approved but, like the sado-masochistic sex, actively encouraged. Indeed, the university community not only feeds upon these phobias/isms but actively propagates them. Most chilling of all, almost all the professors, like almost all the students, are complicit in the outrages. And why should they be exempt? They are, after all, part of the university community, simultaneously producer and product. And at a time when affirmative action is under hostile scrutiny and facing dismantlement at some universities, when minority student enrollment has plummeted in the wake of the revocation of affirmative action programs, when anti-immigration initiatives are sweeping the country, when feminism is still on the receiving end of an anti-feminist backlash, when universities themselves are under attack in certain quarters and their essential usefulness called sharply into question, this text is not discussing a fantastic or supernatural entity as much as the politically conflicted/self-constructed role of the university.

The true horror of *University* is not the living and malignant entity horrifically concretized as the university; it is the social attitudes encapsulated within the metaphor of the university as a monstrous body. *University* was, for me, simultaneously a very uncomfortable and riveting text because, despite the obvious fantastic/horrific elements, in many ways, *University* is very realistically rendered. Much of the dialogue and much of the detail reflects reality; (in fact, I plan to employ the argument with which the professor hero addresses the charge that much horror fiction is dated and irrelevant); students, colleagues, and even the bad hamburgers and slow lines at the school cafeteria are authentically detailed.[22] And yet, authentic and saturated in mundane details as the setting is, this is not a realistic novel, what Ian Watt terms "a production that purports to be an authentic account of an actual experience of individuals."[23] Realistically speaking, universities do not suddenly come to life and physically corrupt the academic community. But the university is a site for the issues of race/class/gender Judith Halberstam locates in the Gothic body, and thus the university is a monstrous body. Donna Haraway's insistence on "Social reality as lived social relations, our most important political construction" figures very strongly in a reading of *University*.[24] Situating the text as Halberstam suggests, "in relation to a whole host of historically specific cultural anxieties about societal decline" is one of the ways in which cultural dread or dis/ease is not only produced but left unresolved.[25] If an institution postulated on tolerance and the pursuit of truth can become this corrupt, what hope is there for the rest of society?

Yet another extremely dis/ease-provoking view of community emerges when a community is readily definable as evil but nonetheless displays what we define as community values. In this pattern, communities composed of werewolves or vampires challenge commonly accepted belief systems. If such a community displays admirable qualities, such reversals and inversions produce dis/ease. The handy black-and-white distinctions between good and evil and us and them, are called into question. Texts like Gary Brandner's *The Howling* and Poppy Z. Brite's *Lost Souls* shift the paradigm of positive to encompass a community defined as evil. Such a pattern is easily as dis/ease provoking as *University*, except that this evil community has a code of values entirely lacking in *University*. These are problematic texts because, while something is indeed affirmed, the embrace of evil, the affirmation present in an essentially evil community does not work like algebra and cancel the evil. Two negatives, in other words, do not a positive make. Thus, these texts occupy the murky boundaries, the debatable lands, between outright dis/affirmative fictions and the fragile compromised fictions of the mid-spectrum, shading substantially closer to dis/affirmative.

Gary Brandner's *The Howling* (1977), which postulates a werewolf community, from which non-werewolves usually disappear, is horrifying not only from the point of view of the unfortunate non-werewolves, but also horrifying in its evocation of community:

In the dark Aarda forest on the border between Greece and Bulgaria there is a dead gray patch of land where no one goes and nothing lives. . . . Four hundred years ago it was a village. It was called Dradja. . . . Even when the village lived it was a place of darkness.[26]

Dradja is finally attacked by enraged inhabitants from around the area, who herd all the inhabitants into a square, and call for the guilty to step forward. Despite threats to obliterate the town à la Lidice, to destroy it and remove all evidence of existence, the townspeople refuse to give up the werewolf in their midst.[27] Even in the face of threats which amount to genocide, they cannot and will not so easily surrender the werewolf, for they are all werewolves. The enraged outsiders execute as many of the accursed inhabitants as they can catch, and in time-honored rites of obliteration, slaughter the animals, burn the bodies, and plow the ashes under. The spot is so accursed that four hundred years later nothing yet will grow there.

But all of the Evil is not destroyed, for the survivors emigrate to America and maintain their community, a secluded village which they name Drago. It is hard to decide what is most horrifying and what issues are at stake. Is this a very conservative/reactionary text, which is anti-immigrant—we never know what diseased monsters we're letting in—or is this a perverse celebration of liberal icons in that no one will move to destroy the sense of communion, no matter how di/per/verse it is? If human- flesh-eating monsters value community and family values, and are willing to die rather than scapegoat and sacrifice one of their own, what does this say about the importance of community? Certainly the werewolf community is strong and vibrant, a community which, unlike many typically "American" communities, refuses to buy its survival at the price of its members, which refuses, so to speak, to throw its members to the wolves. It is, in many ways, a more admirable community than UC Brea, or Castle Rock. The community is not easy prey for the strategies of exclusion; outsiders are generally unwelcome, except as prey, but insiders are protected by a code of behaviour more rigorous than the famed Sicilian *omertá*.

Karyn and Roy Beatty have moved to Drago temporarily because a rapist, another man-as-beast, has made Karyn temporarily sexually dysfunctional, and her therapist, subscribing to the myth of "restful rural surroundings," has recommended a move from L.A.[28] But this move does not benefit Karyn at all; in fact, it makes her even more frigid and depressed. Marcia, a Drago native and therefore *ipso facto* an animal in human form, finds Roy easy prey sexually. She is every wife's nightmare—single, beautiful and wantonly available. Furthermore, Roy dismisses his guilt very easily. "Marcia Lura had been there when he had badly needed someone and he had taken her. . . . The thing had happened, and he knew it would happen again."[29] Roy not only turns his back on his wife's distress, but chooses to have sex outside of marriage; the implication is that he is showing signs of reverting to animal status. Later, he chooses to remain a werewolf, to turn his back on the human and embrace the monstrous. What can Roy embrace in a community which is defined by present-day morals as a village of serial killers? I argued earlier that a double negative, does not, except in algebra, postulate a positive; to embrace Drago is to double the evil present, not reverse it. Any human is legal prey for these monstrous beings who are no different from the Manson family or any of the other cult killers. What price community when a husband turns from a wife, commits adultery, and prefers werewolfdom to the human? The dis/ease arises because it is not only good and affirmative communities which have strong bonds; evil communities exert the same attraction and are also important to their members. Many of the citizens of Drago are portrayed as just like us; Oriole Jolivet likes to gossip, play cards, and always has time for a pot of coffee; Dr. Volkmann makes house calls and seems very sympathetic when Karyn and Inez, a woman who suspects that the Drag-onians are not human, blurt out their concerns. But neither Jolivet nor Volkmann is concerned with hunting werewolves; they are werewolves, part and parcel of Drago. This is what Karyn and Inez do not understand, and what gets Inez killed by Roy. They do not realize in time that Drago is a werewolf community, which has defined itself as non-human and actively embraced evil.

When Karyn flees from Drago, we sympathize because her husband has willingly chosen the werewolves. What resolution or affirmation is possible here? The village of Drago remains, living proof that containing the monster is not possible. "Some of them will get away," says Karyn, "Some of them always get away."[29] Here the outsider chooses to join a non-affirmative community, one we unwillingly understand to be a solid community. The problem, of course, is that being a werewolf, a human beast, means preying on human beings. Roy-the-wolf may prevent Volk-mann-the-wolf from tearing Karyn's throat out in the final climactic escape from Drago, but this alone is not enough to mitigate the dis/ease. The antinomous and dis/easeful pairing of community values with were-wolves makes this book a very disquieting read.

Poppy Z. Brite's *Lost Souls* (1992) also works with the sense of loss engendered by partial victories, questionable compromises, and the problematic choice of an evil community. Her novel defines vampires somewhat differently than is the case in conventional vampire fiction. None of the well known vampire myths apply. Religious artifacts have no standing, and victims cannot become the UnDead. Vampires are another race entirely, and humans are their prey. The bite of a vampire means death and nothing more; sex with a vampire results in obsession, pregnancy, and certain death. Nevertheless, the vampires' victims often embrace the myth that they too will become UnDead, able to prey on their former fellow humans with impunity.

Nothing, the aptly named hero/anti-hero, is a very postmodern, nihilistic hero indeed. The adopted child of upper-middle-class parents, materially indulged but emotionally alienated, he has no history which he can access, no concern for anyone but himself, or anything but death. Once the reader understands his genealogy, however, his attitude is more comprehensible. The ironically named Christian, Zillah, Mordecai, and Twig are the vampires. While Christian represents a kinder, gentler vam-pire, Zillah and company represent the vampires as punks, who prey on the adolescent Goth/deather types. Zillah and Company are ruthless, completely amoral consumers, and Nothing, who is revealed as Zillah's son, is soon corrupted. Nothing, raised and spoiled by human beings and part of the alienated Goth movement, naturally chooses the vampires and has an incestuous and homosexual relationship with his father. Nothing also willingly participates in killing Laine, his best friend who tries to find him when he leaves home, and who trusts him right up until the moment Nothing betrays him.

At first Nothing has not realized that his new-found friends are vampires, ascribing "the sharpened teeth, the bite marks Zillah left all over him, the blood in wine bottles which he had thought an exotic, delicious affectation" to some sort of intense Gothic role-playing. However, when Zillah dips his finger in Laine's blood, both Laine's and Nothing's fates are sealed:

> That was when he realized he could do it. He could tear Laine's pulse open and drink from it . . . because he wanted to. . . .
>
> "*Please*," Laine sobbed, and some small dim part of Nothing realized what he was about to do. . . . Laine had been his friend, in another life.
>
> Zillah smiled a dark smile and said, "Come and be one of us," and Nothing knew he was being told to make his choice.
>
> So he opened his mouth as wide as it would go and bit into the soft flesh of Laine's throat. . . . [T]he last sane part of his mind screamed, *o god, what am I doing WHAT AM I DOING*, and it kept screaming even as his teeth tore out Laine's jugular. . . . The taste of blood meant the end of aloneness.[31]

What is most dis/easeful in this scene is the price of community: to what lengths will Nothing go to avoid feeling alone, to feel he belongs somewhere? He has always felt alienated from human beings, more so than the average fifteen-year-old. But Laine, at least, cared enough to leave his home and try to find Nothing. Ironically, that is exactly what he does find. As in the more disaffirmative horror fiction, part of the horror occurs because Nothing does find community and because he so completely turns his back on community. The antinomy of his character is also dis/ease provoking, particularly the extent to which Nothing will go to satisfy his appetites. As Euripides' *Bachae* so explicitly states, the Dionysian will not be denied, but such intrusions are extremely unsettling for any society which theoretically values order.

Ghost, Steve, and Ann are the humans who come into contact, to their sorrow, with the essentially soulless and completely inhuman vampires when the vampires "join" the small, closely knit community of Missing Mile, North Carolina. Steve and Ghost are close friends and members of the rock band Lost Souls?; Ann and Steve are estranged lovers. Ann, carelessly seduced, impregnated, and abandoned by Zillah, dies as a direct result of her impregnation; Steve, who still loves Ann, blames the vampires and vows vengeance:

"The vampires did it. . . . Does that mean they can just roll into town, fuck up my life and then go party some more? I was fucking up my life just fine on my own. I didn't need them. Ann didn't need them. I still loved her—I would've—I would've—"[32]

And while Steve and Ghost do manage to kill Zillah, who deserves death at Steve's hands, as well as Christian, who does not, they do not succeed in wiping out the vampires. As a result of the two deaths, Nothing becomes the leader of the vampire pack, and as he leaves New Orleans, his essential vampiric nature rises up: "If you wanted something, you didn't wait for the world to hand it to you; you took it."[33] Despite his nature, however, which balances the vampire and the fading human, Nothing lets Steve and Ghost live.

Steve and Ghost, however, almost do lose their sanity if not their souls; badly damaged, they escape back to Missing Mile. They are, however, no longer a part of the sleepy community of Missing Mile. Steve and Ghost have lost the ability to live in a pre-lapsarian state of unawareness. If Missing Mile symbolizes the post-lapsarian, the garden motif, then Steve and Ghost, even though they are not barred from returning, cannot dwell in the garden in serenity. While the town does not consciously exclude them, in fact, their absence is barely noticed, their experience and the awareness it generates does set them apart. Unlike Nothing, they do not gain a community but to a degree lose the one of which they have been a part.

Another problem which makes the novel such a problematic evocation of community is that of defining and confronting evil. On one hand, as Steve asks, "How do you deal with it? Doesn't it fuck you up to know that we touched something evil, that it is still out there in the world?" Ghost's response is this:

I don't think anyone knows what evil is. I don't think anyone has the right to say. . . . So maybe they [the vampires] are just like us. Maybe they did what they had to do to live and tried to get a little love and have a little fun before the darkness took them."[34]

Maybe so. But the vampires' idea of love and fun has cost Ann her life. And the point Ghost does not confront is that while fun may have been involved, the "love" to which Ghost refers is pure and simple lust. Nor do vampires have to worry, as humans do, about darkness taking them untimely.

Ghost's comments reflect a postmodern and relativist sensibility, although the advice comes from his wisewoman/witch grandmother. The words confirm that it is easier to deny the actuality of evil than to confront the issue of evil directly. Unfortunately, such black and white dichotomies do not wear well, either. Can non-human vampires, members of another race, be held to human standards? Vampires are not, by vampire standards, evil; they are merely surviving by preying on human beings. On the other hand, human standards are the only standards we have with which to judge and to try to impose some order over chaos. And certainly the vampires' sustenance can only be read against human death.

There is no clear-cut resolution in this novel as there is in *Dracula* and numerous other vampire texts. Ghost and Steve survive their experience with the vampires; Nothing, Twig, and Mordecai survive their experiences with Ghost and Steve. A sense of community seems to be one of the main casualties, however; as Missing Mile no longer fits Steve and Ghost, who plan to leave it for at least a while, so Nothing and Company cannot stay in New Orleans. Since vampires age very slowly, it is impossible for them to live in a community of humans for any length of time without their immortality becoming evident. Steve and Ghost will age and die and may never be at home in Missing Mile again, but Nothing and Company can outwait time and regain space. Indeed, the book closes fifty years later. Nothing, Twig and Mordecai are still young and restless, now back in New Orleans, as a snuff-rock band, a highly ironic disguise for vampires as well as one which enables them to prey unnoticed on the marginalized groups of society. Little has changed in their lives, while Steve and Ghost, if they are still alive and have managed to outrun their personal demons, are in their early seventies. Like the green bay tree, the vampires still flourish, apparently unaccountable. The dis/ease here springs from the lack of balance implied. Humankind is used to being the careless consumers rather than the carelessly consumed. Humankind as the highest and most powerful species is the touchstone of anthropocentric belief systems. To be relegated to the status of hamburger is thus profoundly dis/ease generating.

The texts I have chosen to discuss are among the many which relentlessly deconstruct the face of community and concentrate on the price someone else pays for community. They show people in head-on collisions with the construct we label community and gruesomely display "the body under the sheet," the term Stephen King employs in discussing the simultaneous fear and fascination evoked by horror fiction.[35]

But these texts do not provide the relief valve or the reassurance so many critics define as the ultimate purpose of horror fiction. Both of King's novels illustrate the impossibility of maintaining an ideal community. The only way to have a community, according to King, is to lose it. Straub, working from a slightly less draconian viewpoint, also points up the difficulty of maintaining community. Bentley Little's work indicates how easily a community can fall into intolerance and hatred,; Brandner's and Brite's evil communities all deconstruct the deeply cherished myth that community is solid, affirmative and a place in which we find the good guys. Indeed, one of Brite's meditations might be taken from any one of these works:

He [Laine] had come away from home because Nothing had; he had followed Nothing, trusting him. But Laine should have learned by now that when you have too much faith in something, it is bound to hurt you. Too much faith in anything will suck you dry. In this way, all the world is a vampire.[36]

8

THE DISCOMFORT ZONE:
WE ALL LIVE ON MAPLE STREET

"It isn't fair," Mr. Hutchinson screamed, . . . and then they were upon her."[1]

Some horror fictions resist even a partial resolution of the dis/ease generated by the text. These fictions, my main interest, occupy the far side of the spectrum. In such fictions, antinomy is foregrounded and the resolution actively resisted. In such fictions, however the demarcations and demonizations play out, whoever is chosen to be the scapegoat/sacrifice, however the insider/outsider motif is handled, the end result is the inability of the mechanisms of denial and resolution to function. Such texts as Shirley Jackson's "The Lottery," Rod Serling's "The Monsters Are Due on Maple Street," Stephen King's "One for the Road" and *The Mist*, Harlan Ellison's "The Whimper of Whipped Dogs," Edward Bryant's "A Sad Last Love at the Diner of the Damned," and Anne Rivers Siddons' *The House Next Door* all deal with communion which practice the previously discussed strategies of exclusion, and which use the most dis/ease-provoking pattern extant: that of the "innocent outsider" sacrificed for purposes that range from preservation of a compromised community to the desires of a purely evil community.[2] There are various reasons for selecting these particular texts from among literally hundreds of works. Jackson, Serling, and Ellison have produced texts in which a particular extratextual dis/ease figures large; King is almost obsessively interested in issues of community, and his own work provides a fascinating contrast with his critical stance on horror fiction; Bryant's very effective use of extremely graphic content reinforces the idea that the community is a cannibal, consuming itself; and Siddons' *The House Next Door*, with its evocation of a seemingly untouchable community, works surpassingly well to point up the slippage between the ideal and the real. In addition, what makes these texts worthy examples is what they do not reflect. The pattern I am discussing shows up in small towns, remote privileged enclaves, and large cities, as well as among various classes and genders. I am struck by the pervasiveness of the structure I have discovered in a wide range of horror fictions. Thus, while the specific texts I have chosen to discuss range widely in literary quality and degree of conventional horror, they all counter widely accepted cultural models. What makes these texts more antinomous and more dis/ease-provoking than texts like Brandner's *The Howling* or Brite's *Lost Souls* is that these communities are composed, not of werewolves or vampires, but of people like ourselves, who turn out to be moral monsters, people who lack some essential connection to humanity, people whose moral compasses have gone seriously awry.

In Shirley Jackson's paradigmatic short story, "The Lottery" (1948), the townspeople seem to be a community in which the storehouse of cultural assumptions is indeed common property. The citizens of this small town gather on a warm day in June to carry out community business in a manner somewhat reminiscent of New England town government. Everyone knows the agenda, so to speak, and if there are any newcomers, we do not know it. On the surface, therefore, this text seems to fit within affirmative fictions. A more important American cultural model than the active citizens of a small town gathering to carry out commonly agreed town business would be difficult to find.

As becomes apparent, however, the details of the gathering lend a sense of spurious ease to this story. The village square, the post office and the bank, the regularly scheduled day, and the reference to "noon dinner" all indicate a time-honored, well-understood village event. There is a great deal of social chitchat and joking back and forth; the children's talk is "still of the classroom and the teacher, of books and reprimands," the men find themselves "speaking of planting and rain, tractors and taxes," the women "exchange greetings and bits of gossip." It is an almost too picture perfect, too homely a vision of small town life in America. "The lottery was conducted—as were the square dances, the teen-age club and the Halloween program by Mr. Summers, who had time and energy to devote to civic activities."[3] The origins of this well-accepted ritual are both cloaked in and privileged by time, and no one dares to change anything. The black box, whose very sight provokes a ripple of disquiet, is hidden from sight 364 days a year and grows shabbier with the years; the specific rituals have been long forgotten; but the lottery takes place without fail each and every year, and the three-hundred-odd villagers willingly participate. The villagers no longer chant or salute, but the basic ritual, the lottery, survives intact.

What values, if any, are actually being affirmed in this dark little fable? The answer, alas, is scapegoating and ritual murder in the service of some dark but unspecified force. The townspeople believe that their rituals of blood sacrifice are their only bastion against barbarism and the failure of the crops. They therefore purchase their economic security, their consumer status, with the unwilling sacrifice of an "outsider," who is, in fact, one of their own members chosen by lot. The generation of a scapegoat will secure their economic security and consumer stability. The outsider, minutes earlier a well-liked villager with whom everyone jokes, becomes an outsider randomly, by choosing the paper with the black circle at the town lottery. As Stephen King points out, quite cogently, it is a very slick maneuver; something as simple and wordless as a blackened dot establishes the lines of demarcation which move the victim from townsperson to outsider.[4] The sacrificial slaying can then follow, for as Jackson sardonically notes, once the victim has been selected, "Although the villagers had forgotten the ritual and lost the original black box, they still remembered the stones." Once the individual has been chosen, all communal and familial feeling disappears. The necessary strategies of exclusion, those of demarcation, demonization, scapegoating and sacrifice, function to deny the victim's status as one of us. Tessie Hutchinson attempts to have her married daughter draw with them to increase the odds of survival, but as Summers points out, daughters are part of their husband's family and draw with them. Tessie does indeed know this, as do all the villagers. The dissipation of any sort of accepted family values continues as "Bill Hutchinson went over to his wife and forced the slip of paper out of her hand. It had a black spot on it. . . ."[5]

Actually, this whole story is a subversion of community. Any argument for this text as positive by virtue of its common values and sense of community is invalid, although whenever I teach this short story, students invariably attempt to make out a case by which Tessie Hutchinson brought her fate upon her own head by some action, unfortunately unspecified within the text. My favorite interpretation is one in which Mrs. Delacroix wants to brain Tessie for having an affair with her husband, an inventive reading supported by nothing more than a desire to construct an ending which is explicable and consequently reassuring.

Demarcation and demonization are well served by the strategy which assigns the victim the responsibility for his/her own demise. One cannot affirm a negative, however, without embracing evil, and the embrace of evil cannot be considered as affirming anything. In *Eichmann in Jerusalem*, Hannah Arendt postulates the banality of evil not because the monster is rare, but precisely because the monster embraces commonality; we all have monstrosity.[6] It shares space on the shelves of that higgledy-piggledy storehouse, stacked right along with the love and cohesiveness of the family unit, the unbreakable bond between husband and wife, and the unlimited love between parent and child. The stoning of an innocent villager, if only innocent in the generic sense that she is neither more nor less culpable than her fellow citizens, in order to keep up a standard of civilization, save the corn crop, and ensure domestic tranquillity, does not hold up to textual scrutiny. Even in the world within the text this custom has been successfully challenged. Jackson makes it quite clear that this village is an anachronism; many other villages have stopped the lottery with no ill effects. These other villages have not as yet been reduced to "eating chickweed and stewed acorns," as the village elder, Mr. Warner, so direly predicts.[7] The grim truth is that the villagers continue this ritual, at least in part, because they enjoy it. When a girl in the crowd whispers, "I hope it's not Nancy," after the Hutchinson family has been identified, Old Man Warner says, "It's not the way it used to be.[8] People ain't the way they used to be." The villagers are uneasy prior to the selection, and guiltily aware of their evil deed when the selection is made, but once the victim is selected, her fellow townspeople surge forward, filled with blood lust: Mrs. Delacroix selects a stone so large that she has to pick it up with both hands. The apotheosis of man's capacity for inhumanity to his fellow travelers occurs when a townsperson puts stones in the hand of Davy, Tess Hutchinson's young son. Tess' move from insider to Judas goat, from one of us to one of them, mirrors the antinomy between affirmation and subversion, between the idealized community and its opposite, which may be much more recognizable than we are comfortable admitting. "'It isn't fair, it isn't right,' Mrs. Hutchinson screamed, and then they were upon her."[9]

This carefully crafted short story intentionally deconstructs the myths of community, marriage, and family so dear to modern American hearts. The tension created within the text, starting with a beautiful day and the carefully established camaraderie, as opposed to the townspeople's action and the reader's horror at that action, also mirrors the lack of reaffirmation. What, after all, can possibly be defined as positive here? How can a reader respond to this text in a positive manner?

The townspeople in "The Lottery," however, are horrified at the non-community-minded attitude of the victim who will not docilely accept her fate—how can she be so selfish as to object to being stoned to death for the good of her fellow citizens? When Tessie objects after her husband "wins" the first round prize, thereby targeting the Hutchinson family, Mrs. Delacroix tells her to be a good sport, as if the lottery were nothing more than a game, and Tessie a sore loser. The reader, on the other hand, also experiences horror and dis/ease, but for a very different reason: we are horrified at the embrace of evil, at the negative values so strongly espoused by a corrupted community. And we are dis/eased because that particular metaphorical community resonates heavily and inexplicably. We cannot reduce this text to Halberstam's very handy and often valid model of race/class/gender as there is no certain evidence that the patriarchal structure has chosen Tess Hutchinson because of her gender. There is, after all, at least one widow in the crowd of villagers, though widowed by what or by whom the text does not state. One can reasonably assume, however, that her husband was one of the lucky winners of a previous lottery. Furthermore, if this is a patriarchally driven action, as may be argued from the male officials and the action of Tessie's husband, it is even more horrifying by reason of complicity; it is the women, after all, who most quickly pick up the largest rocks. The villagers seem to be quite homogeneous; if class and power were at issue, Mr. Summers would be exempted, but he takes his chance with the rest, though it can be argued that he has privileged knowledge since he drew the spots on the paper. If race is a component, none of the surnames in particular give it away. Adams, Allen, Anderson, Delacroix, Dunbar, Hutchinson, Jones, Martin, Overdyke, Percy, Summers, Warner, and Zanini are among the names called. While the preponderance of names are of British extraction, there are two names obviously French and Italian, but neither of these is chosen.

Who knows what particular historical or cultural dis/ease, if any, Jackson may have wished to play upon? The story, although carefully left unspecified as to setting and only loosely chronologically based, could be set in New England; if so, on which Puritanical actions is she commenting? Is Jackson reworking the persecution and execution of witches or of Quakers? Is she playing off Hawthorne's *The Scarlet Letter* or "The Gentle Boy"? Is her interest more contemporaneous? The eleven million victims of the Holocaust, slaughtered for Hitler's mad dreams, come to mind. The black-dot would substitute for the stamped "J" or the yellow armband, and the villagers would make excellent Nazis. The Nuremberg trials were in session the same year Jackson wrote "The Lottery," and the world was still looking for reasonable explanations for Hitler's rise to power and the average German's active complicity in genocide. No one wishes to identify with the Hitler, but no one can explain either why his rise to power was ignored, or why the Germans so willingly carried out mass exterminations on the people who were, previously, their friends and neighbors. On some levels, Jackson's dark fable explains such inhumanities cogently, if not precisely comfortingly. Or is she non-political and more interested in how social constructs play out? Is she discussing something as personal as joining in the ostracization of a classmate for no better reason than that everyone else is doing it? Is she discussing the lamentable human tendency to ostracize and exclude people on various but essentially unimportant grounds? During the writing of this study, the Columbine High School massacre at Littleton, Colorado, occurred, and the entire country asked how such a horrific event could take place. The strategies of exclusion and the types of horror fiction in which I am interested provide an answer. We demarcate and demonize other human beings in a culture where weapon-based violence is not an atypical response and stand amazed as individuals too alienated by the culture to survive it wreak vengeance on their tormentors. Why these two individuals reacted so strongly when other students have not remains unanswerable; why no one took steps to prevent their actions remains unanswered. Perhaps the balance falls on the side of nature. Perhaps the nurturing was ineffective. Perhaps, for some arcane combination of reasons, these adolescents were walking time-bombs. One of the more uncomfortable functions horror fiction performs is to illustrate how the exclusions work and what the possible effects might be.

What is most dis/easeful about this short story is the lack of concrete explanation for the villagers' motives in the first place. An ideal community, after all, would have one brave villager (probably superbly acted by Jimmy Stewart) who would step forward and state that what's going on here just isn't right. In our idealized constructed view of ourselves as Americans, the rest of the village would rise up as one and the ritual would end. But Jackson denies the easy closure, the handy exit out of the ghoulhouse, because other villages have dropped the lottery and her villagers are not only not conscience-stricken but actively complicitous.

"The Lottery" works to generate dis/ease on several levels. There is the actual literal text, with its antinomous elements of community and individual self-preservation linked paradoxically and inextricably together, the model to which I referred earlier in which the degree of dis/ease is extremely high and not resolvable. In addition, the story's widely applicable metaphors generate dis/ease. "The Lottery" is by no means limited to a physical evocation of the outsider or an actual scapegoating ritual. Today one might read "The Lottery" as a parable about the changes in society. Today any member of society might be employed and successful; but if corporate downsizing, or a recession, or any number of uncontrollable factors come into play, unemployment and homelessness might be right around the corner: insider to outsider in one easy move. Moreover, our newly constructed outsider might be no more responsible for the situation that reduces him/her/them to an ex-insider than Tess Hutchinson is responsible for getting the paper with the black dot. What, after all, is the difference between a pink slip and a black-dotted piece of paper? Both generate vast amounts of dis/ease in their unfortunate recipients. Both produce a change from consumer to consumed. And both draw forth the same reaction from the community at large. In some way, we assume, both Tess Hutchinson and our unfortunate pink-slipped worker have brought their fate on themselves, and by so doing have become a threat to the rest of the community. Thus, as Jackson so succinctly points out, they become the scapegoats of our uneasy society. How much of the eager surge forward, stones in hand, is due to blood lust and how much to the fact that, this year at least, it isn't me?

Rod Serling's "The Monsters Are Due on Maple Street" (1962) uses, or seems to use, the time-honored and indeed somewhat hoary conventions of aliens from outer space to achieve much the same commentary on community as do other disaffirmative horror fictions. It is rather ironic in its title as well: as we shall see, the monsters are not due on Maple Street; they already reside on Maple Street. In this respect, "Monsters" is a text much like "The Lottery" or Kosinski's *The Painted Bird*. Serling deftly sets up a 1950's neighborhood, reminiscent of a cultural model in which everyone knows and likes everyone else. The setting emphasizes the domestic/cold war ideology of containment so prominent in America during the 1950s, and herein lies its importance. Maple Street is quite clearly an American community; people own their homes, work together as a cohesive force, exchange neighborhood gossip, and have both respect and tolerance for each other. Absolutely nothing about it indicates that it is a community which can be easily destroyed. But ideal neighborhood or not, it falls with frightening ease.

Again, as in Jackson's text, Serling's description emphasizes the homogeneity of the neighborhood in terms of race and gender, although class is a bit more problematic, and one man's name, Ned Rosen, indicates a Jewish patronymic. Although no one is explicitly linked to a specific paradigm of class, the descriptions of cars, hobbies, and clothing indicate a blue collar neighborhood. Women's work is contained within the house, men's work outside. Nearly everyone has cars, gas mowers, radios, and other consumer gadgets.

Thus, the setting functions to make Maple Street a paradigm for America. But a flash of light in the sky, a series of seemingly random power outages and even more random power surges reveal the inner rooms of this neighborhood in no short order. Anti-Semitism, that long and time-honored definition of the Other, rears its ugly head; harmless habits transmogrify into life-threatening actions; and total chaos, including murder and arson, ensues. The first target, by no coincidence whatsoever, is Ned Rosen. Stunned, he protests his almost immediate demarcation and demonization vehemently. He has, after all, been an accepted part of the community for years. But Ned Rosen, while he can probably be accurately read in terms of race, does not entirely explain the dynamics of exclusion. As the apparently random power surges and outages continue, as nightfall approaches, the neighborhood literally rends itself and its sense of community into pieces. Charlie Farnsworth, the Joseph McCarthy-like demagogue who instigates the demarcation/ demonization ploy, is one of the early victims for no better reason than can be found for the random outages and surges. The sudden and apparently incomprehensible generation of electricity is enough to turn the members of an apparently strongly bonded neighborhood into an hysterical mob intent on discovering a scapegoat.

At story's end, the neighborhood is a lifeless, smoking ruin. Ironically, it is a fit new habitation for the two-headed aliens who plan to walk right in and sit right down. Why? A twelve-year-old child, who has, perhaps, read too many science fiction texts, explains that aliens are secreted among the townspeople:

> "They sent four people. A mother, a father and two kids who looked just like humans. But they weren't."
>
> A twelve year old boy had planted a seed. And something was growing out of the street with invisible branches that began to wrap themselves around the men and women and pull them apart.

As the narrator points out, "Order, reason, logic were slipping, pushed by the wild conjectures of a twelve-year-old boy."[10] Nor is it order alone which is slipping into the Dionysian abyss; it is the long cherished myth of community. In this tale there is finally nothing left to affirm: "When the sun came up the following morning Maple Street was silent. . . . At four o'clock that afternoon there was no more world or at least not the kind of world that had greeted the morning.[11]

There are many ways to interpret this particular text and many didactic lessons to extrapolate; one thing distinctly lacking, however, is a sense of affirmation or resolution. And while it may indeed be a didactic tale, warning as it does against indulgence in the evils of exclusion, the lesson does not seem taken to heart. "Monsters" is also a politically activated tale, which echoes several historical events. Prior to World War II, Jews had lived as members of various communities for decades. It took the rise to power of one demagogue who could call on the imbedded anti-Semitic cultural model and manipulate a highly persuadable populace to completely subvert that sense of belonging. In no time at all, most of the populations across Germany re-realized that the Jews were indeed their enemies and sub-human to boot. In no time at all, the Jews were again branded "Other" and completely excluded from the community. Demarcated and demonized, they were portrayed in cartoons at the time as Satanic.[12] They were transmogrified from thriving members of the society to commodities for that society. Like the unfortunate Mrs. Hutchinson, they were worth considerably more to their fellow country-men dead than alive. It is no coincidence whatsoever that Ned Rosen is the first victim, the first member of the community to whom eyes automatically turn.

Serling could also be exploring the Red-baiting, Commies-under-the-bed mentality of the late 1950s. This short story is polyphonic and multi-layered, and lends itself to the endless generation of societal dis/eases. What makes this story worth discussing is that an apparently coincidental juxtaposition of events unleashes not only the destruction of a neighborhood but also the destruction of civilized values and of community itself. When Ned Rosen comes under immediate suspicion, he says, "You all know me. We've lived here four years. Right in this house. We're no different from any of you," but as the narrator notes, "The people he was looking at hardly resembled the people he'd lived alongside of for the last four years." Steve Brand, the closest figure to a hero in the text, says, "We're on a monster kick. Seems that the general impression holds that maybe one family isn't what we think they are. Monsters from outer space or something. Different from us. Fifth colum-nists from the vast beyond."[13] The dis/ease here undoubtedly has politi-cal as well as social overtones. While the "fifth columnist" concern may be dated, the concern with "the Other," the "not-Us," is not limited but universal. The "phobic pressure points" King postulates exist trans-culturally, but have differing labels in different times and places.[14] Just before events spin inexorably out of control, Brand states a sad universal truth: "And you're with him, all of you. You're standing there all set to crucify—to find a scapegoat—desperate to point some kind of finger at a neighbor. Well, look, friends, the only thing that's going to happen is we'll eat each other up alive."[15]

And in no time at all, metaphorical cannibalism does occur; the citi-zens are literally at each other's throats because the positive aspects of community are never enough to cancel out fear of the other, or fear of dark unknown forces "out there." As the two cogent onlookers, who do indeed turn out to be two-headed aliens, observe, "Throw them into darkness for a few hours and watch the pattern unfold. . . . They pick the most dangerous enemy they can find and it's themselves."[16]

But the myths of community Americans are most comfortable with and reassured by would postulate an ending in which the brave neigh-borhood stands up with the hero against the nasty two-headed aliens and sends them limping, battered and bloody, back to their spaceships. Such recent films as *Mars Attacks*, *Independence Day*, and *Men in Black*, for example, as well as numerous 1950's movies concerned with alien invasion, employ plots in which the idealized view of American society is privileged.[17] In the best affirmative tradition, all of these films whip alien butt and thus dissipate dis/ease over space as well as re-establish American hegemony. This plot is an American icon, non-specific to a particular genre, grounded in and beloved of American cultural tradition. This is a very comforting myth because it allows us to forget, to ignore, and to resolutely disregard the human tendency to turn on each other to avoid personal sacrifice.

The aliens know the truth: all that is necessary to destroy the delicate fabric of the community is to introduce fear and suspicion seasoned with a *soupçon* of threatened loss, then stand back and watch it self-destruct. The reality so vividly delineated by Serling shreds the comforting myth of community and leaves readers very uncomfortable indeed. This dis/ease, this discomfort zone, exists because most people know but do not want to know that community is based on a myth. Most people can probably identify a time when the dark side of community engulfed them. High school cliques, repugnance at a retarded child, avoidance of the different or unpopular, or even uneasy but participatory laughter at a nasty ethnic joke all probably spring to mind. We just don't want to acknowledge the occasion in ourselves. The reality of "The Lottery" and "Monsters" is too disquieting to openly acknowledge. Nor does either of these tales serve to quiet our guilty consciences and affirm that we are not like that: these stories and others like them point out that we are, indeed, just like that. Perhaps worse, these stories point out that we can also be the others. Tessie Hutchinson, Ned Rosen, and various other victims of the mob mentality indicate that almost anyone can suddenly become "the other."

Stephen King consistently explores community-based issues in which the community is often not only not validated but quite often entirely destroyed. Among the many stories which explore community, "One for the Road" and the novella *The Mist* generate that dis/ease which I see as integral to disaffirmative horror fiction. Both texts use the construction of the outsider to illustrate the lengths to which the strategies of exclusion can lead seemingly decent people, and *The Mist* in particular exemplifies the lengths to which a community will go to invoke the strategies of exclusion to protect themselves.

"One for the Road" (1977) is concerned with the demarcation of boundaries and the demonization and subsequent sacrifice of outsiders. Readers of the genre, primed by many and many a text, know one thing about small towns: they very, very rarely house clan Walton. In "One for the Road," a short story that continues the action of *'Salem's Lot*, a vacationing family stumbles onto a small community; the problem is that they stumble into Jerusalem's Lot. They have received directions from other New Jerseyites which send them not safely to their destination, but through 'Salem's Lot and into the clutches of vampires—vampires the citizens of the surrounding towns know perfectly well exist. The townspeople surrounding 'Salem's Lot do not share this knowledge with outsiders, however, partially out of a sort of perverse Maineness, partially because they do not relish being the laughing stocks of the entire state of Maine, and partially because the occasional outsider is useful. The family gets stuck in the worst snow storm in several decades, and Gerald Lumley, the father, leaves the car running and goes for help. Prissy New Jersey urban dweller though he may be, and unaware outsider though he undoubtedly is, he takes reasonable action. He leaves his wife and daughter safe in the car, with the engine running and goes for help.

Although Booth and Herb Tooklander (Tookey) are willing to help, they are not happy about rushing off to 'Salem's Lot. Neither Booth nor Tookey is an unfeeling man, but they have good reason to avoid The Lot. Nevertheless, they do go out to find the man's family, however reluctantly, and they do, even more reluctantly, try to explain about 'Salem's Lot. Gerald, of course, thinks he has fallen into the clutches of madmen. But Gerald and his family are still outsiders, lacking the secret knowledge which would make them part of the protected community. While Booth and Tookey have crosses, or, ironically, Douai Bibles or St. Christopher medals, as residents who live around 'Salem's Lot do, they do not give Gerald one.[18] The vampires get Gerald and his family just as the vampires get the occasional backpacker or tourist, but they do not get Booth or Tookey, although the closing lines indicates that Booth at least, after an encounter with Francie Lumley, who "was going to be seven for an eternity of nights," fears the "little girl out there" [who he thinks is] "still waiting for her goodnight kiss."[19]

The dis/ease provoked here is double-edged. On the one hand, we could be Gerald and his family, turned (over) to vampires to buy someone else time; on the other hand, we could be the townspeople who must, at some level, acknowledge that they are sacrificing innocent men, women, and children to the vampires, for fear of ridicule and becoming vampire bait themselves. In the novel preceding this short story, *'Salem's Lot*, it is apparent that "the Lot" is a dying town, and the surrounding villages would like to avoid a similar fate. They do not want to become actual vampires, but have no objection to sucking tourists' economic blood. And while Booth and Tookey do attempt to save the family, their actions avail nothing. Perhaps the dis/ease produced here concerns which is the worst fate: to be a vampire or to be complicit in their production. And as long as the occasional backpacker or passerby falls prey to the vampire, the citizens surrounding 'Salem's Lot can sleep more easily at night, festooned with the trappings of Papistry.

King's story, "The Mist" (1986), is in many ways a very typical horror story, drawing on Lovecraftian fears that a monstrous other dimension does exist, peopled by monsters waiting to pounce on the unfortunate inhabitants of Earth. Nevertheless, its construction of community occurs in a manner which reflects, in a contemporary New England resort town, the mechanics of community, Puritan style. David Drayton, the narrator, recounts this story in such a way that the reader knows from the start that the ending is compromised but does not know by what. Thus the dis/ease is omnipresent, and all the seeming normality of the opening scenes must be read against the grain.

The title refers to an odd mist which springs up on the lake one fine summer day. Initially, this project generates dis/ease because the inhabitants do not know what the Arrowhead Project is researching or developing, but since it is a government agency, they suspect the worst. This novella is only incidentally about a secret project, however. The secret project is the catalyst for the dual construction of community. The original community seems to be composed of fairly typical people. The Drayton family, David, Steff, and Billie are depicted very traditionally; they are integral parts of the community, well known and well respected. Their next door neighbor, Brent Norton, a middle-aged attorney in the midst of a mid-life crisis, red Thunderbird convertible and all, is a representative of the "new people." He is also a litigious and unpleasant individual. When a sudden and spectacular storm blows down trees and wires, ruins the Drayton's boathouse, and damages Norton's prized Thunderbird convertible, David offers him a ride into town where he is going to report the many live wires snaking around the ground as well as pick up groceries. Just as they leave, a rather inexplicable mist appears, heading straight for them. Uneasy though David is, he and Billie leave for town with Brent Norton. As David writes later, "I didn't like it. . . . Part of it was the unnerving straight edge of its leading front. Nothing in nature is that even; man is the inventor of straight edges." Steff Drayton does not like the way Norton's eyes "crawled over her tight T-shirt" and declines to go to town. The fractures in that most nuclear of communities are presaged by her reaction to Norton. David recounts pulling out of the driveway: "She had put on her old floppy sunhat, and it cast a band of shadow over her face. . . . I haven't seen my wife since then."[20] Thus the original conflict between Norton and Drayton, caused by a land dispute and Norton's abrasive behavior, adds fuel to the coming catastrophe. The narrator's very matter-of-fact tone, his dry, dispassionate, almost Hemingway-like style, is in strong contrast to the events, and it is this slippage which initially creates the reader's dis/ease.

As is typical of much horror fiction, from Shelley's *Frankenstein* on, one catalyst of the breakdown in community is the mad scientist in hot pursuit of forbidden knowledge, in this case the Arrowhead Project, which has opened a hole in the sky, a rip in the fabric of the earthly dimension, so to speak, and let in a large number of rather repulsive creatures, all of which suck blood quickly from human beings and evoke extreme emotions of horror and repulsion. The main action of the story takes place in a largely indefensible supermarket, an edifice dependent on electricity, with very large plate glass windows. In terms of ironic oppositions, the role of the supermarket has been reversed. As often occurs in horror fiction, the consumers have become the consumed; the supermarket, for the creatures outside, differs little from the place where human beings buy their meat, or from the Chicago Stockyards, or a Chinese restaurant at which one can choose one's dinner.

Behind these glass walls, the characters in the story react to the disaster in ways which subvert King's contention that people are all we have, and that the politics of horror fiction are conservative and affirmative, by foregrounding the dis/ease-provoking view that community is inevitably a fragile social construct, built on certain societal values which not only do not stand up to scrutiny, but often deconstruct almost immediately.[21] The people in the supermarket are prey to the melodies of fragmentation and disestablishment, which King somewhat contrarily contends are the music of horror fiction. As soon as the inhabitants of the supermarket, a microcosm of the community, are put under pressure, the same pattern noted in "The Lottery," "Monsters," and "One for the Road" emerges. As more and more people attempt unsuccessfully to take action to escape, the physical decimation of the survivors is paralleled by the destruction of community. One by one the very brave inhabitants are massacred, until of the original proactive group, only six people are left. The rest have either been disestablished through mental breakdowns or have joined a witch-like religious fanatic who raves in Old Testament language of blood sacrifice, repentance, and sins of the flesh, and who exercises a morbid fascination for an increasingly large number of formerly decent people.

The melodies of disestablishment are embodied in the unappealing form of Mrs. Carmody, who believes in omens, has an unsavory reputation, and a negative influence on people who would formerly have disregarded her ravings. Thus, when it becomes apparent that the defensive measures are at best busy work, the very fragile bonds of community break apart. David, Billy, and four other people decide to leave the doomed community. In a scene which reflects a rock bottom belief in blood rituals as propitiation and appeasement, Mrs. Carmody confronts them as they attempt to leave:

> "These are the sort of people who brought it on!" she shouted. "People who will not bend to the will of the Almighty! . . . It is from their number that the sacrifice must come *From their number the blood of expiation!*"
>
> A rising rumble of agreement spurred her on. . . . *"It's the boy we want! Grab him! Take him! It's the boy we want!"*
>
> They surged forward . . . .[22]

The parallel with Jackson's "The Lottery" comes sharply to mind.

Only four of these people make it to the Scout, and the story ends with David writing down his account in a deserted restaurant. It is a cheap ending because we do not know whether or not they make it to safety or are eaten by monsters, but therein also lies the production of dis/ease. "The Mist" illustrates a dis/easeful, non-affirmative paradigm of community. An apparently healthy and cohesive community, when faced with inexplicable pressure and fears of self-preservation, breaks down and exposes the solitary cave-dweller.

As in "The Lottery," the antinomy in "The Mist" is driven by the Janus-like aspect of horror fiction. Community only exists in and is defined by the face of fragmentation and dissolution. Mrs. Carmody and her followers destroy community in an attempt to preserve it. Perhaps this is because there is no such thing as community, only a societal construct which we use to hide the faces of scapegoating and demonization. In each of the stories discussed above, the ritual of sacrifice is employed in the interests of a community and its survival, but the community is a cannibal; it lives, quite literally on the flesh, blood, and bones of those conveniently labeled "others."

But what makes these "others"? Tessie is decentered and "othered" by the simple expedient of picking the wrong paper. This black dot-inscribed paper has tremendous power and authority. Once picked, it defines Tessie. Ned Rosen is really no different at all from his neighbors until one day he is different. The family in "One for the Road" reflects the same random misfortune. The wrong set of directions, and the trip turns to a sacrifice. Mrs. Carmody targets David and his son, Billy, as the cause of the deadly influx of monsters, but why David or Billy, and why does the supermarket community not turn on Mrs. Carmody? They listen to her delusional ravings, because deep down they share the same contagion, the same need to deploy the strategies by which an "us" vs. "them" paradigm is constructed.

The most frightening aspect of these works is that the parameters of sacrifice are so all encompassing. Why Tessie? Why me? These questions resonate within the texts and within the audience. Halberstam's race/class/gender triad would produce dis/ease because this triad is also part of the mechanisms through which community is constructed, but the very fact that we can point to an easily recognizable trait and claim that this race, this class, or this gender makes someone an "other" mitigates some of the dis/ease. True cultural dread arises when there is no handy marker which signals the demarcations. In the absence of an explanation, the demarcations lose power in one way but in another expand to encompass any/everyone. The fact that the demarcations, demonization, and subsequent sacrifice are so arbitrary and yet so unarguable once deployed makes it impossible to achieve any sort of satisfactory resolution. The questions embedded within these texts do not allow a reason for the choice of victimization other than the random vagaries of chance. Such an element is extremely disquieting in itself, implying as it does that we are not in control of our destinies, that any individual choice we make is ultimately meaningless. A further source of disquiet in these stories is the unwilling recognition that we are not as distinct from the victimizers as we might wish to believe. Such a strong search-light, flashing through our hidden rooms and revealing, in King's pungent phrase, "the cave dweller within," is extremely discomforting. However filtered and indirect, however shielded within the conventions and tropes of popular fiction, such exposure still functions in a disaffirmative way. The acknowledgment that we are creatures of the herd does not in any way validate either the culture or the individual who inhabits it.

In Harlan Ellison's "The Whimper of Whipped Dogs" (1973) we move to fiction even further along the spectrum of disaffirmation; I chose this story because Ellison states that the brutal Kitty Genovese murder is the germ of this story, and the lesson of uninvolvement and disengagement is painfully rendered. New York is described by Ray, the antagonist, as a

cesspool of a city. . . . They take rats and they put them in boxes and where there are too many of them some of the little fuckers go out of their minds and start gnawing the rest to death. *It ain't no different here, baby!* It's rat time for everybody in this madhouse. You can't expect to jam as many people in this stone thing as we do. . . . You can't do it without making the time right for some godforsaken other thing to be born.[23]

When Beth, a somewhat naive young woman from the rural niceties of Bennington, Vermont, moves to New York, she finds the city not only an indifferent but an actively malignant entity, a site which thrives on hate. An outsider to the city, she quickly discovers the truth of life in New York. Soon after her arrival in New York she sees a woman slowly and hideously stabbed to death in front of her building. Beth does nothing and notices in shock that her neighbors also do nothing but watch: "The women with . . . their tongues edging from the corners of their mouths, the men wide eyed and smiling. They all looked as though they were at cock fights."[24]

Beth is shocked and appalled, but she soon discovers that the price of survival, of being a cannibalizing rat rather than a cannibalized rat, depends on worshipping a dark god. In a scene which repeats the opening scene of the story, Beth is nearly murdered while her erstwhile community watches. And she has an epiphany: she suddenly understands that Ray, the man who defined New York for her, had brought her to a party as an offer to join the congregation which worships the dark god. She understands why the people who watched the woman slowly hacked to death did nothing:

. . . and she understood with the blood knowledge of survivors *at any cost* that the reason the witnesses to the death of Leona Ciarelli had done nothing was not that they had been frozen with horror, that they didn't want to get involved, or that they were inured to death by years of television slaughter.

They were worshippers at a Black Mass the city has demanded be staged; not once but a thousand times a day in its insane asylum of steel and stone.[25]

In other words, the city provides the excuse for the strategies of exclusion; we are no more responsible than a rat in an overcrowded cage or an inmate in an insane asylum is responsible for the dark realities of life in New York City. This is handy but untrue, of course, because the people living in New York and not the urban space alone construct the environment. Steel and stone are inanimate objects which may mutely witness the human rats in the maze, but which cannot and do not actively propagate evil. The space is infected by humans, not *vice versa*, but it is certainly less dis/ease provoking to blame the urban space. "It made me do it," the plea of the victimizer/ed, is much more acceptable than "I did it to the place myself."

Beth joins the community which worships this dark god and is spared, at least physically. Her assailant is picked up and rended alive, but she joins a community which can take great pleasure and even sexual satisfaction in the sight of another human being murdered. The story ends with a chilling comment: "At last she was unafraid, and it was so good, so very very good, to be unafraid."[26] The epigraph from Rollo May's *Love and Will*, is perhaps more chilling as it is not fictional:

When inward life dries up, when feeling decreases and apathy increases, when one cannot affect or even genuinely touch another person, violence flares up as a demonic necessity for contact, a mad drive forcing touch in the most direct way possible.[27]

Thus, in this text which affirms nothing, not even a sense of community as marginally admirable as the werewolf community of *The Howling*, the same demarcations and victimizations are at work. In a reversal of "The Lottery," the outsider moves to the insider position, and avoids being the scapegoat, but someone else, in this case a black burglar/murderer, is sacrificed. In those texts which expose community as an agenda-driven construct and refuse easy affirmations, there is always someone who is sacrificed, someone who is cannibalized.

Edward Bryant's "A Sad Last Love at the Diner of the Damned" (1989), invariably generates very strong reactions of horror as well as fascinated repulsion whenever I teach it. These responses in many ways make my point: this story is one of the best examples of my thesis that the horror fiction in which I am interested does not reassure its readers or validate cultural norms. This story echoes George Romero's "Dead" films with much the same disquieting twist. "The zombies are us" says the heroine in *Night of the Living Dead*, when she witnesses some good ole boys lynching a zombie.[28] Bryant's text is extremely dis/ease-provoking for many reasons: its accounts of cannibalism, sadism, and graphic rape (both hetero- and homosexual); the casual reversal of basic paradigms; the complete lack of any cause or explanation for the horrifying demise of community. The narrative structure, with its antinomies of death/life, love/lust, sex/death and its openendedness which provide no ready explanation, resolution or closure make of this one of the most dis/easeful horror fictions I have encountered.

In Bryant's story, zombies have appeared all over the country, posing a major threat to America as we know it. Bryant does not deal with exactly why the zombies have erupted; it is some societal contagion from the larger towns, from the rest of the country, but now it has hit Fort Durham. The zombies, as it turns out, are not the primary cause of dis/ease. What is really disturbing is that Bryant reverses the paradigms by which we define evil and completely deconstructs the human vs. other binary opposition which is so handy and so soothing. Zombies, eaters of the dead, are evil, as are all re-animated dead. Demarcated off from the living, generally defined as demons like the Norse *draugr*, revenants, and other animated corpses, zombies are a perversion of the living. They are in many ways antinomous and unknowable: what animates them is unknown, and they embody the paradox of death-in-life.

Living people, by definition, are not dead zombies; they are civilized and hold their unappeasable appetites in check, honor culturally accepted values and, most importantly, are easily recognizable for the decent people they undoubtedly are. Or so we like to think. . . . And if one cannot define a human by his or her adherence to accepted cultural taboos, by means of spiritual factors which distinguish mankind from lesser beings, then how one knows a human being becomes very problematic. The answer, that in the end there is very little difference between the supposedly non-human zombies and the supposedly human inhabitants of Fort Durham is what causes such strong reactions in Bryant's readers.

The story begins in what closely approximates fairytale language: "There was once a beautiful young woman with hair the color of russet gold." Martha Malinowski, whose family has lived in Fort Durham for three generations and who works at the Cuchara Diner, has dreams of escaping Fort Durham. This sounds like a rather conventional tale of small town life in America, where young women do work in diners and do dream of escape. Martha "haunted the illicit dreams of many in the community. She was largely oblivious to this."[29] Martha as illicit but essentially unaware sacrificial victim is thus hinted at rather early in the narrative. She is not content to remain in Fort Durham, listens to public radio, has an analytical turn of mind, high standards, and pride. Martha is the superior "other" who must in some manner be integrated into the community, who cannot be allowed to have different dreams, different goals, or a different and superior set of values. The monstrous community in "Diner" must, to validate its own class and gender-based values, consume Martha. Since little difference exists between humans and zombies, and both are motivated by perverted and therefore monstrous hungers, Martha's eventual fate at the hands/teeth/cocks of both groups of community works very effectively to establish the community's inability to accept a differing outsider.

Bryant's bucolic rendition of small town/rural life is rudely shattered very early in the story. Some of the men are eating at the diner, as usual, when the first zombies appear. A group of little old ladies "scratch ineffectually against the diner's thick plate glass window, their clawed fingers fluttering like the wings of injured birds." After settling the non-essentials, such as where they came from, which turns out to be a local nursing home and is another way of establishing their identity as former insiders, Billy Gaspar asks,

"We gotta kill 'em?"
"Too old to fuck," said Shine. "Too tough to eat."

Somebody closer to the window said, "See the second from the left? that's ol' Mrs. Davenport, Kevin's grandma."

"The one in the center," said Bertie Hernandez, "is my mother. Fuck her. Let's do it."[30]

This rather matter-of-fact conversation reflects several paradigmatic reversals. Killing and fucking women, any women, are synonymous in Bertie Hernandez' worldview; meat and people are the same commodities, and people are nothing more to him than zombies. When Bertie's mother sees him, she speaks his name, and he shoots her. Billy says, "I didn't think they were supposed to remember anything human," and Miguel replies, "Reflexes, I'll bet. You know, like chickens when you pull off their heads."[31] Bertie, having just blown his mother away, sits at the counter and complains that his bacon is overdone. The setting of a diner with a neon sign flashing, "eat, eat, eat;" the complete lack of emotion which Bertie Hernandez, most notably, displays; the total disconnection from humanity in which every emotion defining humanity is missing; the inability to register any emotion which is not base—virtually every detail calls the idea of community into question. Theoretically, their behavior toward the zombies is justified, but this behavior is not limited to the zombies. As the demarcations between accepted standards of civilized behavior fail, the lines demarcating human and zombie also start to fail. In the end, the mindless hungers of Bertie Hernandez and the zombies are no different at all. What kind of community do we have here when the zombies, the frightful walking dead, display more humanity than the theoretically live human beings?

When Bobby Mack Quintana, the deputy sheriff and another outsider like Martha arrives, the men's contemptuous attitude toward him indicates again the deconstruction of the community at work throughout the text. Martha finally manages to confront Bobby Mack over his dislike of her; he denies it, but in his denial the rotten and prurient undercurrent of this community surfaces. Carl Crump, the high school principal's son, has evidently staked a claim to Martha. And Martha, although she pretends to be oblivious, is at least somewhat aware that in this particular community, "There were men who talked about her, speculated, perhaps even claimed to have touched her in the dark. . . . They had all said things that seemed harmless enough on the surface but she knew meant something else if examined closely enough."[32] Martha is an outsider, although as yet she does not really understand just how far outside the community she actually is. As the contempt for an ordered society increases, Bobby Mack's status as an outsider also becomes more apparent. Their budding relationship, in the midst of what amounts to apocalypse, is, of course, doomed, but it serves to foreground the essential loss of humanity and the powerlessness of love. Discussing the zombies, Martha displays sympathy: "They can't be all bad. . . . I don't think I could kill one if it was somebody I'd loved." Bobby Mack replies, "Hard to say. I reckon we'd do most anything if we were pushed."[33]

With the arrival of the zombies, all the previous limitations on behavior that make communities possible are lost because anything done to a zombie is legal. Thus Bertie, instead of being ostracized and demarcated for his behavior towards his mother, is applauded. As the mayor says at the town meeting when speaking of Bertie and his pals, "We all have to be heroes like that. . . . We've got to watch out for each other and do more than our share." Exactly what watching out for others and doing more than our share comprises is open to question. When Martha and Bobby Mack leave the meeting, Martha, seeing the hostile eyes of people, experiences an epiphany. "They hate me, she thought, somewhat startled by the epiphany. They want me, but they hate me, too."[34] Martha and Bobby Mack see the Bertie Bunch stringing up a zombie, which means that civilized behavior, within which is embedded the very idea of community, has declined yet another notch. As I noted earlier, this scene recalls, deliberately I would guess, Romero's *Night of the Living Dead*, in which one of the final scenes makes the dissolution of boundaries between humans and zombies very clear.

The strategies of exclusion are now increasingly aimed at Martha and Bobby Mack. Bertie is one of the men who thinks he has staked out a claim to Martha, and he is openly contemptuous of Bobby Mack:

"You gonna go out for a ride in the deputy's rice-burner?"
"I'm going to give her a ride home," said Bobby Mack.
"See that that's the only ride you give her."[35]

In their next confrontation, Bertie will refer to Bobby Mack as "Deputy Dawg" and "college boy," thereby demarcating him from the good ole boys on three levels: the "rice-burner" he drives, a Suzuki Samurai; his powerlessness as enforcer of the law; and his college education. Bertie Hernandez, once again refused by Martha, drinks himself to a beast-like state and decides to rape Martha, aided in this venture by the members of his community, Miguel and Shine: "What I propose is screw this little girl until my pecker comes out her asshole." When Henry Roybal, a good man, says he cannot let Bertie do that, Bertie shoots him dead. He also tells Martha not to look for rescue from Bobby Mack because Bobby Mack is dead: "I just put him out of his misery. . . . Woulda done the same thing for a dog."[36]

Bertie, however, has underestimated Bobby Mack; as he starts to rape Martha, Bobby Mack comes through the door. Bobby Mack, still himself despite his zombie status, does save Martha. Unfortunately, the residents of Fort Durham do not change their essential natures when they become zombies. As Martha attempts to escape with Bobby Mack, she realizes all her nightmares have come to the Diner: all the men and women who lusted after her in life, whom she refused and tried to ignore, are now after her. Bobby Mack, one against many, is unable to defend her, and in a climactic scene which completely refuses the possibility of any affirmation of community, Martha is raped nearly to death by the zombies and those who hate her dead as they hated her living. The high school principal and his son, both with enormous erections, the pastor and his wife, and the priest are all participants in an unholy communion. Martha manages to get Bobby Mack's pistol, hoping for one bullet:

> The zombies inside her grunted and heaved. . . . Dead eyes looked at her but none of them *saw*. They never had. Her vision grayed.
> The zombies kept coming—
> —and coming—
> Just one bullet, Martha thought.
> There was.[37]

The explicit, graphic sex, the images of humans as beasts and people as meat, and the preoccupation with sexual violence are, as I stated earlier, extremely disturbing elements in this story, and do not pale with a re-reading. This story, in the tradition of Clive Barker's *Books of Blood*, is obviously heavily invested in veil rending. Thus, the graphic and loveless fucking, the lack of demarcation between the "safe" Diner and the outside community, and most horrific, the fact that being a good and decent person does not matter. Martha, Bobby Mack, and Henry, the only arguably good people in the story, the only characters with whom we can engage, end up horrifically dead. When the horror, rather than being safely encapsulated within the "other," is forcibly and graphically shown to reside in "us," the societal dis/ease becomes almost unbearable. Beyond the concern with the graphic sex and cannibalism, what really disquiets the reader is the very unwilling recognition of people we may know.

My last example may seem anticlimactic as a text with which to close a chapter on community. Compared to Ellison and Bryant, the horror is very ambiguous and very understated; but Anne Rivers Siddons' *The House Next Door* (1978) confirms the argument that the most disaffirmative horror centers not on the monster but on the mundane, and provokes a great deal of cultural dread on two levels. First, the people are recognizable as ordinary people even more readily than in other texts I have examined. On the second, the ambiguity of the events is as dis/ease provoking as in a text like Henry James' *The Turn of the Screw*. Siddons does an extremely effective job of revealing the fragility of community and its antinomous nature whereby inclusion is constructed by various exclusions. As she states in her foreword,

. . . the whole point of this book, of course, is not so much the house and its peculiar, terrible power but what effect it has on the neighborhood, and on the relationships between neighbors and friends and between families. . . . This has always been the power of the supernatural to me—that it blasts and breaks relationships between people and other people and between people and their world and in a way between people and the very essences of themselves. And the blasting and breaking leaves them defenseless and alone. [38]

The novel's protagonists, Walter and Colquitt Kennedy, are upper-middle-class, genteel-old-money, old-Southern-family WASPs who inhabit an exclusive Atlanta neighborhood, once again a neighborhood which shares the same values, enjoys the same activities, and has a strong and cohesive bond. The characters are not to everyone's taste. I find Colquitt Kennedy almost a parody of a self-referential Dink type, with her rigid class delineations, complacent self-absorption, and unavailing attempts to keep her life exactly as she wants it on the somewhat facile ground that she and Walter are deserving of such a life. Stephen King, analyzing this tale at some length, notes that "Colquitt herself is particularly unappetizing: vain, class conscious, money conscious, sexually priggish and vaguely exhibitionist."[39] But she and Walter have what they consider a perfect relationship; certainly they have a very solid marriage, as do all the people in the neighborhood. Siddons is writing about a rather elite community in which the people are homogeneous in terms of race, class, and social values: they are all concerned with the surface of their lives, with appearances and class markers, with a way of living that is almost purely self-referential. In this neighborhood, nothing unpleasant intrudes. Since they all hold approximately the same old family traditions, have lived in the neighborhood all their married lives, are in approximately the same financial bracket, educational level, and social status, there is no apparent reason for the strategies of exclusion to emerge.

The House Next Door changes all that. The news that a house is going up is the first crack in the Kennedys', as well as the neighborhood's, carefully constructed life. It will ruin Colquitt's view and her privacy, as the windows of this house will look onto her patio. The house, however, is stunningly beautiful and seems to grow out of the land. It is promising young architect Kim Dougherty's first house, built for a vapid little rich girl and her retiring young husband. The couple, named Pie (for sweetie-pie) and Buddy Haralson, are cloyingly cute but harmless. As the house approaches completion, however, a series of seemingly unrelated mishaps occur. Pie falls down the stairs and miscarries, something kills the wildlife and rends the corpses apart, and Pie's new puppy, a replacement for the lost baby, is also killed. The neighborhood blames a wild dog for the massacred wildlife although animal control cannot confirm this, and the woods are neither dark nor deep enough to hide a truly ferocious wild animal. At Pie's housewarming, utter disaster strikes, which in this neighborhood might mean nothing worse than having spots on the champagne flutes or running short of lobster canapé. In The House Next Door, however, disaster is never trivial. Buddy and Lucas Abbott, his mentor at the law firm, are found locked together in an obviously homosexual embrace, and Pie's father drops dead. The marriage is destroyed and two careers are ruined: exit the Haralsons.

The second couple who buy the house, Anita and Buck Sheehan, also meet disaster. She is an emotionally fragile woman emerging from a complete catatonic breakdown due to the loss of her only son, and he is a former alcoholic who lost his job due to philandering and drinking. They have come to Atlanta to make a new life. The neighborhood genuinely likes them, and they are a much better fit in age and interests than the Haralsons were, but again disaster strikes. Anita mistakes one of Claire and Roger's sons for her dead son, and starts seeing TV movies showing the death of that son in Vietnam, which causes a euphemistically labeled "setback." The Kennedys offer the Sheehan's their beachhouse for a few days, but when Kim goes with Colquitt to water Anita's plants, they suddenly find themselves engaged in entirely involuntary sexual foreplay. Walter appears unexpectedly and almost kills them. It is Kim who yells at everyone to get out of the house; mysteriously, Colquitt and Kim's lust and Walter's killing rage, along with Colquitt's "queer flattened childlike suspension" disappear.

This incident gives Kim the idea that the house is possessed. He has been unable to complete a single project since he designed and built this house, and this, coupled with his and Colquitt's completely inexplicable behavior, convinces him that there is something wrong with The House Next Door. This is an odd assertion because nothing supernatural or inexplicable has happened in the house. Wildlife does die, women do fall and miscarry, men do have unacknowledged sexual proclivities, creative forces do dry up, and a married woman can certainly find herself almost in *flagrante delicto* with an attractive younger man, something to which middle-aged husbands often take strong exception. The Sheehans' problems certainly predated the house, so on the face of the events, this explanation is bizarre. Haunted or possessed houses always have a series of supernatural events, poltergeists, cold areas, clanking chains, or moaning, gibbering voices. This is how one knows they are haunted. This house is less than a year old and has no history. Nevertheless, Kim's original belief is the right one:

> "It is damned, that house. It's a greedy house. It takes. You said, once, Col, that it would bring out the best in whoever lived there. You were wrong. It takes the best. It took that miserable Pie's kid, and her marriage and her daddy. It took that poor sonufabitch Buddy's whole future. It took that Abbott guy's future. It's taking Anita Sheehan's sanity . . . and it took my talent. And tonight it almost took you and Walter from each other for good."

Neither Walter nor Colquitt can accept Kim's premise; as she says,

> "I don't know how or why it happened, and I am ashamed and sick about it, but it's not your fault, and it's *nothing in that house.* . . . It was something in me, something . . . sick and awful that I didn't know I had. . . . But I will not listen to you talking like this anymore. You've let this dry spell you're having make you sick."[40]

The ambiguity and the sense of unresolvable paradox arise again because it is entirely possible that the whole series of events has nothing to do with the house at all. Kim's afternoon visits to Colquitt have aroused some snide neighborhood innuendo, and Walter is a trifle jealous of Kim; it does not take a demonic house to escalate such a relationship beyond platonic, nor is Walter's reaction all that atypical. This doubled perception follows the reader all the way through the text; even at the end, when Walter and Colquitt have decided to burn the house rather than let anyone ever live there again, the reader still wonders.

Meanwhile, Anita gets a telephone call which she claims is from her dead son, that sends her into delusions and an institution; Buck, whose previous adultery was one of the reasons for Anita's catatonic trance, is found engaging in sex with Virginia Guthrie, the most ladylike woman on the block, while his wife, newly home from another hospital stay, watches him and retreats permanently to catatonia. Virginia Guthrie is a woman for whom the appellation "a real Southern lady" has meaning. The whole episode is so unbelievable to Colquitt that it causes her to re-examine her out-of-hand dismissal of Kim's theory and decide that too many catastrophic and inexplicable events have happened for it to be merely coincidence.

Since this community is based, simultaneously and inextricably, on both closeness and distance, Colquitt cannot bring herself to tell anyone except Walter what she saw. This inability either creates or shows up the first cracks in the community. Demarcation based on secret knowledge is at work as has been the case with Ellison's story and King's "One for the Road." Claire, who is Colquitt's best friend, is hurt at Colquitt's refusal to talk as well as the Guthries' sudden departure on a round the world cruise. The issue of trust surfaces, and Claire feels that Colquitt possesses secret knowledge which she is unwilling to share.

The Sheehans disappear and the house goes on the market yet again. This time the Greenes buy it. Norman, Susan, and Melissa Greene are enchanted by the house, the neighborhood, and the exclusivity. Norman Greene is a thoroughly unpleasant man, an abusive bully and a rampant social climber, who married his wife for her money, which he spends attempting unsuccessfully to look like a real live WASP. Ironically, he is referred to as a Nazi type, but he is, according to Claire Swanson, a half-Jew, "trying to pass for an Episcopalian . . . one of those Ivy League Jews who . . . would sell his soul to the devil if his name could be Lowell or Cabot or Lodge." Colquitt also dislikes him, and for good reason; he is patronizing, condescending, and a racist himself.

Norman's function in the text, aside from being "a tight-assed, bullying, pretentious prick,"[41] is to display the forces of demonization lurking beneath the social surface. His unpleasantness does not cancel out either Claire's or Colquitt's covert anti-Semitism. He may, after all, be the world's most abusive husband and father without his Jewish heritage having anything to do with it. Claire's commentary, implying as it does that he would be different if he his name were Lodge, reeks of both class and race biases which cast a new light on this supposedly pleasant community. Since Susan Greene is much like both Colquitt and Claire in background and interests, her pathetic doormat behavior generally goes unchallenged. Thus, the lines of demarcation and demonization are rapidly surfacing in this heretofore happy and cohesive community. It is, at this point, questionable whether the house is demonic in and of itself, or merely a reflection of a privileged enclave who never wished for either a new house or new residents. So far, the demonization is aimed at Norman Greene, an outsider. But when Colquitt, who is feeling increasingly dis/easeful about The House Next Door, tries to warn Claire to keep her distance from Susan Greene, the demarcation/demonization lines abruptly shift, and Colquitt, the neighborhood insider, is on her way to becoming a pariah. Claire reacts angrily, "Are you jealous of Susan Greene? Because if you are, then you're really a spoiler."[42] But Colquitt cannot or will not reveal her knowledge, the knowledge that makes her surer and surer it is the house that is a destructive force. The upshot is the breakdown of the deep and longstanding friendship between Claire and Colquitt. While Colquitt claims she is not jealous but only trying to protect Claire, when she first met Susan, she immediately thought that the friendship between Clair and Susan was dangerous, and then acknowledged her own jealousy.

That community is central to this novel is unarguable, but what exactly are the forces responsible for invoking the strategies of exclusion? Is it a house in which a series of unfortunate but natural events has occurred, or is Colquitt responsible? She narrates the whole tale, after all, starting at almost the end and recounting everything. As in other tales of anti-closure and ambiguity, the narrator is the key. Can we believe Colquitt, or can we not? If she is, in Wayne Booth's terms, reliable, then she is recounting an understated but heroic tale of her attempts to save her community, attempts which result in her and her husband losing their community and probably their lives in their efforts to save it. If she is not, this is the tale of a spoiled and self-centered neurotic, perhaps the victim of an obsession, who brings her ostracization on herself, and ruins her life and her husband's life for no good reason. By novel's end, Colquitt and Walter have lost everything—friends, community membership, status, Walter's ad agency, Colquitt's clients, their two cats, and Kim. Colquitt expects their lives will also be lost, yet still they proceed.

As events unfold, swiftly and horrendously, the Greenes, who want so desperately to fit in and who try too hard to do so, give a Twelfth Night party at which the electricity goes out, and Melissa, their child, soils herself. Again these events are apparently explicable; electricity does go out with winter storms, and children with colitis cannot always control their bodily functions. While the guests are distressed for the child, it is Norman Greene's unbelievable behavior which drives them away. Again, the house, if house it is, has attacked, taking away the quality its owners most wish to have. Norman Greene wished to display his perfect house, wife, and child in a perfect holiday setting, and the evening ends in disaster. Susan Greene, moreover, confides to Claire that she is not the bubble-headed scatterbrain that she appears to be; before buying this house, she ran two houses efficiently, was secretary of the Junior League, and entertained. It is only in this house that she cannot even seem to get the simple everyday things accomplished. And Norman

Greene is so anal that the meat in the freezer is packed by type, weight, and date of purchase.

Colquitt persuades Walter to go tell the Greenes what she thinks is going on. Naturally, since the Kennedys sound increasingly like raving monomaniacs, and since electrical and bowel failures are not supernatural, Norman Greene declines to believe Walter. He chooses to believe that it is a WASP plot to scare him out of the neighborhood. Claire, in a furious reaction to Colquitt's actions, accelerates the strategies of exclusion: "I don't want to see you again, Colquitt, I'm going to tell everyone I know that you're a jealous, vindictive, *crazy* woman. People ought to be *warned* about you."[43] Claire is as good as her word, and Colquitt begins to feel, very acutely, what it is like to be the scapegoat, the butt of ridicule.

Later, however, an hysterical Claire comes to announce that her son Duck has dropped out of Yale and married his long time and now suddenly pregnant girlfriend, Libby. While this moment lacks the feeling of high tragedy, as indeed much of this book does, there is no doubt that it is a devastating blow to Claire. Interestingly, she blames it on the house: "That damned evil, hovering, sneaking, crouching monstrous killer of a house over there." Claire, in another escalation of the deconstruction of the community, admits her fault to Colquitt and Walter—she has indeed been spreading tales about them—but absolutely refuses to help Colquitt take action. She says she and her family will move, and she will deny any conversation on the house took place; she does not, in other words, care what happens to the neighborhood, or to her friend Susan Greene, or what price Walter and Colquitt pay as long as her family is safe:

> "I care about her and the child, but not enough to have everyone talking about me and my family the way they are about you and Colquitt. And I know that will haunt me to my grave. I can never never make it up to you, but it's *not* going to happen to us."[44]

Colquitt and Claire attempt to resume their old friendship, but the demarcations have become too well established, the demonization and scapegoating too advanced. As Colquitt says, explaining why she and Claire could not go back, "The house . . . lay between us like the carcass of some great dead animal.[45] But it is both more and less than the house, even the demonized house in which both believe. Colquitt, accepting the role of the sin-eater, one who takes the burdens of others on her own shoulders, has been scapegoated as well. There is no way back from such a doubled exclusion. Claire Rogers, close to Susan and Colquitt though she is, has decided to save her own family first at the expense of friendship, integrity, and common morality. Instead of telling Susan that what Colquitt has said about the house is true, she abandons two women for whom she claims friendship, and the friendship she and Colquitt share is the kind of friendship by which one defines oneself. Claire is abandoning more than her house and more than her community; she is also abandoning the qualities which make her Claire. As she says, she cares—but not that much. This accounts for her behavior, unless, of course, having failed to get Colquitt to deal with her destructive obsession, Clair has declined to feed the obsession and reluctantly retreated from Colquitt. In either reading, community becomes increasingly fragile and compromised.

Many readers of this text must wonder how important our communities are, and how we choose among communities, but some of the dis/ease is also engendered by the deliberate ambiguities structured within the text. Siddons claimed she wrote it as a ghost story, although a ghost is conspicuously lacking. As Stephen King points out, however,

> . . . much of the walloping effect of *The House Next Door* comes from the author's nice grasp of social boundaries. Any writer of the horror tale has a clear—perhaps even a morbidly overdeveloped—conception of where the country of the socially (or morally or psychologically) acceptable ends and that great white space of Taboo begins. Siddons is better at marking the edges of the socially acceptable from the socially night-marish than most.[46]

Siddons, understanding social boundaries so well, also understands that these boundaries are absolute; overstep them as Colquitt and Walter do, threaten the community with knowledge it would rather not have and perhaps cannot survive, and the community will demarcate, demonize, scapegoat, and sacrifice the offender in no time flat.

At a later party, one Norman bullies Susan into having, the invitations do not get mailed, no one shows except Claire and Roger, and when Norman Greene reveals that Melissa is not his but "that dirty, stinking, *reeking*, whining little bastard I gave my *name* to," the Swansons literally flee.[47] They get almost to their own driveway, their own sanctuary, when they hear the gunshots. Susan Greene has killed her husband, her daughter, and then herself. Colquitt and Walter decide they have no choice but to publicly warn people about the house, but again Claire Swanson refuses to help even though she has now moved and is safely away from the neighborhood. "For all I know there is some kind of . . . contagion that comes from it, some horrible kind of virus." There certainly is, but it is not the external virus which Claire claims; it is an internal virus, the same virus that demonizes the "other," and prefers scapegoating to acceptance. Claire curses Colquitt as her last words:

"You're dead, Colquitt! You're a walking dead woman! Get out of my house!"[48] Thus the ritual of exclusion works. Colquitt, her former best friend, has no existence to Claire. Although we do not know what happens to Colquitt and Walter, there is no reason to assume that they live after destroying the house; nor do we know whether Claire is pleased when her curse comes true. But the strategies of exclusion are certainly in full bloom.

Walter and Colquitt attempt, without success, to make the situation public to keep the house off the market. No media will touch it except the *National Enquirer*-like Ernie Lipschultz who wants to know two things: the degree of exclusivity and the asking price. Walter sells his half of the advertising agency to avoid its failure, and Colquitt's accounts drop her. They are asked to resign from their club, threatened with lawsuits, and isolated from the community. They wonder at times about their sanity but cannot move and let the situation go on as Claire and Roger have done. They fear that the house will kill them, but they fear it will somehow separate them even more. The process of demonization continues inexorably as they are hounded, vandalized, and ostracized by the very people for whom they are doing this. Outcast as they are, however, they are fair game.

The climax occurs when Kim, the once promising architect, returns and plans to buy the house and live in it. Kim is now convinced that "if awful things happened to the people over there, it was because they were awful people to begin with!"[49] This is comforting, perhaps, but not supported by anything we know. Colquitt then realizes, or thinks she realizes, that Kim is the vector, the source of the contagion, which has already killed people in earlier projects and will continue as long as he lives. Walter kills him, and they decide to burn the house down with him in it. Colquitt finds their beloved cats, cats who were alive when Kim came to the house at 9:00 p.m., dead on the patio. The last line of Colquitt's saga is "I wonder how it will happen," but that is not the last line of novel. In the epilogue, the plans resurface, and a young couple prepares to build the house because "It looks like it is growing right out of the ground, doesn't it? It looks like it's alive."[50]

The epilogue denies the resolution that the reader may have painfully achieved. The loss of community, Colquitt and Walter's gallant stand, and all the deaths, have been for nothing; the forces that destroy community are not so easily leashed, the dark gods not so easily propitiated by human sacrifice. Such a text does not really work at all to reaffirm conservative values or reactionary virtues, but it does work to generate and produce the twentieth-century angst so prevalent in discussions of contemporary culture. As *The House Next Door* indicates, these virtues, in the face of the essential constructs of community, matter not at all.

In this particular text, it is difficult to isolate the most important factors generating dis/ease. It is easier to isolate the ineffective mechanisms of denial, which say such things as not my family, let the other guy do it, they deserved it, or they're crazy. Dis/ease is also caused by the possibility, never entirely stilled throughout the narrative, that we may be listening to someone who is paranoid or obsessed; while Colquitt seems very sane, even matter of fact, this is no guarantee of sanity because we must rely on her voice throughout the novel. Even more dis/easeful is the conflict between the family and the community. Is one obligated to put the community ahead of one's family, and if so, where is that line drawn? While Claire is wrong to demonize Colquitt in the eyes of her friends and neighbors, whether she is wrong to refuse to take any action that may further harm her family is another matter entirely. Whether Colquitt and Walter are right or wrong to murder Kim is less problematic than the epilogue, which indicates that all their puny attempts to destroy evil are ineffectual; the *House Next Door* will repeat its demonic behavior as humans will repeat theirs.

Denial of responsibility can only go so far, and one cannot deny that Colquitt and Walter do put their lives on the line for a belief. Very dis/ease-provoking as well is the destruction of the community we witness; that neighborhood is now haunted, if not by a demonic house, by the memories of demarcation, demonization, scapegoating, and sacrifice with which the inhabitants must live. If Colquitt and Walter are indeed killed by the house, what will the neighbors think? This ironic question echoes through the text, but what will the neighbors, who turned their backs on them, feel when the Kennedys are found dead? What price then will their denials and their community fetch? Certainly they can circle the wagons against the dark knowledge that it was not really the house that destroyed the community, but the inhabitants of the community; but such knowledge seeps out at inconvenient times. Unlike the villagers in "The Lottery," they do not have propitiation rituals to hide behind. Unlike the people trapped in the grocery store, they are not under active threat. Unlike Karyn, they cannot simply escape the corrupted community. Unlike the students in University, or the Chowder Society, or Alan Pangborn and Polly Chalmers, they do not take a stand against corruption. Unlike the "Losers Club," they do not take a stand against the destruction of community. Who would be Claire Swanson? Like the villagers who send the tourists to *'Salem's Lot*, or worship a dark and corrupted urban god, and very like the villagers who sacrifice one of their own, they do destroy the vill.[51]

Sorting Out Different Styles of Malignity

INTRODUCTION

"Utopia, this century has learned the hard way,
usually bears a resemblance to hell."[1]

Another aspect of community which generates intense cultural dis/ease appears in novels of apocalypse and novels of utopia/dystopia. Frequently enough these categories are not mutually exclusive. Non-dystopian societies frequently face apocalypse as a result of their dystopian elements; post-apocalyptic novels often play out a compromised scenario of redemption, one which may result in the restoration of a more utopian society, or in the utopia-to-dystopia pattern. Some redemptive/apocalyptic novels explore the possibilities of individual redemption in a dystopian society, although such novels still stress the impossibility of acceptance within the society. Societies which seem to be utopian, and which, in fact, define themselves as utopian, are actually dystopias because the strategies of exclusion often determine which citizens obtain utopia and which are excluded. While dystopian texts do deal with a wide range of scenarios, each of these texts creates dis/ease by confronting the reader with an articulated disjunction between the accepted cultural model of government and the dismal reality.

In general, these texts are to be distinguished from those discussed in the previous chapters because more overt and specific political agendas surface, and an entire political entity is depicted as opposed to one neighborhood or one village. While the communities discussed in Chapters 6, 7, and 8 can often be profitably read in political terms, such as the elements of the Holocaust possibly present in "The Lottery," or the concern with McCarthyism in "The Monsters Are Due on Maple Street," these works focus primarily on the social structures and foundations of community, while a specific political system is often absent or relatively decentered. Conversely, in dystopian texts, important though the individual is, the governmental system portrayed is of primary importance.

The cultural model which exists for most denizens of a particular political system is generally understood to be positive in nature. Americans, for example, have strongly held views on democracy which frequently discount the negatives lurking beneath the surface. "Government of, by, and for the people," a government in which the citizenry is actively and directly involved for the good of the entire population, is a common basis for the American governmental model even though it is largely absent in actual practice. By definition, after all, the country is a republic. But the myths, legends, and handed-down traditions behind the actual government are in many ways more important than the hard, dry truth. Grammar-school children imbibe the myth of a free and equal society with their midmorning snacks; the hard realities, which come later, if at all, are an overlay on the essential myth. The Abraham Lincoln who walked untold miles to return a penny too much which he received in change before he learned to read by firelight is far more real and far more important than the pragmatic politician who did not free all the slaves. In David Brin's *The Postman*, for example, the postal service is honored after one no longer exists much more than was the case either pre-Armageddon, or, indeed, in actual practice.

In actual practice, the government is often perceived as some monstrous and disparate entity and is widely distrusted. "The government" is thought to impinge on the lives of Americans, tax them unjustly, regulate nearly every aspect of their lives, and have almost complete power over them. Such governmental entities as the DEA, ATF, FBI, and CIA can apparently invade our personal space, destroy or confiscate our property, and arrest us for no good reason. Neither the Constitution nor the Bill of Rights, which supposedly protect us from our government's excesses, seem very effective. Scenarios of the government run amuck, which reflect a dis/ease with the government, frequently appear in horror fiction, particularly such novels as Stephen King's *Firestarter* and *The Stand*, and Margaret Atwood's *The Handmaid's Tale*.

The government is commonly treated as though it has a separate life of its own, as some monstrous and alien body. The belief that the government is "them," the Beltway people, those suits in Washington, is increasingly prevalent. The idea that "the government" ought to get out of our lives is commonplace, as if we are not the government and the government is some intruding entity. And yet, underneath the cynical reality, lies a continuing belief in the myth. The idea of the storehouse of popular assumptions with everything jumbled on the shelf is again useful. A large portion of the dis/ease generated by apocalyptic and dystopian texts comes from the antinomous conflict between the ideal cultural model of American government and the citizenry's views of the actual working government. Dystopian horror texts emphasize the monstrous aspect of the government and the corruption to which its abuses of power inevitably lead. Many, if not all, of the strategies of exclusion-figure in these politicized novels, and while the concept of community is by no means absent, novels of apocalypse/utopia /dystopia use specific political systems to reflect and generate cultural dread. In horror fiction, a utopia is constructed on the bodies of those who do not get the promised perfection, on those who are victims of the strategies of exclusion.

Whatever pattern emerges, the reader recognizes that each of these texts, however exaggerated, is firmly based in the material culture of its time and is "about" that culture. All these works subvert the idea that these fictional societies are really different from those in which we live. To read of an alien civilization, a radically othered civilization, which is wiped out by its own stupidity is not as dis/ease provoking, as productive of cultural dread, as to read of a society which does not have tentacles but which does, however stereotypically portrayed, include our friends and neighbors. I stress the absence of the purely alien or fantastic because while the some of the events may indeed appear fantastic, they are carefully rooted within the possible.

Readers might well question why the dystopian texts I have chosen to discuss are horror novels. I could answer this question in several ways. I could say that novels concerned with apocalypse and eschatology naturally fall within the bounds of horror fiction, as death and extinction are extremely dis/ease provoking subjects. I could say that these texts produce at least one of the triad of emotions which are central to horror fiction: if a text evokes terror, horror, or revulsion, as I contend my chosen texts do, then labeling them horror seems reasonable. I could say that most of these texts have freaks, demons, or monsters and are, *ipso facto*, horror novels. I could say that every text I purchased for this study was physically located on the horror shelf of my friendly and helpful used bookstore. In other words, people other than myself, people not trained in literary theory and genre studies, instinctively recognized the horror elements, although they could not articulate them specifically. "What else would you call it?" and "Where else would you stock it?" were typical answers when I asked everyday readers and bookstore owners about the generic question.[2] Such critics as Gene Wolf, David Hartwell, Stephen King, or Jane Tompkins would argue that the bookstore owners and readers recognize the effect, the emotional engagement, the phobic pressure points, or the type.

In Chapter 2, I read Jerzy Kosinski's *The Painted Bird*, a mainstream, canonical text in which dystopia is foregrounded, as horror fiction of the most dis/easeful kind. And if, as I contend, one function of horror fiction is as allegorical vehicle to foreground man's inhumanity to man, dystopian texts fall naturally within such a classification. One answer to why we could define dystopian texts as horror lies in the function of horror fiction: horror fiction reveals the body beneath the sheet, so to speak, and actively denies and resists the more affirmative cultural models which we use to tell reassuring stories about ourselves and our communities. Because the texts I discuss invoke the emotional triad so important to horror fiction and because the resolutions involved are either compromised or absent, because these texts showcase man's inhumanity to man, I define them as within the boundaries of horror fiction.

9

DYSTOPIAS OF THE HUMAN HEART:
APOCALYPSE, REGENERATION AND REDEMPTION

"Evil is anyone outside the tribe. Evil works by dehumanizing the Other."[1]

While affirmative dystopia sounds not only oxymoronic but also outside the realms of horror fiction, I contend that the relevant texts betray the principal characteristics of horror fiction: dehumanizing narratives and situations, deployment of the strategies of exclusion to ostensibly good ends, and fictional communities which are often monstrous bodies, as horrible as any animate figures, human or otherwise. Texts which deal with the antinomous concept of affirmative dystopia call for rejection of or resistance to the dystopia, or an attempt to rebuild a post-apocalyptic community, intentionally avoiding the elements which created the dystopia in the first place. Such texts are irremediably conflicted and generate the cultural dis/ease so intrinsic to horror fiction because rejection, resistance, and rebuilding cannot occur in a vacuum; the dominant culture still informs the process, often contaminating even the most positive conclusions.

Robert McCammon's *Gone South*, Stephen King's *Firestarter*, McCammon's *Swan Song*, and David Brin's post-apocalyptic *The Postman* are good examples of texts which achieve affirmation in the midst of a pervasively dystopic situation. What makes such texts affirmative is that the characters, rather than accepting apocalypse and dystopia, survive and often achieve redemption.

While all four of these texts concern dystopian societies, the first two focus more on an individual reaction to a dystopia, while the final text is more concerned with a societal reaction. My third example, McCammon's *Swan Song* provides a bridge between these two groupings, placed as it is between individual reactions to dystopia and communitarian reconstructions. McCammon's *Gone South* and King's *Firestarter* reflect differing strategies for inhabiting a dystopian world. In both *Gone South* and *Firestarter*, the protagonists discover that such accommodations as are possible call for active rejection of the dominant culture. By invoking and inverting the strategies of exclusion, they make their own accommodations to the dystopian society which exists around

them; furthermore, by refusing to accept either monster status or culpability, they refuse to permit the strategies of exclusion to define them.
These texts foreground the importance of the individual in a dystopian
society which has demarcated and demonized them, while *Swan Song*
provides a third option; instead of either rejecting the society or forcing
her acceptance within it, Swan is the catalyst who provides the impetus
for reconstruction of the society. Like *Swan Song*, *The Postman*, my
final text, concerns the reconstruction of a post-apocalyptic society dev-
astated by nuclear war. *The Postman* reflects the morally problematic
choices this society makes in reconstruction, choices which invoke the
strategies of exclusion to both positive and negative effect.

While these four texts fall within an affirmative model of horror fiction, they do so on two different levels. Both *Gone South* and *Firestarter*
are affirmative, as the protagonists do not accept the dystopian society's
right to demarcate, demonize, scapegoat and sacrifice them; but this
affirmation, as in many other horror texts, is highly conflicted. While
neither protagonist compromises with a dystopian society, their refusal
to interact with the system also negates the possibility of change, and
affirmation is restricted to an individual level. Although the possibility
of another cataclysmic event hangs over the heads of Swan's world,
Swan, the protagonist of *Swan Song*, does apparently accomplish the
miracle of regeneration, making this a highly affirmative text with the
same *caveats* noted in other affirmative horror fictions I have discussed.
By examining the strategies involved in reconstructing societies, *The
Postman*, the final text of this spectrum calls the possibility of defeating
dystopia into question. The last two texts suggest that individual effort
alone is not enough, but they also point out that community cannot solve
all problems, either. All these authors, by acknowledging that dystopic
societies cannot be easily dismantled or reformed, avoid the traps into
which the more facile writers of horror fiction tend to fall.

The title of McCammon's *Gone South* (1992) refers to a moment in
a person's life both apocalyptic and irreversible as well as a literal geographical designation. The first lines of the novel, "It was hell's season
and the air smelled of burning children. This smell was what destroyed
Dan Lambert's taste for barbecued pork sandwiches," clearly place us in
horror territory."[2] These lines, evoking as they do bodies as commodities,
echo dis/easefully throughout the entire novel. One reason that the novel
defines contemporary America so effectively as dystopic and horrific is
the prevailing images of people as bodies, commodities, or units of value.

Dan Lambert, the main protagonist, prides himself on having never
"gone south" during his time in Vietnam, or even afterward when dealing with a souring marriage, Agent-Orange induced leukemia, a child

retarded as the result of Agent Orange, and a society which has no place for him. To "go south" is to give up, accept defeat, or let his fellow soldiers down, an action Lambert has fiercely resisted. He is dying of cancer, out of work in a boom-gone-bust construction cycle, and living increasingly on the edge. When Emory Blanchard, the callous vice-president of the bank, attempts to repossess his truck, the last thing of value Dan possesses and something he must have to try to get work, Dan "goes south." Blanchard's snide commentary about Vietnam vets, "We could have cleaned up over there if so many of you fellas hadn't been on drugs," and his refusal to grant a paltry week's extension pushes Dan over the edge. After Dan pulls a gun on the loan officer and kills him, he thinks, *"I've gone south . . . Gone south, after all this time."* In many ways, this action is a microcosm of the apocalyptic/dystopic form of horror fiction. Lambert experiences his own personal apocalypse, and in order to come to terms with it must reject contemporary American society with all of its materialistic values. While the society might not be dystopian for all the inhabitants, as is the case in the globally apocalyptic texts, both Dan Lambert and Arden Halliday, the female protagonist, are searching for utopia in a world which has discarded them.

As Dan says to Blanchard, in an attempt to refute the man's ignorant commentary on the loss of the Vietnam War:

"It [Agent Orange] could kill a jungle in a week. What it could do to a man didn't show up for a long time later. That's what bein'a good soldier did to me, Mr. Blanchard. I came home full of poison and nobody blew a trumpet or held a parade."[3]

Once his value as a worker, whether as a grunt in 'Nam or a working body in construction is gone, he faces a society that has discarded him. He can try to get a day's work in construction or disappear into a veterans' hospital: in either case, he is a non-person—one of those men lined up hoping for a call, one of those faceless veterans tucked neatly out of sight in some institution or another. Once society has safely contained him, it can also safely ignore him.

Arden Halliday is a young woman who, due to a monstrous, unsightly, and unremovable birthmark, is also a non-person. People do not see Arden; they see a metonymy: a walking disfigurement. Unable to tolerate a society that reduces her to a monstrosity, she has set off on a classic quest; childhood tales of a legendary faith healer who lives in the bayous have enticed her to go and find the "Bright Girl" whom she believes will heal her. She thus also turns her back on a dystopic world in pursuit of a personal utopia.

The other major characters in this novel are also societal misfits, who have no place except on the margins of society. Flint Murtaugh, like Arden, is a freak of nature; by some congenital accident, he has the living infantile remains of his twin brother Clint embedded in his torso. Despite his life as a freak in a traveling carnival, Flint is certain that he came from the gentry and dreams of a plantation-style mansion. Meanwhile, he is a bounty hunter, searching the margins and hidey-holes of society for other misfits, while he is himself both demarcated and demonized by the society he theoretically serves. Cecil (Pelvis) Eisley, an unsuccessful Elvis impersonator, a misfit among misfits, becomes his partner. Ironically, both men are impersonating someone else; Flint believes he is a Southern gentleman, and Pelvis impersonates Elvis. Designating people as freaks echoes the strategies which construct human monsters and also constructs dystopias.

The strategies of exclusion, the processes of demarcation, demonization, scapegoating, and sacrifice, function to define the major characters to various degrees; neither Flint nor Arden has chosen to be demarcated and demonized, but both bear the mark of the "freak." No modern technology can repair their problems, and contemporary society is incapable of looking beyond the marker of a freak. The commonality is that none of these characters fits within a supposedly flexible society; they must go to the bayous, where demarcations between land and water are very uncertain, and where a different set of societal *mores* holds. One cultural model of America, a place where anyone can achieve the American Dream through hard work and one that welcomes difference, must be rejected by the characters in favor of the cultural model of the exiled, displaced and disenfranchised. It is no accident that Lambert goes as far south as he can go and still remain on the margins of the United States; it is no coincidence either that Arden looks for a mystical faith-healer on the margins of society.

The bayous also house those outlaw types, in this case drug lords, whose business is best conducted out of sight. The drug lords echo a materialist, consumerist culture run amuck, the same type of society from which Lambert and Halliday have already been displaced, and have, in turn, rejected. The bayous are not only a path to redemption; like the society Lambert is fleeing, they also house evil. Lambert, Murtaugh, Eisley, and another Vietnam war "refugee," Little Train, ally against the drug lords. As might be expected in this kind of fiction, after the alliance proves successful, Flint has an epiphany and lets Lambert go. Both Cecil and Flint reconfigure their identities and relinquish their self-destructive dreams. Eisley, although a terrible Elvis impersonator, is a musician of some talent; Flint decides to be Eisley's business manager and quit searching for not only the Southern colonial of his fantasies but also the parents who rejected him. Unlike Arden and Dan, however, both Flint and Eisley do decide to return to the society which has rejected them. By contrast, Arden discovers her role as the "Bright Girl," the person who makes the incurably ill feel happier for the sight of her. She finds the island where the current "Bright Girl" lives. There she discovers, not for a cure for her birthmark, but knowledge that the birthmark does not matter. Dan decides to stay on the island and repair the somewhat shabby house.

Gone South, then, reworks the common pattern by reversing and inverting the societally imposed strategies of exclusion. None of the main characters can be successfully demarcated and demonized if they refuse to accept a materialistic society's valuation of them. The sacrifices are actually nominal for Eisley and Flint, as neither was happy with his life, while Arden receives a spiritual cure instead of a physical cure, and Dan not only redeems his homicide but also sees his skills and himself not as marginalized and worthless but valued. This novel is on the left side of "the spectrum of doom" as the reaffirmation is as complete as it can be. In no case does a character realize either his or her innermost desire, and each character must accept a compromised solution. Arden, for example, will always have an ineradicable birthmark and will be the object of revulsion if she leaves her remote island. But as the current "Bright Girl" says, "I could promise you that no one would see that birthmark. . . . They'd see only the face behind it."[4] Dan is still dying of cancer, but has found a peaceful place in which to do so, a place where his skills as a carpenter will keep the refuge going. But nothing can reverse the damage Agent Orange has done to him; furthermore, should he leave the island, he will be hunted down as a dangerous and deranged Vietnam vet. Flint is still a freak, still an unwilling repository for his twin Clint, and Eisely may or may not be successful as a musician instead of an impersonator. Nevertheless, McCammon's work in this and several other novels postulates a world in which certain values are affirmed and, as in de Lint's "Waifs and Strays," a world in which personal redemption, at least, is possible, if one is willing to pay the price. As I have argued earlier, in line with Stephen King's contention that "Terror . . . arises from a pervasive sense of disestablishment . . . that sense of unmaking [which] seems personal and hits you around the heart," it is not necessarily the monster *per se* that causes the emotional engagement, but the implications embodied in the monster.[5] Ironically, the absence of the monster and presence of real but inhumane people generate the horror in this novel.

Stephen King's *Firestarter* (1980) concerns protagonist Charlie McGee's efforts to live within a monstrous system as an accepted human being. On an extra-textual level, *Firestarter* aptly reflects the widespread disenchantment with and distrust of the American government so endemic in the late 1960s and early 1970s and portrays American society as the era of Watergate. The novel is especially useful for delineating the abyss between the ideal and real, and reminding readers, weary from too many political-gates, that such events are not always frivolous. King depicts a genuinely horrific society, horrific and revolting in the sense that Orwell's *1984* or *Animal Farm* is revolting, but affirmative in much the same way that Ray Bradbury's *Fahrenheit 451* is affirmative. Like Bradbury's Guy Montag, who ultimately rejects the dystopian world he inhabits, Charlie refuses to accept dystopia.

Seven-year-old Charlie McGee is a recognizable and definable "other." She is pyrokinetic, and people hate, fear, and consider her unnatural, which indeed she is. Her parents also fall in the monster category, as does the chief representative of the antagonists, John Rainbird, Chief Executioner for "The Shop," a super secret government agency, which exaggerates the worst elements of the FBI/CIA/NSA and is completely without any limits on its power.[6] Charlie and her parents are victims of a government experiment in which they were unwitting guinea pigs. Rainbird, a casualty of the Vietnam War, is also to a degree, monstered by the government. Since Charlie's monstrosity is a direct result of a government experiment carried out on her unsuspecting parents, and since "The Shop" is now attempting to deprive her and her family of life, liberty, and the pursuit of happiness, it becomes quickly apparent that "The Shop," and not young Charlie McGee, is the actual monstrous body.

The novel opens with Andy McGee and his daughter running from an unspecified evil force. The year long nightmare began when agents of "The Shop" broke into his home, tortured and killed his wife, and kidnapped his daughter. Andy has managed to use his powers of mental domination to rescue Charlie, but such power has its price; Andy's reserves are almost entirely consumed.

In a flashback, we discover that Andy was an English grad student in need of some cash who signed up to participate in an experiment run by Dr. Wanless, who is connected to massive (and ultra-secret) government funding. Both Andy and Vicky Tomlinson were selected for the experiment, which called for ingesting "Lot Six," supposedly a well-tested mild hallucinogen, but actually an untested drug which induces telepathy and other paranormal powers. Vicky and Andy wed, have a child, and quickly discover that their child is pyrokinetic. If Charlie is upset, if her bottle is late, if she is frightened or angry, she strikes out with fire. Vicky simply refuses to discuss it as she refuses to acknowledge her own mild telekinetic powers. Andy is aware that he has what he calls "the push," perhaps most accurately defined as autohypnosis, or, more darkly, a power of mental domination. When Charlie is a year old and starts a fire in the middle of a temper tantrum, burning her stuffed teddy bear and very nearly the house, he calls his old roommate and friend, Quincey, who admits that he has heard "things" about the Lot Six experiment. Only four participants are left, and Quincey notes:

"I understand one of them can bend keys and shut doors without even touching them. . . . They keep him in a little room with a door he can't open and a key he can't bend. . . . He's going crazy so two hundred and twenty million Americans can stay safe and free. . . .

"What about the two people who got married? . . . Good thing those people can't do anything like that, isn't it, Andy? . . . Wouldn't they be interested in that child? . . . They just might want to take it and put it in a little room and see if it could help make the world safe for democracy. . . ."[7]

Andy is terrified both on the personal and political levels. Time passes, and Vicky and Andy teach Charlie fire-training along with toilet-training and other socialization skills. And all the while they are under government surveillance. Wanless has "gotten religion," so to speak, and now says that Charlie and her family should be sanctioned. "Cap" Hollister, the head of The Shop, would much rather secure the McGees and use them. Since King deliberately sets this novel in the aftermath of Nixon and Watergate, and since an abusive government permeates the text, the idea of a "government within a government," not subject to any limitations in its treatment of its citizens, is profoundly dis/easeful.

The men who work for the Shop, for the American government, and by extension, for us, are amoral psychopaths who delight in murder, rape, and various other sadistic acts. Blackmailing American citizens is the least offensive action they carry out, torturing and murdering innocent people the most offensive. A retired couple, Irv and Norma Manders, shelter the McGees, and when they see evidence of Charlie's pyrokinetic powers and watch the government vehicles lining up, Irv offers to stand by the McGees, and confronts the Federal agents:

"You men are trespassing," Irv Manders said. "I want you to get the hell off my property."

"We're government agents, sir," Al Steinowitz said in a low courteous voice. "These two folks are wanted for questioning."

"I don't care if they're wanted for assassinating the president," Irv said. "Show me a warrant or get the Christ off my property."

"We don't need a warrant," Al said. His voice was edged with steel now.

"You do unless I woke up in Russia this morning."[8]

Irv's assertion is both true and untrue. Substantiated allegations of CIA/FBI abuse are not unusual. The FBI's role in blackmailing the citizenry under the fascistic J. Edgar Hoover, for example, is too well known for this novel to safely exist in the purely fantastic.

Charlie creates a conflagration, killing several agents, and very nearly burning the Manders' property to cinders. Norma, displacing the blame from where it properly belongs, hisses at Andy to "Take your monster and get away."[9] Irv, assessing blame where it properly belongs, helps Andy and Charlie escape to Andy's grandfather's remote cabin. But the pursuit eventually catches up with them, and the McGees are captured and confined with neither a warrant nor a trial. Despotic and totalitarian governments may routinely mistreat their citizenry, but the ideal cultural model (as well as the law) supposedly prevents such abuses of justice in the United States of America. Thus, further dis/ease arises from the inevitable collision between the ideals and the pragmatic realities of government.

John Rainbird, "an orc, a troll, a balrog of a man . . . [whose] countenance was a horror show of scar tissue and runneled flesh,"[10] and who has been awarded the task of sanctioning Charlie when the government has no more use for her, pretends to be a marginalized and mistreated custodian/orderly in order to gain her sympathy and her confidence. As he says to Cap, "She and I will be great friends," and to Cap's laugh of disbelief, "You look at my face and you see a monster. . . . But I tell you it will happen. . . . You see her, you see a monster. Only in her case, you see a useful monster."[11] Rainbird accomplishes his goal by convincing her that "we're both outsiders—freaks if you will—buried in the bottom of the KGB's American branch."[12] Cap considers this a cheap shot, but the casual linkage of The Shop to the KGB, one of the more loathed intelligence organizations, is also a reminder of the gap between what we believe and what is. Charlie listens to her "friend" John, takes his advice, and eventually agrees to start setting fires for the government in return for small privileges.

Andy manages to revive his dormant powers and plans an escape. Although he has always been extremely careful when using his power to avoid setting up a ricochet, he no longer cares. Andy, like John Smith, has the capacity to be a human monster and is finally pushed into behaving as one. One of the Shop psychologists, Dr. Pynchot, pushed by Andy, not only agrees to another series of tests but finds himself so obsessed with his hobby of cross-dressing and the garbage disposal that eventually, due to the unpredictable echo, he dresses in some women's lingerie and sticks his arm in the running garbage disposal. The dystopian environment in which Andy is living shows clearly when he is told how Pynchot died: "He had pushed Pynchot and started a ricochet and torn the man apart. For all that, Andy could not find it in his heart to be sorry. There was horror . . . and then there was the caveman who capered and rejoiced."[13] Meanwhile, Charlie has learned something very important. Her parents' very carefully constructed "fire complex" has been progressively weakened by the constant testing. Not only have the tests dismantled the complex her parents so carefully built, "the tests . . . had shown her, beyond the shadow of a doubt, who was in charge here. She was."[14]

At the climax of the novel, Charlie goes to the stable to meet her father, and Rainbird traps Charlie there, intending to kill her; Andy intervenes by pushing Rainbird and suffers a massive cerebral hemorrhage. Before Andy dies, he tells Charlie, "Make it so they can never do this again. Burn it down, Charlie. *Burn it all down.*" Rainbird tries to kill Charlie, but she kills him first, literally flash-frying him. In the final conflict, the men shoot the fear-crazed horses, and for Charlie, seeing the slaughtered and wounded horses is the last straw: "*You killed the horses, you bastards. . . .* Yes, she decided. She would make them know they had been in a war."[15] She carries out what is nearly apocalyptic destruction, and when a secretary says she should burn herself up, she responds with the truth: "*None of it was my fault; they brought it on themselves, and I won't take the blame and I won't kill myself.*"[16] She refuses, in other words, to accept demarcation and demonization, preferring instead to assign responsibility where it properly belongs—on the monstrous body of the government.

The Manders, in the interval since Charlie burned down their house, have learned a great deal about their government—knowledge they could easily do without. The government agent who comes to settle their "insurance claim" also comes with files on both Irv and Norma's families. While most of the files record penny-ante infractions, Irv Manders, whose family name is Mandroski, has relatives in the old country. Whitney Tarkington, ignoring their pointed comments on the government's actions, "smiled coldly—a smile reserved for people who foolishly pretend to a knowledge of how the government works." If the Manders refuse to cooperate, the government will make life very difficult for Irv's relatives. And Irv, a moral man, is caught in a painful, undeserved, and impossible dilemma:

"You haff relatives in the old country, yesss?". . . . It was such a cliché that it was funny, but he didn't feel like laughing at all, somehow. *How many removes before they're not your relatives any more? Fourth cousin removed? Sixth? Eighth? Christ on a sidecar. And if we stand up to this sanctimonious bastard, and they send those people off to Siberia, what do I do?*[17]

The vaudevillian German accent is not even remotely humorous, when one considers its overtones of the Third Reich. It becomes even less humorous, when one considers that a representative of the United States government is blackmailing the Manders into silence. Irv and Norma shelter Charlie anyway, but they worry about what retribution sheltering her could bring. Perhaps the most dis/easeful element in the novel is not Andy telling Charlie to make them know they've been in a war and burdening an eight-year-old with an impossible responsibility, but Irv saying, "I love her like my own, and I know you do, too, but. . . . She could get us killed."[18]

By the time The Shop shows up again, Charlie has fled. She goes to New York and asks a librarian for a publication that is "honest, nation-wide and [has] no ties to the government."[19] The novel ends with Charlie telling her story to *The Rolling Stone.* Charlie refuses to be demarcated and demonized, but the essential problem remains unresolved. Staunch and anti-corrupt government though *The Rolling Stone* undoubtedly is, it is still only a single publication. Even if Charlie's account is believed, there is no guarantee at all that she will not end up the government's prisoner.

The troubling questions raised by this novel remain basically unre-solved. What kind of a government do we have, and just how much is the individual at the mercy of the perceived needs of the state? Does the government have a right to lock up one of its citizenry, without that citi-zen's consent, to benefit two hundred and twenty million other Ameri-cans? Assuming, of course, that a benefit exists. Utilitarians would say "certainly," but American values are predicated on a free citizenry. What entity can be trusted to make these decisions is another central concern, as is who exactly the government is. And the dis/easeful possibility that Charlie acknowledges also resonates within the reader. Charlie likes making fires; the more she uses her power, the more she likes that, too. And the more she uses her power, the stronger that power becomes. In Apollonian/Dionysian terms, the fire, a rather antinomous element, might escape her control. And then what? Her status as monster, how-ever undeserved, is not entirely inaccurate. The Shop, after all, has not given up, and Charlie, who hates the government for good reason, may

well decide to unleash her power. While her actions are unarguably justified and the novel ends, on the whole, affirmatively, the element of
dis/ease is certainly present. The government will not leave the now
orphaned eight-year-old alone; the Manders cannot effectively protect
her; and while she can protect herself, the resulting cataclysm could
result in apocalypse. The affirmation lies in the fact that she refuses to
become a tool of a fascistic organization and that she will carry out her
father's instructions to prevent a government cover-up from taking
place. Unlike Dan and Arden, who risk little or nothing by withdrawing
from society, Charlie takes the risk of confronting the society which has
monstrosized her. Perhaps one way to foreground the affirmative is to
note that Charlie has been through the fire and come through relatively
unscathed, while Dan and Arden have chosen the somewhat easier path
of nonresistance.

My third example, McCammon's *Swan Song* (1987), in many ways
responds to my first two examples and provides a third option. Unlike
Charlie, Swan uses her extraordinary powers to effect societal change.
Swan Song opens with the world rushing toward nuclear war. No one
really knows who or what started it, but in the end, the initial strike does
not matter: the United States is a blasted cinder where pitiful individuals
attempt to survive and re-form communities, amidst cataclysmic devas-
tation.

McCammon's main characters include Swan Prescott, the orphan of
a topless dancer; Sister, an alcoholic New York City bag lady, formerly
called Sister Creep; Joshua Hutchins, a wrestler billed as Black Frankenstein, Swan's protector; and Robin, her eventual mate, a member of a
gang of teenage thieves. Sister carries with her a post-apocalyptic circle
of glass embedded with gems from New York's Fifth Avenue Tiffany
store, and this circle is more than a fragment shored against world's ruin;
in some mysterious and inexplicable fashion, the circle is attuned to
Swan, who can feel the earth's pain, and alone can cause the irradiated,
poisoned, and sterile earth to regenerate. When Swan plants seed in the
poisoned, irradiated ground, the land responds. As such, she is the hope
of a blasted world. As such, she is a threat to the opposing forces. Swan,
however, is also a mutant, disfigured with keloids, dense encrustations
which disfigure and eventually obscure her face. "Normal" people are
repulsed by her and also fear her. Like Arden Halliday's birthmark,
keloids are a metonymic device which defines the person as a monstrous
body.

McCammon's evil cast consists of "The Man with the Scarlet Eye,
a.k.a. 'Friend,'" a shapeshifting demon and Dionysian force who wishes
to see the world remain a burned ruin; Colonel James "Jimbo" Macklin,

a washed-up Vietnam war "hero" who murdered his fellow prisoners of war in order to survive; and Roland Croninger, a psychopathic teenager enmeshed in video games who sees himself as a "King's Knight."

McCammon is concerned, not only with the importance of the individual, but also with the politics of community. Swan and Josh travel widely, looking for a community from which they can start the regeneration of the world. Both Swan's and Macklin's people form their own communities. Swan's community, a small and struggling town called Mary's Rest, uses the strategies of inclusion; everyone shares what little "stone soup" is available, the misshapen nuclear freaks as well as the more fortunate. A liberal view of community thus prevails in Swan's community, and the general attitude is strongly reminiscent of the government camps in John Steinbeck's *The Grapes of Wrath*, in which the people come to each others' aid rather than adhering to the conservative model of "to each his own." By contrast, in Macklin's reactionary, militaristic, and totalitarian community, which will inevitably be co-opted by the demon, the strategies of exclusion generate a reactionary and survivalist politics which demarcates and demonizes the keloid-marked nuclear survivors.

In the armed conflict which inevitably arises, the citizens of Mary's Rest are defeated by Macklin's Army of Excellence, the survivors are taken prisoner, the only growing corn crop is ruthlessly destroyed, and the demon "Friend," now the moving force behind the Army, marches the army toward Armageddon. The demon, a figure of Dionysian excess, who has attempted to kill Swan and thus kill the hope of the world, repeatedly defining the nuclear holocaust and its horrible aftermath as "my party," claims that he will make a human hand do the work of final destruction. When the crazed ex-President is finally located, he is easily persuaded to use the weapon. As the President says to Swan,

"The world will be cleansed, don't you see? . . .—[A]nd someday things will start over again, and they'll be good, like they used to be.

"A . . . Doomsday machine," Friend whispered, and a grin skittered across his mouth. . . . "Oh, yes! the world *must* be cleansed! All the Evil must be washed away! like *her*! . . . I told you!" he crowed. "I told you I'd make a human hand do the work!"[20]

Because McCammon is interested in issues of redemption, the Doomsday weapon is disarmed by Swan and catastrophe narrowly averted. Because McCammon is also interested in issues of human responsibility, the evil is carried out, not by the essentially powerless demon, but by men who willingly follow him, or men whose minds, like the President's, have shattered beyond culpability. Because men can choose damnation or redemption, Colonel Macklin tries to atone for his evil; in a manner consistent with McCammon's philosophy, it is Roland the "King's Knight" who shoots Macklin and not the demon. Because McCammon is interested in choice and redemption, it is Colonel Macklin who dies to prevent Roland from shooting Swan. In McCammon's world view, the mistakes which brought nearly total apocalypse cannot be magically erased, but the society which created the apocalypse can be redeemed.

As Swan's community can choose to re-forge the tenuous bonds of community and attempt to rebuild, so Macklin's Army of Excellence can choose to become an exclusionary and vicious force bent on domination. In this novel, the evil comes, not from Talons, not from the demon, not from magic, but from, and only from, the actions of human beings. As the keloid-marked survivors can emerge like butterflies from cocoons, so human beings, says McCammon, can transform themselves. This second chance is not completely unproblematic. Choosing not to commit evil does not disarm or nullify evil; at most it mitigates and contains the evil. The demon's human body is destroyed, but the immortal demon escapes, almost certainly to plague the world at some future time. Thus, evil remains loose in the world, but is more than balanced by the closing images:

And in the years to come, they would talk about the blooming of the wasteland. . . . They would talk about the rebuilding of the libraries and the great museums and of the schools that taught first and foremost the lesson learned from the awful holocaust on the seventeenth of July: *Never again.*[21]

Despite the hint that the demon is immortal and evil will always have a presence, this novel offers a deliberately affirmative structure. Unlike Santayana's dictum that "those who do not learn from history are doomed to repeat it," McCammon's work postulates a world in which the lessons of history are taken to heart. Unfortunately for a completely satisfactory affirmation, humans are more likely to repeat history than to learn from it. The acknowledgment that many people will choose the strategies of exclusion saves this novel from being facilely resolved.

My final example, David Brin's *The Postman* (1985), while still affirmative, moves beyond the individual in dystopia and examines the possibilities and problems of rebuilding society after apocalypse. It is closely related to the thematic concerns of mid-spectrum dystopia. The movement of the novel is affirmative and resolution is achieved, but the affirmation is founded upon "a lie that became the most powerful kind of truth."[22] Like many other apocalyptic novels, *The Postman* describes post-nuclear America. Sixteen years after the blast, the "United States" is completely destroyed and the geographical entity is made up of scattered communities with governmental models which vary from the Holnists, a macho reactionary militia organization, to dictatorships, "machine-type" mayors, and democratic communities. As might be expected, democratic communities which will accept new-comers are few and far between. What almost all do have in common is "the drawbridge syndrome," in which newcomers are generally not welcomed into communities which have barely maintained a subsistence-level existence. Needless to say, the "United States" is a fast fading memory, and unrelenting savagery is the order of the day.

Gordon Krantz, the novel's protagonist, is the last idealist, trekking the country in a vain attempt to find someone who is trying to get things back together, looking for someone to rekindle the dream of America in a world where "*paranoia and depression are adaptive. . . . Idealism is only stupid.*"[23] At one point Gordon spies a glint of glass which turns out to be a postal jeep hidden in a ravine. As he scavenges the jeep, he discovers that the postman was a "bona fide *postwar* postman, a hero of the flickering twilight of civilization, a recollection of America as it was."[24] Gordon "had often wondered if the right symbol might do the trick—the right *idea.*" While he knows that "[t]he legends he offered weren't the kind of sustenance needed in order to overcome the inertia of a dark age," he does not know what symbol might reverse the move to barbarism.[25] The answer is not an individual but a symbol of a communitarian past. The villagers of Pine Crest, who remember and romanticize mailmen, and who eagerly recount the anecdotes, automatically assume that in donning the dead man's uniform he has become the postman. Thus is the "Restored United States of America" reborn. The villagers of Pine Crest give him letters to deliver when he leaves. When he meets with an unfriendly reception at Oakridge, he uses the uniform and some flyers he has made up and takes the lie/dream/illusion a step further. His bluff pays off, and the people, desperate to believe in something, embrace the lie. One lie leads to another and soon Gordon has a whole mythology about the "Restored United States." What started as a survival plan has led to renewed hope in community after community, as well as a sense of commonality which replaces the drawbridge syndrome. Gordon now has not only mail routes but also postmasters and the equivalent of the Pony Express. Ironically, however, for one who wants a place to stay, he can only maintain his image by constantly moving from village to village—in effect, by actively accepting the strategies of exclusion.

One subplot in this novel reinforces the idea of a necessary lie. A giant super computer named Cyclops has survived the war, which "killed" most computers and is supposedly distributing both information and technology. Corvallis, Oregon, the home of Cyclops, is a prospering network of communities; the farmers support the scientist "Servants of Cyclops," and Cyclops answers questions on farming and technology. Cyclops, however, does not exist—in a stratagem exceedingly reminiscent of the Wizard of Oz, the voice of Cyclops is that of the scientist who built him. And the scientist offers the same rationale to the outraged Gordon as Gordon has offered himself: "It offered a way to survive in the coming dark age."[26] Gordon is very disillusioned and leaves, claiming that he is finished with myths, but a phrase embedded in his brain gives him no peace: "*Who will take responsibility now for these foolish children*" resonates in his brain night and day and Gordon is the answer, despite his attempts to deny obligation "to a scrap of ruined tin, or a desiccated spectre found in a rusted jeep."[27] As in *Swan Song*, the answer lies in the formation of communities and not individual efforts; unlike *Firestarter* and *Gone South*, this text claims that community is the only system which might reverse the move toward dystopia.

In the third and problematic part of the novel, the communities of Southern Oregon are locked in a life-or-death struggle with the Holnists, the best organized band of hyper-survivalists. Gordon, four years after he has realized that he cannot simply ride away, is desperately trying to hold an increasingly tenuous line with a ragged band of farmers and the occasional actual soldier. He knows that there is a legendary warrior, George Powhatan by name, who has held the Southern Oregon communities together, and in desperation he goes to him for help. But Powhatan refuses; after all, Holnists attacking Central Oregon mean less pressure on his community. Powhatan, like Gordon, is an unwilling idealist who just wants to be left in peace:

"Where is it written that one should only care about big things? I fought for big things long ago. . . . For issues, principles, a country . . . I discovered that the big things don't love you back. . . . Today I fight for my people, my farm—for smaller things—things I can *hold*."[28]

Captured by the Holnist army, Gordon finally realizes that there are lies and lies, and that the lies he told were necessary and for the common good. As he reads Nathan Holn's *Lost Empire*, which argues that true males dominate, makes Aaron Burr a hero, and demonizes Benjamin Franklin, George Washington, and the "Order of Cinncinatus," the real problem becomes clear. In an imaginary dialogue with Benjamin

Franklin, Franklin asks how one can encourage individual excellence, still afford compassion, and weed out tyrants. Thus, the use of the "lies" that Franklin told, and the lies Gordon has manufactured, become clear. Such lies allow time for an ideal to mature; such lies keep the strong from overpowering the weak. Gordon learns another essential truth: Powhatan's refusal to fight, however understandable, plays out in favor of tyranny; he will end up holding Southern Oregon for the Holnist empire because he refuses to intervene. Powhatan finally shows up and defeats Macklin, the Holnist leader, in hand-to-hand combat. Both Macklin and Powhatan are *augments*, biologically engineered to have superhuman strength. In another dis/ease provoking scenario, the government which Gordon wishes so ardently to restore has created the first generation of *augments*, represented by Macklin, of alpha males, realized its mistake, and chosen to augment men like Powhatan, who, like Cincinnatus, have an aversion to power. The dis/ease exists because Powhatan so nearly refuses to fight; as Gordon says to him, *Did you honestly think your responsibility was ever finished?*" Powhatan finally reveals what moved him to intervene: "It was the women. . . . Ever since your visit and those damned letters . . . They kept after me and after me and *after* me. . . . *The women* made me do it."[29]

Dena, a young feminist scientist in a world which has devalued women and uses them as domestic drudges or sex slaves, has the idea that women were responsible for allowing men to create apocalypse. She theorizes that

"You fellows were doing your jobs well enough—shaping and making and building things. Males can be brilliant that way. But anyone with any sense can see that a quarter to a half of you are also lunatics, rapists and murderers. It was our job to keep an eye on you. . . ."[30]

It is her view that women must "stop the bastards ourselves. We are going to do our job at last . . . to CHOOSE among men and to cull out the mad dogs."[31] Later, when Dena is dying and a prisoner of the Holnists, she tells him that her "Night of the Red Knives" has failed, but notes that she tried.

In another conflicted move toward affirmation, the women reclaim their status. The story of the band of forty women who infiltrated the Holnist camps to try to kill them sweeps Oregon and attains mythic proportions and acceptance and Gordon fears that it could be as dangerous a dogma as Nathan Holn's creed or his own "Restored United States." For one thing, unlike Cyclops and the "Restored United States," this tale of sacrifice is true. His fears arise because the women have realized that they have responsibility, as they whisper among themselves, "the mad ones [men] can ruin the world. *Women, you must judge them. . . .*"[32] Thus Gordon writes to Mrs. Thompson, the mayor of Pine View,

"In my worst dreams I see women taking up a tradition of drowning their sons if they show signs of becoming bullies. I envision them doing their duty. . . . [T]his 'solution' is something that terrifies me."[33]

On the other hand, regeneration is everywhere evident and the Restored United States has become a reality. At tale's end, Gordon leaves a thriving Oregon, a community in which "windmill generators, and humming electric lines, busy machine shops, [and] scores of clean noisy children playing in the schoolyards"[34] proliferate and heads for California: "Once out of town, he did not look back."[35]

On the surface, this is a truly affirmative tale, and yet disquieting questions are central to a reader's response. This novel argues that motivation is all, and that for a good motive, the end justifies the means. To lie to give people hope is not to lie but to create a dream. If, however, the opening sentences of the Declaration of Independence ("We hold these truths to be self-evident . . ."), are nothing more than a scam propagated by Ben Franklin and his constitutional cronies, "propagandists to make Himmler and Trotsky blush as amateurs,"[36] if idealism is a disease and a scam as Gordon supposes at one point, and if the truth is that the victories go to the strong and ruthless, then the idea of any idealism is nothing more than self-defeating proposition.

When one considers that the idealized United States which Gordon so ardently wishes to restore caused the Doomwar, the affirmation is less complete than one might wish to believe. When one considers the uses to which legends can be put by even the most well-intentioned people, the affirmation is called into question. What if male infanticide does become an accepted practice? One of the reasons this is a novel that shades on to the mid-spectrum dystopian is that the strategies of exclusion and the idealized view of nationalism are still alive and well. The women in this tale will employ the Amazon myth to separate the bullies from the caring men, thus themselves becoming the same kind of tyrants against which Dena and her band fought so bravely and futilely. Gordon Krantz, who started the restoration, cannot participate, but must, to keep the "restored United States" believable, leave the Oregon community. Perhaps most disquieting is the ready acceptance of an "end justifies the means" philosophy. Nathan Holn's *Lost Empire*, after all, tells lies for an end which he considers both moral and necessary. Does truth matter or can it be manufactured? And to which manufacturer do we give authority? The idea that one cannot run away from responsibility, that there are some actions worth undertaking, whether victory or defeat is the result, makes this an affirmative novel with a dark undertaste. The strategies of exclusion, by which all strangers are looked upon with suspicion, no one has the inclination to practice any type of charity, and life is reduced to a single concern with "getting mine," are central to this novel and provide the dis/easeful element, as does the pernicious "the ends justify the means" philosophy.

The novels discussed in this chapter are affirmative in nature because, although dystopias do exist and strategies of exclusion do come into play, both dystopias and exclusionary strategies are ultimately discarded. In *Gone South* and *Firestarter*, even though the society remains essentially unchanged, the main characters not only reject the dystopic society but transcend its limitations and achieve at least a personal reaffirmation. *Swan Song* strongly rejects the strategies of exclusion based on the disfigurement of the survivors. In a blasted and irradiated landscape, a landscape which promises nothing but a short, brutish, and losing struggle for life, human beings nevertheless reject political systems which are based on the abuse of power and forge communities which work towards inclusion. While *The Postman* explores several possible post-apocalypse scenarios, and while the strategies of exclusion are very prominent, the characters also eventually reject the exclusionary systems of power in favor of a more inclusionary system. With various degrees of plausibility, then, these works do offer examples of affirmation somewhat shakily achieved within actions which are not simply pleasant fantasies.

10

JAILERS OF THE MIND:
CLAPPING THE MIND-FORGED MANACLES
ON OURSELVES AND OTHERS

"You don't say that the shadow has the same stature as the light."[1]

Mid-spectrum dystopian horror fiction is fiction in which affirmation is not possible, but the situation dramatized does not approach complete and unrelieved dystopia. As in the previous mid-spectrum texts, those dealing with human monsters and social communities, the results are neither affirmative nor disaffirmative, but located somewhere in the middle. The personal redemptions are not as clear as in McCammon's works, the societal restorations are more conflicted, the politics are considerably less clearcut. The three texts I will discuss, F. Paul Wilson's short story "Midnight Mass," Sheri Tepper's *The Gate to Women's Country* and Stephen King's *The Stand*, are seemingly disparate texts bound together by the same thematics of horror as well as the same concern with political systems. Each text discusses the impossibility of an affirmative dystopia and confronts the problems inherent in maintaining affirmative values in a political system in which the ends justify the means. As in Chapter 9, the mid-spectrum advances from "Midnight Mass," in which the dystopia is least compromised, through *The Gate to Women's Country* where an end justifies the means political philosophy rules with frightening success, to *The Stand* in which an inability to break the mind-forged manacles of the past results in a repetition of the same political system which created the dystopia in the first place.

In a story in which Vichy France, the politics of collaboration, and the Holocaust are invoked, Wilson's "Midnight Mass" (1993) explores the consequences of a society turned dystopian: vampires are the super-race, collaboration is the only means to survival, the UnDead prey upon their former friends and neighbors, and affirmative choices like resistance seem not only worthless but futile. At least one belief system is invalidated and another remains questionable at best. Wilson's short story, dealing as it does with the corruption located in both the Catholic Church and the community at large, provokes dis/ease as much from the historical resonances as from the evocation of the Roman Catholic church as both corrupt and complicit. As in such texts as McCammon's *Swan Song*, the role of the individual is foregrounded, but communitarian redemption is somewhat more problematic than in McCammon's work. Both Sheri Tepper's *The Gate to Women's Country* and Stephen King's *The Stand* explore what happens when the myths and idealized cultural models become corrupted and necessary deceit becomes a way of life. Unlike *The Postman*, where the lie buttresses the ideal, both King and Tepper posit a darker vision of myth, ideals, truth, and *Realpolitik*. Both texts deal with the reconstruction of post-apocalyptic societies, and both examine the ways in which these societies are constructed through the strategies of exclusion to accomplish goals of which the rest of the society is ignorant. The dystopian elements come into play because the society at large is unaware of the deceit and manipulations involved and because the danger of recreating the very problems the new society is supposed to avoid remain very great. Like Wilson's story, both of these texts fall midway between an affirmative dystopia and the complete nihilism of a disaffirmative dystopia.

"Midnight Mass" is set in Lakewood, New Jersey, after most of the world has been conquered by vampires. No explanation is provided for this take-over, and it seems to have caught the citizenry by surprise. Certainly no resistance is mentioned. Society has broken into three groups: the vampires, who are now the majority; the Vichy collaborators, who are best defined as vampire wannabes; and the passive and directionless group who are neither, but from whom any resistance must come. Rabbi Zev Wolpin, an Orthodox Jew, is one of the few Jews to survive the vampire take-over. As occurred in World War II, most Jews, particularly Orthodox Jews, have perished at the hands of the Nazis and their own traditions. Wilson, writing a fairly conventional vampire text, privileges Roman Catholic rituals, by which his characters avert consumption by the vampires. The Catholic church, St. Anthony's, with its holy water, crosses, stations of the cross, stained glass, and crucifix, is originally territory forbidden to the vampires. The cross, although available to Jews, comes with an extremely high price tag. If the cross, the most basic symbol of Christianity, or worse, the crucifix, repels evil, the Jews are placed in a position where they must either abandon their religious beliefs, which deny the role of Jesus Christ as the Messiah, or become victims of the vampires. As Zev thinks to himself, "To hold up a cross was to negate two thousand years of Jewish history, it was to say that the Messiah had come and they had missed him."

Unfortunately, Jewish sacred symbols are completely ineffective. Only the cross can save these people and only the cross can doom them. By the time the action of the story starts, all the Orthodox, most of the

Conservative, and many of the Reformed Jews have been either killed by vampires or turned into UnDead. In a mordantly humorous line, Wilson notes, "The great fear had come to pass: they'd been assimilated."[2] In Nazi Germany, the separate status of the Jews made them easy victims; in this text the same separation, a separation from the body politic which the Orthodox Jews have practiced for years, also brings them to destruction. As Zev, who does wear a cross, thinks to himself,

The Reformed and Conservative synagogues started handing out crosses at Shabbes . . . did the Orthodox congregations follow suit? No. They hid in their home and shules and yeshivas and read and prayed.
    And were liquidated.[3]

    Father Joe Cahill, an Irish Catholic priest unjustly accused of sexual misconduct and dismissed from St. Anthony's, is the person around whom resistance could coalesce, but he is understandably extremely bitter that his parishioners believed the accusations against him. He is no sooner accused than the strategies of exclusion come into play and he ends up labeled a rogue priest, a pariah, without a parish or a community. He has taken to heavy drinking and denies any interest in his old parish's problems. Father Alberto Palmeri is the pastor at St. Anthony's; he is also a child molester and a vampire, a priest who has thoroughly rejected his vows and allied himself with the UnDead. Naturally, his best hope of success is to somehow nullify the strength of Cahill. The false accusation, so easily believed, works perfectly to demarcate and demonize Cahill. With Cahill safely removed, Palmeri can allow his unnatural appetites full rein; he deconsecrates the church, installs the vampires, practices black masses and ritual sacrifice, and generally has the time of his UnDead life while his parishioners either cower in their homes or become vampires or their victims.
    Zev, aware that Cahill is one of the few people with the inner strength to resist the vampires and restore St. Anthony's, tracks him down and persuades him to return to the parish. This is a difficult task because as Cahill says, ". . . I can't forget how they [the parishioners] stood quietly by while I was stripped of my position, my dignity, my integrity, of everything I wanted to be."[4] Cahill is unable to resist Zev's arguments as to why he should at least see St. Anthony's; he is also trapped into administering the Last Rites to a vampire who had attacked them the previous night, which leads to an interesting discussion. At the center of this short story lie questions of responsibility: are the people turned into vampires responsible for their actions? Can they resist? Can one judge the collaborators? And again, the ghosts of the Holocaust

inform the discussion. Are the citizens of Lakewood responsible for their actions as vampires? Were the Germans responsible for their transmogrification into Nazis? Surprisingly, it is Zev, whose people have been ruthlessly liquidated, who says to Joe, "You act as if they are responsible for what they do after they become vampires." Cahill argues that since the vampires stay in their home towns, inhabit their basements, and prey upon people they knew when they were alive, that some of their old personalities survive, and that they are indeed responsible for their actions, which in Catholic theological terms means they are culpable for their actions. And he asks the central question of both this text and the Holocaust: "Why can't they . . . resist?"

When Zev asks whether he thinks he would be able to resist, the priest answers, "Damn straight."[5] He observes the desecration of the church by ritual sacrifice reminiscent of a Black Mass, and ponders yet another question, which is why the Vichy collaborate. Again, the historical resonance is impossible to miss, as the role of collaborators and the consequences of resistance are still much debated in World War II and Holocaust studies. The Vichy work for the vampires in return for immortality at a later time, and Cahill, who has become extremely judgmental, says, "I never cease to be amazed at our fellow human beings. Their capacity for good is only succeeded by their ability to debase themselves." Zev responds, "Hopelessness does strange things, Joe. The vampires know that. So they rob us of hope. . . . They transform our friends and neighbors and leaders into their own, leaving us feeling alone, completely cut off." Vampires evidently understand the strategies of exclusion quite well and use them most effectively.

When Joe decides to confront the vampires, saying, "Nobody can do what he's [Palmeri] done and get away with it. I'm taking my church back," he and Zev start by attempting to clean it, a task clearly analogous to cleaning the Augean stables.[6] To his amazement, one of his parishioners comes to help him. Carl Edwards, terrified of the vampires, revolted at the state of the church, and deeply conscious of his past offences, nevertheless offers to help. He tells Cahill, "Ay, an' Fadda, I neva believed any a dem tings dat was said aboutcha. Neva." Cahill responds by saying, "It would have meant a lot to have heard that from you last year, Carl." All Carl can say in return is "Yeah, I guess it would. But I'll make it up to ya, Fadda. I will. You can take that to the bank."[7] This passage provides a way of explaining both the citizens as vampires and the Vichy: deploying the strategies of exclusion while refusing active involvement is much the easier course of action. There is little doubt that Edwards knows Cahill is guiltless; he would be highly unlikely to aid a child molester at the risk of not only his body but his immortal soul. There is no doubt whatsoever, either, that he did not stand up and publicly state that the accusation was false. It is interesting how often in horror fictions the communitarian cultural model is subverted and the strategies of exclusion are actively embraced. If Cahill is the equivalent of the brave sheriff, the townspeople are certainly remiss in rendering him active support.

In order to reconsecrate the church, Father Cahill starts to say Mass: "*Some Mass.* A defiled altar, a crust for a Host, a Pepsi can for a chalice, a fifty-year-old pistol-packing altar boy, and a congregation consisting of a lone, shotgun-carrying Orthodox Jew."[8] Palmeri, the Vichy, and the vampires attempt to stop the Mass, but are unsuccessful. In fact, when Brother Frederick, one of the vampires, jokes about the doctrine of Transubstantiation and drinks from the Pepsi can, he is liquefied on the spot, thus frightening the vampires and their followers out of the church, at least temporarily. Even this victory is compromised; Zev, after all, faced with the reality of "the fearsome . . . incalculable power" of Roman Catholic belief and ritual, has a lifetime of belief stripped away.[9] Not only are his people almost entirely exterminated, it looks as though the *goyim* have been right all along.

The Vichy overpower Joe and Zev, and Palmeri gloats as he tells Joe that he will kill Zev, but turn Joe into the UnDead. And here Father Joseph Cahill faces his own crisis of faith:

> He wouldn't be like them! He would not allow it!
>
> But what if there was no choice? What if becoming Undead toppled a lifetime's worth of moral restraints, cut all the tethers on his human hungers, negated all his mortal concepts of how a life should be lived? Honor, justice, integrity, truth, decency, fairness, love—what if they became meaningless words instead of the footings for his life?[10]

What if these are, in other words, only constructs, believable only as long as the rest of the society accepts them? A consensus reality, after all, only maintains its existence as long as it is accepted.

Cahill offers Palmeri a deal; he will not pursue Palmeri once he becomes Undead, if Palmeri will let Zev go. Just as Palmeri orders Zev killed, the parishioners of St. Anthony's attack, but Palmeri has suspended Zev over a large wooden spike, and Father Cahill cannot bear to kill his friend, the man who gave him back his soul. He again offers a trade, believing that he will still win in the end because he believes in the virtues which Palmeri has rejected. And Palmeri provides a clear articulation of the dis/ease this text produces when he tells Zev, "He's going to lose and we're going to win for the same reason we'll always win. We don't let anything as silly and transient as sentiment stand in the way."[11] Overcoming a moment of despair, Zev sacrifices his life, taking Palmeri with him. The death of the leader causes the remaining vampires and Vichy to flee, and the parish regains its church, at least for one night. Joe thinks that it is "A small victory of minimal significance in the war, but a victory nonetheless."[12] Thus the victory may or may not be the beginning of the end of the vampires' domination; it is, at best, a beginning of the resistance, at worst an anomaly.

Wilson's text creates dis/ease on several levels: it portrays the Catholic Church as a seriously flawed institution; it places the Jews in an impossibly conflicted situation, wherein the price of survival is the abnegation of faith; it deliberately invokes such politicized terms as collaborator, Vichy, genocide, holocaust and liquidation, and it portrays nearly all the citizenry either as actively collaborating Vichy or passive observers who refuse to take a stand against the vampires, and therefore condemn their friends and neighbors to a grisly fate. Placing the story in a New Jersey town completes the sense of troubling inversion. As many Americans will claim, with perfectly straight faces and sincere beliefs, the Holocaust could never happen in the United States of America. Collapsing the distance between 1936 and 1993, between America and Nazi Germany, Wilson provokes great discomfort. The politicized view of the Catholic Church as a corrupt institution vulnerable to the politics of genocide and collaboration also inverts a basic cultural model. In addition, Zev's sacrifice also creates a sense of dis/ease; in the last moments of his life, he thinks "*Futile. . . . Like much of his life it seemed. Joe would die tonight and Zev would live on, a cross-wearing Jew, with the traditions of his life sacked and in flames, and nothing in his future but a vast, empty, limitless plain to wander alone.*"[13] Zev's sacrifice does save St. Anthony's, although the parishioners credit Father Cahill, but in an ending that reprises all Zev's despair, Cahill decides to rename the Church St. Zev's, thus confirming Zev's misplaced faith and even his despair.

While the story seems to offer a compromised affirmation, because the vampires, are temporarily defeated, and the citizens do mount a successful resistance, Churchill's remark, "This is not the end. It is not even the beginning of the end. But it is, perhaps, the end of the beginning,"[14] provides an apt reference. In an affirmative text, the vampires would all have been liquefied at the sight of the crosses, the brave citizens would have retaken the entire town, and Zev would have survived with his faith intact. In a disaffirmative text, Palmeri would have been proven right, and such values as Cahill believed in would have been proof of nothing more than an expensive sentimentality. But, in fact, the parishioners have rallied to him, Father Cahill has recovered from his disgust with them, and they are a unit at least as cohesive as the vampires and the Vichy. Whether Zev's sacrifice is effective is not addressed. Perhaps the brave villagers are liquidated by the vampires as were so many resistance fighters; perhaps they manage to hold their church. The text does not say as Wilson avoids the certitudes of both his affirmative and disaffirmative colleagues.

My second example, Sheri S. Tepper's *The Gate to Women's Country* (1988), is a novel which depicts a society feminist in orientation, dedicated to peace, nurturing and civilization, which nevertheless carries the seeds of dystopia within it. Tepper's carefully drawn society, which in many ways embodies a feminists' paradise, also carries a disquieting message: women are no more immune to the corruption inherent in power than any other oppressed segments of society. Tepper's text concerns a post-apocalyptic society which has been ravaged by nuclear war, referred to as "convulsions," some three hundred years ago. Much technological knowledge has been lost, or in some cases rejected, much of the land is "lost" to radiation, many systems of knowledge have been severely truncated, and most important, the communities which did survive the holocaust, are now defined in terms of gender roles. The men, with the exception of the "servitors," live in martial encampments, the women in the towns, all of which were started by women and are run by a Council of Women, which is neither democratic nor open, though is ostensibly both. Membership in the Council is decided solely by the Council, and their word is absolute. The Council has agendas of which neither the male warriors nor most of the women are aware. The lives of both genders are tightly bound with very inflexible rules, rules which at first seem utterly without rhyme or reason. The price of living within the protected walls of the towns in *Women's Country* is strict and unquestioning adherence to the Women's Country Ordinances.

Questioning authority is not a value in this society, and such an attitude, with its hints of a fascistic society and its parallels in twentieth century history to societies that unblinkingly followed orders is very dis/ease-provoking. Access to knowledge is also severely constrained; while the women are encouraged to accumulate as much knowledge as possible in several areas, the rules concerning transmission of that knowledge are both strict and exclusionary. Warrior men, for example, are permitted neither medical care nor books from Women's Country. The women are willing to dose the severely wounded with hemlock and water, but no precious antibiotics are wasted on the men. The ordinances by which all women swear to live expressly prohibit lending books to warriors. A man who takes the warrior's path renounces the right to read anything other than sagas and martial epics. On the other hand, when a harvest does not meet expectation, it is the women's towns which take a ration cut and not the warriors. The women also do all the work; the warrior garrison's sole responsibility is to guard them and fight in the event of a war. As with the citizens of Women's Country, the acceptance of warrior status binds the men absolutely to their commanders. Thus, there are two interrelated but essentially oppositional communities which both exact absolute unquestioning conformity as the price of admission.

In many ways, depending on one's point-of-view, these communities are both utopian. The warriors play war games, drill for battle, drink beer, sing songs, and do nothing to earn their upkeep. They parade around, lounge around, and are certainly the superstructure to the women's base. Every time the male lust for domination surfaces, some of the brighter warriors point out that if the warriors were to attack the women's towns, they might have to become active laborers, a fate which the warriors would quite literally rather die than contemplate. Since historical knowledge is very limited, the warriors are not aware, except through apocryphal tales, that there were times and places where women did the work and were sexually, physically, and emotionally dominated by the men. Not surprisingly, the women who do have this knowledge prefer to keep it secret.

The women work hard but have towns within which warriors are not permitted. The gate between the warriors' encampment and the town is closed to warriors. Thus, the women live according to their ordinances, without warriors to intrude on their busy, happy, and ordered lives. They do not marry, bear only as many children as they wish, call no man father, take their matronymic from their mother's line and town, have a Goddess-based religion, and are free from the domination of men. Marriage is a cultural artifact as much frowned upon as foot-binding or genital mutilation. The concept of women as subordinate to warriors is absolutely and irrevocably rejected, mainly because the women do have access to pre-convulsion texts and no intention of ever existing within a patriarchal society.

Between these two groups lie such outlanders as gypsies, itinerants and the so-called "servitors." These are men who go to the warrior camp at the age of five years, as the ordinances demand, stay until they are at least fifteen and at most twenty-five, and then reject the warrior life in favor of a seemingly eunuch-like existence in Women's Country. Naturally, the warriors despise them, and some of the women who are caught up in the warrior mystique are also openly contemptuous of them. The servitors seem to be subordinate to women and carry out tasks which the "true men" find despicable, such as gardening, shopping, and basket-making.

At month-long carnivals which occur twice yearly, the women and the warriors mix freely, and sexual liaisons are encouraged. Any male children are turned over to their warrior fathers at the age of five. The daughters, of course, become citizens of Women's Country. Thus, Tepper posits a society which seems not to have worked out gender differences, but to have accepted them as immutable. No woman is abused or subject to a man. "Domestic violence" is an anachronistic term, without meaning. The women know what the term applies to, but none of them have any direct experience with the concept because none of them are under any man's thumb. Their knowledge is theoretical and analogous to the knowledge of a contemporary woman who reads Western history and knows that women could be sold, beaten, imprisoned, and killed with relative impunity in most Western cultures. The warriors are bound to protect the women and the women are equally bound to provide for the garrison, but they occupy separate and equal spheres.

Morgot, a leading member of the Council, her daughters Stavia and Myra, her servitors Joshua and Corrig, and their friends Sylvia and Beneda are the main Women's Country characters. Chernon, Michael, Stephon, and Patras are the main warrior characters. It is through these characters that both the strains between the women and the warriors, and the strains between appearance and reality, utopia and potentially dystopia, are played out. Stavia, the novel's central character, moves from the unawareness characteristic of the majority of women, a move her sister Myra never makes, to both understanding of and complicity in the Council's highly secret agenda. She becomes involved with Chernon, a young warrior, breaks the ordinances because she considers them unreasonable and does not see why warriors must live separately, goes on a forbidden exploration with Chernon, and becomes the captive not only of Chernon, who rapes her at the first opportunity, attempting to impregnate and own her, but also of Holyland, a highly abusive society based on Old Testament patriarchy. In this social order, women are entirely subordinate to their husbands and sons, polygyny is the rule, and, before being sold in marriage, the woman is stripped, beaten, and shorn as a sign of what to expect. What makes the ritual worse is that it is the women who inflict such punishment on each other. Marriage in this society is defined by rituals whose sole purpose is to degrade, hurt, and humiliate the woman. The women carry out such rituals, so the new wife has enough knowledge to try, however unsuccessfully, to avoid being hurt and degraded in a marriage, the sole purpose of which is to degrade her.

Thus, Stavia learns the harsh necessities for the ordinances the hard way. As Morgot has said to her previously, "We all have to do things we don't want to do. All of us here in Women's Country. Sometimes they are things that hurt us to do. We accept the hurt because the alternative would be worse."[15] It is not until Stavia experiences the essential nature of the warrior males and the dystopian "Holyland" community that she understands what is going on in Women's Country. When Chernon, her erstwhile lover, rapes her, cuts out her contraceptive implant in hope he will get a son who will be "his," and later recounts his experiences in Holyland to the Marthatown garrison in an attempt to enslave the women, Stavia finally understands the stakes. She finally understands the purposes of the ordinances: they are indeed repressive, and they do indeed restrict the transmission of knowledge, a commodity which should be free to all who want it. And they are necessary evils if women are to avoid slavery. When the Holylanders talk about breaking her legs to tame and contain her, Stavia realizes that Chernon "understood these animals from a place deep within himself which empathized with them."[16] She understands the seeming harshness of the ordinances, the penalties for breaking them, and the necessity for the gate. She understands, in fact, the necessity for the strategies of exclusion, and her acceptance, once conflicted and problematic, becomes complete.

All, however, is not quite as utopian in the women's towns as it seems. The utopian society has been bought by a deep-rooted network of deceit, Machiavellian in nature. For Machiavelli's prince, as well as for the Council, anything whatsoever is allowable if it is good for the state:

> To preserve the state, he often has to do things against his word, against charity, against humanity, against religion. Thus he has to have a mind ready to shift as the winds of fortune and the varying circumstances of his life may dictate. . . . Everyone sees what you seem to be, few know what you really are. . . . [W]e must always look to the end. . . . Let a prince therefore win victories and uphold his state; his methods will always be considered worthy and everyone will praise them.[17]

Except for the gendered pronoun, this advice could have come straight from Morgot, who would certainly agree with it, quite possibly has read it, and successfully applies it.

The strategies of exclusion, by which some women in the community know what is going on, but most are ignorant pawns, are, paradoxically, what keep Women's Country strong. The Council of Women argues in favor of a policy in which the ends justify the means. Thus, the Council sets all policy without any input from either the citizenry or the garrisons. Eugenics and selection are at the core of the survival of Women's Country, and so most of the childbearing women are as much victims of the deceit as the warriors. The Council of Women has been quietly working since its inception not only to keep Women's Country safe and to try to gain back lost knowledge and an industrial base, but also to breed out male possessiveness and aggressiveness. The warriors who think they have sons do not; the children born to the women are usually servitors' children, and servitors, of course, are the men who have been selected to reject both male aggression and possessiveness. This is one of the completely secret and arbitrary agendas which the Council of Women carry out. To do this, they must practice a deceit so widespread that it permeates and makes a mockery of the very life of Women's Country, which is supposedly based on a free citizenry of women who agree to live within the ordinances and think they are actually participants. The women, however, only think they have a choice in bearing children and choosing the father; actually, they function much as women have functioned through history, bearing sons for people with whose agendas they may or may not agree. This reduces the status of all but the inner circle quite considerably; ironically, women are more or less vessels for children, as they have been in patriarchal societies.

So the question in this mid-spectrum fiction becomes whether or not the end justifies the means. Can one small group of women, who are not elected, distribute absolute power as they wish, control life and death for not only the women but also the warriors, and decide on a eugenics policy for the country, be anything but instruments of eventual dystopia? Although the women do supply the garrison with the necessities of life, the Councils also manufacture situations in which one garrison insults the other; the ensuing bloodshed keeps the warrior numbers within reason. If food is short, the women go without, but it is odd how often an increase in Women's Country population results in a set percentage of the warriors losing their lives in battles. Odder still is how perfectly proportional the increases and decreases are. These battles are always fought over a garrison-to-garrison insult rather than a real threat to the security of Women's Country. The Council itself deals ruthlessly with threats against the security of Women's Country, the favored means being assassination.

Since the women do employ the strategies of exclusion—demarcation, demonization, scapegoating, and sacrifice—but employ them to good ends, this novel is extremely antinomous. Can a community thrive on lies and deceit, or thrive in a situation where nearly every action taken is shrouded in secrecy? In many ways, despite the gate between the women and the warriors, the insistence on the rights of the women to live the lives they wish to live, and the voluntary containment practiced, Women's Country is not all that different from the authoritarian warrior society. And the authoritarian militaristic society is clearly condemned in Tepper's novel.

Several metaphors rule the text: the constant emphasis on the actor/observer, the play *Iphigenia at Ilium*, the reindeer, and the gate of the title. All these metaphors reflect the constant disjunction between appearance and reality as well as indicating how the society we see actually functions. Stavia, for example, is thirty-seven, and has been a member of the Council of Women for some fifteen years. Dawid, her son by Chernon, the result of his rape, chooses to stay with the warriors permanently, and Stavia, who has hoped against unwarranted hope that Dawid would return through the gate, puts on her role. Stavia the actor carries out the final meeting between herself and her son while Stavia the observer weeps helplessly. The disjunction between woman Stavia and Council member Stavia runs throughout the whole text, provoking reader dis/ease. Such a gap between the real woman and the member of the ruling council is based on exclusion, an exclusion which costs the council members an immense amount. Stavia, for example, must listen daily to Beneda and her mother Sylvia praise Chernon, the man who betrayed, beat, and raped her. She cannot admit the truth about Chernon because it is connected with secret Council business; the gap in knowledge between the unobservant Beneda and Stavia forces Stavia to pretend to a friendship she no longer feels. Fifteen years later, Beneda is one of the women who sees nothing that does not lie on the surface, while Stavia has been a member of the inner circle for fifteen years. Stavia's comment, "We used to be best friends," is not the least of the prices she pays for knowledge and the power to shape Women's Country.[18]

Much of the daily life in Marthatown, where the main characters live, is based on pretense. The servitors, who actually father many of the boys who return to the women, are never acknowledged as fathers, for example. The warriors who claim the sons are never told that they are being selected out. The women who consort with the warriors during carnival do not realize that they are artificially inseminated under guise of medical checks post-carnival and are not bearing warriors' sons. Most of the women make no association between the rising population of the women's town and the declining warrior populations as each year more and more men return through the gate. For that matter, no one realizes that whenever the grain reserves get low, war between the garrisons breaks out.

One of the most important features of this novel is the re-telling of a very basic Greek myth. While the play *Iphigenia at Ilium* starts at the same point in time as Euripides' *Trojan Women*, and refers to the play *Iphigenia at Aulis*, the Women's Country version of this drama has an agenda which differs from *Trojan Women* and *Iphigenia at Aulis*. In *Iphigenia at Ilium*, for example, Andromâche, rather than silently acquiescing to her son's death, resists and curses the messenger. In *Trojan Women*, Andromâche puts up no resistance for fear the brave Odysseus will forbid her son burial and leave him for the kites and vultures. In *Iphigenia at Aulis*, Ipheginia dies a willing death; but such is not the case in the Women's Country version. If *Trojan Women* is a commentary on Athens' barbarous treatment of captives during the initial stages of the Peleponnesian Wars, as Richard Lattimore contends, then *Iphigenia at Ilium* is a commentary on men's barbarous behavior toward women.[19] The warriors in this play use the women as indiscriminately as pawns, sacrifice them as unfeelingly as sheep, dispose of them as carelessly as slaves, and in general deny their humanity. The additional characters in *Iphigenia at Ilium* are the ghosts of Polyxena, Iphigenia, and Achilles, and it is their commentary which largely differentiates the two plays. By re/envisioning *Trojan Women*, Tepper foregrounds the women and denies their passivity. The subversion of patriarchal myth and the restoration of women's voices in *Iphigenia at Ilium* tells the women's stories and is also a warning about the consequences of permitting men mastery. Cassandra, for example, rather than being a figure of mockery, is acknowledged as a prophetess.

Iphigenia at Ilium is staged not as the tragedy it undoubtedly is, but as a farce in which Achilles wears a giant dildo, the Trojan women are painted tarts, and the doll representing Astanyax which is thrown off the walls of Troy is fat and red-cheeked. But the staging is at variance with the rhetoric, which is as gutwrenchingly tragic as *Trojan Women*; thus, the actors who understand that the yearly performance is tragic rather than comic are most likely to be the citizens who see beneath the surface of the comedy which the Council enacts. The sharp contrast between the staging and the rhetoric, the serious attention of the Council of Women and the servitors who act the drama, and the laughing women who applaud it, is rather jarring. As the play progresses, it diverges sharply from *Trojan Women*, and deals with the relationship between the ghosts of Iphigenia, Polyxena, Astanyax, and Achilles on the one hand, and Hecuba, Andromâche and Cassandra, the living survivors of Troy, on the other. The sub-text of the play echoes the relationship between the warriors and the women, the necessity for political lies, and also the Council's role. It also lays bare the tawdry lies of glory and honor which cover the pragmatism of power politics. And while the play may be staged as a farce, and ostensibly aimed at the warrior culture, it also underscores the lies the Council promulgates. The ghost of Iphigenia, for example, says that the warriors' songs claim she was a willing sacrifice, but in reality, "They [the poets] say I offered to die for Hellas! What did I know of Hellas?! . . . My father used me as he would a slave or a sheep from his flock."[20] The ghost of Polyxena is more graphic yet: "I wanted to live, but they killed me stinking like a dung-covered animal. . . . [T]hey killed me there in the mess with my skirts hiked up and blood and shit mixed like a stinking stew, damned to remember myself like that."[21]

While the element of farce is hard to see, the parallel to the Council is not. Beneath the necessary lies or myths lies the reality. And the reality in the relationship between men and women is summed up in the question Iphigenia asks Polyxena:

"Tell me. Did the men cry when they slit your throat? . . .

"No, no, they did not," Polyxena cried.

"They didn't cry when they were slitting mine, either," Stavia said through the rasping dryness memory had made of her throat.[22]

At the end of the play, the women tell Achilles what Hades is like:

"Like dream without waking. Like carrying water in a sieve. Like coming into harbor after storm. Barren harbor where the empty river runs through an endless desert into the sea. Where all the burdens have been taken away. . . . Hades is Women's Country."[23]

Thus, although the Women's Council sees the tragedy, sees the reality, the remainder of the women see only the farce, the appearance. They laugh and clap in a cocoon of ignorance that has been deliberately woven, but what they laugh about is far from comic. When the garrison commanders decide to betray their sworn oaths and take over Marthatown, for example, the Councilwomen of Marthatown, in conjunction with the other towns, decide to eradicate the garrison of Marthatown entirely. In this way, they remove the threat of sedition, reduce the useless mouths of the other garrisons, and solve the problem of supporting a garrison riddled with treachery. That some of the warriors may have been innocent is unimportant. Nor is the truth spoken aloud. The Women's Council, realizing that an explanation is needed both for the members of the garrison who were too young to fight and the grieving mothers and lovers, concocts a myth: "The Lady will distinguish the guiltless and the honorable from the traitors. Their honors will be paraded in heaven."[24] The Council thus invokes a lie to avoid having to admit the hard truth. The Council, knowing quite well that some of the garrison is innocent, has chosen to demarcate, demonize, scapegoat, and sacrifice an entire garrison in order to get rid of any traitors and also to reduce the economic drag on Women's Country. Some of the Council members have sons who march away in that garrison, sons who have denied them, but who are nevertheless their flesh and blood. Since they cannot admit that they arranged for the slaughter of the entire garrison, in conjunction with other Town Councils, they use much the same lie as the male poets who claimed Iphigenia died for Hellas. For this reason, the Council members enact the play yearly, as a reminder, not to the unaware women, but to themselves.

A reviewer for *The Washington Post* reveals the dis/ease embedded in this text: "[Tepper] not only keeps us reading, but by carrying several feminist dreams to the point of nightmare, she provokes a new look at old issues."[25] This comment, of course, is double-edged like so many comments on feminist texts. Whose dream and whose nightmare are questions which come to mind. Certainly it is dis/ease provoking to read about a society in which the ruling cabals make all the decisions for the other residents and do not scruple to murder and lie "for the good of the state," a political perspective which has been used throughout history to justify dubious ends. Perhaps the balance between the ruthless behavior more often associated with the male gender, and the idea that women must guard against their nurturing nature is also dis/ease producing. As Septemius Bird, a gypsy entertainer who has accepted a place in Women's Country, points out after Stavia's horrible experience:

"Misplaced nurturing. The biggest chink in your female armor. The largest hole in your defenses. The one thing you cannot and dare not absolutely guard against, for your nature must remain as it is for all your planning to come to fruition."[26]

If Stavia is not a nurturing woman and mother, her children will grow up lacking love; but Chernon successfully played upon this same need to nurture in order to lure her away, under orders from the garrison commanders to uncover the secrets of Women's Country.

The sense of a dream that might turn to a nightmare is hard to avoid in this novel. It is entirely possible that the Council will simply continue selecting out men and women who do not fit the parameters considered appropriate. Such rhetoric and policies sharply reverberate with at least one twentieth-century nightmare. Fascism, which rose to prominence in Europe, particularly in Nazi Germany and Italy, used many of the same strategies the Council uses. The subordination of the individual to the state, unquestioning obedience, and genetic selection come forcibly to mind. And as the question arose in the Greek *polei*, so it arises here: who, asked Plato, will guard the guardians? But then one must ask if the ends are not worth the means, and one must also consider that the women who are carrying out the agendas are aware, sharply aware, of the conflicted nature of their governing.

> "I do wonder, though, sometimes . . ." [comments Septemius]
> "Yes?" [replies Morgot]
> "Whether you ever feel guilty over what you do? You few who do all the doing."
> "I'll tell you what we call ourselves, among ourselves. That will answer your question. . . . We call ourselves the Damned Few. And if the Lady has a heaven for the merciful, we are not sure any of us will ever see it."[27]

But the Damned Few, those who watch *Iphigenia at Ilium* and see the tragedy, are also the bastions of Women's Country. Although many of the actions of the Council produce dis/ease, rendering harsh judgment on the Council women is difficult because their motives are undoubtedly worthy and their actions, risking damnation for the good of the state and the protection of the weaker members, constitute a sacrifice of heroic proportion. But to balance the admiration, the deceit, and the many manipulations create a counter-balance. What if the political balance of the Council should shift radically? Then the recurring question in Brin's *The Postman*, for example, would take on great importance: "Who will take responsibility for these foolish children?" Or in Plato's more dis/easeful terms: "Who will guard the guardians?" The Council could easily abuse the trust the women of Women's Country place in them; as politically unaware as most of the women are, they could easily fall victim to a council which works for the good of itself rather than the good of the country, and then the question of whose nightmare would be answered.

My third and final example, Stephen King's epic novel *The Stand* (1991) is generally considered an affirmative work.[28] In *Danse Macabre*, King acknowledges that "cutting the Gordian Knot simply destroys the riddle instead of solving it, and that the book's last line is an admission that the riddle still remains," but argues that "In spite of its apocalyptic theme, *The Stand* is mostly a hopeful book that echoes Albert Camus' remark that 'happiness, too, is inevitable.'" I read this novel not only against the grain but also against the author's expressed opinion, because I consider that King's conflicted remarks actually reinforce my contention that horror is not always reassuring. The Apollonian elements that

King points out are certainly there, but beneath the affirmative theme of rebirth lies a society that as King says, "carries a kind of germ with it."[29]

The lack of closure, the ambiguous ending, and the subversion of the new beginning effectively resist any attempt to see *The Stand* as affirmative. As in *The Gate to Women's Country*, the basic plot structure of *The Stand* concerns a post-apocalyptic society in which existing societal forms disappear and in which the survivors must reconstruct a society; the novel concerns their interactions and attempts to rebuild all the basic units of society. One subtext of the novel examines the consequences of secrecy and deceit in government and the possible dangers inherent in a government out of touch with its citizenry. As he did in *Firestarter* and *The Dead Zone*, King contends that any government system, however beneficent in origin, will eventually deconstruct because abuse of power is inherent and inevitable. In King's somewhat Gothic view, we cannot escape the chains of the past and are doomed to repeat history.

The main characters reflect a society sinking into dystopian entropy. Stuart Redman, a West Texas good ol' boy, lives in Arnette, a dying town—literally as well as metaphorically: the arrival of the apocalyptic plague will do no more than finish off what a severe economic downturn has started. Larry Underwood is lost in a rock star world of sex, drugs, 'n' rock-n-roll. Despite evidence to the contrary, he is frantically and unsuccessfully trying to convince himself that he's "a nice guy." Franny Goldsmith, unintentionally pregnant and unmarried, has an extremely hostile relationship with Carla, her mother, whose sole interest in life is her family's standing and genealogy. A familial dystopia comes into being when the dead past, the dead ancestors, and the dead history become privileged over the living. Nick Andros is a self-educated deaf-and-dumb drifter, a person who has only the most marginal stake in the American dream. Tom Cullen, another major figure, is mildly retarded. Glenn Bateman is an eccentric professor of sociology. Ralph Brentner is a good ol' boy, the kind of man a technological society is rapidly leaving behind. On the dark side stand prime exemplars of the strategies of exclusion. Lloyd Henried is a small-time crook caught in big-time trouble. Donald "Trashcan Man" Elbert is a psychotic firebug. Harold Lauder is, perhaps, the most tragic figure in the novel, someone who wants desperately to fit in but is prevented by his own personality from doing so. Nadine Cross, the prospective daemon bride, has never fit comfortably into American society. Various other characters mirror the feeling of displacement and emptiness that exists in America, once again depicted as a society whose values are almost entirely materialistic.

The occasion of the novel's apocalypse is a government project gone seriously agley; Project Blue, a virus with a mutating antigen base, an extremely high mortality rate, and no cure, is loosed on the world, and 99.4% of the world's population dies. The first part of the novel deals with the coming of the plague and the inevitable descent into dystopia as well as setting the scene for a new beginning. The United States is depicted as approaching dystopia in any event; the plague simply quickens matters. Such a scenario is rich with possibilities for the production of cultural dis/ease. Unfortunately, it is not beyond belief that such a situation is more realistic than fantastic, and this, I contend, is one of the sites for horror fiction.

One of the more dis/ease-provoking scenes occurs when General Billy Starkey, who has been relieved of duty, tells his replacement that it will be necessary to make certain that the whole world gets the Project Blue virus:

"It's imperative—*imperative*—that the other side never sees this as an artificial situation created in America. . . . [A]ll you need to say is *Rome falls*."

Starkey, whose daughter gave him a book of poems by Yeats, says,

"But there was one poem in that book I have never been able to get out of my mind. . . . [H]e said that things fall apart. The center doesn't hold. I believe he meant that things get flaky, Len. . . . Yeets [sic] knew that sooner or later things get goddamn flaky around the edges."

The poem, of course, is William Butler Yeats' "The Second Coming," and the lines, "Things fall apart; the centre cannot hold; Mere anarchy is loosed upon the world." Starkey continues, "The beast is on its way . . . and it's a good deal rougher than that fellow Yeets [sic] ever could have imagined."[30]

Starkey sees it as an entropic process, although the truth is similar to that expressed in *Swan Song*. Evil does not just happen; human agency is at the center of evil. It is human minds and hands which have created Project Blue, not some amorphous "thing." Things do not just fall apart, and centers do not simply fail to hold. In this case, the military-industrial complex has taken specific steps to attempt to retain weapons' superiority and specific steps to loose the rough beast. America will fall, not because of an external threat or a natural cataclysm, but by purely internal actions. The unsuccessful attempt to recast the responsibility onto the vague "things" and to deny agency is one of the most effective means in *The Stand* for generating dis/ease. The emphasis on secrecy, deceit, and denial of accountability will resurface throughout the novel with what I contend are disastrous results. The rhetoric of disassociation, however, is contrasted with the suicides of those responsible for Project Blue and world's end, and the futility of denying responsibility is made quite clear. Meanwhile, the plague spreads like wildfire, the government engages in a massive cover-up, government mouthpieces spit out soothing advice to simply take aspirin, drink fluids, and stay in bed, while increasing numbers succumb to the fatal flu. As the situation worsens, all semblance of either decency or democracy drops away.

In Ogunquit, Maine, for example, the people call a New England-type town meeting and decide to quarantine Ogunquit from "outsiders," which is a reasonable course of action. The next orders of business, however, reveal the exclusionary tactics. First, a motion is proposed to expel the sick residents. This motion is voted down, as nearly all the Ogunquit residents have sick relatives at home, and "How would they ever be able to look each other in the face again if . . . they had overreacted by putting their own out like pariah dogs?" A further motion is proposed, to whit, that the sick "*summer* people" be expelled. The summer people retort that "If they were treated in such a cavalier fashion, the people of Ogunquit could be sure they would never come back."[31] The breakdown in the social community is discussed in the rhetoric of the political, in terms not of treating people like pariah dogs, but of town services for which the summer people foot the bill. Although saving the corn crop does not seem to be a consideration, Ogunquit could well be the name of Shirley Jackson's unnamed community. Thus, the presence of external plague releases the strategies of exclusion almost immediately, and any ideas of honor or decency are the first casualties of the plague.

The descent into dystopia continues as martial law is harshly enforced, the Constitution is suspended, attempts by the media to tell the truth to the people are met by immediate execution, cities and towns are forcibly quarantined, and plague victims' corpses are either bulldozed under or dumped at sea. In this supposedly conservative text, the Army is on par with Hitler's Gestapo, and the media is heroic. Ray Flowers, a radio talk-show host, is ordered to stop broadcasting and refuses, saying, "I have been ordered to shut down the KFLT transmitter and I have refused the order, quite properly, I think. These men are acting like Nazis, not American soldiers. I am not—"[32] His speech is cut short by a burst from an automatic weapon. The sergeant who kills Flowers is in turn scragged. As the dystopian spiral continues, the Army runs completely amok, soldiers mutiny, ephemeral republics rise and fall, and a graffitto expresses the state of affairs quite nicely: "Dear Jesus, I will see you soon, Your friend, America. P.S. I hope you will still have some vacancies by the end of the week."[33]

Thus, the second part of the book opens with the government in complete disarray. Eventually, of course, things do fall apart, and neither the lies nor the center can hold; less than two weeks after Project Blue surfaces, the American body politic is a rotting corpse. As occurs in *Swan Song* and *The Postman*, America becomes nothing more than a geographical entity composed of wary individuals and straggling groups of survivors attempting to survive in a completely unfamiliar environment. However, as the first wave of shock wears off, people begin the long, slow process of rebuilding communities which have been completely destroyed not only by the flu, but by the institutions of power that are supposed to protect communities.

Two opposing communities, one in Las Vegas, Nevada, and one in Boulder, Colorado with two binarily conflicting political systems form in the wake of the plague, and good and evil are inextricably mixed and conflicted in both communities. If Las Vegas harbors those who have freely chosen evil, it also harbors those who have honestly mistaken totalitarian evil for needed order; if it has Randall Flagg, the Adversary, it also has mothers and children. If Boulder has "the good guys," Mother Abagail's people, it also has its share of slackers, trouble-makers, and those who choose evil in full knowledge of their options.

Abagail Freemantle, a 108-year-old black fundamentalist Christian from Nebraska, is the locus for the good. She has endured slavery, the rise and fall and rise of racism, the Depression, two world wars, and times both good and bad. Mother Abagail believes that she has been called by God to lead the survivors to Boulder, Colorado. She is reluctant to do so, but being a genuinely god-fearing woman, she, like Moses, to whom she is often compared, accepts God's charge to lead the survivors to the "Promised Land."

Randall Flagg, the "Dark Man," is the *locus* for the evil. He coalesces in "troubled times"; indeed his first memory of being born is during the early Sixties in the midst of the Civil Rights Movement. King is very specific about Flagg and his American status: "It was his country and none knew or loved it better."[34] King also closely allies Flagg with the "rough beast" which Starkey has so feared yet brought into existence:

He . . . was going to be squeezed out of the laboring cunt of some great sand-colored beast that even now lay in the throes of its contractions. . . . He had been born when times changed, and the times were going to change again.[35]

Like McCammon's demon, Flagg revels in the coming destruction: "He could *taste* it, a sooty hot taste as though God was [sic] planning a cookout and all civilization was going to be the barbecue."[36] Flagg is a Dionysian creature with no beliefs except the politics of hate: all fanatics are grist to his mill. If, as King plainly states, Flagg is a typical American, and his cowboy boots and denim indicate that this is indeed the case, and if he is also a metaphor for America, "a body politic with its network of roads embedded in its skin like marvellous capillaries . . ." then separating America from the evil associated with Flagg becomes impossible. The reader must acknowledge that such hate groups do exist in America, and that if Flagg is well known by "those who have been taught to hate so well that the hate shows on their faces like harelips . . ."[37] but is also one of us, then the antinomous elements are foregrounded and cultural dis/ease rises sharply.

The most important structures of the novel deal not with the plague but with mankind's inability to forge communities which can successfully resist the inherent corruption of political systems. Both communities are fragmented by the end of the novel and neither political model has been especially successful. Both communities engage liberally in the strategies of exclusion, with disastrous results. The disintegration of the liberal community of Boulder starts when Nick Andros, one of the keystones of the Boulder community, unilaterally decides to exclude Harold Lauder from any participation in the government of the Free Zone. The Boulder community employs the strategies of exclusion as its primary governing mechanism with subsequent catastrophic results.

The Boulder Free Zone is reminiscent of a very liberal city, almost a "do-your-own-thing" liberal commune. As Nick Andros writes, circling the words in a doodles stockade, "*Authority. Organization. . . . How well they went together . . . and what a sorry sound they made.*"[38] He adds politics, and the potentially lethal triad is set. But some governmental body is undoubtedly necessary. The Free Zone's societal values and political model tend toward the liberal traditions, except in terms of the religious model, which is fundamental Southern Baptist in its stark delineation of good and evil. In Mother Abagail's world view, the idea that evil/Satan has no independent existence but is part of every human being is absolutely wrong. As she says, "Mankind disposes nothing in the Lord's sight."[39] On the other hand, there is no attempt to organize a "Free Zone Church" and thus implement a theocracy or a state religion. Thus, in Boulder, Mother Abagail deliberately rejects any worldly power, but reserves the right to be included in all deliberations which concern "the dark man."

Randall Flagg sets up his camp in Las Vegas. The Las Vegas community is totalitarian, with somewhat reactionary and conservative laws, all of which are enacted by Randall Flagg, First Citizen. Flagg, unlike

Mother Abagail, does not refuse earthly power and defines the community he will govern very arbitrarily. In some ways, this community seems to be admirably confronting the problems which plague modern society. Everyone, for example, is gainfully employed, and no shirking is allowed. Drug users are executed, something with which the more conservative element in American society might agree; the method, however, which is crucifixion, might seem a bit extreme. Flagg, in a deliberate echo of the fascistic Mussolini, has the trains running on time, a well-armed and powerful police force, an army, and an air force.

By the time the citizenry realizes he is offering not community but demonization, the destruction of Las Vegas has become inevitable. But while many of these people do not understand what Flagg is or what Flagg stands for, many of the Las Vegasites understand exactly what he stands for and have willingly come West to join him. Some of the people who have gathered around Flagg are those who willingly seek evil; some are societal misfits who feel a need to belong somewhere, and some, feeling that American society is too liberal and too permissive, deliberately embrace the monster. Barry Dorgan, for example, chooses Las Vegas because as a seventeen-year-veteran of the Los Angeles police force, he has seen the effect of "do your own thing." As Glenn Bateman, eccentric professor of sociology and philosopher extraordinare says, "Your experience with a few babykillers, young man, does not justify the embrace of a monster."[40] Once the monster has been embraced, however, it is impossible to step back.

Neither community works. Las Vegas is eventually destroyed when a nuclear bomb found by "Trashcan Man," a psychotic firebug, is brought to Flagg at the public execution of Glenn Bateman, Larry Underwood, and Ralph Brentner. The three members of the Boulder Free Zone Committee have walked to Las Vegas to confront Flagg, at Mother Abagail's direction and as willing sacrifices. As Glenn Bateman inscribes on his jail cell, "*I am not the potter, not the potter's wheel, but the potter's clay; is not the value of the shape attained as dependent upon the intrinsic worth of the clay as upon the wheel and the master's skill?*"[41] The sacrifice, the holocaust, does take place, saving Boulder, at least for the moment, by blowing Las Vegas to kingdom come. While the threat from Las Vegas is nullified, it is not the external threat which proves to be the Free Zone's undoing. The Boulder community loses direction and veers increasingly in the direction of the hyper-conservative political model which Flagg favored, and demarcation of the original residents of the Free Zone is an inevitable result. By novel's end, Boulder is disintegrating, too, and in the process of reconstructing the behaviors that brought apocalypse on the world.

If, as I argue, *The Stand*'s basic premise is that government is essentially corrupt because power eventually corrupts, many of the events described could happen today. The dis/ease generated by the premise that one's own trusted government and not the enemy "other" is responsible for wiping out 99.4% of the entire world is considerably greater than the threat posed by someone like Saddam Hussein. Unfortunately, it is not beyond belief that the United States government could be busily fomenting various biological warfare viruses; it is not, alas, entirely in the realm of fiction that the Army's security measures might fail and a plague be loosed on the American people. Nor is it out of common and recent knowledge that the government might not only lie to us, but also become extremely fascistic in its attempts to control the situation. The nightmarish incidents of martial law in *The Stand*, for example, are horrifying and terrifying, not because they occur in the realms of fantasy, but precisely because they do not. Deliberate cover-ups, martial law, suspension of First Amendment rights, mass burials, forcible quarantines, citizens manhandled into the Center for Disease Control, euphemisms such as "media management" (i.e., media control), and "crowd control," (i.e., shooting and hanging the citizenry), are all entirely possible. King describes a world where anyone brave enough to expose the truth behind the government's cover-up is executed on charges of treason. *The Stand* echoes and exaggerates such American institutions as Japanese internment camps, Watergate, Irangate, Contragate, the power of the FBI, and the ability of the government to cover up the truth.

With the 99.4% death rate, predicted for the virus "Captain Trips," we arrive in horror territory. A plague this effective is a deliberate reflection of the extreme or exaggerated component of horror fiction. No plague in recorded history has been this lethal, this globally effective. The average mortality rate for the "Black Death" pandemic was 40%.[42] The government denying any "superflu" epidemic while quarantining entire towns, advising people to treat the extremely fatal flu like any garden variety influenza to avoid panic, and covertly controlling the news and imposing military law in a vain cover-up attempt are among the really horrific elements. Or perhaps the real dis/ease lies in the fear that this novel does not exaggerate anything but the initial scenario and perhaps not even that. Who, after all, knows what apocalypse our government is busy cooking up in secret labs?

The dis/ease is not provoked, solely by the vision of a dystopian America in its death-throes, though that is horrific enough in its own right; an alternative cultural model of American government, based on subverting democratic institutions is also dis/easeful. It is, after all, the survivors of the government-induced plague themselves, in their attempt to start a new society "right," who subvert the democratic process and bring most of the subsequent tragedy on their own heads. As Glenn Bateman points out, it is necessary to re-ratify such basic tenets of American belief as the Declaration of Independence, the Constitution, and the Bill of Rights. Stu Redman disagrees:

> "Christ, Glen, we're all Americans—"
>
> "No, that's where you're wrong," Glen said. . . . . "Government is an *idea*, Stu. . . . It's an inculcation, nothing but a memory path worn through the brain. . . . Our people here are very soon going to wake up to the fact that the old ways are gone, and that they can restructure society any old way they want. We want—we need—to catch them before they wake up and do something nutty."

Bateman points out that if a motion were formulated to put Mother Abagail in charge, with an advisory staff, the "citizens" of Boulder would agree by acclamation, "blissfully unaware that they had just voted the first operating American dictatorship into power since Huey Long." Stu, shocked, again disagrees:

> "Oh, I can't believe that. There are college graduates here, lawyers, political activists—"
>
> "Maybe they used to be. . . . No, Stu, it's very important that the first thing we do is ratify the spirit of the old society. That's what I mean about recreating America."[43]

In other words, Batemen wants to articulate the old and often unarticulated cultural model of America and bring it to the surface. As Roy D'Andrade points out in "A Folk Model of the Mind," much of the data embedded in a particular folk/cultural model is "treated as if they were obvious facts of the world," and may "not be made explicit." Quinn and Holland note in discussing cultural models that

> It is no doubt true that some knowledge is more habitually, hence more readily, put into words than other knowledge; that some knowledge but not other knowledge is tidily "packaged" in memory, hence easily retrieved for the telling; and that some knowledge is under conscious and voluntary control whereas other pieces are less available for introspection and articulation.[45]

Ironically, the very first action the organizing committee takes brings about the eventual downfall of "the city on a hill." In a classic exclusionary move, they omit Harold Lauder from the list of candidates and then move to subvert the democratic process. Harold Lauder is an extremely bright but troubled and extremely obnoxious adolescent with a whopping superiority/inferiority complex. But by invoking the mechanics of exclusion and targeting Harold, the Committee dooms itself and eventually the community as a whole. Their action in excluding him unilaterally has far-reaching repercussions. Harold falls victim to his own self-image and the Dark Man's wiles, and plans to kill the entire Free Zone Committee prior to leaving for Las Vegas. Demon they have defined him, and demon he will be. Harold realizes that he could simply ignore their action, work with the Committee, and accept the growing admiration many residents have for him: He could, he thinks, "turn himself into a new person, a fresh Harold Lauder cloned from the old one by the sharp intervening knife of the superflu epidemic." But he rejects this option in favor of evil: "In the new Free Zone society, he could only be Harold Lauder. Over there [in Las Vegas] he could be a prince."[46]

The Free Zone Ad Hoc Committee wishes, of course, to be the first elected officials. To make certain that no one not on the Committee is nominated, they decide to ask a friend to nominate each of them and move to empanel the committee by acclamation.

> "We'll see to it that the people who get elected are the same people who were on the ad-hoc committee. We'll put the rush on everybody and get the vote taken before people can do any tub-thumping for their friends. We can hand pick people to nominate us and then second us. The vote'll go through as slick as shit through a goose."
>
> "That's neat," said Stu admiringly.
>
> "Sure," said Glen glumly. "If you want to short-circuit the democratic process, ask a sociologist."[47]

From this well meaning foray into machine politics, an idea and spirit of America that is at least as valid though not as well articulated as the Constitution, comes the eventual dissolution of the Boulder community. Although the omniscient narrator claims that "Boulder was a *tabula so rasa* it could not sense its own novel beauty," this is not accurate.[48] The Boulder society, made up of survivors of a dystopian, post-apocalyptic society, bring the seeds of their own destruction with them. Flagg escapes, Las Vegas is destroyed, and the Free Zone citizenry does not have to worry about being conquered by external forces. But the Boulder community itself, formed by corrupt measures, eventually fragments and starts the re-construction of the same dystopian society from which they have come and from which they cannot escape.

Although the ending of *The Stand* is frequently read affirmatively, such a reading excludes and discounts several important points. The first and most important is that the forces of evil are checkmated temporarily but not destroyed. Flagg, in fact, is hard at work at novel's end shaping a primitive tribe to his own ends. The good guys, in other words, win an extremely limited victory. The second is the contagion and corruption that have so permeated the government and the society that government by the people is an impossibility and yet government by the people is the touchstone of the American Experience. At novel's end, people are in fragmentation mode, and the Boulder community is disestablishing itself. If an American community is supposedly composed not only of the individualistic pioneers heading West, or in this case, East, but is also comprised of strong and effective communities, what happens when the challenge to re-invent, to re-create America, goes awry? I would contend that underneath the surface of the affirmative ending, a great amount of unresolved cultural anxiety lurks. And the ending actually does little to dissipate such dis/ease. What if there is no concrete America? What if government is nothing more than a memory path worn through the brain, an outworn and overgrown path which no longer works? Add in the novel's opening phases with its constant use of the symbolism of "The Second Coming" and the haunting image of "a rough beast, slouching towards Bethlehem to be born," with things falling apart and centers failing to hold, scenarios in which the American government is revealed as corrupt, deceitful and eventually fascistic, and the so-called "happy and affirmative ending" deconstructs along with the community of Boulder and the *idea* of America.

This "brave new world" is as infected with plague as was its predecessor; moreover, the cycle will repeat. The plague, of course, is a metaphor, a litany for all that is intrinsically and irrevocably wrong with contemporary American society. Whether one reads the plague on an absolutely literal level, i.e., the government does have secret testing grounds and is busily generating new improved plagues, or as a commentary on AIDS, or as a politicized metaphor for the dangers of covert and fascistic government, the whole idea of a plague wiping out entire societies, sundering family ties, and leaving people in a dystopian world is very dis/easeful. By the time the novel ends, approximately two/tenths of one percent of the American population has survived the plague and the nuclear explosion in Las Vegas. Yet this community cannot make a stand together, which is a sad commentary on the possibility of government or politics to forge lasting communities in the face of the strategies of exclusion which underlie the subversion of democracy in America.

Stephen King, however, sees *The Stand* as affirming conservative values primarily because the child born to Stu and Frannie survives. It is one of the first infants conceived post-plague and provides an answer as to whether or not the human race will continue. A previous birth has already resulted in two dead infants and Frannie dreams of stillbirths and a mutant child. If, as seems possible, the children do not share their parents' immunity, than humankind faces a short and profitless existence and soon will be as extinct as if the plague had had a 100% mortality rate. The well-intentioned struggle will be ultimately useless and, as in texts like Nevil Shute's *On the Beach*, human beings will cease to matter. Thus, the child born to Frannie and Stu is an important indicator that life will go on, that people will get another chance, that happiness is inevitable. But while one germ, that of Captain Trips, has not proven victorious, the other germ that King sees as emblematic of society has not been defeated. King acknowledges that "the survivors would be the first ones to take up all the old quarrels" and that the problems remain. At the same time, on a level below that of the capering nihilist who does "the funky chicken over the whole world," he trusts that morality, which he defines as coming "from a good heart" and couples with civilization, will triumph.[49]

Unfortunately, the germ that King sees as inherent in society is multiplying quite nicely in the petri dish of Boulder society. If Boulder is not quite Las Vegas this year, what about the next year, or the next decade? The Free Zone is no less contaminated than was Las Vegas and no more immune than that society to the strategies of exclusion and the thinking which loosed the plague on the world. King cannot have it both ways: he cannot deploy Camus and also have the following sentence: "And the righteous and unrighteous alike were consumed in that holy fire."[50]

11

DYSTOPIAN SOCIETIES, MONSTERED BODIES,
THE BODY POLITIC, AND THE PROBLEMS OF COMPLICITY

"There is still time . . . Brother."[1]

This third chapter on dystopia deals solely with those fictional societies which are irremediably, irredeemably dystopian. Some texts achieve this state of affairs by means of a specific type of government which pursues an agenda resulting in dystopia for certain citizens, others by an apocalypse such as a nuclear holocaust, but many texts arrive at this end primarily through the actions of the people who live in the represented societies. The complicity of the inhabitants in producing dystopia is frequently the most dis/ease-provoking element of the texts. While the concept of utopia is extremely problematic, as utopia for one person or class almost invariably means dystopia for the excluded people or classes, and both utopias and dystopias are built by the strategies of exclusion, the texts discussed here are extremely negative examples.

As in Chapter 9, the texts to be treated fall into three closely connected categories. The first category deals with the fate of the individual in a dystopia, the second deals with entire societies which face total extinction through the actions of individuals, and the third category concerns a citizenry's active complicity in dystopia-making.In the first category, Margaret Atwood's *The Handmaid's Tale* explores the concept of a gendered dystopia from the excluded gender's point-of-view. In the second category, Nevil Shute's *On the Beach*, a novel which concerns the aftermath of atomic war, is almost completely concerned with the eschatology of the endgame.[2] In my third category, Ursula Le Guin's "The Ones Who Walk Away from Omelas" examines a utopia which is constructed on the bodies of the innocent and powerless and explores the dark reality behind any utopia, reminding the reader that a utopia which is not for everyone is ultimately for no one at all. What makes this text the touchstone of disaffirmative horror fiction is that, unlike the characters of the other texts cited in this chapter, the Omelans choose a comfortable "utopia" in full knowledge of the evil mechanisms which construct it.

Margaret Atwood's *The Handmaid's Tale* (1985) explores the antinomy between utopia and dystopia, an antinomy that is, like that in *The Gate to Women's Country,* defined almost entirely in terms of gender. Some critics see this novel as political science-fiction, and indeed comparisons to George Orwell's *1984* or Anthony Burgess' *A Clockwork Orange* do apply. While I myself am sharply reminded of Orwell's *Animal Farm,* Atwood sharply foregrounds gender issues.[3] Although the novel centers on feminist concerns, as women are the people who do not get utopia but dystopias which range from being cleaning women in toxic landfills to being Handmaids to the Commanders and their Wives, Atwood has explicitly stated that she is concerned more with the rise of a totalitarian government.[4] Her novel is informed by the fears that a fanatically religious, patriarchally based, totalitarian government, possibly modeled on such fundamentalist groups as the Moral Majority or the Christian Coalition, might take power in the United States and implement its conservative mysogynistic agendas. Tepper's grim evocation of the patriarchal Holyland also comes sharply to mind, but in Atwood's text, escape is much more problematic.

In the Republic of Gilead, women serve several state-approved functions. They are Wives, Handmaids, Aunts, Marthas, or Colonists. Women outside of the first four designations are Unwomen, like the Colonists. Wives are the officially married women of the upper echelons. Handmaids are concubines, based on the Biblical figure of Leah who gave her handmaid Bilbah to her husband so that she, Leah, could have children. In this context, Leah's angry words to her husband Jacob, "Give me children, or I shall die!" take on an ominous resonance.[5] In this society, however, it is not the Wives who will die for lack of children, but the Handmaids. Handmaids are passed from Commander to Commander, and after three unsuccessful placements are transported to the colonies, a virtual death sentence. The Aunts, "the crack female control agency,"[6] are more like the Jewish *Kapos* in the concentration camps or the Polish Blues in Occupied Poland than kin; they carry out the indoctrination of the Handmaids with Biblical verses as corrupt as crediting St. Paul with "From each according to her ability, to each according to his need," a citation which would have surprised not only Paul but Marx, as well as with cattle prods, steel cables, and other instruments of torture.[7] The Marthas are women past child-bearing age fortunate enough to escape the colonies and be domestic servants, permitted to work until they drop. The women sent to the colonies are superfluous (old or infertile) women or feminist trouble-makers who are forced to burn the bodies of insurrectionists, clean toxic landfills or nuclear waste sites, or, more fortunately, grow crops; they are sent to the colonies to be used up.

In this society, women's bodies do not belong to themselves at all. We never know the main character's name, even though it is her narrative in which we become absorbed and her life in which we become enmeshed. She is merely "Offred" (Of/fred), defined by the name of her current assignment, as are the other Handmaids; when she moves on, she will have her name adjusted to reflect her new assignment. She has no space to call her own, no sense of individuality, and no identity outside of her reproductive status. She is a pair of viable ovaries and an empty egg-like shell, one which, moreover, it is her sole responsibility to fill: "There are only women who are fruitful and women who are barren, that's the law."[8] Even though many of the Commanders are sterile, the women are invariably blamed: "It's only women who can't, who remain stubbornly closed, damaged, defective."[9] Since she is only a void, a container, and since her only function is to be filled, she is not only completely commodified, but both valorized and demarcated/demonized. Handmaids are clearly marked by their scarlet dress and restricted mobility, but they have undeniable status. The Wives, the Aunts, and the Marthas hate and resent them but need them as well. The constant discourse by the Aunts on how the Handmaids' sacrifices will eventually benefit society as well as the constant scapegoating define the Handmaids. Their costumes, lengthy asexual/sexual robes in scarlet, blinkered headgear, and red veils; the absolute prohibition on reading with substitution of pictographs for words; the discourse of religious fascism; the block warden mentality; the transportation of "undesirables," i.e., feminists, to the colonies; their complete physical and mental restriction—all bespeak a political dystopia, one which is saturated by the strategies of exclusion on all levels.[10]

Thus, in Atwood's nightmare, women are nothing more than prisoners of their bodies, viable or non-viable ovaries. Not even the Commanders' legal wives entirely escape this status, although as Serena Joy, the wife of the Commander, says to Offred when she joins the household, "As for my husband, he's just that. My husband. I want that to be perfectly clear. Till death do us part. It's final. . . . It's one of the things we fought for."[11] Thus the Wives of the Commanders, though generally past childbearing, are the exception to the women-as-breeder valuation. Serena Joy's status has its ironies, however. Serena Joy used to make speeches "about how women should stay home. Serena Joy didn't do this herself, she made speeches instead. . . . She has become speechless. . . . How furious she must be, to be taken at her word.[12]

No woman in Gilead has any status or identity of her own, only that which, like the Handmaid's names, has been assigned to them. This ciphering of women has a dis/easeful effect on most women readers, especially critical women readers who are aware of the religious and social history of patriarchal domination and who realize that much of what happens to women in Gilead has happened to women before. Much of the gendered discourse in the novel comes straight from the Old Testament. The idea that women can own their own property, keep their own wages, and control their own bodies has, after all, been legal for little more than a century.[13] A review in *The Houston Chronicle* claims that "Atwood takes many trends which exist today and stretches them to their logical and chilling conclusions."[14] The problem lies in the "stretch." How much exaggeration actually exists in this novel? Nothing happens here that has not happened in living memory. The attempted extermination of the Jews of Nazi Germany, for example, proceeded along much the same lines. First their funds were frozen and their property confiscated; they were fired, rounded up, and made into Unpeople, whose only use was as bodies which served the State. Offred, like many of the "sub-humans" in the concentration camps, is tattooed, so she is always identifiable. Like *The Painted Bird*, Atwood's novel is horror without those elements automatically associated with the genre, for the horror here is strictly mundane and all too human, which is what makes it most horrific. It is also extremely dis/easeful to consider how many Moral Majority/Christian Coalition types would see this as utopian, not dystopian, as a society which has restored the proper social order defined by Jehovah.

The Handmaid's Tale is dystopian fiction with several sources of horror. One is almost purely political as the fanatical religious group, The Sons of Jacob, which overthrows the government and establishes the *soi-disant* Republic of Gilead, sets up a totalitarian theocracy in which groups and individuals who are not fanatical Christians are denied participation in the "republic," hunted down, commodified, and disposed of. Roman Catholic nuns, for example, are forced to renounce the vows they have taken as Brides of Christ and either accept Handmaid status or go to the Colonies. While many do choose the Colonies, some break under the torture and accept the red veil. As Offred says, "None of us likes to draw one for a shopping partner. They are more broken than the rest of us; it's hard to feel comfortable with them."[15] Even within the ranks of those subject to the strategies of exclusion, nuns are more demonized than other women, perhaps because a recusant nun, having rescinded her pledge to Christ, makes the other women more sharply aware of the economies of loss and the absolute power of Gilead.

Another source of dis/ease lies in the ease with which the United States of America becomes the Republic of Gilead. The first move on the part of the Sons of Jacob is to machine-gun the President and the entire

Congress and blame it on Islamic fundamentalists; the second move freezes all women's bank accounts, followed in fairly rapid succession by laws prohibiting women from working, laws prohibiting women from holding property, laws assigning their monetary credits to their husbands, laws invalidating second marriages or marriages performed by forbidden churches, laws which not only invalidate second marriages but declare the women morally unfit and confiscate any offspring:

> "There were marches, of course, a lot of women and some men. . . . And when it was known that the police, or the army, or whoever they were, would open fire almost as soon as any of the marches even started, the marches stopped."[16]

When Offred and the other women are "let go," her employer says,

> "It isn't me. . . . I don't want any trouble. If there's trouble, the books might be lost, things will get broken. . . . If you don't go now, they'll come in themselves."[17]

In this society, the employer fears that "things" might get broken or books might get lost. And his fears are well grounded in reality. The problem in this society, however, is that more than things or books, important as the latter are, might get lost or broken. People, all women and some men, might get lost and broken, too. And the employer's action, which reeks of complicity, forces complicity on the women as well. If you don't go now, if you do not accept this status, if you protest the sudden loss of your livelihood, they'll come in.

And when the women have left the office, as Offred notes, "We looked at one another's face and saw dismay and a certain shame. . . . What was it about this that made us feel as though we deserved it?"[18] What indeed? Why would a group of women so tamely accept the loss of such basic rights, and, moreover, feel as though they are in some amorphous, undefinable way deserving of such demonization? Perhaps this acceptance of demarcation and demonization is one of the most disturbing elements of Atwood's novel. To be excluded by the dominant culture is bad enough, but to feel as though one deserved the exclusion is infinitely worse. None of these women have done anything to deserve their fate. In common with the rest of the citizenry, they took for granted certain established freedoms and did not react swiftly enough to their impending disappearance. But who among us would? Like various groups of demarcated, demonized others, they accept scapegoating and sacrifice as a deserved penalty.

Even worse than the political dystopia, however, is the social dystopia thus created. As in many other disaffirmative fictions, Gilead can only work with the complicity of the women. Were the women to stand together, the regime could not be even marginally successful. After all, dead women bear no offspring. But each group is set against the other groups. The Wives despise the Handmaids and treat them as badly as they dare. The Handmaids, rather than uniting as one body, are at odds with each other. As is typical in a dystopic society, the Handmaids, rather than being encouraged to unite, are encouraged to untie. Certainly the indoctrination sessions in which the Aunts and the Handmaids force women who have been raped and abused to take the blame on themselves are dis/ease provoking. Janine, a Handmaid who has been gang-raped at fourteen and also had an abortion, is forced to confess her "crime" while the other Handmaids chant such uplifting and supportive sentiments as "her fault" and "crybaby." "We meant it, [says Offred] which is the bad part. I used to think well of myself. I didn't then." By the following week, Janine has learned her lesson. "It was my own fault. I led them on. I deserved the pain."[19]

When the Handmaids demonize Janine, buying into a sick patriarchal notion that the woman is not the victim but is in some way responsible for her rape and abuse, they are upholding the very system that has reduced them to ovaries. By demonizing Janine, they are abrogating basic human decency and any protection against a similar fate. Addressed as girls, supervised constantly, unable to go to the bathroom without permission, housed in dorms, and indoctrinated night and day, it is perhaps no wonder that the Handmaids turn into spiteful children. After all, everyone knows that women are gossipy and catty by nature. A Handmaid criticizing the regime or attempting to escape will probably be turned in by another Handmaid, so few dare express any opinions for fear of betrayal. The "Aunts," in order to avoid the colonies and sure but lingering death, choose to mistreat the Handmaids. The "Aunts" are not equipped with cattle goads for show; they not only encourage the Handmaids to spy on each other but also use torture at any provocation. These actions ensure that no viable community of women will ever rise up to challenge the patriarchy. The Marthas, subject to the Wives and prospects for the Colonies, dare not offend anyone. Divide and conquer works quite well here: give the Aunts a little power, give the Wives a little power, terrify the Marthas, both privilege and denigrate the Handmaids, and no cohesive challenge will arise.

Thus, instead of a fellowship of women, women standing up for each other and for the concept of sisterhood, as occurs to some degree in Tepper's *The Gate to Women's Country*, we have the strategies of exclusion running rampant. Naturally, such a result is the plan of the governmental leaders. How better to control a large group than through the strategies of exclusion? Women who are suspicious of each other and who are out solely to protect their own lives will never make an effective stand against this abusive patriarchy. What is more, the government leaders use women's emotional strengths against them. The Aunts, calling on the societally inculcated notion that women are natural nurturers, naturally cooperative, attempt to claim that the future will be better:

"The women will live in harmony together, all in one family; you will be like daughters to them [the Wives]. . . . There will be bonds of real affection. . . . But we can't be greedy pigs and demand too much before it's ready, can we?"[20]

Ironically, this same theme surfaces in *The Gate to Women's Country*, in which women are called upon to be the nurturers, the care-givers, the sacrificers. Stavia falls prey to Chernon's blandishments and, as everyone but Stavia sees, she is captured by the usefulness of "that wounded child look. . . . A little obvious suffering to make mama and sister pay attention. . . . So there she is, caught in the middle, feeling she's been the one to hurt him most, all her fault."[21] Offred is caught in the same double bind as Stavia; the Commander, who does not like impersonal sex with Offred in the presence of his wife, establishes a strictly illicit relationship with Offred, behaving somewhat like a shy boy, wanting emotion and tenderness from a woman he has reduced to a pair of ovaries. He wants her to sit in his office in domestic bliss, paging through a forbidden magazine, playing Scrabble, and talking:

"I would like—," he says. "This will sound silly." And he does look embarrassed. . . . He's old enough to remember how to look that way and to remember also how appealing women once found it. "I'd like you to play a game of Scrabble with me."[22]

But these are all qualities from a world he has deliberately destroyed. Indeed, the Commander, somewhat tentatively identified as Frederick R. Waterford, belongs to a group of men whose spokesman says, "Our big mistake was teaching them to read. We won't do that again."[23]

The Commander can engage in nostalgia, pretend that this is something other than what it is, but the plain fact of the matter is that asking Offred "if she will be all right, as if the stairway is a dark street, open[ing] his door, just a crack and listen[ing] for noises in the hall," which she sees "like being on a date, like sneaking into the dorm after hours," asking her to kiss him, "as if you meant it," is nostalgia and dangerous nostalgia at that.[24] The Commander, as Offred thinks to herself, knows all the rules; and while he may be above them, she is not. But she hasn't any real options; caught as she is in an impossible situation between the Wife and the Commander, she can only assess where the real power lies and hope. To further compound her dilemma, Serena Joy, suspecting that her husband is sterile, and wanting the status a child would afford her, has offered to connive with Offred and allow her the opportunity to become impregnated by Nick, the Commander's driver. No matter what choice Offred makes, she faces possible death.

By the time the second meeting with the Commander takes place, Offred has discovered that her predecessor hanged herself: "'Serena found out,'" he says, as if this explained it. And it does. If your dog dies, get another dog."[25] So, while Offred may attempt to fool herself into thinking that she and the Commander are conspiring against the Wife, that the strategies of exclusion do not apply to her, she knows that the Commander is simply indulging in a whim. And whims are expendable. Ironically, her only safety lies in having him treat her as what society has defined her as: "part of the background, inanimate or transparent."[26] Later, when he takes her "out" for an evening to Jezebel's, an old-time bordello, and gets a hotel room, he is disappointed when she cannot respond to him sexually. And what does Offred do? "Fake it, I scream inside my head. You must remember how. Let's get this over with or you'll be here all night. Bestir yourself. Move your flesh around, breathe audibly. It's the least you can do."[27] Offred, deprived of everything that matters in life by this man and his cohorts in crime, does feel an obligation to respond sexually. Thus, yet more dis/ease is generated by the way the representatives of the patriarchy twist women's very natures and better qualities against the women themselves. The most disquieting aspect of the strategies of exclusion lies, not in the application, but in the complicity they engender.

One of the effects of this particular novel is to cast a new light on Tepper's *The Gate to Women's Country*. Perhaps the strategies of exclusion are a necessary evil and women cannot live safely in a man's world. Perhaps it is better to avoid the fate of the women in *The Handmaid's Tale* and form separate societies. Deprived of her identity, her husband, her child, her cat, her home, and everything but her physical life, which only has value as a vessel, sitting in a room carefully furnished to avoid any possibilities of escape, but with "a rug on the floor, of braided rags . . . made by women in their spare time, from things that have no further use."[28] Offred remembers a conversation she and Moira, her radically feminist best friend once had, in another life, in another time, when they were free to associate together, drink coffee, and speak their minds.

Small things, perhaps, but now completely out of reach. Recounting the conversation, Offred recalls,

> "I said there was more than one way of living with your head in the sand, and if Moira thought she could create Utopia by shutting herself up in a women-only enclave, she was sadly mistaken. Men were not just going to go away. You couldn't just ignore them."[29]

Now she is in a society where she cannot ignore men although men, essentially, ignore her. And worse, the dystopia produced by the Gilead-eans poisoned her relationship with her husband. After her bank account has been frozen and her employment terminated, she thinks to herself, "He doesn't mind this at all. Maybe he even likes it. We are not each other's anymore. Instead, I am his." And Offred, isolated now in her room, reduced to a blasted, empty, ovaried shell, thinks, "So Luke. . . what I need to know is, Was I right? Because we never talked about it. By the time I could have done that, I was afraid to. I couldn't afford to lose you."[30]

The contrast between the women of Gilead and the women of Marthatown is painfully obvious. The women of Gilead have no sense of community at all; the Aunts, in addition to using the stick, are holding out a shriveled carrot to the Handmaids and asking them to believe they are making a worthy sacrifice for generations of women yet to come, so these women can grow up to be breeders—illiterate, mindless, identity-less ciphers. Tepper's novel includes as a counterpoint to the Women's Country, a society, the Holyland, much like Gilead in terms of the social and political structures. These two societies illustrate the danger of losing one's community, of letting a mysogynistic patriarchy take charge. The women of Marthatown have built their own community; whatever lacks may exist, a sense of autonomy and selfhood is not among them. In Gilead, as in Marthatown, a women's culture exists. In both societies, certain functions belong to the women. In Gilead, the privilege of attending a Particicution and rending the male malefactor, ostensibly a rapist, into bloody gibbets is specifically a Handmaid's priv-ilege; birth is also women's business.[31] Thus, the women's culture in Gilead is defined entirely by the patriarchy. The Particicution, for exam-ple, functions to allow the women to diffuse their anger; as Professor Pieixoto notes, "It must have been most gratifying for these Handmaids, so rigidly controlled at other times, to be able to tear a man apart with their bare hands every once in a while." The women, however, are no more administering justice than are any other pawns of an oppressive regime. In Marthatown, the Ordinances may or may not be a tool for control, but at least the ordinances were made by some of the people who must follow them and genuinely in the interests of the community.

In the novel's very conflicted epilogue, the authors of an academic paper on Gilead note that

"As the architects of Gilead knew, to institute an effective totalitarian system . . . you must offer some benefits and freedoms, at least to a privileged few, in return for those you remove. . . . [T]he best and most cost-effective way to control women for reproductive and other purposes was through women themselves. . . . [N]o empire imposed by force or otherwise has ever been without this feature: control of the indigenous by members of their own group."[32]

This comment creates dis/ease by pointing up the complicity involved. Women, after all, were half the population, and had long since acquired legal rights. How and why did they submit so tamely to religious slavery? Why would they let religious fanatics demarcate and demonize them, and worst of all, why did they permit and even participate in the scapegoating and sacrifice necessary to successfully enslave other women?

To say they had no choice begs the question. During The Ceremony, during which "the Commander . . . is fucking . . . the lower half of my body," Offred tries to define the experience. It is not making love, and copulating implies two people, "nor does rape cover it: nothing is going on here that I haven't signed up for. There wasn't a lot of choice but there was some and this is what I chose."[33] Both Offred's best friend and mother opt out of the process, but Offred does not. Moira, her best friend, escapes twice; she is caught because the government's Eyes constantly watch for those smuggling precious natural resources, i.e., viable ovaries, out of the country. She ends up in Jezebel's, but at least she is not complicit. Offred's mother ends up in the Colonies rather than submit, but Offred chooses the path of least resistance, thereby clapping the mind-forged manacles on her own wrists. Given a chance to become active in the Resistance, she refuses, and when Ofglen, a member of the Mayday network, commits suicide before she can be interrogated, Offred is only relieved that she was not implicated. Like the men and women in "The Lottery," she is only relieved that it is not she: "So she's dead, and I am safe, after all. . . . I feel a great relief." More disturbing yet, Offred completely capitulates:

I'll repent. I'll abdicate. I'll renounce. . . . I want to keep on living in any form. I resign my body freely, to the uses of others. They can do what they like with me. I am abject.

I feel, for the first time, their true power.[34]

A third source of dis/ease, arguably worse than the others, emerges after Offred has or has not, escaped. In this ambiguously constructed, open-ended, closure-resistant novel, the secret police come for Offred, and Nick, her lover, leads her into the van, telling her that it is all right, that this is Mayday (a rescue organization) and not the Eyes (the Gilead-ean Gestapo). "And so I step up, into the darkness within, or else the light" is the last direct statement we have from Offred.[35]

The section entitled *Historical Notes on the Handmaid's Tale, Being a partial transcript of the proceedings of the Twelfth Symposium on Gileadean Studies held as part of the International Historical Associa-tion convention, held at the University of Denay, Nunavit on June 25, 2195,* is in many ways the most dis/easeful section of the novel. The chair is Mary Ann Crescent Moon, Professor of Caucasian Anthropol-ogy, and the keynote speaker is James Darcy Pieixoto, Director of the Twentieth- and Twenty-first-century Archives. The topic is the short-lived Republic of Gilead and "Problems of Authentication in Reference to *The Handmaid's Tale.*"

The dis/ease arises because none of the academics have learned anything from the Republic of Gilead. Professor Pieixoto's talk is filled with sly sexual innuendo, denigrating women and defining them as sexual objects. Professor Pieixoto sets the tone of the Conference: "I am sure we all enjoyed out charming Arctic Char last night at dinner, and now we are enjoying an equally charming Arctic Chair. I use the word "enjoy" in two distinct senses, precluding, of course, the obsolete third. (*Laughter*)." Of course. Who could possibly doubt it? (*Snigger, snigger*). In the second example, the title is obviously derived from Chaucer, but Pieixoto remarks that Professor Knotly Wade, the Gileadean Studies expert who titled this "document," used "tale/tail" intentionally. As Pieixoto says, to laughter and applause,

". . . those of you who know Professor Wade informally will understand when I say that I am sure all puns were intentional, particularly that having to do with the archaic vulgar signification of the word *tail*; that being, to some extent, the bone, as it were, of contention, in that phase of Gileadean society of which our saga treats."

Later in the same paragraph, tracing the attempts at authentication he and Wade have made, Pieixoto notes that the author refers to "'the Underground Female Road,' since dubbed by some of our historical wags "'The Underground Frailroad' (Laughter, groans)."[36] Pieixoto, in common parlance, does not seem to "get it." Or perhaps there is nothing to get; despite the object of this conference, no one else sees the sexual commentary as problematic. While Gilead may be no more, the attitude which brought such societies as Gilead into being is certainly alive and well. One can imagine the uproar in this conference peopled with Pieixoto, a Basque name, and Crescent Moon and Running Dog, almost certainly Indigenous People names, if minority jokes were told, for example, or comments on "dead Indians" were inserted into the supposedly academic discourse. If the Underground Femaleroad were rendered race specific, it would probably be unacceptable, but sexist commentary is still not only accepted but actively cultivated. Were it not, the hall would empty, silence would reign instead of laughter, and complicity in sexist discourse would be absent. But like the monstrous community in *University*, being a part of académe is no guarantee of either tolerance or common decency.

Further on, Pieixoto discusses the problems of authentication. In a somewhat aggrieved tone, he comments that Offred "does not see fit to give us her real name," and makes the further ignorant comment that "Such names [Offred, Ofglen and Ofwarren] were taken by the women upon their entry into a connection with the household of a specific Commander and relinquished by them upon leaving it."[37] Such an attitude is very dis/easeful; as a scholar of this period, he must be willfully misrepresenting the facts. Offred would have good reason not to give her name in a society in which she could be certain that the Gileadean patriarchy would retaliate against her child. In fact, Pieixoto comments that such a thing occurs. Furthermore, while Offred may have chosen between two evils, she neither "took" the Commander's name nor relinquished it. It was given to her and taken from her by a totalitarian government under which none of these people would wish to live. Such an interpretation is either completely incompetent or a willful misreading in the service of an agenda which demonizes Offred but not the Republic of Gilead. Like the Republic of Gilead's indoctrination methods, which blame the Handmaid for infertility, for rape, for anything that happens, this male blames Offred. The speaker has no problem with judging Offred adversely, as when he says, "She appears to have been an educated woman, insofar as any graduate of a North American College may be said to have been educated (*Laughter, some groans*)" or when he complains that she lacked the instincts of a reporter or a spy. Some of this discourse is understandable, especially from an anthropological point of view; as the speaker points out, "twenty pages or so of print-out from Waterford's private computer" would indeed have provided priceless information.[38] What Offred has to say, dealing with the social and personal sphere, the cultural history of Gilead is, however, just as valuable even though the speaker discounts it.

Provoking even more extreme dis/ease in the reader, Pieixoto invokes cultural relativism to mitigate Gilead's atrocities:

"We must be cautious about passing moral judgement upon the Gilead-eans. Surely we have learned by now that such judgements are by necessity cul-ture specific. Also Gileadean society was under a good deal of pressure, demographic and otherwise, and was subject to factors from which we our-selves are happily more free. Our job is not to censure but to understand (Applause)."[39]

As long as "we," academics, who would be among the first to be purged, understand Gilead, applause ensues; but any attempt to understand and validate Offred evokes contemptuous, denigrating laughter.

Again, such rhetoric would be justifiably dismissed as racist were it directed to American slavery or the Holocaust. Very little reputable dis-course on slavery avoids passing moral judgment; very little Holocaust literature truly disclaims the necessity for judgment. One wonders whether the point of view would have differed had the Gileadeans more centrally targeted Jews and Blacks or white males. Had the Gileadeans enslaved such groups, and had the account discovered been a slave nar-rative, one wonders whether the rhetoric at the conference would have differed. Would the participants have been more conscious of the pitfalls of exclusionary thinking? Atwood seems to see the modern world as all too complicit with the Gileadeans' denial of moral culpability, and her novel therefore generates the feeling that nothing has changed or ever will, that female will always be a profoundly disturbing code word for different or inferior.

Unlike Atwood, Nevil Shute develops a form of horror fiction in which individual choice seems irrelevant. Both Shute's *On the Beach* (1957) and Stanley Kramer's eponymous film (1959) effectively show-case the results of a feloniously stupid nuclear policy. In treating the novel and the film, I shall not distinguish between them except to note the differences, as what interests me here is the dystopian pattern.[40] By concentrating, not on the intangibles of governmental policy, but on the people doomed by it, the novel and film foreground the pathos inherent in a powerless and victimized population, though as I shall demonstrate, such is not really the case. The dis/ease generated by *On the Beach* lies in the virtues espoused, not in the final result. Both texts are in the purely apocalyptic tradition; the dreaded World War III has taken place and in less than a month is all over, as is any future for life on the entire planet. Both novel and film depict a dystopian society in which the only choices left are negative ones: either a slow and lingering death by radiation poisoning, or a quick-acting poison pill. Either way, you lose. And not only do you lose, but your husband or wife, children, friends, fellow citizenry, and even pets, lose as well. As in King's *The Stand*, disaster comes about primarily as the result of politics over which average citizens either have, or think they have, little control. While no single American, for example, can take effective action against the government's nuclear policies, the voters or the citizenry all too frequently fail to take what action they can take. Too many citizens choose to take the easy road of non-involvement since activism is arduous, time-consuming, and often minimally successful.

Shute's novel is set in post-World War III Australia. Radiation is moving steadily southward, all life in the Northern Hemisphere is extinct, and the scientists are predicting six months before all life on earth, defined, of course, as human, comes to an end. None of the relatively few survivors, combatants or non-combatants, really understand how it all started in the first place. A "nuclear accident," in which the first strike led inexorably to other strikes, seems the likeliest scenario. A nuclear accident, however, implying as it does random chance, is comforting but highly inaccurate. The construction of bombs too fearsome to use, bombs that would bring in their wake absolute destruction, was no accident at all, but, like the governmental programs in *The Stand*, the result of intentional policy. After Hiroshima and Nagasaki, there was little if any doubt as to the effects of these bombs. The problem lies not in the existence of the bombs, or even the ignorant first use of atomic bombs, but in the aggressive pursuit of nuclear technology. One of the scientists in *On the Beach* will, rather tardily, question the inherent stupidity of producing weapons that cannot be usefully deployed.

As might be expected, the characters are varied, if slightly stock, in nature. The main character, Commander Dwight Towers, his crew, and his submarine the *U.S.S.Scorpion* (*Sawfish* in the film) represent the stalwart American naval presence. Peter, Mary, and Jennifer Holmes are a young Australian family, with a long and now useless naval tradition. Moira Davidson is a feckless and alcoholic Australian woman facing a wasted life, who falls in love with Dwight Towers; Julian Osborne, a scientist, represents the most nearly demonized character in both novel and film. In addition, various minor characters flesh out the texts and add to the feeling that we know these people or at least people very like them. Such characters diminish the distance between "us" and "them" and resist any possibility of safely demarcating the characters and denying the dis/ease.

The war has ended a year earlier and the structure of central concern is the eschatology of the endgame, a game in which there are no winners. Both texts are concerned with invoking such horrific elements as total annihilation, an eschatological scenario in which death is inevitable, and the fact that the only thing which matters is the way people face life and death, that antinomous pairing again. There is nowhere to go, no escape possible, and nothing to do but prolong the inevitable. While I would like to place this text at the more affirmative side of the spectrum because in many ways the survivors wait for death with great courage, an affirmative reading is problematic. These people are not doomed by a comet from outer space or some other external threat. In films such as *Deep Impact* the comet is not a man-made cataclysm, and the inhabitants of its world bear no responsibility for the encroaching catastrophe.[41] They are, quite simply, in the wrong time and place. Thus, although the strategies of exclusion do come into play, and many hundreds of thousands of people lose their lives, the catastrophe in *Deep Impact* is not disaffirmative, and hope survives. The people in *On the Beach*, however, are doomed not only by the actions of other members of the community, but also by their own negligence in actively opposing nuclear proliferation. They are doomed by humanity's desire for knowledge and pursuit of that knowledge, by advances in science and technology, by the desire to be the strongest kid on the block, perhaps by the very state of being human. An Australian scientist, Julian Osborne, has worked on the bomb; one of the main characters, Dwight Towers, is an American submarine commander; another, Peter Holmes, is an Australian naval officer. As part of humanity, the community of the doomed cannot be neatly separated—the lambs, so to speak, from the goats, the innocent from the guilty.

As the end comes inexorably closer, and the southernmost South American cities fall silent, the government schedules distribution of suicide pills for people who do not want to die the miserable death by radiation which is the only other option. And, pragmatic and humane as this may seem, Peter Holmes, who is coping with his approaching death by continuing on active duty in the Australian Navy, has to tell his wife Mary that she will have to kill Jennifer, their year-old child, if he is unexpectedly away at sea. She is, of course, deeply in denial anyway, convinced that somehow the radiation will not come to Australia. When Peter sees a chemist to find out the exact procedure in case he is not around for the end, the chemist dispassionately describes the horrors of radiation sickness and shows him poison pills for the adults. But as the chemist says, "The baby, or a pet animal—It's just a bit more complicated." Just a bit. Dog, cat, or baby—what possible difference? Stick them with the hypodermic needle. They'll "fall asleep" quite soon. The euphemism points up the dis/ease one feels in reading this novel. Jennifer will stop breathing; her heart will fail; she will die. The one thing she will not do is "fall asleep."

Oddly enough, Mary is not quite so dispassionate. As the narrator sardonically notes, "Of the three presents which Peter Holmes took back to his wife that night, the playpen was the most appreciated."[42] The scene in which Peter tries to explain the coming events to his wife is one of the most horrific in the novel. Initially, Mary refuses to discuss it. Mary's response and Peter's reply indicate the depth of denial at work:

"But, Peter, however ill I was, I couldn't do that. Who would take care of Jennifer?"

"We're all going to get it. . . . Every living thing. Dogs, cats and babies— everyone. I'm going to get it. You're going to get it. Jennifer's going to get it, too."

Again, Peter explains what Mary must know but adamantly refuses to face. The horrific crisis occurs, however, when he tells her that she will have to kill Jennifer if he is not around. Mary, not surprisingly, refuses, and in the process rends the veil from a seemingly happy family:

"The trouble is you don't love her. You never have loved her. She's always been a nuisance to you. Well, she's not a nuisance to me. It's you that's the nuisance. And now it's reached the stage where you're trying to tell me how to murder her."

The trouble is that however melodramatic, exaggerated, and irrational Mary's attitude is, there is some truth to her accusations. Peter routinely refers to the baby as "it," and has very little to do with her. Perhaps this is a typical 1950s nuclear family in which Peter leaves the child-raising duties to Mary; perhaps it is self-defense. Jennifer, after all, must have been born around the time World War III began, and Peter may be protecting himself in the only way he can. Peter, attacked, attacks in turn, and points out some hard truths. Jennifer, he says, "may live on for days, crying and vomiting all over herself in her cot and lying in her own muck, with you dead on the floor beside her and nobody to help her." Peter, in this scenario, is notably absent.

Later, sitting on the verandah, Peter thinks:

These bloody women, sheltered from realities, living in a sentimental dream world of their own. If they faced up to things they could help a man, help him enormously. While they clung to the dream world they were just a bloody millstone round his neck.[43]

Who are the "they," and who is the man? The only "unhelpful" woman of whom we have knowledge is Mary. The agreement error, while common enough in speech, and perhaps intended to refer only to Mary, could also be an accurate sentence and could refer to "his" women, i.e., Mary and Jennifer, who are, perhaps, in his secret thoughts, millstones round his neck. After all, Peter uses a non-existent "duty" to escape whenever he can. At any rate, this scene, with its brutal rending of a marriage and some home truths revealed on both sides, exposes the horror behind the seemingly affirmative qualities of courage and a "stiff upper lip." It is, after all, a bit much to expect to Mary to say "Right-o, old chap. I'll see to it."

What affirmation can possibly be extracted from this situation? The stoic acceptance of disaster? Neither Boethius nor Solon, both proponents of the stiff upper lip point of view, recommend themselves to Mary. Solon's comment to Croesus, while quite stoic, does not address the realities of life. "Until he is dead, you had better refrain from calling him happy and just call him fortunate," does not quite fit this situation.[44] Nor does Boethius' "In all adversity of fortune, the most wretched kind is to have once been happy" quite fit the bill.[45] Whether Mary has been happy in the past is not the point; she is looking at irremediable misery in the future. Psalm 103 may note that "man's days are like those of grass; like a flower of the field he blooms; the wind sweeps over him and he is gone and his place knows him no more," but most people prefer to think that they are slightly more important than flowers or grass.[46] What situation could be worse than to be the giver of life forced to take life? How much more nonaffirming and life-denying can a situation be?

The horror rests on two elements: a circumstance, completely irreversible in nature, and the necessity for negative action. The radiation will, inevitably and inexorably as death, wipe out all human life in Southern Australia as it has wiped out all human life in its journey south. It is not going to dissipate, or go elsewhere, or lose its potency, nor will the government develop a vaccine, nor will some miraculous immunity suddenly surface. The only event that will come to pass is death. As the novel draws to its grim end, and Brisbane and Sydney go silent, the last wretched survivors are faced with purely negative choices. These doomed people, as doomed as Kosinski's painted bird or broken-legged horse, can either commit suicide or die wretched, lingering deaths from radiation poisoning. Starkly presented, these are the circumstances that create dystopic horror fiction. People clutch at love, duty and obligation: Dwight Tower takes his submarine on its journey "home," and Moira watches it leave before she takes her pill, whispering, "Dwight, if you're on your way already, wait for me."[47] Peter and Mary have a last cuppa together, Osborne chooses to take his pill in his beloved Grand Prix winning Ferrari, in the film the Australian Commander-in-Chief and his secretary drink a sherry to "a blind, blind world," and on and on and on, but nothing wipes out the last image of a sterile and hollow world, populated by corpses, poison, and the detritus of a vanished civilization.[48]

The horror in *On the Beach*, arises from many of the same mechanisms that provoke horror in the texts discussed in previous chapters, mechanisms that point out that the constructions of values we take for granted are not always positive. In many ways, it would appear that these people are no more responsible for World War III than the people in *Deep Impact* for the comet that hit the earth. As Mary Holmes says, "But we didn't have anything to do with it all, did we—here in Australia? . . . Couldn't anyone have stopped it?" In many ways they are victims as Peter says:

"Some kinds of silliness you can't stop. . . . [I]f a couple of hundred million people all decide that their national honour requires them to drop cobalt bombs upon their neighbors, well, there's not much you or I can do about it. The only possible hope would have been to educate them out of their silliness.

"You could have done something with newspapers. We didn't do it, no nation did because we were all too silly. We liked our newspapers with pictures of beach girls and headlines about cases of indecent assault, and no government was wise enough to stop us having them. But something might have been done with newspapers if we had been wise enough."

Ironically, it is Mary Holmes who exposes the denial and the problems behind affirmative interpretations of this novel. "I'm glad we haven't got newspapers now," she says "It's much nicer without them."[49] A look at the supermarket checkout line or the typical television news program in contemporary American society will confirm the above comment; we do not want serious news now, either. We want snappy, witty news, funny news, human interest news, scandalous news, etc, etc., but not hard news. To directly face potentially apocalyptic news is too discomforting. "It's much nicer without it." But the government and the people are not separate entities; one cannot wriggle off the responsibility hook by saying, in effect, "the government wasn't wise enough to stop us having them" as though the government is Lakoff's stern parent who tells the children that candy before dinner is not good for them.

As one re-reads and re-views the novel and the film, an affirmative ending becomes more and more difficult to argue. The strategies of exclusion resonate through the entire novel, culminating in the final scenes as fatal radiation sickness reaches Southern Australia. Dwight

Towers, while intended to be sympathetically viewed, is in many ways an extremely dis/ease-provoking character, especially in Shute's novel. He throws away a chance for happiness, however transient, with Moira because he has a family in Connecticut. This is admirable, even though he no longer has anything in Connecticut. There is no Connecticut. The audience for both the book and the film can sympathize with this attitude, which functions on much the same level as Mary Holmes' denial. But in the novel's final scenes, he takes his submarine out to sea to sink her. When Moira, who loves him passionately and who has, as he says, "meant a lot to me," asks if she can go with him, he says:

> "I've been asked the same thing this morning by four men. I've refused them all because Uncle Sam wouldn't like it. I've run this vessel the navy way right through and I'm running her that way till the end. I can't take you, honey. We'll each have to take this on our own."[50]

Moira has done a great deal to make Dwight's final days bearable; common decency would indicate that he allow her to go with him on the final journey. What possible harm could it cause? Dwight has, in the novel, nothing whatsoever to hide; as he has told Moira, he fully intends to tell Sharon and his children all about her. To cut her adrift and put duty, honor and obligation first makes of these virtues a hollow mockery.

This attitude, while purportedly admirable, is arguably what caused the dystopic, doomed society in the first place. It leads to a world where we are each alone, where love does not matter, and duty to a non-existent country or, for that matter, an existent one, is more important than any other value. Does Dwight Tower indeed have an obligation to "run this boat the navy way"? One might well question what purpose such a stand serves. Like Connecticut and Dwight's family, it does not exist. As commander-in-chief, he could disband the crew, but he chooses to put the empty and meaningless forms of duty ahead of humanity. This current, which runs through the entire book as well as to a slightly lesser degree in the film, does a great deal to mitigate the affirmative way in which the people meet their ends. Stephen King's comment,

> I believe we are all ultimately alone and that any deep and lasting human contact is nothing more and nothing less than a necessary illusion. . . . [T]hey [feelings of love and kindness] are the emotions which bring us together, if not in fact then at least in a comforting illusion that makes the burden of mortality a little easier to bear,[51]

resonates disquietingly throughout these texts. There really are very few comforting illusions for either the characters or the audience: in the novel, Moira will swallow her pills watching the submarine sail away and share the threadbare fantasy that "she could be very near him when he started home. If then she turned up by his side . . . perhaps he would take her with him and she could see Helen hopping on the pogo-stick." But what really happens is that she says, "There's nothing left to go on living for," to which one of the other women watching the submarine depart says, "Well, ducks, you won't have to." Then, driving to a point where she can see the Scorpion, "dumbly watching as the low grey shape went forward," she swallows her suicide pills.[52]

The film makes the point even more sharply. In the film, the men vote to "go home" and Dwight, who had hoped to stay with Moira to the end, feels that he must go with his men. He tells her he loves her and then departs. After Moira swallows the pills, watching the submarine leave, the camera cuts to the empty and desolate city. A banner which proclaims "There is still time . . . brother" flaps ironically in the breeze, and trash rolls down the deserted streets.[53] Dwight and Moira, who each must die, are thus deprived of the solace, however slight, that each other's company might have brought. A thoughtful reader/viewer might well wonder what purpose is served by sailing the boat outside Australia's territorial waters and sinking her there. What shibboleths will be observed? And although moral decisions should not constructed on who will know, the decision is Dwight's to make. To put meaningless duty ahead of humanity helps set this film within the spectrum of the dissaffirmative fictions which comprise the most effective horror.

The sense that this is a conservative text, in which duty, honor, and country are valorized and affirmed, is in irresolvable conflict with the novel's anti-nuclear, and to some degree, anti-militaristic message. Dwight Towers, commander-in-chief of the American navy, cannot function effectively both ways; if he is a duty-bound officer, which in the novel he most certainly is, then he cannot escape his tradition, which is heavily complicit in bringing the entire globe to extinction. If we are to see him as upholding traditional values, what are these? If the militaristic values of duty are valorized at the expense of common decency, compassion and love, the conflict becomes unresolvable. Even in Kramer's film, the idea that the men would vote and Towers abide by the vote raises questions. A further problem arises because his executive officer could take the vessel out ten miles and sink her, thereby resolving the individual over duty conflict so central to the novel. And since it is, more or less, duty and policy over considerations of individual rights which put the world at the mercy of atomic weapons, the lack of resolution and the closure-resistant resolution is very dis/ease-provoking. This contradiction works to create the dis/ease in somewhat the same way dis/ease is generated in Brandner's *The Howling*. Monstrous though the werewolves are, they will not buy their safety with one of their own: monstrous though these creatures are, they face extinction bravely. One of Osborne's comments that "The war started when people accepted the idiotic principle that peace could be maintained by arranging to defend themselves with weapons they could not possibly use without committing suicide" expresses the dis/easeful antinomy at the center of the text as well as a modern dilemma.[54]

This is a horrific text because it de-centers the importance of the individual and the community and valorizes an empty set of ideals, because the emotions which bring us together are those emotions which are decentered in the novel while apparently being affirmed, because the characters are good people undeserving of so harsh a fate, and the injustice of the situation is irremediable. Because, in effect, the monster wins, and we are the monster. While demonization is almost entirely absent, scapegoating is not deployed, the sacrifice is too all encompassing to be part of the strategies of exclusion, and such absences should make for a more affirmative novel, the demarcations in favor of duty and obligation only serve to point up the dreadful strength such demarcations have. *On the Beach* may be momentous or thought provoking, or arguably, "the most important and dramatic novel of the atomic age,"[55] but it is not really located on the affirmative spectrum at all.

My last text, Ursula K. Le Guin's "The Ones Who Walk Away from Omelas" (1974), may seem a rather odd choice for the final example of an irremediably dystopic society. Despite its indeterminate setting, which seems slightly on the fantastic, "swords and sorcery" side, "Omelas" is nevertheless intimately concerned with the political realities of utopia/dystopia. Omelas is, at first encounter, a utopia, a city where all people have what they need and desire, and all are happy. Indeed, the narrator speaks quite cogently about the importance of happiness:

The trouble is that we have a bad habit, encouraged by pedants and sophisticates, of considering happiness as something rather stupid. . . . How can I tell you about the people of Omelas? . . . They were mature, intelligent, passionate adults whose lives were not wretched. . . . Happiness is based on a just discrimination of what is necessary, what is neither necessary nor destructive, and what is destructive.[56]

The narrator, who seems to be in an intimate relationship with the Omelans without being an Omelan, continues to describe the Festival of

Summer and the joy of living in Omelas. And lest we not believe in the joy of the Omelans, the narrator describes one additional facet of life in Omelas the utopia. A small broom closet exists under one of the spacious public buildings in Omelas. And in that room "a child is sitting. . . . It is feeble minded. Perhaps it was born defective, or perhaps it has become imbecile through fear, malnutrition and neglect."[57] Anyone who wishes, in this brave and joyful utopia, can come in and kick the child. The child has absolutely no protection whatsoever. What is more, people avail themselves of this permission:

> [T]he child, who has not always lived in the tool room, can remember sunlight and its mother's voice, sometimes speaks. "I will be good," it says. "Please let me out. I will be good!" The child used to scream for help at night and say a great deal, but now it only makes a kind of whining, "eh-haa, eh-haa," and it speaks less and less often. It is so thin there are no calves to its legs; its belly protrudes. . . . Its buttocks and thighs are a mass of festered sores, as it sits in its own excrement continually.
>
> They all know it is there, all the people of Omelas. . . .

And some of these people come to stare at the child in disgust, and some of them to get the fun of kicking it. A corrupt bargain with forces unknown exists. All understand that

> their happiness, the beauty of their city, the tenderness of their friendships, the health of their children, the wisdom of their scholars, the skill of their makers . . . depend wholly on this child's abominable misery. . . .
>
> The terms are strict and absolute; there may not even be a kind word spoken to the child.[58]

And so, one sees that the underpinnings of Omelan utopia, and arguably any other utopia, depend on the same strategies of exclusion that form dystopias. Demarcation, demonization, scapegoating, and sacrifice preserve the utopia. The Omelans, at first upset, usually come to the handy and convenient conclusion that the child is too far gone to appreciate sunlight or a kind word anyway. The reasons are many: it is "too degraded and imbecile" to know real joy. It would be "wretched" without walls and darkness and its own excrement to sit in. Indeed, it would. Quite likely, it would miss the festering sores too and wouldn't recognize its mother were it to see her. And, of course, it likes being kicked.

The narrator comments that the Omelans' tears dry as they realize "the terrible justice of reality and accept it." It is not the "terrible justice" being invoked here but the nineteenth-century utilitarian concept of the greatest good for the greatest number. The narrator asks if the Omelans are now more credible. Sadly, the answer is yes. Utopias, after all, must always be paid for by someone. And as long as it is a helpless child, an unwilling sacrifice to the greatest good, and not an Omelan who has volunteered, the citizens are free to pursue untrammeled happiness at the expense of someone else. This is the terrible "paradox" the Omelans face; this is the antinomy of utopia/dystopia, "resolved" by the handy strategies of exclusion. "It" knows nothing better. "It" had a mother and promises amendment for whatever horrible act resulted in imprisonment, but it "is too degraded and imbecile," now, to appreciate any restitution. Since it has become degraded and imbecilic, the actions of the people who stuffed it in the tool room to become, in the absence of any care, sub-human, are exonerated.

This is perhaps the most deceptively disaffirmative text I have discussed because the narrator implies that happiness depends on and is made credible by the existence of communal evil. All the inhabitants know that the child is there, and most accept its necessary misery. The narrator states that the knowledge of the child's misery makes them, in effect, better people: "They know that if the wretched one were not there sniveling in the dark, the other one, the flute player, could make no joyful music."[57] But one thing is even more incredible than the acceptance of the child's misery as the fount of compassion:

At times, one of the adolescent boys or girls who go to see the child does not go home to weep or rage, does not, in fact, go home at all. . . . They leave Omelas, they walk ahead into the darkness, and they do not come back. . . . But they seem to know where they are going, the ones who walk away from Omelas.[59]

The disquieting question, of course, is not from what dis/ease they flee, but to what dis/ease they head? Should everyone leave Omelas, or is it true that a utopia always depends on someone else's dystopia? And if this is the case, if dystopias always win, why bother making a moral choice that will lead you, not to justice or morality, but to another deceptive utopia? What secret rooms exist in societies that the inhabitants of the brightly lighted, warm, and clean houses do not wish to acknowledge? If a place away from Omelas does not exist, and the narrator thinks it might not, what alternatives are left, except acceptance of the secret room? And, of course, what alternatives are left if one rejects that room? According to authors such as Le Guin as I read them, nothing but a tool room by another name.

CODA:
WORTH STUDYING OR SUITABLE
FOR WRAPPING THE GARBAGE?

En ma fin est ma commencement.[1]

In this project, I have ranged over a fairly large number of texts, major texts in the horror canon, relatively unknown horror texts, badly written texts, literary texts, texts unmistakably horrific, texts seemingly unhorrific, even texts which seem to belong to other genres entirely—all have been grist for my mill. We have traveled deep into horror territory, a place demarcated off from "us" at the same time it is intrinsic to us. By stressing antinomy and the strategies of exclusion, I have attempted to illustrate that the best and most effective horror fiction provides neither resolution nor affirmation. And the reason is self evident: if the best horror fiction is that which evokes the greatest degree of terror, horror, or revulsion, then logically, the fiction that leaves the reader in that state of dis/ease without ameliorating it is the most effective, for either resolution or an affirmation of commonly accepted cultural values works to displace the monsters in our lives and to deny the dis/ease. The reader is inevitably dis/eased if the text resists the resolution, the closure, and the emotions called into being by horror fiction remain in play.

In the spectrum I have established, affirmative horror fiction texts, those texts which avoid the facile papering-over so characteristic of hack or formulaic fiction, although resolved affirmatively, still retain some degree of dis/ease. As David Hartwell notes, in his introduction to Stephen King's "The Reach," "it is a virtuoso performance in which the horror is distanced but underlies the whole."[2] Of all the texts discussed, King's short story best exemplifies the lingering, niggling tinge of dis/ease that distinguishes affirmative horror fiction from the facile and *faux*. On first reading, "The Reach" contains very little horror, except perhaps the disturbing image of Stella Flanders "at long last in her grave." But this undercurrent, slight though it is in the story as a whole, serves to underscore the essential alienation at the root of the human experience. Alden, her son, understands that questions of the dead lie in the forbidden realms, yet he believes that the dead do sing and do love. Nevertheless the image of Stella, "at long last," dead is a disquieting one. The further along the spectrum one advances, the more conflicted the resolution and the greater the degree of dis/ease becomes. In mid-spectrum horror fiction, such as Thomas Harris' novels (particularly *Red Dragon*), King's *It*, and Sheri Tepper's *The Gate to Women's Country*, the resolution, while fragile, tenuous and compromised, is still in place, or, as is the case in such texts as Gary Brandner's *The Howling* or King's *The Stand*, the society, while still intact, may be one which is hopelessly corrupted. In disaffirmative horror fiction, the most dis/ease-provoking texts I have examined and the central concern of this project, neither resolution nor affirmation is possible. Texts such as Brett Easton Ellis' *American Psycho*, Anne Rivers Siddons' *The House Next Door*, and Nevil Shute's *On the Beach* reflect a society in which no affirmation is possible. These texts indicate that making moral choices or amoral choices, taking action or doing nothing, embracing affirmative cultural values or denying them make no difference. In such disaffirmative texts as Joyce Carol Oates' "Extenuating Circumstances," Shirley Jackson's "The Lottery," and Edward Bryant's "A Sad Last Love at the Diner of the Damned," love does not matter; in a society which has turned cannibal and devoured itself, love is meaningless and death triumphant.

In my introductory chapter, I defined horror fiction as any text which has extreme or supernatural elements, induces, as its primary intention and/or effect, strong feelings of terror, horror, or revulsion in the reader, feelings which remain to some degree unresolved, and which metaphorically or allegorically generates a significant degree of unresolved dis/ease within society. The key definition employed was that of a significant degree of unresolved unease or conflict, a dis/ease significant enough that the reader who inhabits the society cannot simply gloss it over and return to business as usual. Spreading glossy white frosting over the burned and lumpy cake is not enough; people know that the frosting only hides the ghouls without destroying them. It is the knowledge that horror fiction is metaphorically or allegorically discussing everyday horrors which is so dis/ease-generating. The human monster who is a part of society, the community which deploys the strategies of exclusion against its own residents, the dystopias which we cannot escape despite our best intentions, the realization that unconflicted happy endings rarely occur and then always at someone else's cost: all of these are part and parcel of horror territory.

The reader cannot close such books with a satisfied thump, but is haunted by the text. As I noted earlier, Terry Heller contends that certain texts, by their very ambiguity, "haunt the reader" and force him or her to construct a resolution to nullify the "anti-closure" elements in the text.[3] Much of the disaffirmative horror fiction I have discussed is haunting and much of it defies a reader to achieve resolution. A reader can construct an ending to Stephen King's "The Mist," but not a satisfactory one; another reader can debate Colquitt Kennedy's motivations, much as readers have debated Henry James' *The Turn of the Screw*, and with much the same result. But how can a reader comfortably close the book on Brett Easton Ellis' *American Psycho*, or Harris' *Red Dragon*? If these texts are, in Jane Tompkins' words, "agents of cultural formation," one must ask, how exactly? It is easy enough to say they are didactic or minatory, wailing of catastrophe, Cassandra-like, but where does that get us?

If we could safely keep the horror within the pages of a text, we would live in a society which has no need of horror fiction, except, perhaps, as tales for children. Literature, however, as Mao Tse-Tung posits, "does not fall from the heavens, but is the product of social practice . . . inescapably part of a material process . . . the product of reflection, the life of a given society," and cannot be safely contained within the covers of a text. And if a society is more comfortable ignoring such a reality, and "the first and last command-ment in its ideology is 'Thou shalt study all forms of struggle, save that which determines thine own self,'" horror fiction resists such an exclusion and concentrates on the exposure and deliberate non-resolution of the ideological repressions and contradictions in a way which much other literature does not.[4]

Effective horror fiction holds up a carnival house mirror which reveals the often warped but ironically true image of our society, our community, and ourselves, and while this may be, as Stephen King says, "the most important and useful form of fiction a moral writer may command," it is also a subject about which people do not wish to think.[5] The "magic mirror" device, which reveals the nature beneath the smiling surface, the monster under the man, and the skull beneath the skin, is a device common in horror fiction, like the carnival mirror which delivers the warped/true image. By concentrating on the skull beneath the skin, on the reality of the skeleton society instead of on its smoothed-out skin, horror fiction lays bare one truth: all of the qualities on which we pride ourselves as Americans are as subject to alienation and subversion as they are to validation and reaffirmation. Thus, the most effective horror fiction works, not by revealing the monster and then denying the monstrosity, but by forcefully pointing out that not only must we be on the watch for monsters, but we might also need to be on the watch for ourselves, because monsters-r-us. Stephen King's view that horror texts are agents which validate cultural norms is often true, but only part of the truth; many of the texts I have discussed not only do not validate the cultural norms, but reveal the problems in taking them at face value. Such a text as *On the Beach*, for example, seems to validate all the iconic values of courage and grace under pressure; yet, the empty streets at novel's end validate nothing. Other texts, especially disaffirmative texts like Atwood's *The Handmaid's Tale*, King's *Carrie*, and Jackson's "The Lottery," seem to indicate that regardless of how often warnings are given, the warnings fall on deaf ears. We are creatures of exclusions, these authors say, and the demarcations, demonizations, scapegoating, and sacrifices which define exclusion are too intrinsic to society for it ever to shed them.

If horror fiction has any value at all, if it is not to be accurately derided as one of the most facile and worthless of fictions, its real effect must be foregrounded more than has often been the case. I have attempted to delineate a new way to read horror fiction and a new use to which it might be put. My interest in the texts I see as most effectively horrific, those which actively resist resolution and closure or reaffirmation or resolution/restoration motifs is one of long standing, and one I do not feel this study has entirely worked out. Like horror fiction itself, this study has no clearly demarcated boundaries, no unassailable answers, no comfortable solutions.

So we end where we began. Horror fiction, antinomous to the core, is either worth studying or suitable for wrapping the garbage, a serious literature or hack fiction, affirmative and conservative, or radical and disaffirmative. People who read it seriously are either readers willing to confront the hard and uncomfortable truths which comprise our societies or sick puppies. It would be nice to think the former is true, but the subject itself denies our more comforting assumptions.

NOTES

Chapter 1

1. Old Scots invocation, widely quoted.

2. Dis/ease, a neologism I coined for this project, is the disturbing effect and the sense of unease which the texts I discuss generate; a sense more active than un- and generating a greater amount of the horrific emotions. The slash is less axiomatic of current literary theory and criticism and more to separate the word from disease.

3. Stephen King, "One for the Road," *Night Shift* (New York: Doubleday, 1978) 319.

4. Jane Tompkins, *Sensational Designs: The Cultural Work of American Fiction, 1790-1860* (New York: Oxford UP, 1985) xi.

5. Tompkins xvi-xvii.

6. David J. Skal, *The Monster Show: A Cultural History of Horror* (New York: Penguin, 1993) 354.

7. Clive Barker, qtd. in Linda Badley, *Writing Horror and the Body: The Fiction of Stephen King, Clive Barker, and Anne Rice*. Contributions to the *Study of Popular Culture*, 51 (Westport: Greenwood P, 1996) 75.

8. Judith Halberstam, *Skin Shows: Gothic Horror and the Technology of Monsters* (Durham: Duke UP, 1995) 3-8.

9. Halberstam 88.

10. Tvetsan Todorov, *The Fantastic: A Structural Approach to a Literary Genre*, trans. Richard Howard (Cleveland: P of Case Western Reserve U, 1973), and Rosemary Jackson, *Fantasy: The Literature of Subversion* (New York: Methuen, 1981).

11. Gene Wolf, qtd. in Badley 3.

12. Stephen King, *Danse Macabre* (New York: Berkley, 1981) 9. Perhaps because my son Michael was two years old and my daughter Erica eight, when I read *Pet Sematary*, this particular novel hit me very hard; someone without children might find it substantially less horrifying.

13. Todorov 57.

14. Jeffrey Jerome Cohen, ed., preface, *Monster Theory: Reading Culture* (Minneapolis: U of Minnesota P, 1996) viii-ix.

15. Heller 98.

16. Howard Phillips Lovecraft, *Supernatural Horror in Literature* (1945; New York: Dover, 1973) 16.

17. David G. Hartwell, ed., introduction, *The Medusa in the Shield*, vol 2. *The Dark Descent* (New York: Tor, 1987) 7.

18. King, *Danse Macabre* 99.

19. The idea of terror, horror, and revulsion being the significant emotional markers of horror fiction is commonly accepted. From Walpole's commentary on Gothic and Burke and Coleridge's commentary on the use of the sublime to the early twentieth criticism of Edith Birkhead's *Tale of Terror*, including contemporary critics, critical consensus agrees that the primary purpose of horror fiction is to cause horror, terror and revulsion, as well as delight. The antinomous phrasing of delightful terror is paradigmatic of the genre. The differences of opinion lie in how these emotions and delight work, and what effect horror fiction has on the reader and the society. Critics like Edith Birkhead, David Punter, Joseph Grixti, Terry Heller, Daryl Twitchell, Walter Kendrick, William Gibson, Stephen King, et al., see horror fiction as in some way purging the horror or using the horror as vicarious rituals of shame or validation. Most of these critics see horror fiction's role as affirmative and conservative. Such critics as Edward Ingebretsen, Martin Propp, David Skal, Louis Gross, and Clive Barker question the idea of affirmation and see horror fiction in a different light.

20. Mark Edmundson, *Nightmare on Main Street: Angels, Sadomasochism, and the Culture of Gothic* (Cambridge: Harvard UP, 1997) xv.

21. In "Contemporary Tragedy: Stephen King's *Pet Sematary*," *Studies in Weird Fiction*, 16 (1995), I argue that King's novel fits Aristotle's definition of tragedy quite closely. Two major differences between horror fiction and tragedy are status and catharsis. Tragedy is the most valorized genre, horror fiction one of the least. Catharsis is more problematic in horror though the idea that catharsis always occurs in tragedy is questionable. It is more than possible to see Euripides' *Bacchae* or *Trojan Women*, or Sophocles' *Oedipus Rex*, or Shakespeare's *King Lear*, as horror fiction, especially if one invokes reader response or questions the degree of catharsis which actually takes place in these texts.

22. Eric S. Rabkin, *The Fantastic in Literature* (Princeton: Princeton UP, 1976) 83.

23. Steffen Hantke, "Deconstructing Horror: Commodities in the Fiction of Jonathan Carroll and Kathe Koja," *Journal of American Culture*, 18.3 (1995) 41.

24. Kristeva 5-6.

25. Noel Carroll, *The Philosophy of Horror* (New York: Routledge, 1990).

26. King, *Danse Macabre* 25.

27. Tompkins xv-xvi.

28. Tompkins xv-xviii.

29. Tompkins xvi.

30. Heller 6.

31. King, *Danse Macabre* 5.

32. Hantke 42.

33. King, *Danse Macabre* 4.

34. Skal 386.

35. The corpse candle, the predictor of death, which appears before the house of someone about to die.

Chapter 2

1. Jerzy Kosinski, *The Painted Bird*, 2nd ed. (New York: Grove, 1976) 233.

2. Naomi Quinn and Dorothy Holland, "Culture and Cognition," *Cultural Models in Language and Thought* (New York: Cambridge UP, 1987) 4.

3. James B. Twitchell, *For Shame: The Loss of Common Decency in American Culture* (New York: St. Martin's, 1997) 142; Tompkins, *Sensational Designs* xi, King, *Danse Macabre*.

4. Quinn and Holland 3.

5. Donna J. Haraway, *Simians, Cyborgs, and Women: The Reinvention of Nature* (New York: Routledge, 1991) 149.

6. King, *Danse Macabre* 31.

7. Cohen 6.

8. Halberstam 92.

9. Frederich Nietzsche, *The Birth of Tragedy* and *The Case of Wagner*, trans. Walter Kaufmann (New York: Random, 1967) 33 ff., and King, *Danse Macabre* 75.

10. Nathaniel Hawthorne, "The Minister's Black Veil," *Tales and Sketches* (New York: Literary Classics of the United States, 1982) 374.

11. Hawthorne 384.

12. King, *Danse Macabre* 75.

13. King, qtd. in Badley 43.

14. King, *Danse Macabre* 395.

15. David G. Hartwell, introduction, *The Medusa in the Shield,* vol. 2 of *The Dark Descent* (New York: Tor, 1987) 14.

16. Ancius Boethius, *The Consolation of Philosophy*, trans. Victor Watts (London: Penguin, 1969). Boethius' argument concerning the powerlessness of evil, while it may be valid for the after-life, or accurately reflect sixth-century A.D. philosophy, has little relevance to the twentieth century where evil is seen as intrinsically powerful. We no longer inhabit an Age of Faith where the belief that worldly concerns are valueless has validity; as the world has become more complex, so has the province of evil. 121 ff.

17. Lance Morrow, "Evil," *Time*, 10 June 1991: 48.

18. Jerzy Kosinski, Afterword, *The Painted Bird*. 2nd ed. (New York: Grove P, 1976) xxv.

19. Kosinski 51.

20. Kosinski 81-82.

21. Kosinski 233.

22. Stephen King, *'Salem's Lot* (New York: Signet, 1975) 203.

23. Tompkins 200.

COMMUNITIES, MONSTERS, AND "US"

1. Katey Painko, "Perspectives," *Newsweek,* 23 Aug. 1999: 17.

2. Robert Louis Stevenson, *Dr. Jekyll and Mr. Hyde 1886* (New York: Penguin, 1987) 43-44.

3. Richard Tithecott, *Of Men and Monsters: Jeffrey Dahmer and the Construction of the Serial Killer* (U of Wisconsin P, 1997) 7.

4. James R Kincaid, Foreword, *Of Men and Monsters: Jeffrey Dahmer and the Construction of the Serial Killer* by Richard Tithecott (U of Wisconsin P, 1997) ix.

5. See Mark Seltzer, *Serial Killers: Death and Life in America's Wound Culture* (New York: Routledge, 1998) 9-10; Robert K Ressler, *I Have Lived in the Monster* (New York: St. Martin's P, 1997) 65ff.

6. Kincaid ix.

7. Stephen King, *Danse Macabre* 39.

Chapter 3

1. Stephen King, *The Dead Zone* (New York: Viking, 1979) 277.

2. Although some of King's readers may point out that *Cujo*, in which a rabid St. Bernard exemplifies evil, is an exception to the good dog archetype, in general dogs uphold positive cultural values and wolves are evil beasts. In *The Stand*, wolves are clearly servants of the Dark Man, while Kojak, a Golden Retriever, exemplifies all the good dogs of the world.

3. Farley Mowat, *Never Cry Wolf* (Boston: Little, Brown, 1965) 103-06.

4. Robert R. McCammon, *The Wolf's Hour* (New York: Pocket, 1989) 133-34.

5. McCammon 153.

6. McCammon 230.

7. McCammon 268.

8. McCammon 502.

9. Jane Caputi, *The Age of Sex Crime* (Bowling Green State U Popular P, 1987) 63-67.

10. King, *The Dead Zone* 14.

11. King, *The Dead Zone* 107. I noted earlier that King usually employs the wolf archetype negatively; in Johnny's trance, during which he reveals that Sam Weitzak's mother is not dead, one of the images Johnny uses is "*the nazi war wolf is loose in Europe.*"

12. King, *The Dead Zone* 114.

13. King, *The Dead Zone* 141.

14. King, *The Dead Zone* 148.

15. King, *The Dead Zone* 158.

16. King, *The Dead Zone* 224.

17. King, *The Dead Zone* 227.

18. King, *The Dead Zone* 232.

19. King, *The Dead Zone* 241.

20. King, *The Dead Zone* 7.

21. King, *The Dead Zone* 277.

22. King, *The Dead Zone* 283.

23. King, *The Dead Zone* 292.

24. King, *The Dead Zone* 304.

25. King, *The Dead Zone* 367.

26. Carr is working in a long-standing tradition, which ranges from evil mothers as in "Hansel and Gretel," evil stepmothers as in "Cinderella" and "Snow White," Grendel's monstrous mother, through such biting social commentary as Guy de Maupassant's "The Mother of Monsters," and present day contemporary horror writers such as Thomas Harris who obsessively return to the mother as the source of dis/ease.

27. Caleb Carr, *The Angel of Darkness* (New York: Ballantine, 1997) 749.

28. The Beecham case involves an insane and psychopathic serial killer living in New York City in the late 1890s; the story is recounted in Carr's first novel, *The Alienist*.

29. Carr 4-7.

30. Carr 10.

31. Carr 440-41.

32. Carr 127.

33. Carr 441.

34. Carr 180-81.

35. Carr 676.

36. Carr 709.

37. Carr 712.

38. Carr 714.

39. Carr 745.

40. Stephen King, *Rose Madder* (New York: Viking, 1995) 17.

41. King, *Rose Madder* 153-54.

42. Not only is King invoking the long, rich mythic tradition of the man-beast, he is also invoking the long tradition of problematic pictures and magical mirrors. Sheridan Le Fanu's "Schalken the Painter," Hawthorne's "Prophetic Pictures," Poe's "The Oval Portrait," and Conan Doyle's "The Silver Mirror," are among the many texts which work with a dualed representation.

43. King, *Rose Madder* 391.

44. King, *Rose Madder* 392.

45. King, *Rose Madder* 396.

46. All of these interviews were conducted under strictest confidentiality, and I agreed that I would not, in any way whatsoever, identify these women.

47. King, *Rose Madder* 414-16.

48. King, *Rose Madder* 420.

Chapter 4

1. Thomas Harris, *The Silence of the Lambs* (New York: St. Martin's, 1989) 6.

2. Jonathan Kellerman, *Over the Edge* (New York: Signet, 1988) 113-14.

3. Charles King, *Mama's Boy* (New York: Pocket, 1992) 85.

4. Charles King 88-90.

5. Charles King 93.

6. Charles King 193.

7. Charles King 195.

8. Charles King 195

9. Charles King 375.

10. Richard Tithecott 20.

11. Psychopomps, a term King evidently borrowed from Lovecraft, are usually defined as harbingers or messengers of the dead. In his case the psychopomps are sparrows. When Thad is operated on to remove the part of his twin that is ostensibly causing the headaches, thousands of sparrows gather; one of the phrases that recurs in the *Dark Half* is "the sparrows are flying." Thad eventually manages to call the sparrows, the harbingers and messengers of the dead, to remove George Stark from the land of the living, which seems to solve the problem quite nicely. In later novels, we find out this is not the case. Beaumont ends up a divorced alcoholic, unable to write or function without his *doppelganger*. Liz has left him, taking their children, because she realizes that George and Thad are far from separate entities. Since she hates and fears Stark and cannot forget that Stark and her husband are the same being, her actions, while perhaps unfair, are not surprising.

12. Stephen King, *The Dark Half* (New York: Signet, 1990) 426-27.

13. Eleven-year-old Thad has excruciating headaches, which occur when he starts writing; when the surgeons perform brain surgery, they discover that Thad should have had a twin, but he consumed his twin *in utero*, leaving only a few minute scraps of tissue which the surgeons excised. Since these headaches occur when Thad starts to write, the buried persona of Stark signals not only Thad's creative genius, but also his conflicted personality.

14. Stephen King, *The Dark Half* 432.

15. Stephen King, *The Dark Half* 430.

16. Stephen King, *The Dark Half* 433-34.

17. Stephen King, *The Dark Half* 464.

18. Hantke 41.

19. Paul Krendler is an exception to this case, but his role is minor; *Hannibal*, Harris's latest work, changes this affirmative paradigm rather drastically.

20. Thomas Harris, *Red Dragon* (New York: Dell, 1981) 8.

21. Harris, *Red Dragon* 15.

22. Harris, *Red Dragon* 21.

23. Harris, *Red Dragon* 30.

24. Harris, *Red Dragon* 152.

25. Harris, *Red Dragon* 66-67.

26. Harris, *Red Dragon* 67.

27. Harris, *Red Dragon* 313.

28. Harris, *Silence* 73.

29. Harris, *Red Dragon* 193-94.

30. Harris, *Silence* 194.

31. Harris, *Red Dragon* 354.

32. Harris, *Silence* 6.

33. Harris, *Silence* 22.

34. Harris, *Silence* 230.

35. Harris, *Silence* 290-91.

36. Harris, *Silence* 82.

37. Harris, *Silence* 366.

38. Harris, *Red Dragon* 195.

39. Harris, *Red Dragon* 78.

40. Harris, *Red Dragon* 262-63.

41. Dolarhyde identifies with Blake's etching, *The Dragon and the Woman Clothed in the Sun* and is/is not controlled by the Dragon, who obviously represents that which he desires and that which he also dreads.

42. Harris, *Red Dragon* 281.

43. These indicators or markers refer to the triad of behaviors which indicate the possibility of disturbances that lie in the realm of the serial killer: bedwetting, fire setting, and cruelty to animals.

44. Harris, *Red Dragon* 54.

45. Harris, *Silence* 366.

Chapter 5

1. Rita Rippetoe, a friend and colleague, probably best described the effect produced by Ellis' disgusting work: "After I read a few pages, I put it down and went to the nearest ladies' room to wash my hands." While the temptation to mitigate this problem and wear metaphorical gloves has occurred to me, it is one of the best examples extant of a dis/ease provoking novel. And yet another friend, picking up the text and idly leafing through its pages became quite

uncomfortably riveted—she is still trying to figure out why she is fascinated by something so repellent. Perhaps after she reads it she will provide me with an answer.

2. In many ways, King's *Carrie* both predicts and explains the many student shootings. It is a pity that more people do not appreciate the polyphonic elements in King, too often dismissing him as facile and predictable. The demonized students at Columbine, unable to walk the halls without being thrown into lockers and labeled fags by the popular and immune jocks, took much the same revenge *Carrie* did, and for much the same reasons. In the final result, what differences existed between assault rifles and psychometry? We are talking degree here, not difference.

3. Stephen King, *Carrie* (New York: Signet, 1974) 4.

4. King, *Carrie* 7.

5. King, *Carrie* 21-22.

6. King, *Carrie* 11.

7. King, *Carrie* 19.

8. King, *Carrie* 32.

9. King, *Carrie* 76.

10. King, *Carrie* 115.

11. King, *Carrie* 150.

12. King, *Carrie* 168.

13. King, *Carrie* 183.

14. King, *Carrie* 187.

15. King, *Carrie* 204.

16. King, *Carrie* 233.

17. King, *Carrie* 88.

18. Joyce Carol Oates, "Extenuating Circumstances," *Haunted: Tales of the Grotesque* (New York: Plume, 1994) 153.

19. Oates 152-53.

20. Oates 148.

21. Oates 151-53.

22. Oates 151-53.

23. Patrick Süskind, *Perfume: The Story of a Murderer,* trans. John E. Woods (New York: Pocket, 1987) 3.

24. Süskind 3.

25. Süskind 13.

26. Süskind 21.

27. Süskind specifically refers to the infant Grenouille as "it." Until he is placed with Mme. Gaillard, the author refers to the child as "it," thus reinforcing his essential monsterdom.

28. Süskind 26.

29. Süskind 24.

30. Süskind 25.

31. Süskind 176.

32. Süskind 183.

33. Süskind 189.

34. Süskind 230.

35. Süskind 273.

36. Süskind 288.

37. Süskind 294.

38. Süskind 297.

39. Süskind 309-10.

40. Thomas Tryon, *The Other* (Greenwich: Fawcett, 1971) 13.

41. Tryon 15.

42. Tryon 202.

43. Tryon 209.

44. Tryon 228.

45. Tryon 265-66.

46. Tryon 268-69.

47. Tryon 270.

48. Tryon 288.

49. Tryon 287.

50. Although *American Psycho* is variously regarded as parody or an over-the-top satire on yuppiedom, I intend to read it as though it were a serious novel, i.e., one that expects the reader to take the action seriously and to react to the events as if they happened.

51. David Skal 376-78.

52. Skal 376. The text I am using was published by Pan (Great Britain); the American version, to which Skal refers, by Random House (Vintage).

53. Brett Easton Ellis, *American Psycho* (London: Pan, 1991) 387.

54. Ellis 20.

55. Ellis 313.

56. Ellis 214.

57. Ellis 345.

58. Ellis 379.

59. Ellis 90.

60. Ellis 89.

61. Since they broke up over Bateman's violent behavior, which in his undergraduate days was restricted to breaking her arm and blacking her eye, at which point she called the relationship off, Bethany has some inkling what a relationship with Bateman entails. This being so, it is hard to understand why she invites him to lunch and then accompanies him to his apartment. Felony stupidity seems to account for it, however.

62. Ellis 245-47.

63. Ellis 327.

64. Ellis 329.

65. Ellis 343.

66. Nora Rawlinson and Joe McGinnis, back cover of Ellis.

THE CONSTRUCTION OF SOCIAL COMMUNITIES

1. Rod Serling, "The Monsters Are Due on Maple Street," from *The Twilight Zone* (Garden City: Doubleday, 1962) 77.

2. Nancy Gibbs, "The Backbone of America," *Time*, 7 July 1997: 44.

3. Pam Lamborn qtd. in Gibbs, 45.

4. Edward J. Ingebretsen, *Maps of Heaven, Maps of Hell: Religious Terror as Memory from the Puritans to Stephen King* (Armonk: Sharpe, 1996) xvii.

5. Ingebretsen 43.

Chapter 6

1. Stephen King, "The Reach," *Skeleton Crew* (New York: New American Library, 1985) 566.

2. David Punter, *The Literature of Terror: Gothic Fictions from 1765 to the Present Day* (London: Longman, 1980) 423.

3. Heller 4.

4. Dean R Koontz, *Midnight* (New York: Berkley, 1989) 176.

5. Koontz 68.

6. This motif is a recurring one for Koontz; in *The Watchers* a sentient Golden Retriever battles his evil counterpart, and the family claims he is dead, so that the government will not recapture him; naturally, the dog is not dead, but lives happily ever after with the family he has enabled to come into being Dean R. Koontz, *Watchers* (New York: Berkley, 1988).

7. Rabkin 83.

8. Hartwell 7.

9. Charles de Lint, "Waifs and Strays," *Journeys to The Twilight Zone*, ed. Carol Sterling (New York: Daw, 1993) 236.

10. de Lint 239-40.

11. de Lint 242-44.

12. de Lint 247.

13. de Lint 258.

14. de Lint 264.

15. de Lint 271.

16. de Lint 266.

17. de Lint 249.

18. Carol Orlock, "Nobody Lives There Now. Nothing Happens," ed. Kathryn Ptacek, *Women of Darkness* (New York: Tor, 1988) 136.

19. Orlock 137.

20. Orlock 137.

21. Stephen King, "The Reach," *Skeleton Crew* (New York: New American Library, 1985) 546.

22. King 556.

23. King 565-66.

24. King 566.

Chapter 7

1. Poppy Z Brite, *Lost Souls* (New York: Dell, 1992) 159.

2. King, *Danse Macabre* 261. While my earlier reference to five elderly men may appear to contradict King's quote, Edward Wanderley, the fifth member of the Chowder Society dies shortly before the novel begins.

3. George Lakoff, *Moral Politics: What Conservatives Know That Liberals Don't* (Chicago: U of Chicago P, 1996) 18.

4. Lakoff 65.

5. Peter Straub, *Ghost Story* (New York: Pocket, 1979) 480.

6. Straub 508.

7. Straub 469.

8. Straub 396.

9. Stephen King, *It* (New York: NAL, 1986) 974.

10. King, *It* 1074-75.

11. King, *It* 1073.

12. Technically Hebrew for shit, this term has been generalized in American English to mean any worthless object.

13. King, *Needful Things* (New York: Signet, 1992) 254-55.

14. King, *Needful Things* 554.

15. King, *Needful Things* 604.

16. King, *Needful Things* 339.

17. "Little Red Riding Hood," *The Old Wives' Fairy Tale Book*, ed. Angela Carter, The Pantheon Fairy Tale and Folklore Library (New York: Pantheon, 1990) 208-10. The last line in the original text, translated from Perrault's *Histoires ou Contes du Temps Perdu* (1697) tale is, "At that, the wicked wolf threw himself upon Little Red Riding Hood and gobbled her up, too."

18. King, *Needful Things* 730.

19. King, *Needful Things* 736.

20. King, *Danse Macabre* 12.

21. Bentley Little, *University* (New York: Signet, 1995) 416.

22. Little 98. The professor, in discussion, notes that the line between "popular" literature and "serious" literature is very difficult to draw; in addition, when questioned as to whether King's brand name consumerism will not irremediably date the fiction, he comments, "You know, that's the same problem I have with Steinbeck. His work is so dated. All those references to the Depression."

23. Ian Watt, *The Rise of the Novel: Studies in Defoe, Richardson and Fielding* (Berkeley: U of California P, 1957) 27.

24. Haraway 149.

25. Halberstam 77.

26. Gary Brandner, *The Howling* (Greenwich: Fawcett, 1977) 7.

27. Lidice is the town completely destroyed by the Nazis as a reprisal for the execution/assassination of Reynard Heydrich, then Governor of Czechoslovakia.

28. Brandner 22. One of the things horror fiction *aficionados* understand is that the rural places are never ever safe; they do not house Ma and Pa Walton, but monsters. And the nicer the town appears, the worse is the fate which will overtake the unwary.

29. Brandner 115.

30. Brandner 122.

31. Poppy Z Brite, *Lost Souls* (New York: Dell, 1992) 156-58.

32. Brite 335.

33. Brite 343.

34. Brite 349.

35. Stephen King, foreword, *Night Shift* (New York: Doubleday, 1978) xvii.

36. Brite 159.

Chapter 8

1. Shirley Jackson, "The Lottery," *The Magic of Shirley Jackson*, ed. Stanley Edgar Hyman (New York: Farar, 1966) 145.

2. "Innocent" is, of course used semi-facetiously; some of the victims are innocent, or at least unaware, but many become outsiders at the caprice of the community and have previously been complicit in various community busting actions.

3. Jackson 137-38.

4. Stephen King, *Danse Macabre* 31.

5. Jackson 145.

6. Hannah Arendt, *Eichmann in Jerusalem* (New York: Viking, 1964) 252.

7. Jackson 142.

8. Jackson 145.

9. Jackson 145.

10. Rod Serling, "The Monsters Are Due on Maple Street," *From The Twilight Zone* (New York: Doubleday, 1962) 81-82.

11. Serling 93.

12. Robert Wernick, *The Nazis* World War II (Alexandria: *Time-Life*, 1980) 121-33.

13. Serling 84.

14. King, *Danse Macabre* 5.

15. Serling 88.

16. Serling 92.

17. It is possibly a bit more than coincidental that these three films have been produced when space exploration is reemerging in the culture, the Cold War has dissolved, and the United States is reemerging in its role as the world's policeman.

18. It is ironic because most of the characters are Protestant, and believe in religions that utterly reject all the Popish symbols and rituals. However, King is adhering to conventional vampire tales here and one of the conventions privileges Roman Catholic rituals and symbols.

19. King, "One for the Road," *Night Shift* (New York: Doubleday, 1978) 322.

20. King, "The Mist," *Skeleton Crew* (New York: Signet, 1986) 47.

21. King, *Danse Macabre* 14-16.

22. King, "The Mist," 143.

23. Harlan Ellison, "The Whimper of Whipped Dogs," *The Horror Hall of Fame*, ed. Robert Silverberg and Martin H. Greenberg (New York: Carroll & Graf, 1991) 356.

24. Ellison 348.

25. Ellison 363.

26. Ellison 364.

27. Rollo May, qtd. in Ellison 364.

28. George Romero, *Night of the Living Dead*, 1968.

29. Edward Bryant, "A Sad Last Love at the Diner of the Dammed," *The Year's Best Fantasy and Horror*, ed. Ellen Datlow and Terri Windling (New York: St, Martin's 1990) 124-45.

30. Bryant 125.

31. Bryant 126.

32. Bryant 129.

33. Bryant 130.

34. Bryant 131.

35. Bryant 132.

36. Bryant 141-42.

37. Bryant 145.

38. Siddons qtd. in *Danse Macabre* 273-74.

39. King, *Danse Macabre* 279.

40. Anne Rivers Siddons, *The House Next Door* (New York: Ballantine, 1978) 135.

41. Siddons 184-85.

42. Siddons 188.

43. Siddons 215.

44. Siddons 227.

45. Siddons 231.
46. King, *Danse Macabre* 278.
47. Siddons 238.
48. Siddons 242-43.
49. Siddons 269.
50. Siddons 277-79.
51. The term *vill* is used intentionally to echo the Vietnam War usage with its ironic connotations, which my dissertation also reflects. My thanks go to Peter Halloran of the Northeast PCA/ACA; Oscar Patterson III, University of North Florida; Ed Palm, Glenville State College; and Steven L. Reagles, Bethany College, among others, for their timely response to the question of *vill* as appropriate terminology.

SORTING OUT DIFFERENT STYLES OF MALIGNITY

1. Lance Morrow, "Evil," *Time,* 10 June 1991, 51.
2. Thanks to Dave and Pearlie of Vintage Books, who tirelessly and faithfully located and discussed my choices with me, and thanks, too, to the many anonymous people who took the time to answer my questions on what they thought horror fiction was and why they read it.

Chapter 9

1. Lance Morrow, "Evil," *Time,* 10 June 1991: 50.
2. Robert McCammon, *Gone South* (New York: Pocket, 1992) 1.
3. McCammon 27.
4. McCammon 387.
5. Stephen King, *Danse Macabre* (New York: Berkley, 1981) 9.
6. "The Shop" is slang for the Department of Scientific Intelligence. King's governmental department of horrors makes secret police like Hitler's Gestapo, the dreaded KGB, or "Papa Doc" Duvalier's Ton-Ton Macoute look like absolute pikers. The Shop is an utterly secret, amoral, and completely ruthless organization with unlimited powers. King, of course, uses them to illustrate a dystopic organization within a dystopic government.
7. King, *Firestarter* (New York: Viking, 1980) 52-54.
8. King, *Firestarter* 107.
9. King, *Firestarter* 111.
10. King, *Firestarter* 76.
11. King, *Firestarter* 181.
12. King, *Firestarter* 193.
13. King, *Firestarter* 271.
14. King, *Firestarter* 286.
15. King, *Firestarter* 342-44.
16. King, *Firestarter* 351-52.

17. King, *Firestarter* 357-59.

18. King, *Firestarter* 367.

19. King, *Firestarter* 370.

20. Robert McCammon, *Swan Song* (New York: Pocket, 1987) 920.

21. McCammon, *Swan Song* 956.

22. Review of *The Postman*, back cover, no source.

23. David Brin, *The Postman* (New York: Bantam, 1986) 19.

24. Brin 31.

25. Brin 36-37.

26. Brin 164.

27. Brin 166-67.

28. Brin 229.

29. Brin 306.

30. Brin 193.

31. Brin 226.

32. Brin 312.

33. Brin 316.

34. Brin 317.

35. Brin 321.

36. Brin 279.

Chapter 10

1. Lance Morrow, "Evil," *Time* 10 June 1991: 49.

2. F. Paul Wilson, "Midnight Mass," *The Best of Weird Tales*, ed. John Gregory Betancourt (New York: Barnes and Noble, 1995) 8.

3. Wilson 7.

4. Wilson 9.

5. Wilson 15-16.

6. Wilson 24-25.

7. Wilson 27.

8. Wilson 35.

9. Wilson 40.

10. Wilson 42.

11. Wilson 48.

12. Wilson 50.

13. Wilson 48-49.

14. Winston Churchill, "Speech at the Mansion House in Reference to the Battle of Egypt," *Dictionary of Quotations*, 2nd ed. (London: Oxford, 1953) 143.

15. Sheri S. Tepper, *The Gate to Women's Country* (New York: Bantam, 1988) 12.

16. Tepper 251.

17. Niccolo Machiavelli, *The Prince*, ed. and trans. Robert M. Adams, 2nd ed. (New York: Norton, 1992) 49.

18. Tepper 19.

19. Richard Lattimore, introduction, *The Trojan Women, Euripides III*, ed. David Grene and Richard Lattimore, trans. Richard Lattimore (Chicago: U of Chicago P, 1958) 124.

20. Tepper 56.

21. Tepper 314.

22. Tepper 264.

23. Tepper 315.

24. Tepper 312.

25. Review of *The Gate to Women's Country* in *Washington Post* review, front page.

26. Tepper 290.

27. Tepper 290-91.

28. Stephen King, *The Stand* (New York: Signet, 1991). *The Stand* is 1,138 pages in length, with an epic cast of characters and numerous sub-plots; I am concerned in this reading with the notion of dystopia, so a great deal of the novel goes unmentioned. While I am working with the revised novel, the original *Stand* was published in 1978; thus, the actual original preceded McCammon's *Swan Song* by nearly a decade.

29. King, *Danse Macabre* 402-03.

30. King, *The Stand* 167-68.

31. King, *The Stand* 235.

32. King, *The Stand* 209.

33. King, *The Stand* 220.

34. King, *The Stand* 171.

35. King, *The Stand* 176.

36. King, *The Stand* 175.

37. King, *The Stand* 173.

38. King, *The Stand* 654.

39. King, *The Stand* 902.

40. King, *The Stand* 1052.

41. King, *The Stand* 1054

42. Tuchman, Barbara W., *A Distant Mirror: The Calamitous 14th Century* (New York: Knopf, 1984) 95-101.

43. King, *The Stand* 636-37.

44. Roy D'Andrade, Quinn and Holland 113.

45. Quinn and Holland 8.

46. King 671-72.

47. King, *The Stand* 637.

48. King, *The Stand* 672.

49. King, *Danse Macabre* 401-02. King states that *The Stand* is quadruply leveled. Beneath the conventions of the Apollonian society temporarily disrupted by a Dionysian force, lies the real werewolf, the Mr. Hyde figure who is not treading an upward path, the horror writer who enjoys destroying the whole world. But beneath that, says King, lies the horror writer as moral and civilized, and *The Stand* as a novel about starting with a nihilistic premise and relearning old lessons and old human values. This is, of course, why I classify this novel as mid-spectrum.

50. King, *The Stand* 1072.

Chapter 11

1. In Stanley Kramer's brilliant film version of *On the Beach*, the last evocative scene shows trash already blowing down the deserted street and the forlorn banner, a mute reminder of the last frantic religious meetings, flapping in the wind

2. Although the first two texts are Commonwealth, Atwood is widely read in the United States and Atwood's text intimately concerns American society, as Gilead is her view of American society. As with Atwood, Shute's novel is also intimately concerned with American society; indeed, the driving force behind the novel is arguably America's nuclear development program. Certainly the American presence within the novel is instrumental in creating the dystopia. And, of course, all my examples are published by major American publishers.

3. Reviewers in *The Washington Post Book World* and *Playboy* comment on the likenesses to both Burgess and Orwell. Bradbury's Fahrenheit 451 is an obvious resonance. I always seem to hear the ironic "Some animals are more equal than others" and am sharply reminded of *Animal Farm* and the continuing adjustments to the rules.

4. Margaret Atwood, interview with Geoff Hancock, "Tightrope Walking Across Niagra Falls," *Margaret Atwood: Conversations*, ed. Earl G. Ingersoll (Princeton: Ontario Review P, 1990) 216.

5. Genesis 30:1, *The New Oxford Annotated Bible*, ed. Bruce M. Metzger and Roland E. Murphy (New York: Oxford UP, 1994).

6. Margaret Atwood, *The Handmaid's Tale* (New York: Fawcett Crest, 1985) 390.

7. Atwood 151.

8. Atwood 79.

9. Atwood 264.

10. Although Professor Pieixoto, the speaker in the problematized epilogue, claims that one of the Commanders, Frederick R Waterford, got the idea for the red colour from the German POWs in Canadian POW camps, this seems highly unlikely; crimson, the colour of harlotry, of loose women, provides a much more cogent example of how the Handmaids were actually perceived.

11. Atwood 21.

12. Atwood 61.

13. Arthur M. Schlesinger, Sr., "The Rise of the City, 1878-98," *A History of American Life,* ed. Mark C. Carnes, Arthur M. Schlesinger, Sr., 1948 (New York: Simon & Schuster, 1996) 914.

14. Rev. in *Houston Chronicle, The Handmaid's Tale* by Margaret Atwood, frontispiece.

15. Atwood 285-86.

16. Atwood 232-33.

17. Atwood 228.

18. Atwood 229.

19. Atwood 93.

20. Atwood 209-10.

21. Tepper 230.

22. Atwood 178-79.

23. Atwood 389.

24. Atwood 180-81.

25. Atwood 243.

26. Atwood 209.

27. Atwood 331.

28. Atwood 9.

29. Atwood 223.

30. Atwood 236.

31. Particicution is the term used for the execution of a male who has either raped a Handmaid or caused a miscarriage. The Handmaids form a circle, an Aunt blows a whistle, and they are free to do what they will until the whistle blows again. All of which sounds quite just; the only time this ritual is described, however, the women unknowingly do the government's work. They attack and rend a man who, far from being a rapist, is a member of the Mayday organization attempting to free women. Thus, in Atwood's world, the patriarchy always wins.

32. Atwood 390.

33. Atwood 121.

34. Atwood 367-68.

35. Atwood 378.

36. Atwood 380-81. The issue of authentication is genuine. The document is a transcription of 30 cassettes found in a sealed military locker, with two or three songs initially and then a voice detailing the narrator's day-to-day life as Handmaid. While the narrator is accepted as Offred, her real identity and ultimate fate is still unknown.

37. Atwood 387.

38. Atwood 393.

39. Atwood 383.

40. Robin Wood, "Cat and Dog: Lewis Teague's Stephen King Movies," *Gender, Language and Myth: Essays on Polpular Narrative*, ed. Glenwood Irons (Toronto: U of Toronto P, 1992) 303-18. I am indebted to Robin Wood's article for an elegant method to discuss parallels in novel and film without getting bogged down in the minutiae.

41. *Deep Impact*, dir. Mimi Leder, perf. Robert Duvall, Morgan Freeman, Tea Leoni, Elijah Cook, and Vanessa Redgrave, Dreamworks, Paramount, 1998.

42. Shute 136.

43. Shute 139-41.

44. Herodotus, *The Histories*, trans. Robin Waterfield (Oxford: Oxford UP, 1998) I; 32.

45. Boethius, *The Consolation of Philosophy*, trans. Victor Watts (London: Penguin, 1969) ii, prose 4, 61.

46. Psalm 103: 15-16, *The Holy Bible*, New Catholic Edition (New York: Catholic Book, 1957).

47. Shute 278.

48. *On the Beach*, dir. Stanley Kramer, perf. Gregory Peck, Ava Gardner, Anthony Perkins. Fred Astaire. MGM, 1959.

49. Shute 268.

50. Shute 274.

51. Stephen King, *Danse Macabre* 12-13.

52. Shute 275-77.

53. Kramer, *On the Beach*.

54. Kramer, *On the Beach*.

55 Rev. by *The Washington Post* and *The Times Herald*, front cover of *On the Beach*.

56. Ursula Le Guin, "The Ones Who Walk Away from Omelas," *The Norton Anthology of Short Fiction,* ed. R. V. Cassill, 5th ed. (New York: Norton, 1995) 968.

57. Le Guin 970.

58. Le Guin 971.

59. Le Guin 972.

Coda

1. Motto of Mary, Queen of Scots, qtd. in Antonia Fraser, Mary Queen of Scots (New York: Delacorte, 1969) 413.

2. David Hartwell, ed., introduction to Stephen King's *The Reach*, in *The Dark Descent* (New York: Tor, 1987) 15.

3. Terry Heller, *The Delights of Terror: An Aesthetics of the Tale of Terror* (Urbana: U of Illinois P, 1985) 6.

4. Mao Tse-Tung, *Talks at the Yenan Forum on Literature and Art*, qtd. in Ettienne Balibar and Pierre Macherey, *On Literature as an Ideological Form*, *Oxford Literary Review* 3 (1987): 36.

5. Stephen King, introduction, *The Arbor House Treasury of Horror and the Supernatural*, ed. Bill Pronzini, Barry Malzberg, and Martin H. Greenberg (New York: Arbor House, 1981) 5.

BIBLIOGRAPHY

Critical Works

Andriano, Joseph. *Our Ladies of Darkness: Feminine Dæmonology in Male Gothic Fiction*. University Park: Pennsylvania State UP, 1993.

Arendt, Hannah. *Eichmann in Jerusalem: A Report on the Banality of Evil*. New York: Viking, 1964.

Aristotle. *The Poetics of Aristotle*. Trans. Stephen Halliwell. Chapel Hill: U of North Carolina P, 1987.

Atwood, Margaret. *Strange Things: The Malevolent North in Canadian Literature*. Oxford: Oxford UP, 1995.

Badley, Linda. *Writing Horror and the Body: The Fiction of Stephen King, Clive Barker and Anne Rice*. Contributions to the Study of Popular Culture, 51. Westport: Greenwood, 1996.

Baldick, Chris. Introduction. *The Oxford Book of Gothic Tales*. Oxford: Oxford UP, 1992.

Barron, Neil, ed. *Horror Literature: A Reader's Guide*. Garland Reference Library of the Humanities, vol. 1220. New York: Garland, 1990.

Baym, Nina. *American Women Writers and the Work of History, 1790-1850*. New Brunswick: Rutgers UP, 1995.

——. *Feminism and American Literary History*. New Brunswick: Rutgers UP, 1992.

Belford, Barbara. *Bram Stoker*. New York: Knopf, 1996.

Bettelheim, Bruno. *The Uses of Enchantment: The Meaning and Importance of Fairy Tales*. New York: Knopf, 1976.

Bhalla, Alok. *The Cartographers of Hell: Essays on the Gothic Novel and the Social History of England*. New Delhi: Sterling, 1991.

Birkhead, Edith. *The Tale of Terror: A Study of the Gothic Romance*. London: Constable, 1921.

Bouza, Tony. *The Decline and Fall of the American Empire: Corruption, Decadence, and the American Dream*. New York: Plenum P, 1996.

Briggs, Julia. *Night Visitors: The Rise and Fall of the English Ghost Story*. London: Faber, 1977.

Briggs, Robin. *Witches and Neighbours: The Social and Cultural Context of European Witchcraft*. New York: Viking, 1996.

Buell, Lawrence. *New England Literary Culture: From Revolution through Renaissance*. Cambridge: Cambridge UP, 1986.

Bussing, Sabine. *Aliens in the House: The Child in Horror Fiction*. New York: Greenwood, 1987.

Butler, Judith. *Gender Trouble: Feminism and the Subversion of Identity.* New York: Routledge, 1990.

Butts, Mary. "Ghosties and Ghoulies." *The Bookman*, 1933.

Caputi, Jane. *The Age of Sex Crime.* Bowling Green, OH: Bowling Green State University Popular P, 1987.

Carnes, Mark C., Arthur Schlesinger, Sr., and Dixon Ryan Fox, eds. *A History of American Life.* Rev. & abr. ed. New York: Simon & Schuster, 1996.

Carroll, Noel. *The Philosophy of Horror or Paradoxes of the Heart.* New York: Routledge, 1990.

Cheever, Leonard. "Apocalypse and the Popular Imagination: Stephen King's The Stand." *Artes Liberales* 8.1 (1981): 1-10.

Chodorow, Nancy. *The Reproduction of Mothering: Psychoanalysis and the Sociology of Gender.* Berkeley: U of California P, 1978.

Clover, Carol. "Her Body, Himself: Gender in the Slasher Film." *Gender, Language and Myth: Essays in Popular Narrative.* Ed. Glenwood Irons. Toronto: U of Toronto P, 1992.

——. *Men. Women and Chain Saws: Gender in the Modern Horror Film.* Princeton: Princeton UP, 1992.

Cohen, Jeffrey Jerome. *Monster Theory: Reading Culture.* Minneapolis: U of Minnesota, 1996.

Collings, Michael. "The Stand: Science Fiction into Fantasy." *Discovering Stephen King.* Ed. Darryl Schweitzer. Starmount Studies in Literary Criticism 8. Mercer Island: Starmount House, 1985. 83-90.

Combs, James. *Phony Culture: Confidence and Malaise in Contemporary America.* Bowling Green, OH: Bowling Green State U Popular P, 1994.

Crawford, Gary William. "Stephen King's American Gothic." *Discovering Stephen King.* Ed. Darryl Schweitzer. Starmount Studies in Literary Criticism 8. Mercer Island: Starmount House, 1985.

D'Andrade, Roy. "A Folk Model of the Mind." *Cultural Models in Language and Thought.* New York: Cambridge UP, 1987.

Datlow, Ellen, and Terri Windling, eds. *Snow White, Blood Red.* New York: Morrow, 1993.

——. *The Year's Best Fantasy and Horror.* New York: St. Martin's, 1990.

Day, William Patrick. *Circles of Fear and Desire: A Study of Gothic Fantasy.* Chicago: U of Chicago P, 1985.

De Cuir, Andre L. "Power of the Feminine and the Gendered Construction of Horror in Stephen King's 'The Reach.'" *Imagining the Worst: Stephen King and the Representation of Women.* Ed. Kathleen Margaret Lant and Theresa Thompson. Contributions to the Study of Popular Culture. Westport: Greenwood, 1998. 79-89.

Delbanco, Andrew. *The Death of Satan: How Americans Have Lost Their Sense of Evil.* New York: Farrar, Straus and Giroux, 1995.

Derleth, August. Foreword. *Sleep No More: Twenty Masterpieces of Horror for the Connoisseur.* New York: Farrar & Rineheart, 1944. v-x.

Docherty, Brian. Introduction. *American Horror Fiction: from Brockden Brown to Stephen King.* New York: St. Martin's, 1990.

Donovan, Josephine. *New England Local Color Literature: A Women's Tradition.* New York: Continuum, 1988.

Douglas, John, and Mark Olshaker. *The Anatomy of Motive.* New York: Scribner, 1999.

Egan, James. "Antidetection: Gothic and Detective Conventions in the Fiction of Stephen King." *Clues: A Journal of Detection* 5.1 (1988): 131-46.

———. "Sacral Parody in the Fiction of Stephen King." *Journal of Popular Culture.* 23.3 (1989): 125-41.

———. "Technohorror: The Dystopian Vision of Stephen King." *Extrapolations* 29.2 (1988): 140-52.

Ellis, Kate Ferguson. *The Contested Castle: Gothic Novels and the Subversion of Domestic Ideology.* Urbana: U of Illinois P, 1989.

Fraser, Antonia. *Mary Queen of Scots.* New York: Delacorte, 1969.

Frazer, Sir James George. *The Golden Bough: A Study in Magic and Religion.* New York: MacMillan, 1950.

Gelder, Ken. *Reading the Vampire.* London: Routledge, 1994.

Gibbs, Nancy. "The Backbone of America." *Time* 7 July 1997: 44.

Glover, David. *Vampires, Mummies and Liberals: Bram Stoker and the Politics of Popular Fiction.* Durham: Duke UP, 1996.

Goldhagen, Daniel Jonah. *Hitler's Willing Executioners: Ordinary Germans and the Holocaust.* New York: Vintage, 1997.

Grixti, Joseph. "Consuming Cannibals: Psychopathic Killers as Archetypes and Cultural Icons." *Journal of American Culture* 100.1 (1995): 87-96.

———. *The Terrors of Uncertainty: The Cultural Contexts of Horror Fiction.* London: Routledge, 1989.

Gross, Louis. *Redefining the Gothic: From Wieland to Day of the Dead.* Ann Arbor: U of Michigan P, 1989.

Halberstam, Judith. *Skin Shows: Gothic Horror and the Technology of Monsters.* Durham: Duke UP, 1995.

Hanson, Claire. "Stephen King: The Powers of Horror." *American Horror Fiction: From Brockden Brown to Stephen King.* Ed. Brian Docherty. New York: St. Martin's, 1990. 135-54.

Hantke, Steffen. "Deconstructing Horror: Commodities in the Fiction of Jonathan Carroll and Kathe Koja." *Journal of Popular Culture* 18.3 (1995): 41-57.

Haraway, Donna J. *Simians, Cyborgs and Women: The Reinvention of Nature.* New York: Routledge, 1991.

Hartwell, David, G. Introduction. *The Dark Descent.* New York: Tor, 1987.

Heldreth, Leonard. "The Ultimate Horror: The Dead Child in Stephen King's Stories and Novels." *Discovering Stephen King*. Ed. Darryl Schweitzer. Starmount Studies in Literary Criticism 8. Mercer Island: Starmount House, 1985. 141-52.

Heller, Terry. *The Delights of Terror: An Aesthetics of the Tale of Terror*. Urbana: U of Illinois P, 1985.

Holland, Dorothy, and Naomi Quinn, eds. *Cultural Models in Language and Thought*. Cambridge: Cambridge UP, 1987.

Holland-Toll, Linda J. "Contemporary Tragedy: Stephen King's *Pet Sematary*." *Studies in Weird Fiction* 16 (1995).

Hoppenstand, Gary. *Clive Barker's Short Stories*. Jefferson: McFarland, 1994.

——, and Ray Browne, eds. *Landscape of Nightmares: The Gothic World of Stephen King*. Bowling Green, OH: Bowling Green State University Popular P, 1997.

Indick, Ben. "Stephen King as an Epic Writer." *Discovering Stephen King*. Ed. Darryl Schweitzer. *Starmount Studies in Literary Criticism* 8. Mercer Island: Starmount, 1985. 56-67.

Ingebretsen, Edward J., S. J. *Maps of Heaven, Maps of Hell: Religious Terror as Memory from the Puritans to Stephen King*. Armonk: Sharpe, 1996.

——. Monster-Making: A Politics of Persuasion." *Journal of American Culture* 21.2 (1998): 25-34.

Irons, Glenwood, ed. *Gender, Language and Myth: Essays on Popular Narrative*. Toronto: U of Toronto P, 1992.

Jackson, Rosemary. *Fantasy: The Literature of Subversion*. New York: Methuen, 1981.

Joshi, S. T. *The Weird Tale*. Austin: U of Texas P, 1990.

Kendrick, Walter. *The Thrill of Fear: 250 Years of Scary Entertainment*. New York: Grove P, 1991.

Kerr, Howard, John W. Crowley, and Charles L. Crow, eds. *The Haunted Dusk: American Supernatural Fiction. 1820-1920*. Athens: U of Georgia P, 1983.

King, Stephen. *Danse Macabre*. New York: Berkley, 1981.

——. Introduction. *The Arbor House Treasury of Horror and the Supernatural*. Ed. Bill Pronzini, Barry Malzberg, and Martin H. Greenberg. New York: Arbor House, 1981.

——. *Nightmares & Dreamscapes*. Introduction. New York: New American Library, 1994.

——. *Nightshift*. Introduction. New York: New American Library, 1979.

——. *Skeleton Crew*. Introduction. New York: New American Library, 1985.

Koelb, Clayton. *The Incredulous Reader: Literature and the Function of Disbelief*. Ithaca: Cornell UP, 1984.

Kristeva, Julia. *Powers of Horror*. New York: Columbia, 1982.

Lacayo, Richard. "Law and Order." *Time* 15 Jan.1996: 48-56.

Lakoff, George. *Moral Politics: What Conservatives Know That Liberals Don't.* Chicago: U of Chicago P, 1996.

Lant, Kathleen Margaret, and Theresa Thompson, eds. *Imagining the Worst: Stephen King and the Representation of Women.* Contributions to the Study of Popular Culture 67. Westport: Greenwood, 1998.

Lovecraft, Howard Phillips. *Supernatural Horror in Literature.* New York: Dover, 1973. reprint. Abrahamson, 1945.

MacAndrews, Elizabeth. *The Gothic Tradition in Fiction.* New York: Columbia, 1979.

MacDonald, John D. Foreword. *Night Shift.* New York: New American Library, 1979.

Magistrale, Tony. "Hawthorne's Woods Revisited: Stephen King's Pet Sematary." *The Nathaniel Hawthorne Review* 14.1 (1988): 9-13.

——. *Landscape of Fear: Stephen King's American Gothic.* Bowling Green, OH: Bowling Green U Popular P, 1988.

——, ed. *The Dark Descent: Essays Defining Stephen King's Horrorscape.* New York: Greenwood P, 1992.

Martin, Jay. *Harvests of Change: American Literature, 1865-1914.* Engelwood Cliffs: Prentice Hall, 1966.

Massumi, Brian, ed. *The Politics of Everyday Fear.* Minneapolis: U of Minnesota P, 1993.

May, Elaine Tyler. *Homeward Bound: American Families in the Cold War Era.* New York: Basic, 1988.

Morrow, Lance. "Evil." *Time* 10 June 1991: 48-53.

Mowat, Farley. *Never Cry Wolf.* Boston: Little, Brown, 1963.

Newman, Judie. "Shirley Jackson and the Reproduction of Mothering: The Haunting of Hill House." *American Horror Fiction: From Brockden Brown to Stephen King.* Ed. Brian Docherty. New York: St Martin's, 1990. 120-34.

Price, Robert M. "Fundamentalists in the Fiction of Stephen King." *Studies in Weird Fiction* 5 (1989): 12-14.

——. "Stephen King and the Lovecraft Mythos." Discovering Stephen King. Ed. Darryl Schweitzer. *Starmount Studies in Literary Criticism* 8. Mercer Island: Starmount 1985. 109-22.

Punter, David. *The Tale of Terror: A History of Gothic Fictions from 1765 to the Present Day.* New York: Longman, 1980.

Quinn, Naomi, and Dorothy Holland, eds. *Cultural Models in Language and Thought.* New York: Cambridge UP, 1987.

Rabkin, Eric S. *The Fantastic in Literature.* Princeton: Princeton UP, 1976.

Reino, Joseph. *Stephen King: The First Decade, Carrie to Pet Sematary.* *Twayne's United States Authors Series.* Ed. Warren French. Boston: Hall, 1988.

Ressler, Robert K., and Tom Shachtman. *I Have Lived in the Monster.* New York: St. Martin's P, 1997.

Reynolds, David S. *Beneath the American Renaissance: The Subversive Imagination in the Age of Emerson and Melville.* New York: Knopf, 1988.

——. *Walt Whitman's America.* New York: Knopf, 1996.

Roberts, Thomas J. *An Æsthetics of Junk Fiction.* Athens: U of Georgia P, 1990.

Ross, Andrew. "New Age Technoculture." *Cultural Studies.* Ed. Lawrence Grossberg, Cary Nelson, and Paula Treichler. New York: Routledge, 1992. 531-55.

Schechter, Harold. "The Bloody Chamber: Terror Films, Fairy Tales, and Taboo." *Gender, Language and Myth: Essays in Popular Narrative.* Ed. Glenwood Irons. Toronto: U of Toronto P, 1992.

Schneider, Kirk J. *Horror, and the Holy: Wisdom Teachings of the Monster Tale.* Chicago: Open Court, 1993.

Seltzer, Mark. *Serial Killers: Death and Life in America's Wound Culture.* New York: Routledge, 1998.

Senf, Carol. *The Critical Response to Bram Stoker.* Westport: Greenwood P, 1993.

Shattuck, Roger. *Forbidden Knowledge: From Prometheus to Pornography.* New York: St. Martin's, 1996.

Skal, David J. *The Monster Show: A Cultural History of Horror.* New York: Penguin, 1993.

Spencer, Anita. *A Crisis of Spirit: Our Desperate Search for Integrity.* New York: Plenum, Insight, 1996.

Storey, John, ed. *Cultural Theory and Popular Culture: A Reader.* 2nd ed. Athens: U of Georgia P, 1998.

Stroby, W. C. Interview. "Digging Up Stories with Stephen King." *Writer's Digest* May 1990.

Tithecott, Richard. *Of Men and Monsters: Jeffrey Dahmer and the Construction of the Serial Killer.* Madison: U of Wisconsin P, 1997.

Todorov, Tvetsan. *The Fantastic: A Structural Approach to a Literary Genre.* Trans. Richard Howard. Cleveland: P of Case Western Reserve U, 1973.

Tompkins, Jane. *Sensational Designs: The Cultural Work of American Fiction, 1790-1860.* New York: Oxford UP, 1985.

Tropp, Martin. *Images of Fear: How Horror Stories Helped Shape Modern Culture, 1818-1918.* Jefferson: McFarland, 1990.

Tse-Tung, Mao. "Talks at the Yenan Forum on Literature and Art." Qtd. in *Ettienne Balibar and Pierre Macherey*, "On Literature as an Ideological Form." *Oxford Literary Review* 3 (1978): 34-54.

Tuchman, Barbara W. *A Distant Mirror: The Calamitous 14th Century.* New York: Knopf, 1984.

Twitchell, James B. *For Shame: The Loss of Common Decency in American Culture.* New York: St. Martin's, 1997.

Underwood, Tim, and Chuck Miller, eds. *Fear Itself: The Early Works of Stephen King.* San Francisco: Underwood-Miller, 1982.

——. *Kingdom of Fear: The World of Stephen King.* San Francisco: Underwood-Miller, 1986.

Watt, Ian. *The Rise of the Novel: Studies in Defoe, Richardson, and Fielding.* First American Ed. Berkeley: U of California P, 1957.

Wernick, Robert. *The Nazis.* World War II. Alexandria: Time-Life Books, 1980.

Williams, Anne. *Art of Darkness: A Poetics of Gothic.* Chicago: U of Chicago, 1995.

Winter, Douglas E. *Stephen King.* Series Editor: Roger C. Schlobin. Starmont Reader's Guide 16. Mercer Island: Starmont House, 1982.

——. *The Art of Darkness.* New York: Penguin, 1986.

Wohleber, Curt. "The Man Who Can Scare Stephen King." *American Heritage* Dec. 1995: 82-90.

Wood, Robin. "Cat and Dog: Lewis Teague's Stephen King Movies." *Gender, Language and Myth: Essays in Popular Narrative.* Ed. Glenwood Irons. Toronto: U of Toronto P, 1992.

Wright, Robert. "The Evolution of Despair." *Time* 28 Aug. 1995: 50-57.

Anthologies & Collections

Betancourt, John Gregory, ed. *Best of Weird Tales.* New York: Barnes & Noble, 1995.

——, and Robert Weinberg, eds. *Weird Tales: Seven Decades of Terror.* New York: Barnes & Noble, 1997.

Boucher, Anthony, ed. *The Complete Werewolf.* 1969. New York: Carroll & Graf, 1990.

Brite, Poppy Z, ed. *Love in Vein: Twenty Original Tales of Vampire Erotica.* 1994. New York: Harperprism-Harper, 1995.

Campbell, Ramsey, ed. *Fine Frights: Stories That Scared Me.* New York: Tor, 1988.

Carter, Angela., ed. *Old Wives' Fairy Tale Book.* Pantheon Fairy Tale and Folk Tale Library. New York: Pantheon, 1990.

Crossley-Holland, Kevin, ed. *Folk Tales of the British Isles.* Pantheon Fairy Tale and Folk Tale Library. New York: Pantheon, 1985.

Cuddons, J. A., ed. *The Penguin Book of Horror Stories.* London: Penguin, 1984.

Curran, Ronald, ed. *The Weird Gathering and Other Tales: "Supernatural" Women in American Popular Fiction, 1800-1850.* New York: Fawcett Crest, 1979.

Dalby, Richard, ed. *The Mammoth Book of Ghost Stories*. New York: Carroll & Graf, 1990.

——, ed. *Mistletoe Mayhem: Horrific Tales for the Holidays*. Psychics: Castle, 1993.

——, ed. *Victorian and Edwardian Ghost Stories*. New York: Barnes & Noble, 1995.

Derleth, August, ed. *Sleep No More: Twenty Masterpieces of Horror for the Connoisseur*. New York: Farrar and Rineheart, 1944.

Doyle, Arthur Conan. Selected and introduced by E. F. Bleicher. *The Best Supernatural Tales of Arthur Conan Doyle*. New York: Dover, 1979.

Etchison, Dennis, ed. *Masters of Darkness*. New York: Tor, 1986.

——. *Metahorror*. New York: Dell, 1992.

Ferman, Edward L., and Anne Jordan, eds. *The Best Horror Stories from the Magazine of Fantasy & Science Fiction*. Vol 2. New York: St. Martin's, 1988.

Gilliam, Richard, Martin H. Greenberg, and Edward E. Kramer, eds. *Confederacy of the Dead*. New York: Penguin, 1993.

Gorman, Ed, and Martin H. Greenberg, eds. *Night Screams*. New York: Penguin, 1996.

——, ed. *Predators*. New York: Penguin, 1994.

Grant, Charles L, ed. *After Midnight*. New York: Tor, 1986.

——, ed. *Greystone Bay*. The First Chronicle of Greystone Bay. New York: Tor, 1985.

——, ed. *In the Fog*. The Last Chronicle of Greystone Bay. New York: Tor, 1993.

——, ed. *Midnight*. New York: Tor, 1985.

——, ed. *The Sea Harp Hotel*. The Third Chronicle of Greystone Bay. New York, 1990.

——, ed. *Shadows 3*. New York: Berkley, 1985.

——, ed. *Shadows 4*. New York: Berkley, 1985.

——, ed. Shadows 6. New York: Berkley, 1986.

Greenberg, Martin H., and Charles G. Waugh, eds. *Back from the Dead*. New York: Daw, 1991.

Haining, Peter, ed. *The Nightmare Reader*. Vol. 2. London: Pan, 1976.

Hamilton, Laurell K. *Guilty Pleasures* Anita Blake, Vampire Hunter. New York: Ace, 1994.

Hartwell, David G., ed. *Bodies of the Dead and Other Great American Ghost Stories*. New York: Tor, 1997.

——, ed. *The Dark Descent*. New York: Tor, 1987.

Holmes, Ronald, ed. *Macabre Railway Stories*. London: Allen, 1982.

Jackson, Shirley. *The Magic of Shirley Jackson*. Ed. Stanley Edgar Hyman. New York: Farrar, 1965.

Jones, Stephen, ed. *The Mammoth Book of the Best New Horror.* New York: Carroll & Graf, 1997.

Jones, Stephen, and Dave Carson, eds. *H. P. Lovecraft's Book of Horror.* New York: Barnes & Noble, 1993.

Kahn, Joan, ed. *Some Things Dark and Dangerous.* New York: Avon, 1970.

Kaye, Marvin, ed. *Weird Tales.* New York: Barnes & Noble, 1988.

——, ed. *Witches and Warlocks: Tales of Black Magic, Old & New.* Garden City: Guild America, 1989.

Lamb, Hugh. *Victorian Tales of Terror.* New York: Tapplinger, 1975.

Lovecraft, H. P. Selected and introduced by Joyce Carol Oates. *Tales of H. P. Lovecraft.* Hopewell: Ecco, 1996.

McSherry, Frank D. Jr., Charles Waugh, and Martin H. Greenberg, eds. *Great American Ghost Stories.* Vol. 1. New York: Berkley, 1992.

——, ed. *Great American Ghost Stories.* Vol. 2. New York: Berkley, 1992.

Norton, Alden H., ed. *Horror Times Ten.* New York: Berkley, 1967.

Owen, Betty, ed. *Stories of the Supernatural.* New York: Scholastic Book Services, 1967.

——. *Eleven Great Horror Stories.* New York: Scholastic Book Services, 1973.

Pronzini, Bill, Barry Malzberg, and Martin H. Greenberg, eds. Introduction by Stephen King. *The Arbor House Treasury of Horror and the Supernatural.* New York: Arbor House, 1981.

Ptacek, Kathryn, ed. *Women of Darkness.* New York: Tor, 1988.

Serling, Carol, ed. *Journeys to the Twilight Zone.* New York: Daw, 1993.

Serling, Rod. Adapted by Walter B. Gibson. *Rod Serling's Twilight Zone.* New York: Wings, 1983.

——. Adapted by Walter B. Gibson. *Rod Serling's Twilight Zone.* New York: Grosset and Dunlap, 1964.

——, ed. *From the Twilight Zone.* Garden City: Nelson Doubleday, 1962.

Shephard, Leslie, ed. *The Dracula Book of Great Vampire Stories.* Psychics: Citadel, 1977.

Silverberg, Martin, and Robert H. Greenberg, eds. *The Horror Hall of Fame.* New York: Carroll & Graf, 1991.

Thompson, G. Richard, ed. *Romantic Gothic Tales, 1790-1840.* New York: Harper & Row, 1979.

Wagner, Karl Edward, ed. *The Year's Best Horror Stories, XXII.* New York: Daw, 1994.

Winter, Douglas E., ed. *Prime Evil.* New York: New American Library, 1988.

Wise, Herbert A., and Phyllis Fraser, eds. *Great Tales of Terror and the Supernatural.* New York: Random, 1972.

Wolf, Leonard, ed. *Wolf's Complete Book of Terror.* New York: Potter, 1979.

Novels and Short Stories*

Atwood, Margaret. *The Handmaid's Tale.* 1985. New York: Ballantine-Fawcett Crest, 1987.

Austen, Jane. *Northanger Abbey.* 1818. New York: Bantam-Doubleday-Dell, 1989.

Barker, Clive. *Books of Blood.* Vol. 1. 1984. New York: Berkley, 1986.

——. *Books of Blood.* Vol. 2. 1984. New York: Berkley, 1986.

——. *Books of Blood.* Vol. 3. 1984. New York: Berkley, 1986.

——. *Cabal.* 1985. New York: Poseidon, 1988.

——. *The Damnation Game.* London: Sphere, 1985.

——. *The Hellbound Heart.* New York: HarperPaperbacks, 1991.

——. *The Inhuman Condition.* 1985. New York: Pocket-Simon & Schuster, 1987.

——. *In the Flesh.* 1986. New York: Pocket-Simon & Schuster, 1988.

Bierce, Ambrose. *The Complete Short Stories of Ambrose Bierce.* Comp. Ernest Joseph Hopkins. Lincoln: U of Nebraska P, 1970.

Blackwood, Algernon. *Best Ghost Stories of Algernon Blackwood.* 1938. Introduction by E. F. Bleiler. New York: Dover, 1988.

——. *Strange Stories.* Supernatural and Occult Fiction. New York: Arno P, 1976.

Blatty, William Peter. *The Exorcist.* 1971. New York: Bantam, 1972.

——. *Legion.* 1983. New York: Pocket-Simon & Schuster, 1984.

Bloch, Robert. *The Night of the Ripper.* 1984. New York: Tor, 1986.

Borton, Douglas. *Shadow Dance.* New York: Signet-Penguin, 1991.

Bradbury, Ray. *Fahrenheit 451.* 1953. New York: Del Rey-Ballantine, 1983.

Brandner, Gary. *Carrion.* New York: Ballantine-Fawcett, 1986.

——. *The Howling.* Greenwich: Fawcett, 1977.

Brin, David. *The Postman.* 1985. New York: Bantam, 1986.

Brite, Poppy Z. *Drawing Blood.* New York: Abyss-Dell, 1993.

——. *Lost Souls.* New York: Abyss-Dell, 1992.

——. *Wormwood.* New York: Dell, 1996.

Brontë, Emily [Ellis Bell]. *Wuthering Heights.* 1847. Oxford: Oxford UP, 1995.

Brown, Charles Brockden. *Wieland or the Transformation.* 1798. New York:Russell and Russell, 1966.

Bryant, Edward. "A Sad Last Love at the Diner of the Damned." *The Year's Best Fantasy and Horror.* Ed. Ellen Datlow and Terri Windling. New York: St. Martin's, 1990.

Cady, Jack. *The Jonah Watch.* 1981. New York: Avon, 1983.

Campbell, Ramsey. *Ancient Images.* 1989. New York: Tor, 1990.

——. *Dark Companions.* 1982. New York: Tor, 1985.

——. *The Doll Who Ate His Mother.* 1976. New York: Tor, 1985.

——. *The Face That Must Die.* 1983. New York: Tor, 1985.

——. *The Hungry Moon.* 1986. New York: Tor, 1987.

——. *The Long Lost.* 1994. New York: Tor, 1996.

——. *Incarnate.* 1983. New York: Tor, 1984.

——. *The Influence.* 1988. New York: Tor, 1989.

——. *Midnight Sun.* New York: Tor, 1992.

——. *The Nameless.* 1981. New York: Tor, 1987.

——. *Obsession.* 1985. New York: Tor, 1986.

——. *The Parasite.* New York: Tor, 1989.

Carcaterra, Lorenzo. *Sleepers.* 1995. **City:** Ballantine-Random House, 1996.

Carr, Caleb. *The Alienist.* 1984. New York: Ballantine-Random House, 1995.

——. *The Angel of Darkness.* 1997. New York: Ballantine-Random House, 1998.

Chambers, Robert. *The King in Yellow.* 1895. Rpt. 1976. Cutchogue: New York, 1976.

——. "The Yellow Sign." *The King in Yellow.* 1895. Rpt. 1976. Cutchogue: New York, 1976.

Coyne, John. *Child of Shadows.* New York: Warner, 1980.

——. *Hobgoblins.* 1981. New York: Berkley, 1982.

——. *The Hunting Season.* New York: Warner, 1987.

——. *The Piercing.* 1979. New York: Berkley, 1980.

——. *The Searing.* 1980. New York: Berkley, 1981.

Crawford, F. Marion. *With the Immortals.* New York: Arno, 1988.

D'Ammassa, Don. *Blood Beast.* Pinnacle-Windsor, 1988.

Derleth, August. *The Trail of Cthulhu.* 1962. New York: Carroll & Graf, 1996.

——, ed. *Tales of the Cthulhu Mythos.* Vol. 1. 1969. New York: Ballantine, 1973.

Dos Santos, Audry Joyce. *Henri and the Loup-Garrou.* New York: Pantheon, 1982.

Ellis, Brett Easton. *American Psycho.* 1991. London: Picador-Pan, 1991.

Ellison, Harlan. "The Whimper of Whipped Dogs." *The Horror Hall of Fame.* Eds. Robert Silverberg and Martin H. Greenberg. New York: Carroll & Graf, 1991. 345-64.

Etchison, Dennis. *Dark Side.* New York: Charter, 1986.

——. *The Fog.* New York: Bantam, 1980.

Farris, John. *All Heads Turn When the Hunt Goes By.* New York: Popular Library, 1997.

——. *Fiends.* New York: Tor, 1990.

——. *Wildwood.* New York: Tor, 1986.

Fowles, John. *The Collector.* 1963. New York: Laurel-Dell, 1990.

——. *The Magus.* 1965. New York: Dell, 1973.

Gaskell, Elizabeth Cleghorn. *Mrs. Gaskell's Tales of Mystery and Horror.* Ed. Michael Ashley. New York: Scribner, 1978.

Gibson, William. *Neuromancer.* New York: Ace, 1984.

Grant, Charles L. *Dialing the Wind.* New York: Tor, 1989.

——. *The Tea Party.* New York: Pocket-Simon & Schuster, 1985.

Harris, Thomas. *Hannibal*. New York: Delacorte-Random House, 1999.

——. *Red Dragon*. 1981. New York: Dell-Bantam, 1990.

——. *Silence of the Lambs*. 1988. New York: St. Martin's Paperbacks, 1989.

Hawthorne, Nathaniel. *The House of the Seven Gables*. 1851. New York: Signet-NAL, 1961.

——. *The Scarlet Letter*. 1850. New York: Signet-NAL, 1980.

——. *Tales and Sketches*. New York: Library of America, 1982.

——. *Twice Told Tales*. 1837. New York: Airmont, 1965.

Herbert, James. *The Dark*. New York: Signet-NAL, 1980.

——. *Deadly Eyes*. 1974. New York: Signet-NAL, 1975. Rpt. of *The Rats*. 1974.

——. *Domain*. New York: Signet-NAL, 1985.

——. *The Fog*. 1975. New York: Signet-NAL, 1975.

——. *Haunted*. 1988. New York: Jove, 1990.

——. *The Magic Cottage*. New York: Onyx-NAL, 1988.

——. *Moon*. 1985. New York: Onyx-NAL, 1987.

——. *Sepulcher*. New York: Signet, NAL, 1983.

——. *Shrine*. New York: Signet-Penguin, 1984.

——. *The Survivor*. 1976. New York: Signet-NAL, 1977.

Holt, John R. *When We Dead Awaken*. New York: Bantam, 1990.

Howard, Robert E. "The Black Stone." *Sleep No More: Twenty Masterpieces of Horror for the Connoisseur*. Ed. August Derleth. New York: Farrar and Rineheart, 1944.

——. *Skull-Face*. 1929. New York: Berkley, 1978.

Irving, Washington. *The Sketch Book*. 1820. New York: Signet-NAL, 1961.

Jackson, Shirley. *The Haunting of Hill House*. 1959. Cutchogue: Buccaneer, 1987.

——. "The Lottery." *The Magic of Shirley Jackson*. Ed. Stanley Edgar Hyman. New York: Farrar, 1965. 137-45.

——. *The Sun Dial*. New York: Ace, 1958.

——. *We Have Always Lived in the Castle*. 1962. New York: Popular Library, 1963.

James, Henry. *The Turn of the Screw and Other Short Stories*. New York: Signet-NAL, 1962.

James, Montague Rhodes. *Collected Ghost Stories*. Ware: Wordsworth, 1992.

Johnstone William W. *Them*. New York: Zebra-Kensington, 1992.

——. *Toy Cemetery*. New York: Zebra-Kensington, 1987.

——. *The Univited*. New York: Zebra-Kensington, 1982.

Kafka, Franz. *The Metamorphosis*. 1915. Trans. and ed. Stanley Corngold. New York: Bantam, 1988.

King, Charles. *Mama's Boy*. New York: Pocket, 1992.

King, Stephen. *The Bachman Books*. New York: Signet-NAL, 1986.

——. *Bag of Bones*. New York: Scribner, 1998.

——. *Carrie*. 1974. New York: Signet-NAL, 1975.

——. *Christine*. New York: Viking, 1983.

——. *Cujo*. New York: Viking, 1981.

——. *The Dark Half*. 1990. New York: Signet-Penguin, 1990.

——. *The Dead Zone*. 1979. New York: Signet-NAL, 1980.

——. *Desperation*. New York: Viking. 1996.

——. *Dolores Claiborne*. 1993. New York: Signet-Dutton, 1993.

——. *The Eyes of the Dragon*. 1987. New York: Signet-NAL, 1988.

——. *Fire-starter*. 1980. Book Club Edition. New York: Viking. 1980.

——. *Four Past Midnight*. New York: Viking, 1990.

——. *Gerald's Game*. 1992. New York: Signet. 1993.

——. *The Green Mile*. Vol. 1-6. New York: Signet-Dutton, 1996.

——. *Hearts in Atlantis*. New York: Scribner, 1999.

——. *It*. 1986. New York: Signet-NAL, 1987.

——. *Needful Things*. 1991. New York: Signet-NAL, 1992.

——. *Nightmares and Dreamscapes*. 1993. New York: Signet-Dutton, 1994.

——. *Night Shift*. 1976. Garden City: Doubleday, 1978.

——. *Pet Sematary*. Garden City: Doubleday, 1983.

——. *Rose Madder*. New York: Viking, 1996.

——. *'Salem's Lot*. 1975. New York: Signet-NAL, 1976.

——. *The Shining*. 1977. New York: Signet-NAL, 1978.

——. *Skeleton Crew*. 1985. New York: Signet, 1986.

——. *The Stand*. 1978. Rpt. As *The Stand: The Complete and Uncut Edition*. 1991. New York: Signet-NAL, 1991.

——. [Richard Bachman]. *Thinner*. New York: Viking, 1984.

King, Stephen, and Peter Straub. *The Talisman*. 1984. New York: Berkley, 1995.

Klein, T.E.D. *Dark Gods*. 1985. New York: Bantam, 1986.

Koja, Kathe. *The Cipher*. New York: Dell-Bantam, 1991.

Koontz, Dean R. *The Bad Place*. Dedication. New York: Berkley, 1990.

—— [Leigh Nichols]. *The House of Thunder*. 1982. New York: Berkley, 1992.

——. *Lightning*. New York: Berkley, 1989.

——. *Midnight*. 1989. New York: Berkley, 1989.

——. *Night Chills*. New York: Berkley, 1983.

—— [Brian Coffey]. *The Voice of the Night*. 1980. New York: Berkley, 1991.

——. *Watchers*. 1987. New York: Berkley, 1988.

Kosinski, Jerzy. *The Painted Bird*. 2nd ed. New York: Grove, 1976.

Kramer, Stanley. *On the Beach*. MGM, 1959.

Lee, Tanith. *Dark Dance*. 1992. New York: Abyss-Dell, 1992.

Le Fanu, Sheridan. *The Watcher and Other Weird Stories*. New York: Arno, 1977.

Le Guin, Ursula. "The Ones Who Walk Away from Omelas." *The Norton Anthology of Short Fiction*. 5th ed. Ed. R. V. Cassill. New York: Norton, 1995. 968.

Leiber, Fritz. *Conjure Wife*. 1953. New York: Ace, 1977.

——. *Our Lady of Darkness*. 1977. New York: Berkley, 1978.

Leroux, Gaston. *The Phantom of the Opera*. 1911. New York: Warner, 1986.

Levin, Ira. *Rosemary's Baby*. 1967. New York: Signet-Penguin, 1997.

——. *The Stepford Wives*. New York: Random, 1972.

Little, Bentley. *Dominion*. Signet-Penguin, 1996.

——. *The Ignored*. New York: Signet-Penguin, 1997.

——. *University*. New York: Signet-Penguin, 1995.

Lofts, Norah. *Gad's Hall*. 1978. New York: Fawcett Crest, 1980.

——. *The Haunting of Gad's Hall*. 1977. New York: Fawcett Crest, 1980.

——. *Hauntings: Is Anybody There?* 1965. Greenwich: Fawcett Crest, 1974.

Lovecraft, H. P. *The Dunwich Horror and Others*. Ed. S.T. Joshi. Sauk City: Arkham, 1984.

Mandel, George. *Scapegoats*. New York: Dell, 1970.

Manley, Mark. *Blood Sisters*. New York: Charter, 1985.

Marasco, Robert. *Burnt Offerings*. New York: Dell, 1973.

Masterton, Graham. *Mirror*. New York: Tor, 1988.

——. *The Pariah*. New York: Tor, 1983.

Maturin, Charles. *Melmoth the Wanderer*. 1820. Oxford: Oxford UP, 1989.

McCammon, Robert R. *Boy's Life*. New York: Pocket, 1991.

——. *Gone South*. New York: Pocket, 1992.

——. *Mystery Walk*. New York: Pocket, 1983.

——. *Stinger*. New York: Pocket, 1988.

——. *Swan Song*. New York: Pocket, 1987.

——. *The Wolf's Hour*. New York: Pocket, 1989.

McDowell, Michael. *Gilded Needles*. New York: Avon, 1980.

McNab, Oliver. *Horror Story*. New York: Pocket, 1979.

Monninger, Joe. Rpt. *Incident at Potter's Bridge*. 1991. New York: Avon, 1993.

Morrell, David. *The Totem*. New York: Fawcett Crest, 1979.

Oates, Joyce Carol. *Bellefleur*. 1980. New York: Warner, 1981.

——. *Haunted: Tales of the Grotesque*. New York: Plume, 1994.

——. *Mysteries of Winterthur*. 1984. New York: Berkley, 1985.

Poe, Edgar Allan. *Complete Stories of Edgar Allan Poe*. Garden City: Doubleday, 1966.

——. *The Narrative of Arthur Gordon Pym of Nantucket*. 1838. New York: Penguin, 1986.

Reynolds, Bonnie Jones. *The Truth About Unicorns*. 1972. New York: Ballantine, 1973.

Rice, Anne. *The Feast of All Saints*. 1979. New York: Ballantine, 1992.

——. *Interview with the Vampire*. Book I of the Vampire Chronicles. 1976. New York: Ballantine, 1977.

——. *The Witching Hour*. 1990. New York: Ballantine, 1991.

Rickman, Phil. *Candle Night.* 1991. New York: Jove, 1995.

——. *Curfew.* 1993. Rpt. of Crybbe. New York: Berkley, 1994.

——. *December.* 1994. New York: Berkley, 1996.

Shelley, Mary. *Frankenstein.* 1818. New York: Signet Classic, 1983.

Shute, Nevil. *On the Beach.* 1957. New York: Bantam, 1968.

Siddons, Anne Rivers. *The House Next Door.* 1978. New York: Ballantine, 1982.

Simmons, Dan. *Carrion Comfort.* 1989. New York: Warner, 1990.

——. *Children of the Night.* 1992. New York: Warner, 1993.

——. *Summer of Night.* 1991. New York: Warner, 1992.

Skipp, John, and Craig Spector. *The Light at the End.* New York: Bantam, 1986.

Slade, Michael. *Ghoul.* 1987. New York: Signet-NAL, 1989.

Stableford, Brian. *The Empire of Fear.* 1988. New York: Ballantine, 1993.

Stevenson, Robert Louis. *Dr. Jekyll and Mr. Hyde.* 1886. New York: Signet, 1987.

Stoker, Bram. *Dracula.* 1897. New York: Penguin, 1979.

——. *The Jewel of the Seven Stars.* New York: Carroll & Graf, 1989.

Straus, Peter. *Ghost Story.* 1979. New York: Pocket, 1980.

——. *Houses without Walls.* 1990. New York: Signet-Penguin, 1991.

——. *Koko.* 1988. New York: Signet-NAL, 1989.

——. *Mystery.* 1990. New York: Signet-NAL, 1991.

——. *Shadowland.* 1980. New York: Berkley, 1981.

——. *The Throat.* 1993. New York: Signet, 1994.

Süsskind, Patrick. *Perfume: The Story of a Murderer.* 1985. Trans. John E. Woods. New York: Pocket, 1987.

Taylor, Domini. *Teacher's Pet.* 1987. New York: Jove, 1989.

Tem, Melanie. *Revenants.* New York: Abyss-Dell, 1994.

Tepper, Sheri S. *The Gate to Women's Country.* 1988. New York: Bantam, 1989.

——. *Gibbon's Decline and Fall.* 1996. New York: Bantam, 1997.

——. *Grass.* 1989. New York: Bantam, 1990.

Tryon, Thomas. *Harvest Home.* 1973. Greenwich: Fawcett Crest, 1977.

——. *The Night of the Moonbow.* 1989. New York: Dell, 1990.

——. *The Other.* 1971. Greenwich: Fawcett Crest, 1972.

Vance, Steve. *The Abyss.* New York: Book Margins, 1989.

——. *The Hyde Effect.* New York: Leisure, 1986.

Walpole, Horace. *The Castle of Otranto.* 1764. Oxford: Oxford UP, 1982.

Walters, R. R. *Ludlow's Mill.* New York: Tor, 1981.

Wells, H. G. *The Island of Dr. Moreau.* 1896. New York: Lancer, 1968.

——. *The Time Machine: An Invention. A Critical Text of the 1895 London First Edition, with an Introduction and Appendices.* Ed. Leon Stover. Jefferson: McFarland, 1996.

Wescott, Earle. *Winter Wolves.* 1988. New York: Bantam, 1989.

Westall, Robert. *The Stones of Muncaster Cathedral.* New York: Farrar, 1991.

Wilde, Oscar. *The Picture of Dorian Gray.* 1891. New York: Magnum, 1968.

Wilson, F. Paul. *The Keep.* 1981. New York: Jove, 1986.

——. "Midnight Mass." 1993. *Best of Weird Tales.* Ed. John Betancourt. New York: Barnes & Noble, 1995.

Wright, T. M. *A Manhattan Ghost Story.* New York: Tor, 1984.

Wyndham, John. *The Day of the Triffids.* New York: Fawcett Crest, 1951.

Yarbro, Chelsea Quinn. *Nomads.* New York: Bantam, 1984.

* A representative selection of texts is included in this bibliography, which by no means represents my entire reading on the subject.

INDEX